Restructuring Britain

DIVIDED NATION:
Social and Cultural Change in Britain

A Reader

edited by

Linda McDowell, Philip Sarre
and Chris Hamnett

at the Open University

HODDER AND STOUGHTON
LONDON   SYDNEY   AUCKLAND   TORONTO
in association with the Open University

Restructuring Britain

Uneven Re-Development: Cities and Regions in Transition
edited by Doreen Massey and John Allen

Divided Nation: Social and Cultural Change in Britain
edited by Linda McDowell, Philip Sarre and Chris Hamnett

A State of Crisis: The Changing Face of British Politics
edited by James Anderson and Allan Cochrane

The following are the associated Open Texts published by Sage Publications in association with the Open University

The Economy in Question
edited by John Allen and Doreen Massey

The Changing Social Structure
edited by Chris Hamnett, Linda McDowell and Philip Sarre

Politics in Transition
edited by Allan Cochrane and James Anderson

This reader is one part of an Open University course and the selection is therefore related to other material available to students. Opinions expressed in it are not necessarily those of the course team or of the University.

British Library Cataloguing in Publication Data

Divided nation: social and cultural change in
 Britain: a reader. — (Restructuring Britain.
 D314; v.2)
 1. Great Britain. Economic development.
 Geographical aspects
 I. Sarre, Philip II. McDowell, Linda III.
 Hamnett, Chris IV. Open University V.
 Series
 305'.0941

ISBN 0 340 50161 8

First published in Great Britain 1989

Typeset by Wearside Tradespools, Fulwell, Sunderland
Printed in Great Britain for Hodder and Stoughton Educational, a Division of Hodder and Stoughton Ltd, Mill Road, Dunton Green, Sevenoaks, Kent, by Richard Clay Ltd, Bungay, Suffolk

Contents

Acknowledgments

The editors and publishers would like to thank the following for permission to reproduce copyright material in this volume:

Edward Arnold for 'Beyond housing classes: the sociological significance of private property rights in means of consumption' by Peter Saunders reprinted from *The International Journal of Urban and Regional Research*, Vol. 8, No. 2 (1984); Drake Marketing Services for the extract from *All Day, Every Day* by Sallie Westwood (1984); Gower Publishing Group for 'Clerical "proletarianization": myth or reality?' by Rosemary Crompton and Gareth Jones reprinted from *Diversity and Decomposition in the Labour Market*, ed. G. Day (1982), published in association with the British Sociological Association. (The original research on which this paper is based is fully reported in *White Collar Proletariat*, Macmillan (1984) and *Doing Research in Organisations*, ed. A. Bryman, Routledge (1988).); Greenwood Press Inc. for 'Fiscal reorientation, centralization and the privatization of council housing' by Ray Forrest and Alan Murie from *Housing Markets and Policies Under Fiscal Austerity*, ed. Willem van Vliet (*Contributions in Sociology*, No. 62, 1987, pp. 15–32). Copyright © 1987 by Willem van Vliet. Reprinted with permission of the editor and publisher; HMSO for 'Social trends since World War II' by A. H. Halsey from *Social Trends*, 17 (1987); Macmillan for 'Word processing and the secretarial labour process' by Juliet Webster reprinted from *The Changing Experiences of Employment*, ed. K. Purcell *et al.* (1986); Manchester University Press for 'Minority settlement and the local economy' by Robin Ward reprinted from *New Approaches to Economic Life* by B. Roberts, R. Finnegan and D. Gallie (1985); *Marxism Today* for 'In the land of the dispossessed' by Charlie Leadbeater published in *Marxism Today*, April 1987, pp. 18–25; Methuen, London for 'Brideshead re-revisited' by Robert Hewison from his book *The Heritage Industry* (1987); Routledge and Kegan Paul for 'Racism and class structure: migrant labour in contemporary capitalism' by Robert Miles from his book *Racism and Migrant Labour* (1982) and for 'Wealth and the two nations' by Chris Pond reprinted from *The Wealth Report 2*, ed. Frank Field (1983); Sage Publications for 'Cultural change and contemporary holiday-making' by John Urry reprinted from *Theory, Culture and Society*, Vol. 5, 1988, pp. 35–55; Unwin and Hyman for 'The corporation and the class structure' by John Scott from his book *Corporations, Classes and Capitalism* (1979) and for 'Two sides of anti-racism' by Paul Gilroy from his book *There Ain't no Black in the Union Jack* (1987); Verso for 'The ghosting of the inner city' by P. Wright from his book *Living in an old Country* (1985).

Section I   Setting the scene: restructuring social divisions?

Introduction

This book is part of the Open University course *Restructuring Britain*.* The purpose of the course as a whole is to explore a series of key questions about the nature of social and economic change in the UK today. The course is divided into three parts concerned with, respectively, the economy, the social structure, and politics and the state, and for each part there is an Open Text and a Reader. The part on the social structure comprises this Reader and the Open Text *The Changing Social Structure*, edited by Chris Hamnett, Linda McDowell and Philip Sarre (London: Sage/The Open University, 1989).

'Restructuring' is a term that came to prominence in social science literature in the 1980s. Despite being an imprecise concept, used in several different ways, its utility lies in the notion of structural change that is embodied within it. By focusing on restructuring in the course, the intention is to look at the major changes and to raise the possibility that there has been a radical break with the past. Most discussions of restructuring focus on the economic restructuring brought on by the 1970s oil crisis and subsequent changes in the international divisions of labour; this was covered in the first part of the course. The questions raised in this book are about the extent to which economic restructuring is associated with equally significant social and cultural changes, whether it is possible to point out major structural changes in social divisions in the UK today, and whether the distribution of income, wealth, life chances and opportunities is being transformed.

It is the notion of a radical shift or transformation in the social structure that is at issue here. For, in advanced industrial societies like the UK, there is little doubt that there has been continuous social change over many decades. Taking the years since the end of the Second World War, for example, there have been marked changes in the nature and type of jobs available, reflected in changing occupational divisions. Increasing numbers of men, and more recently of women, have entered new types of white-collar and service-sector employment, with very different working conditions from the old, heavy industrial jobs of previous decades. There have been shifts in the distribution of income, new lifestyles have arisen based on the growth of consumer goods industries, and patterns of shopping and leisure behaviour have changed fundamentally. An associated change has been a rise in the proportion of households who own their own homes.

---

* Details of this course, D314 *Restructuring Britain*, are available from the Student Enquiries office, The Open University, PO Box 71, Milton Keynes MK7 6AG.

There have been changes in other areas too: the nature of provision in health, education and welfare has changed since the war. Free secondary schooling for children was introduced in 1944; the Beveridge Report of 1942, which proposed to rid Britain of the five giants of Want, Disease, Ignorance, Squalor and Idleness, introduced the concept of a free National Health Service and an insurance-based social security system. In many areas, the opportunities and life chances that face a child born in the 1980s are significantly different from those that existed in the 1940s.

Throughout the decades of relative affluence, social scientists focused on a series of questions about the changing class structure. The 'affluent worker' study (Goldthorpe and Lockwood, 1969), for example, was based on a series of hypotheses about how relative affluence and an increasingly privatized, family-based lifestyle was altering traditional working-class attitudes associated with community solidarity and workplace militancy. Theses about larger-scale social change such as the advent of a post-industrial society (Bell, 1974) seemed to promise a smooth transition to a better society in which the supermarket theory of social change – what the middle class have today the working class will have tomorrow – was dominant. But even during this period, research on poverty, on income distribution, on educational opportunities was a significant reminder that the *structural divisions* in British society remained unaltered (Townsend, 1979). Class differentials in earned and unearned incomes, in access to higher education, even in health and well-being, remained substantially unchanged. During these decades, too, in-migration of Afro-Caribbean people and, later, migrants from the Indian subcontinent and East Africa revealed more clearly not only the structures of class inequality in the UK but also the racist nature of British society. The majority of the in-migrants ended up working in the least well-paid positions in the economy and living in the poorest housing.

So what has changed? Has there been a radical transformation of British society in more recent decades or is it more accurate to focus on the continuance of earlier patterns? In many ways, the contributions to this reader emphasize the stability of the structures of social divisions in Britain. But perhaps the best answer to the question is to argue that both approaches are correct. There have been enormous changes in certain areas, in others the continuities are more noticeable.

There is little doubt that the 1980s have witnessed major changes in social divisions in Britain. The most important of these is undoubtedly the enormous rise in the numbers of the unemployed in the early 1980s, resulting in millions of individuals and families experiencing the decline in income associated with no wages and dependence on state benefits. Unemployment brings with it not only loss of income, but also, because of the central significance of paid employment in a capitalist society, the severe loss of status, physical and mental health and a whole range of social problems. But unemployment has not affected the UK population in an even way. It has had a disproportionate impact on particular groups and regions. Despite press coverage of middle-class and middle-management unemployment, it has been the most vulnerable sections of the population who have been most seriously affected by loss of work. The already low-paid and low-skilled members of the workforce, young workers and older workers, especially in the declining regions of the country, and members of ethnic minority groups in the inner areas of Britain's towns and cities are over-represented among the unemployed.

The exclusion of large numbers of individuals and families from waged work, and from access to many of the social and political organizations in Britain has led some commentators to write about a growing 'underclass'. The rise of this underclass largely coincided with the advent of a radical right-wing Conservative government with a rhetoric and set of ideological assumptions that challenged many of the conventional beliefs and assumptions about the role of the state and the individual. Widespread attitudes about the 'right' to state benefits, about the nature and the extent of state provision of health, housing and education have been re-evaluated. Moral assertions about the responsibilities of the individual, the superiority of self-help, and the importance of the private market now dominate discussions about the role of the welfare state. Economic and taxation policies have also been based on assumptions about the need for an 'enterprise' culture and rewards for those who take risks. Changes in the structure of taxation have fundamentally challenged the principles of progressive redistribution. It is in this context that we need to examine carefully the evidence for and against the assertion that there has been a fundamental restructuring of social divisions in contemporary Britain.

The examination of this assertion raises the question of which social divisions should be considered. The areas that we have chosen to concentrate on in this Reader are class, race and gender – without doubt three of the key social divisions in the UK today – and a set of related issues about the distribution of wealth, income and consumption between individuals and classes. As well as income from waged work, the ownership of wealth and access to a set of goods and resources distributed both in the market and by the state are fundamental determinants of life chances. Thus, an examination of the structure of ownership and consumption is a central part of the Reader. As well as material changes, it is often argued that contemporary Britain is a culturally different place from earlier decades. Increasing emphasis on individualism, an 'enterprise' culture, and the rise of a new service class characterize Britain in the 1980s. This contrasts with the more solidaristic and collectivist values of previous decades, which were entrenched, if not in Britain as a whole, in the old working-class heartlands that used to be dominated by heavy industry. We have included a number of articles that examine these social and cultural changes and the extent to which they are resulting in Britain becoming a more homogeneous society.

The Reader is divided into Sections that reflect these divisions, starting with an introductory article by Halsey. This is followed by three Sections which focus on class, race and gender issues respectively. Section V includes articles on inequalities in the distribution of income and wealth and then turns to examine the way in which a set of new social divisions, based on whether or not households or classes have access to publicly or privately provided housing, education and health services, cuts across production-based class divisions. In Section VI the nature of cultural change in the restructuring of contemporary Britain is at issue.

All the contributions to this Reader deal in different ways with the question of social change and the extent to which there has been a radical reshaping of social relations. Some emphasize the continuity with past forms, others the break; yet again, others present a more complicated argument about how the past itself is reshaped to achieve the new transformation. The introductions to the following Sections also consider questions of change and continuity and the ways in which the key social divisions of class, race and gender themselves intersect and are intercut by divisions based on the distribution of income, wealth and public and private goods and services.

Halsey (Chapter 1) examines the extent to which new forms of social polarization are apparent in the late 1980s. His belief is that we are at a historical watershed and he marshals an impressive array of evidence to support his contention. Halsey dates the emergence of the new division from the oil crisis of the mid-1970s. He argues that a new version of Disraeli's 'two nations' is appearing in late twentieth century Britain.

The most marked change in the class structure of Britain as a whole has been its growing diversity, decomposition and feminization. Taking occupational categories as an indication of the growing divisions, a more complex distribution has developed. At one end of the spectrum, there appears to have been a 'managerial revolution' that, with the rise of large corporations, has increasingly separated ownership from control. In the middle ranks of occupations, economic restructuring, greater educational opportunities and the growth of the arts and the media as employers has led to a new 'service class' of salaried professionals. On the other hand, at the bottom end of the occupational structure, changes in the labour process associated in particular with the introduction of new technology have led to the growing proletarianization of many previously non-manual or skilled occupations. Some discussions of this process associate it with the feminization of the labour force as increasing numbers of women are drawn into the new forms of proletarian work. Certainly one of the major changes of the last few decades has been the rapid rise in the extent of women's participation in the waged labour force.

In Sections II to IV of the Reader, the causes and consequences of these changes are examined. Heath and McDonald (Chapter 2) evaluate the debate about the decline of the working class, as male employment in heavy industries falls, and the consequences for voting patterns. The decline of the Labour vote is often explained by the decline of Labour's traditional heartlands of support, but this argument is only partly borne out by the evidence. Leadbeater (Chapter 3) also concentrates on the working class but looks at new divisions *within* the working class. He argues that changes in the labour market, in particular the growth of contract, temporary and casual labour, have created a growing underclass composed of the unemployed and those workers employed on non-permanent contracts.

This shift has opened up a new division between a core of relatively well-off, securely employed workers and their families and a 'periphery' of disadvantaged groups. Many of the periphery are black and women workers. In Chapter 4, Crompton and Jones examine the interrelationship of changes in the gender composition of the clerical labour force and deskilling in the labour process, and the impact of these changes on the hierarchies of control and structures of promotion in office occupations. They argue that the proletarianization of previously middle-class occupations is a consequence of the intersection of these changes. Finally in Section II, Scott (Chapter 5) focuses on the upper end of the class structure, looking at questions of privilege and ownership. It is sometimes argued that a new class of propertyless, well-educated managers has replaced older structures in which the landed aristocracy controlled industrial and finance capital, but Scott shows that the upper class still dominate because they provide most of these key managers.

Section III deals with issues of race, starting with an overview by Miles of the ways in which different theorists view the class situation of the ethnic minorities (Chapter 6). In the 'enterprise' culture of Thatcher's Britain, the role of the small businessman (*sic*) is often extolled as exemplifying *par excellence* the new economic trends, and in Chapter 7, Ward demonstrates how alternative explanations of Asian settlement and employment patterns apply to different areas and their role in the UK economy. Then, from a different perspective, Gilroy evaluates the success of anti-racist policies at two different periods, the mid-1970s and the early 1980s, focusing in particular on the links between anti-racist and class politics (Chapter 8).

Section IV examines the relationship between gender and economic and social change. Both chapters show how current changes in the labour market – restructuring, deskilling and the shift towards service sector jobs – have reinforced women's position as low-paid workers, despite the introduction of equal pay and sex discrimination legislation in the mid-1970s designed to improve women's position relative to men's. In a case study of secretarial work, Webster (Chapter 9) shows how a seemingly objective term such as 'deskilling' hides not only a diverse set of changes but also social attitudes about the nature of 'women's work'. The ways in which attitudes about gender and femininity structure work are the focus of the three extracts in Chapter 10, from a book by Sallie Westwood. She extends the argument about the links between social and economic change and gender in three specific ways. First, she looks at how the relationship between class and gender has been theorized in an assessment of the debate about capitalism and patriarchy. Secondly, she argues that the cultural construction of femininity is both used and produced in the workplace, and finally she integrates a discussion of racism into her conclusions about women's place in the labour market, thus drawing together the three key social divisions considered in Sections II to IV.

In Section V, the focus is on distributional issues. The examples chosen are the distribution of income and wealth, and housing. Here the evidence about structural change is more difficult to assess. In Chapter 11, Pond shows how the concentration of wealth in the hands of a minority divides the nation, linking back to a theme in Chapter 1. The next three chapters look at different aspects of change in the housing market. The expansion of home ownership has been a feature of the entire post-war period, albeit encouraged by particular policies of the Thatcher governments. Saunders (Chapter 12) suggests that the growth of owner occupation has opened up a new social cleavage between those who own and those who rent. The significance of owning a house is that it is a tradable capital asset as well as a security for raising loans and, as such, potentially opens access to large amounts of capital for owners or their dependants that do not accrue to those who rent their homes. The growth of home ownership has been the major factor in the reduction in differentials in the ownership of wealth in post-war Britain, although marked regional differences in house prices have made the impact geographically uneven.

Since 1979, there has been a growing emphasis on private means of provision to replace previous forms of collective provision in many areas of the welfare state. Private education and health care are growing sectors, but it is in the area of housing that collective provision – council housing – has been under greatest attack. The other two articles in Section V examine different aspects of the privatization of housing.

Finally, Section VI considers the question of cultural change in the UK and its effects in different parts of the country. The changing social structure of contemporary Britain takes a specific geographical form. The new managerial and service class, the core workers, the affluent and secure tend to live in different areas of Britain from the poor and deprived members of society, the peripheral workers and the underclass. Broadly, the former live in suburban and rural areas of the prosperous South-East, whereas the latter are trapped in peripheral regions, in the inner areas of large cities and on decaying estates at the edges. In the former, prosperous areas, the reworking of Britain's rural heritage and bucolic past form potent images that attract the service class to its particular residential environment and also enable the countryside and the past to be marketed. Hewison (Chapter 16) examines the role of the country house as a potent symbol in this. In deprived areas, quite different images of an industrial past are sometimes one of the main economic assets of the area – cotton mills, old foundries, even coal mines are opened in increasing numbers as industrial museums and tourist attractions. It is less easy to remodel the inner city into a satisfactory image, but Wright (Chapter 17) shows that it is possible, given the right mix of history, Victorian housing and current demand from particular types of households.

The theme of leisure, partially examined by Hewison, is picked up again by Urry (Chapter 15). His article looks at a relatively neglected effect of the changing class structure and changing patterns of consumption – the impact on holiday-making. Affluence for many, advertising, the role of the mass media have all altered people's images of themselves as tourists and their expectations about holidays. Urry draws links between changes in the class structure, family relationships, the distinction between home and work and holiday-making.

The issues covered by these articles and the evidence presented about the nature of social change are diverse. It is clear that contemporary Britain is very different from the Britain of forty years before. But change has occurred at a different pace in different parts of the country. Social divides, on the basis of class, race or gender, are affected by the history of local areas and their previous social structure and local culture, and it is clear that the UK remains a socially and geographically divided country, although whether there has been a radical break with the past remains debatable.

References

BELL, D. (1974) *The Coming of Post-Industrial Society*, New York, Basic Books.

GOLDTHORPE, J. H. and LOCKWOOD, D. (1969) *The Affluent Worker in the Class Structure*, Cambridge, Cambridge University Press.

TOWNSEND, P. (1979) *Poverty in the United Kingdom*, Harmondsworth, Penguin.

1   Social trends since World War II

A. H. Halsey[1]

Social Trends was introduced in 1970 by the Head of the Government Statistical Services.[2] From the outset it included trend statistics from offical sources reaching back to the 1951 census and even further back towards the beginning of the century on some demographic topics.[3] The publication also included some attempt to compare Britain with other countries, especially the 'first world' states with membership of the Organization for Economic Cooperation and Development (OECD). By 1987, therefore, an arithmetic post-war history of a large number of facets of British social structure had been compiled with at least some comparative international reference.

So the purpose of this article could be to elaborate its title. But that simple definition is impracticable: a focus, even an arbitrary one, is necessary if only for reasons of space. And even so there could be no unique and objective recipe for choosing particular social trends. Selection is inevitable, stemming from an implicit or explicit interpretation as to what social processes have been significant. More fundamentally there is always an underlying theory of social structure and social change. [. . .]

Moreover it must be remarked in caution that the very concept of a trend may generate unintended distortion. Trends are absurdly easy to find. If between two points of time a series of observations yields neither random fluctuation nor absolute stability there must be a trend. But so what? Even stability may be significant; for example a zero rate of population growth would have momentous social implications in most countries in our time. There is no escape from interpreting the significance of a phenomenon, whether rising, falling or trendless. Moreover bias may come in subtle forms from contentious, unproven, or false theories of history. There are no established laws of historical development or decline. Thus modern scepticism towards the view that social institutions evolved and culminated in Victorian liberal society – the so-called Whig version of British history – could be said to be an extravagant preference for graphs moving upwards to the right. The underlying theory is a belief in progress and in the superiority of European civilization, especially the activities of British men. Similarly the Marxist theory of history, at least for 'capitalist' societies, looks for downward trends, for example in the rate of profit or the income of proletarians, towards a revolutionary crisis.

These cautions notwithstanding, the trends identified as significant by one observer can at least serve to invite other readers to specify or sharpen their own interpretations of [social changes]. I have chosen from a thousand possibilities to consider how the evidence from official statistics bears on two widely accepted generalizations in the contemporary social sciences. The first is that Britain has experienced a comprehensive renegotiation of the division of labour over the past forty years. The second is that a post-war period can be identified as having come to an end in the mid-1970s, followed by a decade exhibiting a new form of polarization in British society.

The Context

Britain's position in the world is the anxious subject of popular debate at the present time. The United Kingdom is still a major figure in the world as a whole. It has a gross domestic product (GDP) of over £300 billion (about 6⅓ per cent of the GDP of the OECD countries). However, its relative economic position has been weakening for many years. In the decade 1975 to 1984 the GDP of the OECD block grew by 12 per cent more than in the United Kingdom. On the other hand the first quarter century of the reign of Elizabeth II was one of mounting prosperity. Between 1951 and 1976 real disposable income per capita at 1980 prices rose from £1,375 to £2,536. The average real weekly earnings of male manual workers aged 21 or over rose from £60 in April 1951 to £109 and further to £111 in April 1983.[4] Basic paid holidays for manual workers increased from one and three quarter weeks to three and a half weeks; ownership of cars rose from about 14 per cent of households to 56 per cent (62 per cent in 1985) and, in general, post-war Britain has been an increasingly prosperous society.[5]

In April 1986 the newspapers were carrying comment on the possibility of new rules concerning the retirement of women from employment and their entitlement to pensions. This single news item is sufficient to dramatize how much British society has changed in the period since the end of the Second World War. Today the underlying assumptions are that men and women should be treated equally with respect to employment and that laws with respect to gender and employment relations could originate in Europe and have a claim to adherence in Britain. Both assumptions would have seemed weird to British citizens under an Attlee government. Women at that time were thought of as belonging primarily and essentially to the domestic economy, social equality was thought to be about class rather than gender, and the idea of any kind of primacy for European over British law would have been swamped by the shared conception of Britain as an imperial world power, of London as the centre of the world through which the Greenwich meridian appropriately ran, and by awareness that a quarter of the world's population as well as a quarter of the land surface were under British control. [. . .]

In 1945 the island society, on this perspective, comprised the upper echelons of a worldwide commonwealth. In the 40 subsequent years the size of the UK population, though 16 per cent up in absolute numbers, has declined from constituting one fiftieth to contributing a mere one hundredth to the population of the world as a whole. For better or worse, the first industrial and the greatest imperial nation has been displaced within the memory of those aged 50 or more from the centre of the economic, military and political stage, if not to a marginal offshore station of Western Europe, at least to a relatively minor position among the world's major powers.

So much then for context and as a safeguard against the interpretation of British statistics as representing the inevitable historical pathway of all industrial societies. Every country has its peculiar genius. Britain's post-war record is not a reliable proxy for the recent history of Western, European, industrial, capitalist, 'first world', 'post-industrial', democratic, or any other postulated type of society. It is within the context of British experience that our two theses concerning the renegotiation of the division of labour and the passing of the post-war period into a new phase of polarization may be discussed.

The division of labour

Behind its virtue and its victory Britain emerged from the Second World War as a classical industrial economy, a centralized democratic polity, and a familistic social structure. It was a society with historical roots in a social order in which there had been minimal government, and in which welfare had been dominated by the relation between the family and the workplace through the market for labour. The institutional division of labour of prototypic industrialism was an essential triangle joining the family, the economy, and the state. Families had raised children, men had worked, women had run households. The economy produced, the family reproduced and consumed, and the state protected and redistributed.

All this was to change. In political terms there was a national consensus built during the war on the need for a welfare state which, in an earlier political language, constituted 'interference' in the exchanges between the family and the economy. The rise of the welfare state required an elaboration of the collection of taxes (partly from households, partly from enterprises, and partly from the labour market transactions between them) to be used as redistributive resources for the education of children, the relief of men temporarily out of work, the maintenance of women without men to connect them to the economy, the sustenance of the old, and the protection of the health and safety of the population as a whole.

In the following generation a different and more elaborate pattern of relationships was developed. Thus the family produces as well as consumes. People take recreation, or 'live', as well as work in factories and work as well as live in houses. The family has fewer children and breaks up as well as re-forms more frequently. Women have become more incorporated into the formal economy and men have been drawn back more into the houshold and the informal economy. Adults as well as children learn. More children than in the past labour competitively for qualifications during their compulsory years at school. The state, especially in the early part of the period, was drawn more into the productive system, partly through the taxation and regulation of firms but also in the direct production of goods and of an increasingly complicated array of social services. In short, all of the words used to describe the classical triangle now have modified meanings because each of the major institutions has invaded or absorbed the traditional functions of the other two. Leisure in the family includes do-it-yourself activities, business enterprises and trade unions have taken on some of the regulatory functions of government, and the state, through its employment of policemen, doctors, nurses, teachers, and social workers, has comprehensively invaded the traditional role of the parent. All of these shifts, institutional and individual, together add up to a renegotiated division of labour in the Britain of the 1980s compared with that of the 1940s.

Accordingly, it should be possible to identify statistical trends reflecting, manifesting, or exemplifying the movements in the division of labour which I have sketched. Comparing the beginning and the end of the period we should find that the following changes have occurred.

In the family (see Table 1.1)
1   more women, especially married women, in employment
2   less childbirth, but more illegitimate childbirth
3   more divorce and remarriage and more one-person households
4   more men economically inactive whether as unemployed, retired, or drawn into the domestic economy
5   more men and women in adult education
6   more children in extended schooling
7   a population with higher formal qualifications

Statistics taken from the various editions of *Social Trends* confirm these expectations. Between the end of the war and the mid-1980s the proportion of economically active women has risen from just over a third to nearly half, and the proportion of economically active married women, albeit mainly in part-time jobs, has more than doubled. In the same period fertility, though peaking in 1964, has fallen below replacement levels and there has been a multiplication of nearly four in the proportion of illegitimate to total births. Moreover, not only has reproduction made this marginal but significant movement out of the framework of the traditional family, but the family itself is less stable in the sense that there was a more than fivefold increase in the divorce rate between 1961 and 1985 and remarriages now account for over a third of all marriages. The fragility of the family is also represented in a different way by the rise of the one-person household from less than a tenth of all households before the Second World War to a quarter of them now. Some of this trend is, of course, attributable to the ageing of the population.

The reciprocal movement of men into domesticity is also revealed by the evidence in Table 1.1. But again the reduction in the percentage of men who are economically active is mainly caused by the retirement of increasing numbers of men over 65.

Table 1.1 Trends in the family, United Kingdom

	1931	1951	1961	1966	1971	1976	1981	1985
1. *Percentage of all women aged 16 or over economically active*[1]	34[6]	35[7]	37[7]	42[7]	43[7]	47	48	49
Percentage of married women aged 16 or over economically active[1]	10[6]	22[7]	30[7]	38[7]	42[7]	49	49	52
2. *Total period fertility rate*[1,2]		2.16	2.78	2.78	2.40	1.72	1.79	1.78
Illegitimate births as a percentage of all births	5	5	6	8	8	9	13	19
Persons divorcing per 1 000 married population[3]		3	2	3	6	10	12	13
3. *Remarriages as a percentage of all marriages*	11[1]	18[1]	15[1]	16[1]	20	31	34	35
One-person households as a percentage of all households[1]	7	11	12	15	18	21	22	24
4. *Percentage of all men 16 or over economically active*[1]	91[6]	88[7]	86[7]	84[7]	81[7]	79	76	74
Men in the domestic economy			See Table 7.2					
5. *Thousands of students*[4]								
In part-time higher education[5]: Men			107	115	142	168	207	212
Women			6	8	23	50	87	107
Aged 21 or over in								
Non advanced further education					1 987	2 260[8]	1 986[9]	2 200
of which adult education							1 169[9]	1 349
Part-time higher education[5]						201[8]	236	269
Full-time higher education[5]					216	266[8]	235	252
6. Children in extended schooling			See Figure 1.1					
7. Formal qualifications			See Figure 1.2					

1 Great Britain only.
2 The average number of children which would be born per woman if women experienced the age specific fertility rates of the period in question throughout their child-bearing life-span.
3 England and Wales only.
4 Data are for academic years ending in the year shown.
5 Includes Universities, Open University, and advanced courses in major establishments of further education.
6 Aged 14 or over.   7 Aged 15 or over.   8 1976/77.   9 1981/82.

Source: British Labour Statistics Historical Abstract; Population Trends, Office of Population Censuses and Surveys; Department of Education and Science; Central Statistical Office

Figures for enrolments of adults aged 21 or over on both leisure and vocational courses illustrate the rising tendency for adults to learn, while Figure 1.1 shows the trend towards extended schooling among children. The tendency to voluntary extension has continued into the recent difficult years on top of the raising of the school leaving age from 15 to 16 in 1972.

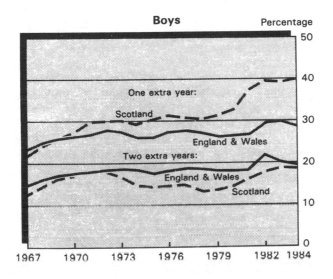

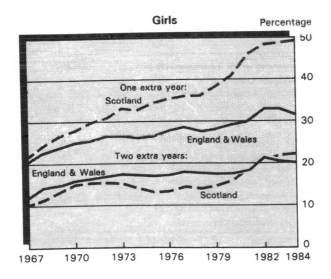

Figure 1.1 Pupils staying on at school for at least 1 extra year, and at least 2 extra years: by sex, England & Wales and Scotland

Source: Department of Education and Science; Scottish Education Department; Welsh Office

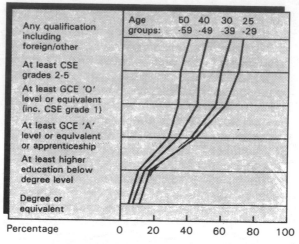

Figure 1.2   Highest qualification level of the population: by age, 1985, Great Britain

Source: Labour Force Survey, 1985, Department of Employment

And Figure 1.2 illustrates the marked rise in the level of qualifications held in the population during the past 30 years. This particular form of illustration also brings out how trends of this kind form, so to speak, geological strata of age cohorts in the population at a given point of time. In this case, in 1985, 72 per cent of the population in the 25 to 29 age group held an educational qualification, whereas only 40 per cent of those aged 50 to 59 did so.

In the economy (see Table 1.2)
The expected correlative changes in the economy include:
8   a higher GDP per capita
9   a less manual workforce
10   shorter hours of work
11   longer holidays

These changes are illustrated in Table 1.2. The national income continued to rise. At 1980 prices GDP grew from 1961 (£148 billion) to 1973 (£215 billion) at about 3 per cent per year. Growth from 1973 to 1980 slowed to about 1 per cent per year. Between 1973 and 1984 the increase in GDP per capita was 1 per cent compared with 1½ per cent for all the OECD countries.

   The proportion of both men and women in manual occupations declined. This gradual transformation of what was, at the beginning of the century, the most proletarianized country in the world (i.e. composed

Table 1.2　Trends in the economy, United Kingdom

	1931	1951	1961	1966	1971	1976	1981	1985
8. Gross domestic product at market prices								
1980 prices (£s billion)		112	148	171	195	220	228	253
Index (1980 = 100)		49	64	74	85	96	99	110
Per head (£s)		2 226	2 811	3 138	3 495	3 918	4 037	4 465
9. *Percentage of men in manual occupations*[1]	77	72			62		58	
Percentage of women in manual occupations[1]	76	64			53		44	
Percentage of total in manual occupations[1]	77	70			59		52	
10. *Average weekly hours of work*[1,2]*, for full-time male manual employees*	48[4]	48	48	46	46	45	44[2]	44
11. *Percentage of manual employees*[3] *with basic holiday entitlement of over 3 weeks*		—	—	—	4	81	98	100

1　Great Britain only.
2　At April. Prior to 1983 data cover males aged 21 or over; since then they cover males on adult rates.
3　Employees covered by national collective agreements or Wages Council Orders.
4　October 1938.

Source: Guy Routh, *Occupation and Pay in Great Britain*, Cambridge University Press, 1965; British Labour Statistics Historical Abstract; Central Statistical Office; *Social Trends*

Table 1.3   Self-rated social class, 1986, Great Britain

	Percentages and numbers	
	Self	Parents
Social class (*percentages*)		
Upper middle	*1*	*2*
Middle	*24*	*17*
Upper working	*21*	*12*
Working	*48*	*59*
Poor	*3*	*8*
Don't know/no response	*3*	*2*
Sample size (= 100%) (numbers)	3 066	3 066

Source: British Social Attitudes Survey, 1986, Social and Community Planning Research

mainly by the industrial working class), appears in a different guise in Table 1.3. In 1984, 29 per cent of a national sample of adults thought of themselves as having moved into a higher social class and only 9 per cent thought of themselves as having come down in the world compared with their parents. Between the two generations, hours of work were reduced and holidays enlarged. Whereas at the end of the war no manual workers were entitled, now virtually all have the right to four weeks paid holiday.

In the state (see Table 1.4)
With respect to statistics concerning government we would expect to find:
12   higher expenditure on education
13   increased numbers of parent surrogates in the employment of the state (police, teachers, doctors, social workers, etc)
14   increased nursery provision for the under fives
15   a higher proportion of the GDP spent by the state

These invasions of the traditional realm of the family are illustrated in Table 1.4. Expenditure and manpower in education, health, and the social services are higher today than they were at the end of the 1940s. The state spends more than it did then out of a much bigger national purse. There are in fact more policemen, doctors, nurses, and social workers and there are more children in school or otherwise in the care of the public authorities. [. . .] Between 1976 and 1983 the total of those employed in the health and personal social services increased by nearly 13 per cent. It is true that the numbers working in the NHS in England fell by about 2 per cent between 31 March 1983 and 31 March 1985.[6] But this is an element in the second of our theses to which we can now turn having given the first a reasonable foundation in the statistical record.

Table 1.4 Trends in the state, United Kingdom

Percentages and thousands

	1931	1951	1961	1966	1971	1976	1981	1985
12. *Government expenditure on education as a percentage of gross domestic product*[1]					5.2	6.3	5.5	5.1
13. Manpower in social services[2] (thousands)	769	1 188	1 725	2 088	1 978[5]			
Regional and District Health Authorities Staff (thousands)						926	1 026	1 023[7]
Family practitioner professionals (thousands)						49	54	58[7]
Personal social services (thousands)						228	251	273[7]
14. *Under fives in education as a percentage of all 3 and 4 year olds*				15	20	34	44	47
Day care places for under fives (thousands)[3] at end March		51[4]	54[4]	128[4]	409	511	540	609
15. *General government expenditure as a percentage of gross domestic product*			35	38	41	46	46	45

1 Financial years ending in the year shown.
2 Education, health, welfare, and social security. Includes part-time.
3 England and Wales only.
4 At end December.
5 Estimated full-time equivalent total for 1970.
6 1972.
7 1984.

Source: *Social Trends* (various), Central Statistical Office.

Economic transformation and social polarization

It is now generally recognized that the post-war period for Britain and for other 'first world' countries came to an end with the oil crisis of 1973–74. The preceding 30 years had been a period of economic boom in the form of high rates of economic growth and full employment with burgeoning public sector activity. The more recent period has been one of declining employment, shifting economic activity out of classical towards 'high tech' or service industry, struggles with inflation, determination to move decision-making out of Westminster and Whitehall into the market and the locality, and policies designed to move activity from the public to the private sector. The question is not so much as to whether this historical watershed is a reality; that is not in serious dispute. It is rather to ask how it is reflected in the statistics pertaining to the process of renegotiating the division of labour. Clearly the post-war boom and the current period of transition are fairly sharply distinguished by their rates of unemployment and their shifts out of manufacturing industry, into the service sector[7]. Meanwhile the arrest of upward trends if not the 'rolling back of the frontiers of the state' is indicated by expressing total government expenditure as a percentage of GDP (though the latter does *not* include transfer payments such as social security). It was 35.5 per cent in 1961, peaked at 48.6 per cent in 1975, and was 45.2 per cent in 1985. But most of the trends in the reorganization of family and economic life are the result of forces other than those which operate as relations between government and the governed. The changing structure of relations between classes, sexes, and age groups may or may not be modified by political activity but, at least in the case of Britain since the Second World War, have not been fundamentally changed in the direction of their development.

There remains, however, the question of whether the distribution of life chances – and the modern national state is, after all, the principal redistributive agent in society – has been crucially altered since the mid-1970s and particularly since the new administration which came in in 1979. This brings us to the hypothesized new trend towards polarization – a widening gap between two components of the population as a whole.

A hundred years ago, discussion of Disraeli's 'two nations' was the stock-in-trade of political arithmeticians. In the 1880s most social observers in Britain agreed that the Marxist polarization thesis of the 1840s, with its prophecy of mass pauperization, of exploited labour and the accumulation of surplus value into fewer and fewer capitalist hands, had been tested and found wanting in the natural laboratory of Victorian history. By and large, the social trends ran in the opposite direction and, however slowly and haltingly, continued to do so through the first three quarters of the twentieth century. But now the question is raised as to whether a new version of the two nations has appeared in the last decade in the form of a widening division between a prosperous majority in secure and increasingly well remunerated employment by contrast with a depressed minority of the

Table 1.5 Distribution of original, disposable, and final household income, United Kingdom

Percentages

| | Quintile groups of households | | | | | |
	Bottom fifth	Next fifth	Middle fifth	Next fifth	Top fifth	Total
Original income[1]						
1976	0.8	9.4	18.8	26.6	44.4	100.0
1981	0.6	8.1	18.0	26.9	46.4	100.0
1983	0.3	6.7	17.7	27.2	48.0	100.0
1984	0.3	6.1	17.5	27.5	48.6	100.0
Disposable income[2]						
1976	7.0	12.6	18.2	24.1	38.1	100.0
1981	6.7	12.1	17.7	24.1	39.4	100.0
1983	6.9	11.9	17.6	24.0	39.6	100.0
1984	6.7	11.7	17.5	24.4	39.7	100.0
Final income[3]						
1976	7.4	12.7	18.0	24.0	37.9	100.0
1981	7.1	12.4	17.9	24.0	38.6	100.0
1983	6.9	12.2	17.6	24.0	39.3	100.0
1984	7.1	12.1	17.5	24.3	39.0	100.0

1 Households ranked by original income.
2 Households ranked by disposable income.
3 Households ranked by final income.
Source: Central Statistical Office, from Family Expenditure Survey

unemployed, the sick, the old, and the unsuccessful ethnic minorities.

Evidence on three aspects of this thesis can be examined. First there are the trends recorded in *Social Trends* on the distribution of income and wealth between the better and the worse off families, shown here as Table 1.5. Between 1976 and 1984, the movement of original or market incomes was towards greater inequality. The bottom fifth of households dropped their share fom 0.8 to 0.3 per cent and the top fifth moved up from 44.4 to 48.6 per cent. The redistributive activity of the state modified this inequality but did not change the direction of movement. The bottom group had final household incomes amounting to 7.4 per cent of the whole in 1976 reduced to 7.1 per cent in 1984, while the top fifth raised their share from 37.9 to 39.0 per cent.

On the side of wealth the story shown in Table 1.6 is less clear. In 1984, the richest 1 per cent and 10 per cent of the adult population owned 21 and 52 per cent respectively of marketable wealth. With the addition of pension rights (both occupational and state) these shares declined to 12 and 35 per cent. In the early 1970s the share of marketable wealth owned by the

Table 1.6   Distribution of wealth, United Kingdom

			Percentages and £s billion	
	1971	1976	1981	1984
Marketable wealth				
Percentage of wealth				
owned by:				
Most wealthy 1%[1]	*31*	*24* [3]	*21*	*21*
Most wealthy 5%[1]	*52*	*45*	*40*	*39*
Most wealthy 10%[1]	*65*	*60*	*54*	*52*
Most wealthy 25%[1]	*86*	*84*	*77*	*75*
Most wealthy 50%[1]	*97*	*95*	*94*	*93*
Total marketable				
wealth (£s billion)	140	*263*	*546*	762
Marketable wealth plus				
occupational and				
state pension rights				
Percentage of wealth				
owned by:				
Most wealthy 1%[1]	*21*	*14*	*12*	*12*
Most wealthy 5%[1]	*37*	*27*	*24*	*25*
Most wealthy 10%[1]	*49*	*37*	*34*	*35*
Most wealthy 25%[1,2]	*69-72*	*58-61*	*55-58*	*56-59*
Most wealthy 50%[1,2]	*85-89*	*80-85*	*78-82*	*79-83*

1 Of population aged 18 or over.
2 Estimates vary with assumptions.
3 Between 1979 and 1980 there was a change in methodology as described in
   Inland Revenue Statistics 1986.
Source: Inland Revenue

richest groups was reduced by a marked fall in the prices of stocks and shares. The late 1970s and early 1980s brought very little change in the pattern of ownership.

With respect to social mobility John Goldthorpe and Clive Payne have concluded unequivocally from their analysis of the 1983 General Election study that 'the stability of relative rates or chances of inter-generational class mobility, which our analyses of the 1972 data suggested went back to the 1920s, has *not* been disturbed to any appreciable degree in the first decade after the ending of the post-war era'.[8] But these authors then go on to examine whether absolute rates have been affected by the new period of transition and particularly whether there has been a freezing of mobility and especially the upward mobility of working class and lower-middle class sons into the middle-class professions, salariat, or 'service class'. The evidence is that absolute rates of upward and of total mobility have continued to rise. A comparison of the 1972 and 1983 samples of these national enquiries is given in Table 1.7. In 1972, 16.0 per cent of the men of working-class origin had found their way into the middle class; by 1983 the

Table 1.7   Class distribution: by class of father, 1972 and 1983, England and Wales

Percentages

| | Respondent's class | | | |
	Middle	Lower-middle	Working	All
Father's class				
1972				
Middle	*57.7*	*23.2*	*19.1*	*100.0*
Lower-middle	*31.2*	*31.9*	*37.0*	*100.0*
Working	*16.0*	*22.7*	*61.2*	*100.0*
1983				
Middle	*62.0*	*22.2*	*15.8*	*100.0*
Lower-middle	*34.2*	*34.3*	*31.5*	*100.0*
Working	*23.6*	*23.8*	*52.6*	*100.0*

Source: Trends in Intergenerational Class Mobility in England and Wales 1972–83, John Goldthorpe and Clive Payne, *Sociology*, Vol. 20

percentage had risen to 23.6. Again, in 1972, 61.2 per cent of those of working-class parentage were themselves in working-class jobs; by 1983 the percentage had fallen to 52.6. Thus there is considerable support for the optimistic liberal theory of a technologically led expansion of middle-class opportunities. But the picture has then to be modified by considering unemployment.

In 1972, the unemployment rate was virtually negligible. In 1983 it was in double figures at over 12 per cent, and more than a million had been out of work for at least a year. The unemployed could reasonably be viewed as an additional depressed class which has objectively to be analysed as a 'destination status' in mobility tables. So, while the expansion of the professional and technical middle class remains a feature of late twentieth century Britain, as it was in the long boom from mid century, unemployment has also emerged as a structure of negative opportunity which tends to polarize mobility chances, especially of those who begin in the working class.

A similar process of social division has also been observed in housing. The dominant trend in the twentieth century has been towards owner occupation and much encouraged in recent years. From this study of trends in housing tenure, Hamnett[9] concludes that, as between owner occupation and local authority renting, there has been 'an increasing degree of social polarization'.

Finally, we may consider the evidence of spatial polarization assembled in the Archbishop of Canterbury's report on Urban Priority Areas, *Faith in the City* (1985).[10]

Using the most recent studies of the Economic and Social Research Council,[11] the Archbishop's Commission assembled a comparison of types of area in Britain in terms of a composite measure of advantage and

Table 1.8   Inner city polarization: by type of area, 1971 and 1981

	Numbers and percentages	
	Advantage and deprivation index 1981[1]	Population change (%) 1971 to 1981
Metropolitan inner cities		
Inner Birmingham	− 2.37	− *19.3*
Inner Manchester	− 1.77	− *25.5*
Peripheral council estates		
Knowsley	− 1.36	− *15.3*
Other old city centres		
Inner Derby	− 1.97	− *20.1*
Other old industrial urban areas		
Outer Derby	0.58	+ *7.4*
Rest of Greater Manchester	0.67	+ *0.4*
Rest of Outer London	1.42	− *9.0*
Fringe areas		
West Midlands south fringe	1.43	+ *16.6*
Mersey north fringe	1.22	+ *17.1*
Manchester south fringe	1.29	+ *5.3*
London south fringe	2.32	− *3.8*

Source: Faith in the City, Report of the Archbishop of Canterbury's Commission on Urban Priority Areas

deprivation.[12] The measures include such indicators as the proportion of people unemployed (negative), in professional jobs (positive), the infant mortality rate, the proportions of owner occupiers and of car owners, and many other manifestations of prosperity or poverty. Column 1 of Table 1.8 shows that there is a gradient of advantage ascending from the inner city districts and the peripheral council estates to the fringe areas outside classical industrial Britain. The second column of Table 1.8 shows the shifts in population between 1971 and 1981. Column 1 shows the clear gradient of multiple inequality from the urban priority areas to the fringe areas. Column 2 shows that the urban priority areas are losing population. The process is one of deprived people being left in the urban priority areas as the successful move out to middle Britain.

Of course, the poor are not confined to the urban priority areas. As the Archbishop's Commissioners put it: 'The city remains part magnet to the disadvantaged newcomer, part prison to the unskilled, the disabled, and the dispirited, part springboard for the ambitious and vigorous who find escape to suburbia, and part protection for enclaves of affluence.'[13]

Summary conclusion

The search for trends necessarily involves selection and interpretation. It is moreover a procedure which intrinsically emphasizes change rather than continuity. The perspective adopted here focuses on changes in the relations between family, economy, and government – what I have called the institutional division of labour – and shows a process of renegotiation of function between them. Government has taken on more familial and more economic functions; industry has absorbed more regulatory duties; the family has weakened in the stability of its marriages and its fertility. The traditional meanings and loci of masculinity, femininity, adulthood, childhood, work, leisure, and learning have all changed as the division of labour has shifted.

The post-war period to the mid-1970s was one of economic growth, full employment, and prosperity against an international background of rapid dismantling of imperial power and relative decline of economic productivity. The managerial, professional, and technical classes waxed and the industrial working class waned. Women, particularly married women, moved increasingly into paid employment.

Then, after the oil crisis of the mid-1970s, a new phase of economic and social transformation appeared. The shift away from nineteenth century urban industrial manufacturing was accelerated, unemployment rose, and population movement away from the inner cities towards suburbia, the South East, and new towns was discernable. And, in the process, a pattern has emerged of a more unequal society as between a majority in secure attachment to a still prosperous country and a minority in marginal economic and social conditions, the former moving into the suburban locations of the newer economy of a 'green and pleasant land', the latter tending to be trapped into the old provincial industrial cities and their displaced fragments of peripheral council housing estates. In short a still recognizable Britain is facing new challenges in the late twentieth century as it carries on its ancient struggle to combine freedom and equality in a United Kingdom.

Notes

1   Professor Halsey is Director of the Department of Social and Administrative Studies at the University of Oxford. The views expressed in this article are those of the author.

2   Now Sir Claus Moser, Warden of Wadham College, Oxford.

3   Independently my colleagues and I had attempted to trace the main trends from the beginning of the century. See A. H. Halsey (ed.) *Trends in British Society Since 1900*, Macmillan, 1972. [Revised edition published as *British Social Trends 1900–1986*, Macmillan, 1988.]

4   *British Labour Statistics Historical Abstract*, Tables 42, 90, and 94, and various editions of the *Employment Gazette*.

5   c.f. Daniel Bell, 'Report on England: the Future that Never Was', *The Public Interest*, No. 51, 1978, pp. 35–73. For statistics on basic holiday entitlement see Table 1.2. The figures for car ownership are rough estimates for 1951 and from the General Household Survey for 1976 and 1985.

6   *Social Trends 16*, p. 130.

7   The number of employees in manufacturing industry reached its highest point in 1956 (see *British Labour Statistics Historical Abstract*, Table 135).

8   John Goldthorpe and Clive Payne, 'Trends in Intergenerational class mobility in England and Wales 1972–83', *Sociology*, Vol. 20, No. 1, 1986, p. 9.

9   C. Hamnett, 'Housing the Two Nations: Socio-Tenurial Polarisation in England and Wales 1961–81', *Urban Studies*, Vol. 43, 1984, pp. 384–405.

10   *Faith in the City: a call for action by Church and Nation*, Church House Publishing, 1985.

11   See especially Victor A. Hausner (ed.) *Critical Issues in Urban Economic Development*, Vol. 1, Oxford University Press, 1987.

12   The analysis was supplied by David Eversley and Ian Begg. Essentially the method was to collect data at ward level of over 70 indicators of advantage and disadvantage and to standardize them as Z scores. By this means an average Z score was produced for every territorial grouping over a range of favourable and adverse social indicators. It is a robust and stable score which provides a refined map of inequality. See Eversley & Begg, 'Deprivation in the Inner City: Social Indicators from the 1981 Census; in Victor A. Hausner (ed.) *op. cit.*

13   *Faith in the City*, 1985, p. 25.

Section II Change in the class structure

Introduction

Class has as much fascination for social scientists as it does for British society. The four extracts chosen from the vast literature are primarily intended to provide evidence about recent changes in the British class structure, but to do so in a way which reflects important theoretical debates about class in capitalist society. These debates are still very much influenced by the ideas formulated by Karl Marx and Max Weber. Neo-Marxists still concentrate on abstract analysis of economic class position and the exploitation by owners of those who must sell their labour. Neo-Weberians tend to focus more on the way classes are defined and interrelate in practice, and therefore deal with economic, social, political and cultural aspects of class. There have been attempts, notably by Giddens (1973) to integrate aspects of economic class position and the social processes which influence individuals' class affiliation, societies' beliefs about the class structure and collective action in the process of *class structuration*, but much of the literature remains antagonistic between the two broad approaches.

The main change in the British class structure this century, as in other capitalist societies, has been the growth in the middle classes. This growth apparently contradicts the basic Marxist prediction that capitalist class structures would polarize into two classes – bourgeois and proletarian. It has provoked a surge of theoretical work by neo-Marxists (e.g. Carchedi, 1975; Poulantzas, 1975; Wright, 1978) which theorizes the middle classes in various ways, most of which rely on the notion that in advanced capitalism control over investment, production and labour is increasingly separated from ownership of the means of production. In recognizing a new middle class of employees exercising control, these neo-Marxists have moved nearer to Weberian views, which have long recognized a middle class of high status, often credentialled, managers and professionals, who can offer much more than unskilled labour power in the labour market. In some formulations (Roemer, 1982; Wright, 1985) the new middle class is seen as containing some groups who are more privileged in class position than the petty bourgeoisie (the old middle class) and some, especially clerks and sales workers, who are less privileged. In so doing, they come close to the common sense view of the salaried middle class as divided into upper-middle and lower-middle, but continue to show the traditional Marxist virtue of spotlighting the vital importance of the numerically small upper class.

The acceptance in general terms of the growth in size of the middle classes poses two new 'boundary problems', which have led to the selection of two of the extracts included here. At the upper bound, what is the division between upper and upper-middle classes and is the upper-middle class, by taking over control functions from capitalists, carrying out a *managerial revolution*? At the lower bound, how should we conceptualize the boundary between proletarian and lower-middle class? Twenty years ago, the debate was about the embourgeoisement of affluent manual workers, more recently it has concerned the *proletarianization* of clerical workers. The literature dealing with the two 'boundary problems' gives an insight into the development of advanced capitalism, both at the level of ownership and control and at the level of the labour process, on the office floor if not that of the factory. Yet, along with the increase in numbers in middle-class positions, the numbers in manual jobs have been reduced by mass unemployment and in many cases reduced from permanent full-time jobs to part-time, temporary or agency work. This transformation of the working class raises the question of the effects of the fragmentation of the economic position of the working class for British politics, and especially for the Labour Party.

This question is addressed by Heath and McDonald in Chapter 2. Our concern is not so much with the implications for the Labour Party as with the succinct summary they give of change in the occupational structure and the other influences on voting patterns. The data they present on changes in occupations quantifies the statement made above: since 1951, the professional and managerial category has doubled to 25 per cent of the workforce, while the manual groups have fallen to a minority of those employed. The influence of housing tenure, union membership and class mobility on voting show that economic class position does not automatically determine class consciousness or action. This is a point developed in later chapters. Every occupational class except the traditional petty bourgeoisie was found to be internally varied: the salariat is divided between private sector and state employees; the intermediate class (equivalent to the lower-middle class) ranges from unionized council tenants to non-union homeowners; the working class has its unionized council tenant core but also marginal groups 'above' and 'below' the integrated group. The view is far from the traditional Marxist stereotype of two internally homogenous and polarized classes. The problem now is to make sense of a highly differentiated society where large and small private organizations create a bewildering variety of combinations of ownership, control and labour market situations as well as a range of social institutions which explicitly or implicitly engage in class structuration. Some writers have argued that the upper and lower class have reduced in importance to such a degree that the class structure is in practice dominated by the 'middle mass'.

As an antidote to the notion that class position has become unimportant in a society dominated by the 'middle mass', Leadbeater (Chapter 3) starkly portrays the effects of the economic restructuring brought on by the recession of the late 1970s and early '80s. He sees the working class as fragmented into five groups by the changing labour market. These groups may create three fractions in a future working class: at the top are the skilled workers in secure employment who, together with less skilled core workers, have seen rising wage levels since 1982; in the middle are a plethora of 'peripheral' positions – part-time, temporary, home and agency workers – whose employment is low paid, shorn of fringe benefits like sick pay and insecure, so that it involves short periods of unemployment; finally, the long term unemployed have in a sense lost their claim to be 'working class' in economic terms, though they may be so in origin and affiliation. A vital point made by Leadbeater, which has implications beyond the working class, is that women and black people are under represented in the more favoured parts of even the working class. This challenges the traditional stance of most class theory, which explicitly focuses on men and implicitly treats them as undifferentiated except in occupation. The real effects of gender and race (as socially perceived) on employment and class are treated here as significant and pervasive.

Perhaps the most significant impact of gender on class is in the area of intermediate non-manual occupations. One of these, clerks, is the focus of Crompton and Jones' discussion of the question of proletarianization (Chapter 4). They identify the dispute between followers of Braverman (1974) – who sees clerical work as increasingly de-skilled, hierarchically controlled and low paid – and their critics, mainly of neo-Weberian persuasion – who see a class which is favoured by good working conditions and security of employment and often a stepping stone in upward mobility from the shrinking working class to the growing upper-middle class. Their resolution of this dispute depends centrally on the effects of gender: the majority (70 per cent) of clerical workers who are deprived of opportunities for upward mobility are women; a minority (30 per cent) are men, but it is they who are promoted to managerial positions, encouraged to acquire qualifications and hence maintain at least an affiliation to the established middle classes. However, a second strand in their argument is that change in the labour process, as offices grow bigger, more hierarchical and more computerized, has actually reduced nominally managerial positions to the white-collar equivalents of skilled worker or foreman rather than 'genuine' managers. In turn, this raises questions about the way some recognize a middle class characterized by the exercise of control. Where in a hierarchical structure does one find a clear division between control, autonomy and subservience?

The upper bound of the middle class is the concern of Scott in Chapter 5, who also presents a sceptical view of the proposal that propertyless managers are in effect taking over control of financial and industrial capital. On the contrary, Scott argues that the upper class have increasingly moved into corporate management, and especially into influential positions of multiple directorships. Although the pattern has moved away from direct ownership and control of family firms, the upper class has largely maintained its wealth and control over investment capital. Restricted access to upper-class positions through inheritance, public school and Oxbridge attendance plus personal contacts at formal and informal social occasions both promotes class solidarity and creates an impression that senior managers are chosen for their educational qualifications rather than their social background. In fact, Scott's findings show that Britain remains a capitalist society in which ownership brings many benefits, including access to positions of control, although the social organization and the processes that sustain class inequality have changed significantly.

References

BRAVERMAN, H. (1974) *Labour and Monopoly Capital: The Degradation of Work in the Twentieth Century*, New York, Monthly Review Press.

CARCHEDI, G. (1975) 'On the economic identification of the new middle class', *Economy and Society*, No. 4, pp. 1–86.

GIDDENS, A. (1973) *The Class Structure of the Advanced Societies*, London, Hutchinson.

POULANTZAS, N. (1975) *Classes in Contemporary Capitalism*, London, New Left Books.

ROEMER, J. E. (1982) *A General Theory of Exploitation and Class*, Cambridge, Mass., Harvard University Press.

WRIGHT, E. O. (1978) *Class, Crisis and the State*, London, New Left Books.

WRIGHT, E. O. (1985) *Classes*, London and New York, Verso.

2 Social change and the future of the left

Anthony Heath and Sarah-K McDonald[1]

One of the reasons for Labour's electoral decline over the past twenty years has been the contraction of its social base. Labour has typically been strongest in the working class, among council tenants, and among union members. But all three groups have been shrinking in size in recent years. The economic developments of late industrialism have led to an expanding number of jobs in professional, managerial and technical work and declining numbers in traditional manual work. This has been associated with a decline in union membership, while in the housing market we have seen the spread of owner occupation, helped by the Conservatives' policy of council house sales.

Labour's 'core' of working-class, unionized, council tenants has shrunk. The Conservative's 'core' of salaried, non-union home owners has grown, as have 'cross-pressured' groups such as working-class home owners.

It is now, therefore, widely believed that the 'natural' level of the Labour vote is quite modest, say around 35 per cent of the national vote. Some commentators therefore believe Labour realistically cannot expect to win an overall majority in Parliament unless it radically changes its social appeal and attracts the votes of the growing numbers of owner occupiers and non-union members.

There is certainly some truth in this analysis of social change. But it is easy to exaggerate the magnitude of the changes and to draw incorrect political implications from them. In our view, social change should not be made the scapegoat for Labour's electoral failures. Nor is an appeal to non-union home owners necessarily the only political response to social change.

2.1 Social change in post-war Britain

Let us begin by looking more carefully at the social and economic changes of the post-war period. Table 2.1 describes the changes in the occupational structure since 1951.[2]

The most striking trend is, of course, the growth in non-manual employment, particularly of managers and professionals, who have doubled in proportion from 12 per cent to 25 per cent of the labour force. Clerical and sales work has shown a more modest expansion from 16 per cent to 19 per cent. And all three categories of manual work have contracted. By 1981 manual employees had fallen from 62 per cent of the total to 45 per cent. They were now a minority of the labour force.

Table 2.1 Distribution of the economically active population by occupational category, 1951–1981, Great Britain

	1951	1961	1971	1981
Employers and own account	6.7	6.4	6.5	6.4
Managers and administrators	5.4	5.3	8.0	10.1
Professionals and technicians	6.6	9.0	11.1	14.7
Clerical and sales	16.3	18.6	19.5	19.3
Supervisors and foremen	2.6	2.9	3.9	4.2
Skilled manual	23.8	24.1	20.2	16.0
Semi-skilled manual	26.6	25.1	19.3	19.0
Unskilled manual	11.9	8.5	11.6	10.4
Total	99.9	99.9	100.1	100.1
N (000s)	22 514	23 639	25 021	25 406

The expansion of professional and managerial jobs, and the contraction of skilled manual, continued unabated during the 1970s. Recent evidence suggests that these trends have continued into the 1980s.[3] We must assume that they will continue for the foreseeable future.

This fall of 17 percentage points in the proportion of manual employees is certainly bad news for Labour and good news for the Conservative and Alliance parties. [In 1987, the Alliance consisted of the Liberal and Social Democratic parties; in 1988, they combined to form the Social and Liberal Democrats, leaving a residual SDP.] But there are two caveats to bear in mind when assessing its political significance. First, the contraction of manual employment has been associated with upward mobility for many people from manual origins; and the political partisanship of the upwardly mobile tends to be half-way between that typical of stable members of their classes of origin and destination respectively.[4] This will tend to mitigate, although not eradicate, the political losses to Labour.

Secondly, the expansion of non-manual work has been associated with increasing numbers of married women entering the labour market. But this increased female participation has not come equally from all social classes. The wives of working-class men have always been relatively likely to take paid employment (no doubt through economic necessity) and the increase has come disproportionately from the wives of white-collar men.[5] These women already would have tended to favour the Conservative Party. Again, this will tend to mitigate, though not eradicate, the losses to the Labour Party.

Table 2.2 takes up the story of union membership.[6] It shows a rather different pattern. Instead of contracting, union membership increased steadily from 1951 to a peak of 12 million in 1981. Membership then dropped quite sharply from that peak, but it was still higher in 1984 than it had been at any time in the 1950s or 1960s.

This increase in union membership was due in part to the increased size of the labour force (the increase in women's participation mentioned above). But Table 2.2 shows that the *density* of membership (actual

Table 2.2 Union membership, 1951–1984, United Kingdom

	Actual membership (000s)	Potential membership (000s)	Density of membership (per cent)
1951	9 530	21 177	45.0
1961	9 916	22 527	44.0
1971	11 135	22 884	48.7
1981	12 106	24 551	49.3
1984	11 086	24 194	45.8

members as a percentage of potential members) also increased over this period. Although density too fell back somewhat after 1979, it was still as high in 1984 as it had been for much of the 1950s and 1960s.[7]

Table 2.3 looks at changes in housing tenure over time.[8] Again, the story it tells is not a wholly straightforward one. In 1951, just over half of the housing stock in the United Kingdom was rented from private landlords. By 1985 this had fallen to 11 per cent, with owner occupation taking its place as the predominant form of housing tenure. But public housing (primarily rented from local authorities) also had increased over this period from 18 per cent to 27 per cent. True, the expansion of local authority housing came to a halt in the later 1970s; Table 2.3 shows that since 1981 there has been a decline of over 3 percentage points in the proportion of public housing. As with union membership, however, the fall has not wiped out all the gains of the 1950s and 1960s. In short, for most of the post-war period *both* home ownership *and* public, local authority housing were increasing at the expense of privately rented accommodation.

We must be careful, therefore, not to over-dramatize these changes or their political implications. Since 1979, to be sure, all three trends have been moving against Labour and are likely to continue in the same direction for the foreseeable future. But in all three cases the long-run trends are somewhat more complicated than appears at first sight, and their political implications are not wholly unambiguous.

Table 2.3 Housing stock by tenure, 1951–1985, United Kingdom (per cent)

	Owner occupied	Rented from local authority or new town corporation	Rented privately and miscellaneous
1951	30.1	18.2	51.7
1961	42.9	26.8	30.4
1971	50.3	30.8	19.0
1981	57.1	30.9	12.0
1985	62.1	27.2	10.7

2.2   The composition of the electorate

Tables 2.1 and 2.2 present information about key changes in the characteristics of the labour force, while Table 2.3 summarizes trends in the housing
stock. To understand the implications of these changes for the political
parties, however, we need to know about the changing proportions of
registered electors with the characteristics in question and, even more
importantly, with particular combinations of characteristics. For this wc
have to turn to sample surveys of the electorate. Our main sources are the
British election surveys which have been conducted since 1964.[9] Data from
the 1987 election survey are not yet available, but we can extend the series
up to 1986 by drawing on the British Social Attitudes Surveys.[10]
    Table 2.4 charts the trends in the proportion of the electorate with
particular combinations of characteristics from 1964 to 1986.[11] We should
note that these estimates are derived from relatively small sample surveys
and therefore are subject to sampling error. Table 2.5 shows how the
members of these different categories have typically divided between the
parties over the period 1964–86.[12]
    In Table 2.4 we distinguish first between four occupational classes: the
petty bourgeoisie (composed of employers and own account workers); the
salariat (composed of professionals and managers); the intermediate
classes (composed of clerical and sales workers together with foremen);
and the working class (rank and file manual employees).[13] We also
distinguish between trade unionists and non-unionists, and between home
owners, council tenants and private tenants. We have not attempted to
look at all possible combinations of characteristics, since in some cases the
numbers involved are very small. Few professionals and managers, for
example, have ever rented council houses. Hardly any of the self-employed
belong to trade unions. We have not, therefore, reported separately the
trends in tiny categories such as these, but have included them in residual
categories such as 'other petty bourgeois'.[14]
    We should note that the interpretation of these three variables is not
always wholly straightforward. In particular, union membership will tend
to be associated with certain types of employment (for example in the
public sector), and we should be cautious in making causal interpretations
of the patterns described below. We should also note that there are
complex patterns of class mobility and class intermarriage that would also
be relevant for a full understanding of the changing structure of British
society.

The petty bourgeoisie

The petty bourgeoisie is by far the most homogeneous of all the classes,
homogeneous that is with respect to the two characteristics we distinguish
here. Throughout our period it has been composed predominantly of

Table 2.4 Social change, 1964–1986

| | Percentage | | | | Change |
	1964	1970	1979	1986	1964–86
Petty Bourgeoisie					
non-union, home owners	5	4	6	7	+ 2
other petty bourgeois	2	2	2	2	0
Salariat					
non-union, home owners	8	11	13	13	+ 5
union members, home owners	1	2	6	7	+ 6
other salariat	5	5	5	4	− 1
Intermediate class					
non-union, home owners	8	8	8	11	+ 3
non-union, private tenants	3	3	2	1	− 2
non-union, council tenants	4	4	3	3	− 1
union members, home owners	2	2	4	4	+ 2
union members, council tenants	1	1	2	1	0
other intermediate	2	1	1	0	− 2
Working class					
non-union, home owners	10	11	9	13	+ 3
non-union, private tenants	7	6	3	2	− 5
non-union, council tenants	11	11	10	10	− 1
union members, home owners	5	6	6	8	+ 3
union members, private tenants	4	3	1	1	− 3
union members, council tenants	7	6	8	4	− 3
other working class	3	1	2	0	− 3
Unclassified	11	11	10	8	3
TOTAL	99	98	101	99	
N (weighted)	1817	1287	1893	3066	

non-unionists and home owners. And it has typically supported the Conservative Party by a handsome majority. The petty bourgeoisie has consistently been the class with the largest Conservative lead. This is the Conservative heartland, although it is only a tiny proportion of the electorate and one that has grown little.

The salariat

The salariat presents a marked contrast to the petty bourgeoisie. As we saw from Table 2.1, it has grown substantially, and unsurprisingly a large proportion of the salariat are non-unionists and home owners. The patterns of political support of this non-unionized section of the salariat are quite close to those of the petty bourgeoisie, with a Conservative lead of around 40 points. The growth of this section should clearly have brought the Conservatives a substantial net gain in support, other things being equal.

Table 2.5 Party identification: average levels for 1964–86

	Conservative	Labour	Liberal/SDP & Other Parties	None	Missing	Total
Petty bourgeoisie						
non-union, home owners	66	13	14	6	2	101
other petty bourgeoisie	46	28	13	11	2	100
Salariat						
non-union, home owners	58	13	19	8	3	101
union members, home owners	41	27	22	9	2	101
other salariat	36	33	18	11	3	101
Intermediate class						
non-union, home owners	51	20	18	8	3	100
non-union, private tenants	44	27	18	7	4	100
non-union, council tenants	28	46	15	8	3	100
union members, home owners	31	38	17	10	3	99
union members, council tenants	14	59	15	9	5	102
other intermediate	37	40	12	8	2	99
Working class						
non-union, home owners	37	36	15	8	4	100
non-union, private tenants	26	48	13	10	4	101
non-union, council tenants	18	61	11	8	3	101
union members, home owners	22	56	11	8	2	99
union members, private tenants	17	63	11	9	1	101
union members, council tenants	14	68	9	8	2	101
other working class	36	36	9	7	6	94
Unclassified	39	34	14	8	5	100

However, we see that there is also a second, unionized section of the salariat that is markedly different from the first in its political preferences, and it too has grown substantially. These union members in the salariat are typically home owners (reflecting their advantaged material circumstances) but only a minority of them support the Conservative Party. While the Conservatives are still in the lead here, that lead is reduced to 14 points.

We would expect to find that these two sections of the salariat differ in a number of other important respects too. The trade union wing of the salariat is likely to be made up of employees in the public sector – teachers, nurses or local government officials – rather than in the private sector as managers. They are likely to have had different routes into the salariat, and while they both share the security that salaried employment offers, we suspect that the public sector trade unionists will be relatively better-educated than the private sector non-unionists but less well paid.

We can also see that the unionized section of the salariat is where the Alliance is relatively strongest. Many political commentators persist in the belief that Alliance support lacks a social base and is drawn equally from all sections of the electorate.[15] Table 2.5, however, shows a clear pattern to Alliance (and previously Liberal) support. It is relatively weakest in the Labour 'core' of working-class council tenants who are union members, and it is generally weaker in the working class than in the intermediate classes or the salariat. And, controlling for class, it is relatively stronger among home owners than among council tenants. The political implication is thus that the electoral advantages of the spread of home ownership and the expansion of the salariat have to be divided (albeit unequally) between the Conservatives and the Alliance.

The intermediate class

This is the most heterogeneous of the four classes. One section – non-union home owners – are close to their equivalents in the salariat in their political preferences; another section – union members renting from local author-ities – are close to their equivalents in the working class.

Overall, the intermediate class has not changed in size, but within it the balance has shifted, the non-union home owners showing a marked increase. This increase has come, however, largely at the expense of private renting, a section which was already fairly similar to the home owners in political partisanship. For example, 51 per cent of non-union home owners supported the Conservatives, compared with 44 per cent of non-union private tenants. Although the actual flows of people from one category to another will have been quite complicated, it strongly suggests (as has other evidence) that people who move into home ownership may have been relatively Conservative-inclined beforehand.[16] At any rate the net political impact of an increase in home ownership within the inter-mediate class at the expense of private renting will have been very small.

The working class

The working class has, of course, been contracting, and within the working class the balance of the different categories has been changing. Two points, however, have not been generally recognized. First, the so-called 'core' of union members renting from local authorities was only a small fraction of the working class even in 1964.[17] Our data suggest that it was only 7 per cent of the electorate, and around 14 per cent of the working class, at that time. Secondly, the so-called 'new working class' of non-union home owners was already present, and at least as big as the core, in 1964. Our data indicate that it was 10 per cent of the electorate, and around 20 per cent of the working class. In other words, divisions within the working class are long-standing. There is nothing particularly new about the 'new' working class.

Our data also suggest that the division between old and new working class is not particularly helpful from a political point of view. We can see from Table 2.5 that, in the working class as in the intermediate classes, non-unionists who rented privately were fairly similar to non-unionist home owners in their political support for the different parties. Table 2.5 also indicates that the various categories of union members and local authority tenants within the working class are all relatively similar to each other in their political preferences.

We can therefore divide the working class into two politically. On the one hand there are the non-union home owners and private tenants; on the other there are the union members and local authority tenants. This does not yield a division between the old and the new working class, for private renting and indeed non-membership of trade unions are very old phenomena. If anything, they are the very oldest sections of the working class! Rather it is a distinction between the *marginal* sections of the working class and the more central or *integrated* sections. We would expect to find that these sections differ in a number of important ways. The integrated section, for example, is more likely to belong to homogeneous residential communities, to be employed in large enterprises and thus to be working alongside other manual workers on the shop-floor, and to be relatively stable with respect to geographical and social mobility.

From this perspective we obtain a rather different view of changes within the working class. The 'integrated' working class was, and remains, substantially larger than the 'marginal' working class. Both have contracted, as the working class as a whole has contracted, but they have done so by rather similar proportions. The marginal wing of the working class has contracted from 17 per cent of the electorate in 1964 to 15 per cent in 1986; the integrated wing has contracted from 27 per cent to 23 per cent.

This rather paradoxical finding emerges because the spread in home ownership within the working class is more than compensated for by the decline in the private rented sector. As Table 2.4 shows, private renting was primarily a working-class phenomenon, and the category of non-union private renters is the one that has shown the largest decline.

2.3 Political implications

By combining the information in Tables 2.4 and 2.5 we can now calculate the net impact of social change on the fortunes of the parties between 1964 and 1986. With the 1964 social structure, and an average level of support in each category, the Conservative Party would have been expected to obtain the support of 35 per cent of the electorate, Labour 40 per cent and the Liberals 14 per cent (with 11 per cent uncommitted). With the 1986 social structure and an average level of support in each category, the Conservatives would have been expected to gain 4 percentage points, Labour to lose 5 points and the Liberals to gain 1 point.

While these figures confirm the adverse nature of the social trends for Labour, they also show very clearly that *more votes are won and lost through political fluctuations than through social changes*. Social change can account for a drop of five points in Labour support, but the Labour share of the vote has fluctuated from 48 per cent in 1966 to 28 per cent in 1983.

As we said earlier, then, social change must not be made the scapegoat for Labour's decline. The gap between Conservative and Labour that our calculations suggest in their 'expected' levels of support can easily be bridged by political fluctuations. Thus if Labour had 'overperformed' in 1987 as it did in 1966 it would certainly have been the largest single party in the House of Commons and would probably have commanded an absolute majority. *Social change may be on balance adverse for Labour, but even now it does not rule out a Labour victory*.

It is perhaps worth noting, too, that in the summer of 1986 Labour was indeed achieving around 40 per cent in the opinion polls. This suggests that the reason for Labour's defeat in 1987 must be sought in Labour's political mistakes (and the Conservatives' political successes) between the summer of 1986 and the summer of 1987, not in the social changes between 1964 and 1986. The social changes are real enough, however, and are likely to continue in much the same direction. It is therefore worth considering possible responses to them.

A realignment of the left?

One response is to seek a realignment of the left and centre with an electoral pact between the Labour Party and the SDP/Liberal Alliance. Now it is clear from Table 2.5 that *the Alliance is much more similar to the Conservatives than it is to Labour in the social profile of its supporters*.[18] The Conservatives and the Alliance were competing for much the same

social territory, and this is reflected in the well-known pattern of consti-
tuency support for the parties, with the Alliance running second in 61 per
cent of Conservative-held seats in 1987 but in only 14 per cent of
Labour-held seats.

This means that an electoral pact between Labour and the Alliance looks
particularly expedient, since they are competing for largely different seats.
But it must surely raise a question mark about the ideological affinity of the
parties.

Analysis of the 1983 election survey showed that Labour and Alliance
supporters were indeed quite close to each other on the 'caring' issues,
such as the welfare state. On these issues it would not be difficult to reach
agreed policies that appealed to both sets of supporters. These are not,
however, the issues which most divide the electorate.

The issues which most divide the electorate are those concerned with the
trade unions and with economic equality.[19] These can be thought of as the
ideological bases of party competition in Britain. On these issues Alliance
supporters tend to be midway between Labour and the Conservatives, but
the gap between Labour and Alliance on trade union legislation, for
example, is as big as that between Labour and Conservative supporters on
the welfare state. A rapprochement between the parties on these issues
may not be easy to achieve without alienating existing supporters.

An appeal to the centre ground?

Labour may have a handsome lead within the 'integrated working class',
but this part of the working class now amounts to only 23 per cent of the
electorate (although it is a geographically concentrated section of the
electorate that brings a substantial bonus of parliamentary seats).[20]

The Conservative heartlands of the petty bourgeoisie and the non-union
home owners in the salariat also amount to 20 per cent of the electorate. In
between, and comprising half the electorate, are the intermediate class and
the two marginal sections of the salariat and the working class – unionized
members of the salariat and non-unionized owner occupiers in the working
class respectively.

It is tempting to argue that this centre ground of the electorate is where
elections are won and lost, and that Labour therefore needs to target these
groups. Logically this must be true, since the majority of votes to be won
and lost are here. Politically, however, it is only a half-truth. Labour's poor
showing in 1983, and probably in 1987 as well, was not confined to the
intermediate class and the marginal section of the working class. *Labour
under-performed in the central or integrated sections of the working class as
well.* Labour needs to improve its showing in all sections of the electorate.

It is useful to make a distinction here between the long run and the short
run. In the long run, a party's social profile will reflect its ideology (and
vice versa). There are, certainly, examples from Europe of parties
gradually changing the social profile of their supporters.[21] In the short run,

however, support is won and lost as a result of factors that seem to operate across the board. A party that is disunited and has lost its sense of direction, for example, is likely to lose support among both central and marginal groups alike. This suggests that, if Labour wishes to revive its fortunes in the short run, it would be unwise to rely on targeting specific groups such as non-union home owners, since its decline between summer 1986 and summer 1987 may not have been confined to this group alone. The remedy might be based on a faulty diagnosis of the illness.

The point we are making is clearly demonstrated by some results from the 1983 Election Study. Respondents were asked: 'If the voting paper had required you to give *two* votes, in order of preference, which Party would you have put as your second choice?'[22] People who gave the Labour Party as their second choice should surely be Labour's primary targets. They are already relatively sympathetic to Labour and would probably be the easiest to 'convert'.

But people who put Labour as their second choice were not concentrated among so-called 'target groups' like the new working class. They were, in fact, remarkably evenly distributed across all sections of the electorate. Thus, within the working class, 9 per cent of non-union home owners reported that they would have given Labour as their second preference compared with 12 per cent of home owners who were union members and 12 per cent of local authority tenants who were union members.[23]

Expanding the social base?

Trying to find an appropriate remedy for short-run changes in support, although clearly necessary for a party that hopes to win power, will scarcely be sufficient to ensure long-run success. Labour clearly cannot ignore the expanding numbers of non-union home owners.

A different perspective on this problem is gained, however, if we think in terms of expanding Labour's social base rather than accepting contraction as an inevitable feature of the later twentieth century. True, there is little that the Labour movement can do at present about the contraction of the working class or the expansion of home ownership. These trends are not within Labour's power to change, certainly not while it is out of office and perhaps not easily when in office either.

It is by no means obvious, however, that trade union membership falls into the same category. The Scandinavian countries (Sweden and Denmark in particular) have not dissimilar occupational structures from that of Britain. Like Britain they have powerful socialist parties which are stronger in the working class than in the petty bourgeoisie or salariat, and stronger among unionists than among non-unionists. However, one major difference between these countries and Britain is that their levels of unionization are much higher. In Sweden and Denmark the density of union membership among manual workers is around 80 per cent compared with around 60 per cent in Britain.[24]

It is not obvious, therefore, that the decline of union membership should be accepted as inevitable. And since, historically, the rise of the Labour Party was much more closely associated with the spread of union membership than it was with other social changes, it may be not only the most possible but also (in electoral terms) the most profitable source of change for the Labour movement.

Targeting the centre ground and extending union membership both aim at the same categories of people. In that respect both strategies aim to deal with the same problem. But the tactics and policies involved are very different. 'Targeting the centre ground' is based on the assumption that voters' interests and policy preferences are somehow exogenously determined and that the Labour Party needs to adapt its policies to appeal to these interests and preferences. It treats the voter as a rational consumer and the parties as vote-maximizing businesses.

Extending union membership is based on the assumption that, through workplace organization, voters can become involved in the Labour movement and can come to share its aspirations and values. On this view, voters' perceptions of their interests are not exogenously determined, but are the outcome of social processes of communication and organization.

Notes

1   Anthony Heath is an Official Fellow of Nuffield College, Oxford. He is Director of the Oxford/SCPR British General Election Studies for 1983 and 1987. Sarah-K. McDonald is Research Officer at Nuffield College for the 1987 Election Study. Previously she was Social Science Analyst at the Center for Survey Methods Research, U.S. Bureau of the Census.

2   The sources for Table 2.1 are as follows. The figures for 1951 and 1971 are primarily derived from Guy Routh, *Occupation and Pay in Great Britain 1906–79*, Macmillan, London, 1980 (Table 1.1). The comparable table for 1981 has been made available personally to us by Guy Routh, and we are very grateful to him. Our practice departs from Routh's in a number of respects, however. First, we have grouped own account workers (other than professionals) with employers and proprietors. Secondly, we have grouped sales workers with clerical workers, whereas Routh includes them in the semi-skilled manual category. The figures for the number of sales workers have been taken from Robert Price and George Sayers Bain 'The Labour Force', in A. H. Halsey (ed.) *British Social Trends 1900–1986*, Macmillan, London, (1988), Table 4.1. We have assumed that the sales workers were all employees. The figures for 1961 have been taken from George Sayers Bain, Robert Bacon and John Pimlott 'The Labour Force', in A. H. Halsey (ed.) *Trends in British Society since 1900*, Macmillan, London, 1972, Table 4.1. All these sources in turn derive from the Census.

3   See *Social Trends 17: 1987 Edition*, HMSO, London, 1987. Table 4.13.

4   See David Butler and Donald Stokes *Political Change in Britain*, 2nd edition, Macmillan, London, 1974, Table 5.6.

5   See Heather Joshi 'Motherhood and Employment: Change and Continuity in Post-war Britain' in British Society for Population Studies, *Measuring Socio-Demographic Change*, Occasional Paper 34, OPCS, London, 1985.

6   The source for Table 2.2 is Robert Price and George Sayers Bain 'The Labour Force' in A. H. Halsey (ed.) *British Social Trends 1900–1986*, Macmillan, London, (1988), Table 4.11. We are very grateful to Professor Halsey for permission to use this material. Potential membership is defined as the economically active population, including the unemployed but excluding own account workers and employers.

7   There are substantial differences in union density between manual and non-manual employees, but both increased between 1951 and 1979. In the case of manual employees, density rose from 49 per cent to 66 per cent and in the case of non-manual employees from 31 per cent to 45 per cent. See *Social Trends 12: 1982 Edition*, HMSO, London, 1981, Table 11.16.

8   The source for Table 2.3 is *Social Trends 17: 1987 Edition*, HMSO, London, 1987, Table 8.1. We are grateful to the Central Statistical Office for supplying us with the detailed percentages and to the Controller of HMSO for permission to reproduce the information.

9   Details of the British Election Surveys are given in Anthony Heath, Roger Jowell and John Curtice *How Britain Votes*, Pergamon, Oxford, 1985, Appendix II. We would like to acknowledge the help of our colleagues on the 1983–7 election study team – Roger Jowell, John Curtice, Julia Field and Sharon Witherspoon – and of the previous investigators – David Butler, Donald Stokes, Ivor Crewe, Bo Sarlvik, James Alt and David Robertson. The interpretations made in the present paper of their data are, of course, wholly our responsibility. We would also like to thank the ESRC Data Archive for making the data available to us.

10   The British Social Attitudes surveys are conducted by Social and Community Planning Research and core funded by the Sainsbury Trusts. For details of the 1986 survey see Roger Jowell, Sharon Witherspoon and Lindsay Brook (eds), *British Social Attitudes: the 1987 Report*, Gower, Aldershot, 1987. We would like to thank SCPR for making the data available to us.

11   We should note that there are some differences between the trends derived from the sample surveys and those shown in the 'official statistics' of Tables 2.1, 2.2 and 2.3. In particular the sample surveys show a larger increase in the proportion of owner occupiers than would have been expected from Table 2.3.

12   Table 2.5 shows the trends in 'party identification' rather than in vote. The party identification question was asked in somewhat different ways in the Election surveys and the Social Attitude survey, but methodological work has shown that they are functionally equivalent. See Anthony Heath, Roger Jowell, John Curtice and Sharon Witherspoon 'Methodological Aspects of Attitude Research' End of Award Report to the ESRC, December 1986. In Table 2.5 identifiers with other parties (such as Plaid Cymru and the SNP) have been combined with Liberal and SDP identifiers.

13   The classifications used in Table 2.4 have been designed to be as close as possible to those used in Tables 2.1, 2.2 and 2.3. Some changes are required, however, since we are now dealing with the electorate. Thus in the case of class, economically active and retired respondents have been classified on the basis of their own occupations; married women who are economically inactive (not retired) have been classified according to their husbands' occupations. To achieve comparability the class schema is based on a collapse of the OPCS socio-economic group scheme. See Office of Population Census and Surveys, *Classification of Occupations 1980*, HMSO, London, 1980, Appendix B1. The petty bourgeoisie is composed of SEGs 1.1, 2.1, 12, 13 and 14; the salariat is composed of SEGs 1.2,

2.2, 3, 4, 5.1 and 5.2); the intermediate class is composed of SEGs 6 and 8; the working class is composed of SEGs 7, 9, 10, 11 and 15. Note that this is very similar, but not identical to, John Goldthorpe's class schema used in the 1983 Election Study.

14   The 'other' categories also include people living in institutions or for whom housing tenure or trade-union membership was unknown. The 'unclassified' category includes all those who could not be assigned to a class under the procedures described in footnote 13.

15   For example, Rose and McAllister, who use the same data but employ a much cruder division of the electorate into categories of class, union membership and housing tenure, conclude that 'Whatever the subdivisions of the electorate, Alliance support is normally within a few per cent of being an exact cross-section of the electorate. The distinctive feature of the Alliance vote is its social representativeness'. See Richard Rose and Ian McAllister *Voters Begin to Choose: From Closed-Class to Open Elections in Britain*, Sage, London, 1986, p. 81.

16   See Anthony Heath *et al.*, *How Britain Votes*, Table 4.4.

17   It is, however, likely that economically inactive respondents married to trade unionists will differ in their political preferences from those of respondents married to economically active non-unionists. If we reclassified such respondents according to their spouse's union membership, this would of course increase the size of the unionized categories and decrease that of the non-unionized throughout. It would also tend to increase the political distinctiveness of the categories.

18   We can use the index of dissimilarity to calculate the difference between the parties in their patterns of social support. Using the categories of Tables 2.4 and 2.5 we find that the dissimilarity between the Alliance (combined with minor parties) and Labour was 28.3 but that between the Alliance and the Conservatives was only 13.1.

19   See Anthony Heath *et al.*, *How Britain Votes*, chapter 8.

20   *op. cit.*, chapter 6.

21   See the example of the Swedish Centre Party described in Torben Worre 'Class Parties and Class Voting in the Scandinavian Countries' *Scandinavian Political Studies* 4 (1980) p. 310.

22   This is question Q9C in the 1983 Election Survey (reprinted in Anthony Heath *et al.*, *How Britain Votes*).

23   One exception to this rule that Labour second preferences were distributed evenly across the different sections of the electorate was that they were unusually common among members of the salariat who were both home owners and union members. 18 per cent of this category said that they would have given Labour their second preference.

24   See Diane Sainsbury 'The Electoral Difficulties of the Scandinavian Social Democrats in the 1970s: The Social Bases of the Parties and Structural Explanations of Party Decline' *Comparative Politics* 18 (1985) pp. 1–20.

3   In the land of the dispossessed

Charlie Leadbeater

The terrain of British politics has shifted irrevocably since 1983. It is not just that Thatcherism still occupies the ideological high ground through its sustained colonization of the public political discourse. Nor that it has forced through change in institutions which gathered their strength in the post-war era – trade unions, the welfare state, the nationalized corporations.

The most fundamental change is the development of new lines of division within British society. These divisions are the product of irrevocable changes in Britain's 'employment base': the rise and *persistence* of mass long-term unemployment, and recurrent short-term unemployment; while the growth of a peripheral workforce of part-timers, temporary workers, and the self-employed, has accompanied rising security and prosperity for those in full-time employment.

Thatcherism is attempting to mould this radical polarization in British society into a stable political order. Thatcherism is encouraging the development of cultural identities, social and economic interests, to channel the expression and resolution of conflicts between the groups which inhabit divided Britain.

It is attempting to construct a 'post-recession settlement' to match the coherence and comprehensiveness of the 'post-war settlement' of old. [. . .]

Before examining in detail the new divisions in Britain, it is worth recalling the character of the employment base for the 'post-war settlement'. In the 1960s the unemployment rate was about 2.3 per cent. Less than 20 per cent of those unemployed were out of work for more than a year. In the sphere of employment the norm was male full-time employment, often with a large company. Part-time employment was about 2 per cent of all employment in the 1950s. Temporary workers, and the self-employed also made up a small proportion of employment.

In the 1960s many conflicts were expressed within the context of full employment. Through the machinery of corporatism, the trade unions, the state and employers harnessed these conflicts so they could be resolved in a way that was compatible with the social democratic ethos of the times. There was a kind of fit between the grassroots of the employment base, the institutions of politics, and the overarching ideology. In the 1980s, that employment base for post-war politics has broken apart. The differences which existed within the full employment labour market, differences of earnings and skills, have been superseded by a much more radical polarization between those secure within the labour market, those bobbing in and out of employment, and those stuck firmly on the edges in long-term unemployment. The task of the late 1980s is to fashion institutions and a political strategy to cope with the conflicts created by what is a new *fivefold* segmentation of the labour market (See Figure 3.1).

The most dramatic change in the employment base is the rise in unemployment from 1.14 million or 4.3 per cent in 1979 to 3.19 million or 11.7 per cent last year on official figures. But this rise masks important shifts in the composition of unemployment over the last five years.

The first of the five groups in the segmented labour market are the long-term unemployed.

About a quarter of men unemployed in 1977 had been out of work for more than a year. By 1986, the proportion had risen to 44 per cent, or about 1.02 million men. The growth of long-term unemployment is a dramatic turn-around from the 1960s. In 1963, for instance, about 800000 men per quarter were registering as unemployed. But they were quickly moving out of unemployment and finding jobs again. So the *level* of male unemployment was 500000. In 1985, the flow into unemployment was lower than in 1963 with about 750000 men per quarter becoming unemployed. However, the level of male unemployment was 300 per cent above its level in 1963 at over 2 million. The explanation for this apparently paradoxical development is simple: in the 1980s, unemployment has risen because a larger group are unemployed for a *longer* period.

The vast majority of the long-term unemployed are more or less permanently outside the labour market. As a result of ill health, depression and the loss of skills, the long-term unemployed are severely disadvantaged in competing for vacancies. Through their unemployment they become isolated, and fatalistic. They lack any sense of individual power, for instance through the freedom to consume, or collective power through institutions such as trade unions. The long-term unemployed suffer a kind of permanent exclusion from society.

The importance of the growth of long-term unemployment should not deflect attention from a second group among the unemployed: those who suffer short-term unemployment. There were about 1.23 million men unemployed for less than 52 weeks last year. A study published by the Policy Studies Institute in 1983 showed that workers who have experienced unemployment frequently have irregular and discontinuous patterns of employment thereafter. This is because when they are recruited to jobs it is most likely to be on the bottom rung of the ladder in companies. Even when they are in employment they are the group most vulnerable to redundancy.

The short-term unemployed are within the labour market, but on its fringes as they move in and out of employment. Their income and contact with the socialized world of work, their sense of their position within society, fluctuates with their employment prospects.

The third segment is the peripheral workforce – a growing army of part-timers, temporary workers, home-workers and the self-employed,

Figure 3.1 Divided Workforce

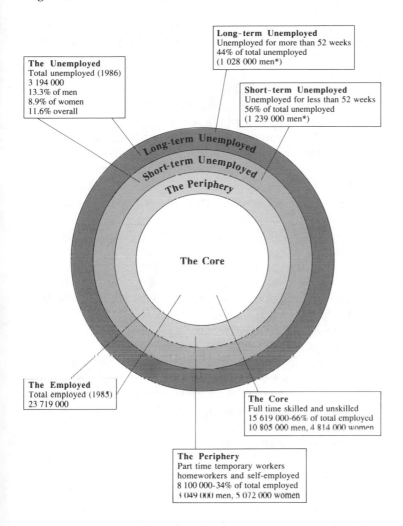

Long-term Unemployed
Unemployed for more than 52 weeks
44% of total unemployed
(1 028 000 men*)

The Unemployed
Total unemployed (1986)
3 194 000
13.3% of men
8.9% of women
11.6% overall

Short-term Unemployed
Unemployed for less than 52 weeks
56% of total unemployed
(1 239 000 men*)

Long-term Unemployed
Short-term Unemployed
The Periphery
The Core

The Employed
Total employed (1985)
23 719 000

The Core
Full time skilled and unskilled
15 619 000-66% of total employed
10 805 000 men, 4 814 000 women

The Periphery
Part time temporary workers
homeworkers and self-employed
8 100 000-34% of total employed
3 049 000 men, 5 072 000 women

* no figures available of numbers of women unemployed

Britain's workforce is acquiring, in the late 80s, a new shape, characterized by new and deep-seated divisions. It divides into five main categories: the skilled core, the unskilled core, the periphery, the short-term unemployed.

The long-term unemployed are now virtually permanently excluded from the labour force. They have borne the brunt of the recession. The short-term unemployed are on the fringes of the labour market. The peripheral workers, such as part-time and temporary workers, bob in and out of the workforce. They are now the fastest growing sector of the labour force.

The unskilled core is in work but finds itself increasingly losing out in the battle of differentials with the skilled. The skilled core not only enjoys job security but has in recent years benefited from rising real wages.

who are suspended in a grey area between unemployment and full-time employment.

The first national estimates of the size of the permanent and peripheral workforces, published by the Department of Employment in February (1987) shows that the peripheral workforce expanded by 16 per cent between 1981 and 1985 to 8.1 million workers, while the permanent workforce of full-time employees declined by 6 per cent. While some of this growth is a continuation of trends established in the 1970s, it seems to mark a permanent change in the structure of employment.

It seems that after the dramatic loss in full-time jobs, employment growth in Britain might be concentrated on peripheral jobs. A recent study of future employment trends by the Institute of Employment Research at Warwick University forecast that, in the next four years, full-time employment will decline by a further 1 million while the number of peripheral workers will rise by 900000.

Several factors explain this shift from permanent jobs to peripheral jobs. First, most companies do not pay peripheral workers non-wage benefits such as sick pay, holiday pay and pensions. This allows savings on labour costs. Secondly, through the use of part-timers and temporary workers, companies can easily vary employment levels to match fluctuating levels of production. Thirdly, it reflects the ambiguous position of trade unions. Trade union weakness has undoubtedly been one reason why companies have been able to push through these changes.

But peripheral workers are also used to provide security for full-time employees. Several unions have allowed companies to introduce more temporary workers under an agreement which says that these workers will be the first to be laid off during a downturn, thereby giving greater security to the full-time employees.

All this adds up to a deep cleavage between the security and status of peripheral and permanent workers within a company. This is reflected more broadly in the legal position of peripheral workers. Labour law has traditionally categorized workers as either employees dependent on an employer or independent and genuinely self-employed. This leaves peripheral workers in a grey area. Temporary workers are clearly not self-employed. But, according to the law, because they do not establish a permanent relationship with a single employer, they are not 'employees', a status reserved for full-time workers.

In the most important legal case in this area in 1983, an industrial tribunal ruled that a regular casual waiter, who worked solely for Trust-house Forte, and attended for duty when summoned, was actually self-employed and had no legal redress against the company for redundancy pay regardless of years of service. Peripheral workers thus go without many of the protections against unfair dismissal or redundancy afforded to full-timers.

The final two segments are those 15.6 million workers in full-time employment. In recent years many of those in full-time employment have enjoyed a combination of rises in earnings of around 7–8 per cent, and low inflation. The contrast between the apparent security and rising prosperity of the full-timers and the vulnerability of peripheral workers has led some to identify full-time workers as 'core' employees. However, the last few years have not just seen a radical polarization between those in work and those out of work; the gap between skilled and unskilled workers has also widened.

The unskilled and semi-skilled in employment make up the fourth segment of the labour market. The earnings of the worst paid 10 per cent of male workers fell from 65.9 per cent of the average male wage in 1979 to 60.2 per cent in 1986, while the earnings of the best paid 10 per cent rose from 156.9 per cent of the average to 173.3 per cent.

This widening gap between the earnings of the top and bottom of the labour market reflects the way that companies have restructured production in recent years. The workers most vulnerable to unemployment are the unskilled, particularly the young and the old. They are the first to be laid off in recession so they are the most vulnerable to pressure to reduce labour costs.

A related development is the changing skills companies demand with new technology. The introduction of microelectronics into manufacturing has not just contributed to lower overall employment, it has shifted the skills demanded. There is a premium on programmers, systems analysts and multi-skilled maintenance workers who can understand both the electronics and the mechanics of a robot. These workers have benefited from the introduction of new technology, with expanded responsibilities and new wider jobs covering a range of activities. However the work of unskilled operatives may have become increasingly deskilled. So, while many among the skilled have become reskilled in line with the new production methods, many among the unskilled have become further deskilled. The growth of labour intensive services, and the abolition of the wages councils have also contributed to this widening of differentials.

Unskilled workers are in an increasingly fiercely fought differentials race with the skilled. They are likely to identify themselves in terms of their relative position within the world of employment, rather than with unemployed workers. For this reason they must have a predisposition to see promotion through companies' internal labour markets as the main route to advancement rather than improvement in the overall level of employment.

Finally in the fifth segment are the genuinely core workers, permanent, skilled workers, with stable employment prospects. The source of continued high earnings growth is companies' approach to motivating these skilled, well paid 'core' employees.

As the CBI makes clear in a recent submission to the National Economic Development Council, companies are increasingly attempting to maximize demand for products through exploiting market niches to the full. While price competition remains important, other 'non-price' elements of competition have increased in importance. As a result, companies are putting more emphasis on design, marketing, reliability and after sales service.

This shift in companies' strategies to competition has carried important consequences for the way they organize, motivate and pay their workers. There is an increasing stress on agreements to allow workers to be used more flexibly in line with shifting marketing strategies, as well as to control labour costs. Employees are also being asked to play more of a role in quality control, reduction of wastage, preventive maintenance, and incremental product innovation. The CBI concludes: 'It is impossible to obtain the best performance from employees through detailed work rules, constant supervision and threat. The only way this can be achieved is by establishing a skilled and motivated workforce, committed to the goals of the enterprise.'

Combined with this, more companies are introducing new technology production processes. This puts a premium on skilled workers. But it has also led to a change in industrial relations, with more companies attempting to wrap workers into the goals of the business through employee involvement, quality circles and profit sharing.

This fivefold division of the workforce is not the only dimension to division in Britain. These divisions within the working class may be overshadowed by the obscenity of the boom in City and executive salaries. Nor are these five groups homogeneous. Running through these labour market divisions are others. There are regional divisions. The job losses of the early 1980s were concentrated on manufacturing and thus its heartlands in the midlands, north and Scotland. Within regions there are differences between areas, for instance between the depression of Merseyside, and the affluence of nearby Cheshire.

There is also a gender dimension to these divisions. While the male long-term unemployed are outside the labour market, women's unemployment is largely invisible, unrecorded by official statistics. Women with husbands in work cannot claim benefit: the state is effectively telling them they were not really working, not in real, i.e., male jobs. Women also make up a disproportionately large part of the peripheral labour force. Over 60 per cent of peripheral workers are women. There are also significant ethnic divisions with unemployment rates among ethnic minorities far higher than among whites.

But it is not just that the labour market has segmented in this way. What is important is that these divisions have created new and conflicting interests, and as a consequence set up a new distributional dynamic for politics. Thatcherism has set about managing and moulding these divisions and conflicting interests to form the stable base for a coherent political order.

When Thatcherism rose to power in the late 1970s, it came with policies very different from those of other post-war governments. But Thatcherism also maintained one important element of continuity. The ethos of post-war consensus politics was *inclusive*. Through full employment and the welfare state all were offered an opportunity to share in the growth.

The initial monetarist cure offered by Thatcherism was also *inclusive*. It claimed to be a popular national government addressing Britain's malaise. The monetarism looked clinical and neutral. And indeed Britons did plunge into the recession together. As unemployment rose, so did pressures on business. As trade unions protested, so ICI posted its first ever loss and the CBI warned of a bare knuckle fight with the government. The clear message was that we could all suffer through the cure but we would all benefit from the inclusive market economy that would emerge.

As we have seen, what has emerged is a radically divided Britain. With the emergence of those divisions Thatcherism's basic political strategy has changed. It is no longer attempting to build a popular base by offering itself as a national, crusading, inclusive political force but rather through the opposite. Its political strategy now depends on *exclusion*. The government is attempting to create a new political equilibrium based on stabilizing the new economic divisions. This is not just a matter of satisfying the economic and material interests of various constituencies. It is a project to wrap them into a new political order which gives members of these groups a sense of a legitimate place within society. At the core is a strategy to legitimize a society where roughly two thirds have done, and will continue to do, quite well while the other third languish in unemployment or perpetual insecurity.

Those who retained their full-time jobs through the recession are doing better than during the mid-1970s. Then, the growth of their earnings of 14.3 per cent in 1976, and 9.8 per cent in 1977, was outstripped by high inflation, 15.3 per cent and 14.7 per cent respectively. In the last three years those in full-time employment have seen their earnings outstrip inflation by 1 per cent, 2.2 per cent and 4.3 per cent respectively. It is not the British economy that has gained from low inflation but those who have remained in employment. The government has acquiesced in these earnings gains, despite its professed belief that pay is the crucial determinant of employment. Clearly it believes its support can best be deepened and maintained by appeasing wage earnings rather than trying to curtail the rise in earnings.

Moreover, the better paid have benefited from income tax cuts, and the power of this group has warned the government away from reforming taxes on mortgage interest relief and pensions. It is the earnings of this group which has created the consumer boom of the last year [1986/7], accompanied by spiralling credit card debt, and rising imports.

The boom on the high streets in affluent areas, continually rising house prices, the comfort of new consumer durables in homes, building societies and banks competing for their savings, new cars in drives, all create the impression for those doing the spending that the bad times are over.

One reason they are able to do that is the invisibility of the depression and insecurity of the long-term unemployed and the outsiders. While the southern service sector booms, in the north the long-term unemployed have been deserted and forgotten. While Hampstead blossoms, Hackney wilts. But the invisibility of the outsiders in British society is not just a matter of geography. Government schemes to create work for the long-term unemployed are as much aimed at salving the consciences of the insiders. Unemployment becomes an inevitability, akin to a motorway pile-up people drive around gawking at, but glad they were not caught up in it as they speed on. Above all, it is not something which is the creation of economic and social processes, in which they play a part.

This deliberate state policy to make unemployment invisible is compounded by the fatalism of the long-term unemployed excluded from the social institutions of work and pleasure. Increasing privatization through consumption in the core is accompanied by privatization through depression on the fringes.

This coexistence of depression and prosperity has been reinforced by a major shift in economic policy. The higher public spending announced last autumn, the tax cutting budget, all suggest that the need for belt tightening is over. Moreover the increases in spending are a nod to the insiders' consciences over the state of the health service and education.

The development of this strategy to legitimize divided Britain has been facilitated through changing the role of key institutions.

The trade unions are being forced further into a non-political, purely industrial role representing workers within the narrow confines of their particular place of work. The labour movement is caught between attempting to maintain and maximize its organization among those still in employment and being able to represent workers who are unemployed.

Along with a generalized curtailment of the legitimate sphere of state activity, the government has changed the way the state operates, centralizing many functions, taking them out of the arena of political bargaining. The state no longer plays a guardian, managing role with the wide compass it had during the post-war years, but it has become a tool to deal with problems on a selected basis, within financial constraints. The Fowler review of social security, which emphasized the targeting of spending on those deserving and in need, is a clear example.

Finally, private companies have come to play a much more important role in shaping the foundations of politics. The crucial divisions created by the fracturing of the employment base are the accumulation of companies' policies. By passing responsibility to companies, Thatcherism has depoliticized these divisions, which are presented as the result of common sense economic imperatives. With the state disowning the obligations it once had, and companies insisting they are only responsible for what goes on within their walls, the whole notion of social obligation has disappeared into a black hole. Where business does operate in the community it is presented as an enlightened act of charity.

Enveloping these in the economic, cultural and institutional roots of the 'post-recession settlement' is a powerful ideology. Apparently neutral, applying equally to all, it brims with common sense, while justifying the new divisions. The economy must be driven by consumers' desire for value for money. We are all consumers, we all like high quality/low priced goods. So the dictum must bring benefits for all. But not if there are some in a position to enjoy consumption while others scrabble to get by. Another 'neutral' catchword is flexibility. More flexible production must be more competitive, it must yield better value for money. But if the UK labour market has become more flexible it is because particular groups have been weakened: the low paid have created flexibility; the insecurity of peripheral workers has allowed companies the flexibility to vary employment levels.

Most importantly the strategy has dramatically lowered the outsiders' judgements of what they deserve, while simultaneously relieving the insiders of any sense that they or their society has 'obligations'. As the gap between them grows, something fundamental happens to insiders' sense of their place in society. The outsiders become to look less and less like the kind of people insiders mix with at work and socially. They become less recognizable as members of the same society, with a similar right to claim a decent standard of living. At best they are an unsettling embarrassment to be treated with charity. At worst they are an unwanted burden. [. . .]

4   Clerical 'proletarianization': myth or reality?

Rosemary Crompton and Gareth Jones

Although the word is of ancient origin, the concept of 'proletarianization' is invariably associated with Marx and Engels' account of the development of industrial capitalism. In the *Communist Manifesto*, they describe the proletariat as 'the modern working class . . . a class of labourers who live only so long as they find work, and who find work only so long as their labour increases capital'. Inseparable from the notion of the 'proletariat' is that of the 'bourgeoisie': 'In proportion as the bourgeoisie, i.e. capital, is developed, in the same proportion is the proletariat . . . developed'. As Marx and Engels' simple definition makes clear, an essential element of the proletarian condition is wage labourer status. However, if the 'proletariat' is simply taken to include those of wage labour (or employment) status, it is immediately apparent that there exist (and indeed, have always existed), considerable variations in condition within the heterogeneous group so identified. These variations in condition (for example, income, working conditions, etc.) produce empirically a hierarchy of 'employment consequences'. Rather than a dichotomy of 'bourgeois' and 'proletarian', the investigation of condition reveals 'upper', 'middle' and 'lower' levels of employment, and it is in the 'middle levels' that clerical workers have traditionally been located.

Not surprisingly, the emergence and persistence of the 'middle layers' has been a persistent focus of debate in class theory. Those unsympathetic to Marx have been able to claim that the existence of the 'middle classes' 'disproves' Marx's analysis; whilst those more sympathetic have endlessly debated the precise manner in which they should be 'located' within a Marxist framework. Much of the debate has been explicitly concerned with 'condition', with a description of incomes, attitudes, working conditions, and so on. Writing in the 1930s, Klingender, for example, argued that clerks, both in terms of their income and status as propertyless employees, were properly to be identified with the industrial proletariat. To the extent that clerks denied their 'true' class situation – for example, by not joining trade unions – they suffered from false consciousness. On the other hand, Lockwood's influential work (published at the end of the 1950s) concluded that, despite their common employment status, the class situation of the clerk differed significantly from that of the manual worker. In terms of their 'work' and 'market' situations, the benefits enjoyed by the clerks both at work and in the market were such as to differentiate them from manual workers, and clerks were not therefore falsely conscious of their class situation if they failed to join trade unions or seek common cause with manual workers.

As a useful heuristic device, Lockwood and Klingender's common strategy may be described as being to examine the conditions of clerical work and compare them with those of manual work – the latter being assumed to represent the 'ideal' proletarian condition. (This representation is, in fact, somewhat unfair to both authors.) This examination is both interesting and useful. Nevertheless, it can be argued that such a strategy, whilst documenting inequalities of condition, does not explain them (Nichols, 1979, p. 153).

We would suggest that this is because, in the 'proletarianization' debate the examination of the proletarian *condition* has become separated from the analysis of the proletarianization *process*. We want to argue that static descriptions of conditions cannot, on their own, adequately test a thesis about process and social dynamics. Braverman's *Labour and Monopoly Capital* attempts to bring together both process and condition. Briefly, Braverman, following Marx, argues that the initial subjection of labour to capital was 'formal' – that is, although the craftsman sold his labour to the capitalist (and therefore did not control the material means of production) he retained control over his own labour power and thus over important aspects of the labour process. The real control of capital over labour (and the labour process) was only achieved via the 'deskilling' of labour, the separation of 'conception' from 'execution' rendering work into a series of simple, fragmented tasks and removing any control by the workers over the labour process. Deskilling is seen by Braverman as the inevitable outcome of the internal dynamics of the capitalist mode of production, in which by (1) reducing labour costs and (2) enhancing the productivity of labour, the 'degradation of work' serves to maximize accumulation.[1]

As with manual work, Braverman argues that non-manual work has, with the development of monopoly capitalism, been similarly deskilled and thereby rendered truly 'proletarian'. To quote directly: to ascribe 'middle class' or 'semi-managerial' functions to the 'millions of present-day clerical workers' is a 'drastic misconception of modern society', yet this is 'exactly the practice of academic sociology' (1974, p. 293). On the contrary, clerical work has become the province of 'an immense mass of wage-workers. The apparent trend to a large non-proletarian "middle class" has resolved itself into the creation of a large proletariat in a new form. In its conditions of employment, the working population has lost all former superiorities over workers in industry, and in its scales of pay has sunk almost to the very bottom' (ibid., pp. 355–6).

It is clear that Braverman, like Klingender and Lockwood, makes his case for clerical proletarianization by pointing to the similarities between routine clerical and manual work. Although Braverman was working within an explicitly Marxist framework, and his position apparently rejects that of Lockwood, the argument he presents is by no means incompatible. The empirical data presented in his chapter on clerical workers chart the impact of 'scientific management' on the office and the decline of clerical salaries – clearly important aspects of 'work' and 'market' situations. What

separates Braverman and Lockwood, we would suggest, is not a fundamental difference of approach, but twenty years of social development.
Although writing from differing perspectives and reaching varying conclusions, one feature common to all three authors discussed above is the
assumption that it is the manual worker who exemplifies the proletarian
condition. That is, to be a 'proletarian', it is not sufficient to be employed,
in addition the worker must also be subject to control, work discipline and
generally 'less favourable' conditions of employment. Such an analysis of
incqualities of 'condition' has been contrasted by Nichols with the analysis
of '*place*' where this term refers to place within the social division of labour
as a whole.

In common with many other recent authors (e.g., Poulantzas, 1975;
Carchedi, 1975; Wright, 1976), we would emphasize that 'place' in the
social division of labour characteristic of contemporary capitalism is not
'given' simply by virtue of individual ownership or non-ownership of the
means of production, but also by the extent of *control* of productive forces.
Therefore, for example, a senior manager who effectively controls production, investment and/or labour is clearly carrying out the function of capital
even in the absence of legal ownership, and the 'place' of such an
individual in the social division of labour is identified with that of the
bourgeoisie. We would take this argument further by suggesting that,
historically, the 'middleness' of the 'middle classes' may have reflected not
only their relatively superior condition *vis-à-vis* the mass of manual
workers, but also the fact that, within the social division of labour, many
carried out both capital and labour functions. (Crompton and Gubbay,
1979; Crompton, 1976; Wright, 1976). Clearly, the extent to which the
conditions of non-manual employment approximate to the conditions of
manual employment is an important issue which should not be ignored; we
would emphasize, however, that this analysis of 'condition' should not be
divorced from the analysis of 'place'. In other words, 'place' may prove as
important a test of proletarianization as 'condition'. Proletarianization has
been described as 'the complex historical process which produces a
working class' (Larson, 1980, p. 132). That is, proletarianization is a
process which generates proletarians – a class which not only lives by the
sale of its labour but also does not exercise control in respect of capitalist
functions – in short, is hired simply *as* labour and is itself controlled and
directed accordingly.

Braverman brings together the analysis of condition with the analysis of
social dynamics and process by focusing on the removal of 'skill' from
clerical work. This is essentially concerned with the *individual's* control of
his or her own labour. Whether or not an individual's control in this respect
renders their place in the social division of labour significantly different (in
class terms) from those who do not is not an issue that we can resolve here
(Wright, 1976; Crompton and Gubbay, 1979). However, we would suggest
that, by focusing on the possession of skill by individuals and the
implications this has for the control of their own labour Braverman has

ignored the question of other aspects of control. As we have argued above, 'work' can involve carrying out not only skilled or unskilled activities regarding the labour process, but also the exercise of control and authority over both the work of others and/or the material means of production. Changes in the organization and content of clerical work may affect not just the 'skill' of the clerk but also the extent of the clerk's control in these respects, and thus their position in the social division of labour (Crompton and Reid, 1982). However, despite these critical comments, we would emphasize that both Braverman and Lockwood (and to a lesser extent Klingender), place the nature of the clerical work process at the centre of their enquiry. We would agree that such an examination remains important for both the analysis of proletarian condition and the proletarianization process.

Two recent contributions to British sociology have strongly rejected the thesis of clerical 'proletarianization' (Goldthorpe, 1980; Stewart *et al.*, 1980). Although the bases of the rejections are apparently similar, there are in fact important differences between the two approaches which we shall attempt to identify in our account.

Goldthorpe's rejection is brief. First, notions of the '"proletarianization" of lower-level non-manual employment, and in particular . . . that of the emerging "office-factory"' are dismissed as 'facile'. We interpret this statement as being largely concerned with the *empirical* question about the nature of lower level white-collar work. If we are correct, we would simply note that the authorities cited by Goldthorpe in support of his case (Mercer and Weir, 1972; Lockwood, 1958; Dale, 1962) can hardly bear the weight of the rejection, which would itself be contradicted by a number of more recent empirical studies (Mann and Williams, 1960; Jaeggi and Weidemann, 1965; Hoos, 1961; Stymne, 1966; Whisler, 1970; Braverman, 1974).

Secondly, Goldthorpe questions the 'proletarianization' thesis by pointing to the fact (revealed by the Nuffield mobility studies) that the social groupings in which routine clerical workers are commonly located 'are known to be ones with highly fluctuating memberships even over a relatively short-run period' (Goldthorpe, 1980, p. 258), thus undermining 'the potentialities for class-based socio-political action' amongst these groups. More particularly,

> Even if one were to accept (and the point is debatable) that the market and work situation of the employees in question have tended overall to move closer to those of manual wage-workers, the import of such a shift is not all that apparent if, as we have shown for males at least, there is a high frequency of work-life mobility from routine non manual positions to both manual *and* higher-level white-collar ones. (ibid., p. 259)

That is, *male* clerks have not been 'proletarianized' because proletarian status – if it exists at all – is left behind in the move to higher-level white-collar positions. Women have been removed from class analysis, as, for the decades covered by the Nuffield study, their class position (or rather, the class position of the family unit) was effectively 'mediated' through that of men (ibid., p. 288).

Stewart *et al.*'s rejection of the 'myth' of clerical proletarianization is more substantial but, we would argue, in certain important respects resembles that of Goldthorpe. (Indeed, Goldthorpe cites their evidence in his own critical comments on the thesis.) Again, a central point of their argument is the empirical finding that men do not usually remain in occupations classified as 'clerical': 'Careers starting out in clerical work and moving on to better things remain the dominant feature of (male) clerical employment' (1980, p. 193). Thus the apparent status discrepancy – identified by writers such as Lockwood – of the well-educated but lowly paid clerk disappears when it is appreciated that such an individual will no longer be a clerk by his mid-thirties. Today, clerical work is carried out by women, younger men and older, ex-manual men. With respect to 'proletarianization', Stewart *et al.* summarize the position of these three groups as follows:

> Certainly the ex-manual workers are not proletarianised; they are, by both past and current experience, proletarian. Those (men) who entered at an early age, for the most part, are not proletarianised. The vast majority leave clerical work, mostly in an upward direction. . . . Whether the women are proletarianised raises complex questions . . . but it seems the answer must be no. They have always been employed in routine positions, mainly in specifically female jobs. (*ibid.*)

These criticisms of the thesis of clerical proletarianization by both Goldthorpe and Stewart *et al.* therefore centre on the empirical finding that men who begin their careers as clerks do not remain clerks for the whole of their working lives. In the latter case, however, it must be appreciated that their rejection of clerical 'proletarianization' reflects a theoretical perspective more generally critical of conventional stratification theory. A common misconception of such theory, they argue, is to assume that it is the nature of the *job* which locates an occupation in a particular class. Although some occupations which encompass a career (for example, the professions) may give a reasonably accurate indication of the class situation of the incumbent, this is not true for many others. The present occupation of a male clerk, viewed strictly in terms of work content, gives no indication of future career development, which will almost inevitably ensue. Clerical workers, therefore, do not belong to a single class (as is assumed, for example, by the Registrar General), and 'the very question(s) "What is the class position of clerks?" is invalid, because "clerks" does not define a meaningful reality in stratification terms' (Stewart, *et al.*, p. 113).

Clearly, this argument has important implications. For the moment, however, we would frankly admit that serious consideration lies outside the scope of this paper, which focuses more narrowly on the thesis of clerical 'proletarianization'.

In evaluating these arguments, we would emphasize that both rest on the fact that few, if any, *individuals* have been 'proletarianized' (ibid., p. 194).

We would certainly agree that this fact, if correct, has important consequences. We would also agree that it has received insufficient attention from exponents of the 'proletarianization' thesis. However, does it constitute a sufficient basis on which to reject it? To put the question another way, is there anything in the original thesis which indicates that 'proletarianization' only occurs when it happens *to* somebody? A moment's reflection should be sufficient to realize that this cannot be so. We have earlier described proletarianization as a process which generates proletarians; it is essentially a concept about the social division of labour. To write of 'the growth of the industrial proletariat', for example, does not commit the author to the assertion that every person so identified had once worked on the land. To be sure, individuals *may* be 'proletarianized', but it would be placing impossible restrictions on the concept if this was the *only* sense in which it could be applied.

It becomes apparent, therefore, that the two sides in the proletarianization debate are arguing from different premises, different conceptions of the theory and different accounts of the data appropriate to it. We would only note that the contributions of Stewart *et al.* and Goldthorpe *et al.* do have some features in common. They locate their 'refutations' of clerical proletarianization at the level of class *formation*. Both Goldthorpe *et al.*'s observations about social mobility and Stewart *et al.*'s arguments about the problematic relation between occupation and class raise problems concerned with the structuration of classes. The points they raise may have considerable relevance for such questions but they do not strictly bear on the question of class *location*. As a consequence their analyses have moved away from a consideration of the social division of labour and have emphasized the individual's experience of his (never her) occupation. Stewart *et al.* regard this move as crucial with regard to the proletarianization thesis, indeed they remark that 'we enter this debate not in the hope of final settlement, but to seek to transform it' (ibid., p. 91).

Our objectives are more modest. At the present time, we would suggest, the proletarianization debate has effectively been rendered sterile by recent interventions. Given the different bases of the argument assumed by the two 'sides', the only course open is to 'choose' one interpretation or the other. In the discussion that follows, therefore, we shall look more closely at two substantive areas highlighted by recent exchanges – male mobility and female participation in the non-manual labour force. In so doing, we hope to emphasize that, although the protagonists of the thesis of clerical 'proletarianization' may certainly be criticized for their failure to consider these problems, their detractors, in failing to take account of recent developments in the non-manual labour process, may equally be subject to criticism.

Male mobility

Although the empirical fact of male mobility is crucial to the refutation of the proletarianization thesis by both Goldthorpe and Stewart *et al.*, they differ in their interpretation of the processes involved. Goldthorpe's account retains an assumption, conventional in stratification theory, that occupations can be utilized as reasonable indicators of class position. Therefore, a move from 'clerical' to 'managerial' work would be a move from Class III to Class II (Goldthorpe *et al.*, 1980, pp. 40–1); that is, the class position of the individual is actually changed by such a move.

Stewart *et al.*, as we have seen, make an explicit break with conventional stratification theory by denying that (except in particular cases) occupations give an unproblematic account of the class position of the individual. Rather they suggest that it is misconceived to think that 'the significance of occupation in determining class resides in the nature of job', while ignoring the relations between jobs and their occupants (1980, p. 93). With respect to clerical proletarianization they argue that:

> If clerical work has been in any sense proletarianised it is only in the limited sense that proletarians now undertake clerical work which was previously the preserve of those middle-class careers. No actual groups of individuals or type of employee has been proletarianised (ibid., p. 194).

What is suggested in this statement is that 'proletarian' (or 'non-proletarian') status is given not by place in the social division of labour, but rather, by the characteristics of the individuals who occupy these places. That is, what may be termed the 'mobility potential' of the men effectively renders them 'non-proletarian'. Yet, as is made equally clear, *some* people who do clerical work *are* proletarians.

In this paper we are not concerned to adjudicate on the relative merits of these two approaches. What we would emphasize is that both approaches treat the boundary between 'clerical' and 'managerial and administrative' work as unproblematic. Goldthorpe, because such a move is a common move across a class boundary which inhibits class formation. Stewart *et al.* because they want to stress that reasonably well-qualified men do not stay in clerical work but are promoted out of it fairly quickly. Therefore, to be a 'clerk' does not, in this case, indicate a stratification position. If the 'non-proletarian' status of the male clerk is given by their capacity to 'move on', then, logically, their destination – managerial work – must be non-proletarian.

Our research, which was designed to focus on the non-manual labour process, gave us ample opportunity to examine the nature of this boundary. As our discussion will show, we found it to be highly contentious.[2] In the first place, the use of 'clerk' as an occupational title has undergone a considerable transformation. Although, since the middle of the nineteenth century, the 'clerical' category has always included individuals performing routine clerical functions on low pay (Anderson, 1976), the category of 'clerk' also included many (if not the majority – at least until the early years of this century) whose work role – and corresponding rewards – could more properly be described as 'managerial' (Pollard, 1968; Lockwood, 1958). The heterogeneity of the 'clerical' category is reflected in the apparent difficulties in the social class allocation of this occupation in the census. In 1911 clerks were allocated to Social Class I, by 1921 they were demoted to Social Class II, and in 1931 to Social Class III, which is where they remain at the last census (Hakim, 1980).

Although the 'clerical' category is still heterogeneous, it is reasonable to suggest that the occupational title has shown a long-run tendency to be increasingly reserved for only the lowest levels of non-manual employment. This assumption is reflected in, for example, Goldthorpe's description of Class III, as including 'routine non-manual – largely clerical – employees in administration and commerce' (1980, p. 40). As one personnel manager put it to us: 'Nobody wants to be known as a clerk'.

However, although there is perhaps now a greater consistency in the use of 'clerk' as an occupational title, the changing manner of its use does raise problems with regard to empirical evidence in considering the historical development of the occupation. For example, earlier census classifications will have included in the 'clerical' category occupations which today would be considered 'managerial'; therefore to compare, say, the 'clerical' category of 1911 with the 'clerical' category of 1971 – a practice which is common to many longitudinal representations of the occupational structure – is to run the risk of simply not comparing like with like. (Comparisons after 1931 would be valid if one assumes, along with the census, that the Social Class/SEG of clerks has not changed since then!) Similarly if our assumptions about the use of the occupational title are correct, the 'growth' of the clerical category during this century will have been increasingly a 'growth' of routine non-manual occupations. That is, the decline in status of the occupational title has been paralleled by a change in clerical work content.

We have stressed that these changes have been long-term, and our research revealed several examples of the progressive specificity of the title as an occupational label. For example, in a major clearing bank, a 'second clerk' became, on job evaluation in the mid-'60s, a 'branch accountant', and a 'chief clerk' a 'sub-manager'. Similarly, in an insurance company, a 'chief clerk' became a 'departmental manager' (Executive Grade 4), and a 'section clerk' an Executive Grade 2 on job evaluation at the end of the 1960s. In all of the examples we have quoted above, these changes in occupational labels were not accompanied by any change in job content.[3]

Although the progressive removal of 'managerial' occupations from the clerical category may have had the effect of rendering 'clerical' status less contentious in respect of the occupational hierarchy, we would point out that, as a consequence, the 'administrative and managerial' category is rendered more contentious. That is, 'administrative and managerial' grades appear at lower levels in the hierarchy than hitherto. Further evidence in support of this assertion is suggested by the fact that the 'managerial' category is getting younger (Stewart *et al.*, 1980, p. 181). We are not suggesting, by any means, that the whole of the increase in 'administrative and managerial' grades is to be explained by this 'labelling shift'; clearly, the growth of administrative and managerial employment is part of a wider development of the occupational structure which also includes the growth in routine clerical employment mentioned earlier.

In summary, we would argue that the changes in the use of the occupational title of 'clerk' should make one sensitive to the possibility that the 'administrative and managerial' category might be more heterogeneous than hitherto. This possibility is further explored in the second issue we will examine in this section; that is the nature of the non-manual labour process and its implications for male mobility.

Not surprisingly, the 'clerical proletarianization' debate has tended to focus rather narrowly on *clerical* work. Although there are those who would challenge this assertion (Shepard, 1971; Goldthorpe *et al.*, 1980), the balance of evidence seems to indicate that much clerical work has been effectively 'deskilled'. Viewing non-manual work as a whole, therefore, one possible scenario is of a mass of routine clerks controlled by 'management'. From this perspective, the gulf between 'clerical' and 'managerial' work would be considerable, and unambiguously express a 'class' boundary (Becker, 1973). In reality, however, our preliminary research findings indicate that the situation is not nearly so simple. Our discussion has already indicated that there exists a considerable 'grey area' between 'clerical' and 'managerial' work. In particular, many of the jobs we examined which were described as 'administrative' or 'managerial' proved to be largely clerical in terms of actual work content – that is, the 'manager' did the same work as his or her subordinates.

Few social scientists would locate managers and their subordinates in the same class. However, does it follow that all *managers* are therefore in the same class situation? For the 'managerial' category is, without exaggeration, the most heterogeneous of those with which the class/social stratification theorist has to grapple. A 'manager' may be an effective controller within a large organization, perhaps with a considerable ownership interest, or, as we have intimated above, a relatively subordinate employee. The heterogeneity of managerial employment has increasingly led to the suggestion that the class position of many managers is highly ambiguous (Westergaard and Resler, 1975; Carchedi, 1975; Wright, 1976). These ambiguities, we would suggest, make it increasingly difficult to represent with any confidence the transition from 'clerical' to 'managerial' work as a 'class' move.

In abstract terms, a manager may be said to be carrying out capital functions when he or she effectively controls either labour power or the material means of production.[4] Such criteria may be too rigid to act as infallible fieldwork guides but they are useful to situate the work of many of the managers in our study. As we have already noted, many 'managers' did the same work as their subordinates.[5] A typical case would be, say, a Team Leader in a Local Authority (AP 4/5), or an Executive Grade 2 in the Insurance Company (still widely referred to as a 'section clerk'). Invariably, such individuals, although doing the same work as their subordinates, would also deal with or give advice on the difficult or unusual cases or problems which arose in the course of the work. Here, we would suggest, the manager was effectively acting as a 'skilled worker' – as opposed to the relatively less experienced, semi- or unskilled clerk.

It is true that the vast majority of these managers did have a formal supervisory role. However, 'supervision' was defined by both the managers and their subordinates as 'helping out with problems' rather than 'policing', serving further to emphasize the view of the manager as 'skilled worker'. In any case, it would have been extremely difficult for such managers to *directly* control their subordinates, even had they wished to do so. Hiring, firing, staff evaluation and discipline were all carried out by the Departmental Manager (or his assistant) in co-operation with a Central Personnel Department. Even timekeeping, traditionally an area where first-line supervision exercises direct control, had been effectively centralized through the introduction of 'flexitime'.

Even if these managers did not have effective personal control over their subordinates, it is still possible that they exercised control in other respects – over the organization of the work, decision-taking on resources, and so on. As far as the organization of the work was concerned, this again seemed an area in which lower-level managers had very little control. With the widespread computerization of non-manual work, both work organization and pace are effectively shaped by the computerized system. These managers may possibly allow, for example, informal job rotation, but even this was more usually arranged at the discretion and initiative of the Departmental Manager or his assistant. One area in which many of these managers *could* be said to exercise a degree of control, however, was in the authorizing of decisions concerned with various payments. For example, it might be possible for a salaries Team Leader to authorize an interim payment to someone whose medical condition was not fully clear; or, in insurance, the payment of a claim, up to a certain limit could be authorized. Even here, however, the criteria governing such decisions tended to be explicit and rule-bounded; unusual cases or large amounts would be dealt with by the Departmental Manager.

In summary, our evidence suggests that many middle to lower level 'managers' spend very little, if any, of their time at work exercising what would be thought of as 'managerial' functions. Rather, they act as skilled and/or experienced workers. This view seems to be endorsed by the attitudes of their subordinates. When asked to say who they thought of as 'management', the lowest level identified by the vast majority of clerks was the Departmental Manager or his assistant, or, in the case of the Bank, the Branch Manager. In making this point, we would emphasize that intermediate positions were clearly seen as *promotion*, but not, apparently, as a move to 'management'.

Although the empirical evidence we can produce at this stage of the project is rather sketchy, we have been able to show that, apparently, the 'deskilling' of non-manual work has not been confined to the clerical section of the non-manual labour force. Much lower-level managerial work has also been routinized, control functions have been effectively centralized leaving the 'manager' more like a skilled employee. Additionally, we would suggest that, on the basis of our evidence, Braverman's assertion of the 'polarization of office employment and the growth at one pole of an immense mass of wage workers' (1974, p. 355) is not entirely correct. Although the growth of non-manual employment *has* been in large part that of routine employees, between these workers and the more senior levels of management there exists a substantial portion of the non-manual workforce.

In the terms in which occupational categories are conventionally employed, therefore, we would suggest that the move from 'clerical' to 'managerial' work should not invariably be assumed to be a move across class boundaries. Although it is true that most men are promoted out of clerical work, the work to which they are (initially) promoted in many cases differs only marginally from that of ordinary clerks. If this represents the full extent of male mobility, then the significance of this mobility in undermining the 'proletarianization' thesis must be weakened. This must be the case whether male mobility is taken to indicate a move across a class boundary (Goldthorpe), or male 'mobility potential' seen as determining class position (Stewart *et al.*).

The class position of women

Again, the position of the two authors under discussion would seem, apparently, to differ on this issue. For Goldthorpe, women are effectively excluded from the debate:

> It is the class position of males which has been the overwhelmingly direct determinant of the class 'fate' of the large majority of families and households: in other words, the way in which women have been located in the class structure has tended to reflect their general situation of dependency. (1980, p. 67)

Stewart *et al.* would seem to regard female clerks as 'proletarians'. This seems to be implied by their statement that 'proletarians now undertake clerical work'. These 'proletarians' clearly cannot be the younger men, for they are promoted out of clerical work. Therefore they must be the women and ex-manual men who they have identified elsewhere as major components of the clerical workforce (1980, p. 93 and pp. 136ff.). However, the proletarian status of women is largely irrelevant as women have not personally experienced 'proletarianization'. This latter interpretation gives rise to an intriguing paradox. If the development of non-manual work has drawn increasing numbers of women, as proletarians, into the non-manual labour force, then surely a process of 'proletarianization' is occurring? Alternatively, is it being suggested that women are invariably proletarian by virtue of their gender and therefore cannot possibly be 'proletarianized'? Yet another possible interpretation of this assumption is that the female component of the routine non-manual labour force is exclusively drawn from women whose families of origin are 'proletarian'. Neither of these latter possibilities seems reasonable, and we would endorse West's statement that:

> Although the proletarianization of white-collar work is far from an undisputed reality, analysis of it is hindered, not helped, by a refusal to consider it just because women happen to be the occupants of the jobs in question. (West, 1978, p. 229)

Nevertheless, Goldthorpe's assumption that class position is effectively given by the location of the family, which in turn means the class position of the male breadwinner has, until recently, been widespread in sociology. We would not claim any originality in challenging this view, and indeed, the major points we would make in countering this argument have already been summarized elsewhere (West, 1978).

First, there is the problem of locating those unattached and/or non-dependent women whose social position is not derived from either their families or male head of household. In the UK, it has been recently estimated that at least one in six households are substantially or solely supported by women (West, 1978, p. 225). Do such households not have a class position, or, alternatively, should they be automatically categorized as reflecting the 'general situation of dependency' of women as a whole? Alternatively, should independent women/female heads of households be 'granted' a class position in the same terms as male heads of households?

Secondly, with the increasing employment of women (particularly married women) it is clear that women's earnings have a considerable impact on family 'life-chances' even where the woman is not the 'main' bread-winner. To the extent that women's employment becomes the norm, then clearly, the life chances of the family will be crucially affected by a woman's capacity to work. To make a final point: in excluding women from consideration as proper subjects of stratification theory, it is being implicitly asserted that the class position of particular occupations depends, not on the occupation *per se*, but on the gender of the occupant. That is: 'the character of certain jobs in [the] market depends on who occupies them' (ibid., p. 233).

However, although we would reject the view that gender excludes women from consideration in class and stratification theory, it is obvious that women are, on the whole, considerably disadvantaged in the non-manual labour market by virtue of their gender. In all of the three organizations we studied, women predominated at the lowest levels of the organizational hierarchy, and few had risen to 'managerial' positions – even the somewhat attenuated managerial positions described in the previous section. Although we did find some evidence of overt discrimination, far more important in the explanation of the women's lowly position in the non-manual hierarchy were the difficulties they encountered in displaying 'promotion qualities' given the constraints of their domestic roles. In a previous paper based on just one of our case studies (Crompton *et al.*, 1982), we have shown that promotion depended on a combination of factors including (1) long, unbroken service, (2) the acquisition of formal post-entry qualifications, and (3) a willingness to be geographically mobile. Breaks in service due to childrearing, the conflicting demands of family and work, and a perceived inability to move because of the husband's job, all conspired to severely handicap women as far as promotion was concerned. However, to recognize that women who enter employment may be encumbered by serious handicaps with regard to promotion does not, logically, lead to the conclusion that they have no place in the class or stratification system. For example, it has never been seriously suggested that an unqualified male school leaver is similarly 'declassed' by the very real problems he would face.

If a wider perspective is taken on non-manual employment as a whole, the position of women appears less problematic. Our own position is very simple. As non-manual employment has grown, non-manual labour costs have become an ever increasing proportion of total costs. (The exact reasons for the growth of non-manual employment need not concern us here.) Faced with ever-rising labour costs, employers have been under pressure to (a) increase the productivity of labour and/or (b) reduce the costs of labour. (We would point out that there is nothing particularly radical in this assertion; from the employers' point of view, it is just sensible 'management' of resources.) One consequence of these pressures is that much non-manual work has been routinized and broken down into its constituent elements. As Braverman so graphically demonstrates – and his assertion is not contradicted by our research findings – Taylorism is applied in the office as it has been in the factory. This process has been facilitated by the introduction of a machine, the computer, that can manipulate symbols as earlier machines manipulated wood, iron and cotton. As non-manual work has been routinized and simplified, employers have found it possible to hire less skilled and cheaper labour than hitherto. In this particular case, women were highly suitable. We would emphasize that there is *nothing* particularly unusual in this. For example, women were brought into the textile industry in the nineteenth century for very similar reasons.

Although the reasons for the increasing participation of women in the labour force have been often examined (Amsden, 1980; Bowen and Finegan, 1969; Greenhalgh, 1980) we can briefly review here some which are particularly relevant to the recruitment of women to clerical work:

1   Both rising demand for, and routinization of clerical labour occurred during a period of full employment (the decades following the Second World War). Additionally, changes in family patterns and control of fertility 'released' women for employment for longer periods than hitherto.
2   Women's labour, as *relatively* short term, unskilled, and immobile, was

cheap. Additionally, women's traditionally dependent status has always been associated with lower wages (Beechey, 1977).

3   The work available (routine clerical) was highly suitable for women – i.e. light, not shift work, etc. (Computer operators, who often work shifts, are usually male.) There are also positive advantages to employers in employing women in socially visible work; as one Bank Manager put it, 'customers like to see a pretty face behind the counter'.

4   There was little or no resistance to the increasing employment of women by the existing workforce, unlike, for example, the Engineers' resistance to 'dilution' (Hinton, 1973). In part, this was probably due to the fact that the existing workforce was only weakly unionized, but more important must have been the fact that women were (on the whole correctly) not seen as a threat to male prospects.

With the increasing recruitment of women into clerical work, it has been suggested that the non-manual labour force has been effectively structured into two tiers which broadly correspond to gender (see Stewart *et al.*, 1980, pp. 93–4, and Giddens, 1973, p. 288). In the lower tier are those in routine clerical jobs with few promotion opportunities (mainly women), in the upper tier those (mainly men) who will make a career in non-manual work. (These two tiers are neatly encapsulated in Bank argot as 'jobbers' and 'careerists'.) Presented in this light, the structure appears extremely stable. There are a number of reasons, however, for believing that this apparently stable two-tier structure may not be smoothly reproduced in the future.

Not all jobs in the lower tier are entirely devoid of opportunities. This clearly cannot be the case, as men pass through the lower tier on their way upwards. It is also probable that a substantial part of the growth of female clerical employment has been in occupations from which upward mobility is possible. For example, in insurance, clerks in branch offices have *always* been women. No promotion is possible from clerical jobs in branch offices, because branch office managers are always recruited from (male) agents. It follows, therefore, that the increase in female employment in insurance has been concentrated in the larger head offices of insurance companies, where promotion from routine clerical grades is a real possibility. It was in the large office, rather than the smaller branches, that we found women expressing discontent with their lack of promotion. In the smaller offices, the women's response was resigned – as promotion was clearly impossible, no strong feelings were expressed on the issue.

Much of the expansion of female clerical employment *has* been 'in the most menial clerical tasks with limited opportunities for promotion' (Stewart *et al.*, 1980, p. 94). We would include here the secretarial ghetto, data preparation and small administrative units whether these are offshoots of larger organizations or, for example, a solicitor's office, or the office of a small manufacturing company. The extent to which women are confined in such clerical occupations, however, can be exaggerated, and many women, perhaps even the majority, will be in clerical occupations in which promotion possibilities exist. In some of these cases, women will effectively be 'forced' into the lower tier by, for example, organizational demands for geographical mobility such as exist in banking (Heritage, 1977; Graham and Llewellyn, 1976).

However, where these constraints are absent, there are a number of factors that suggest that women may not necessarily continue to accept extended service in lower-grade jobs. In the first place, more women are working for longer periods, and this includes women with dependent children. As women's earnings are increasingly accepted as a regular source of family income (rather than as a supplement or 'pin money') it would be unusual if women did not seek to maintain or increase this source of income. Secondly, the change in attitudes brought about by such things as the activities of the women's movement and Equal Opportunities legislation may be difficult to quantify, but they cannot be entirely ignored. Initial results from our study suggest that it is the younger women who are most concerned about their promotion prospects, and, more importantly, there are some indications that they are beginning to acquire the post-entry qualifications so necessary to career development. Lastly, as we have indicated, lower-level managerial jobs have been considerably routinized and are well within the capacities of most women (we are *not* suggesting that they are incapable of undertaking higher-level posts, however), a fact which many women in our study were not slow to appreciate. As a twenty-one-year-old clerk said in explaining her desire for promotion: 'Just to learn a different job – to get in with different people. [There's] no power attached – no more responsibility to being an E1 than a C4!'

In summary, we would not dismiss the increasing employment of women in clerical jobs as irrelevant, rather, we would cite it as evidence for the proletarianization of non-manual work. As non-manual work has been 'deskilled', and as control has been centralized, so many women have been recruited (amongst others) to fill the essentially 'proletarian' positions so created. However, many of these 'proletarian' jobs still provide opportunities for upward mobility – although the *extent* of mobility must be called into question because of the routinization of much 'administrative and managerial' work. Women's mobility chances are certainly severely constrained by their domestic roles. Nevertheless, we are somewhat sceptical of the assumption that women will be content to remain in low-level clerical positions in those circumstances where opportunities for upward mobility exist.

Summary and conclusions

In this paper, we have suggested that the debate on clerical proletarianization as presented by Klingender, Lockwood and to a lesser degree Braverman, has focused on the proletarian *condition* at the expense of the proletarianization *process*. That is, the argument has been presented somewhat statically, and the major question to be answered has been whether or not clerical work approximates to the proletarian condition. In the case of all three authors, manual work is taken to be the exemplar of the proletarian condition. Recent critics of the proletarianization thesis (Goldthorpe, Stewart *et al.*), have, on the other hand, tended to disregard (or treat as relatively unimportant) the question of proletarian condition. An important consequence of this shift in emphasis is their claim that, because men do not remain in clerical work throughout their careers, clerical proletarianization has not occurred and is in fact a 'myth'.

Our position is that a proper examination of the debate on clerical proletarianization must include both condition and process. That is, although earlier theorists may be criticized for their lack of attention to process, their critics may be criticized equally for their treatment of the proletarian condition. In particular, it is our contention that a sustained examination of what may be loosely described as the 'non-manual labour process' provides a mechanism whereby both condition and process may be examined. To be sure, a detailed examination of non-manual work is, at first sight, largely a characteristic of the first approach we have described. However, we would emphasize that an examination of the non-manual labour process does not imply a static approach. Rather, it forces the consideration of processes which change and restructure non-manual work, and which are closely associated with proletarianization.

To illustrate our position, we examined two substantive areas highlighted by the recent debate – male mobility and female participation in the clerical labour force. The importance of male mobility to the critics of the proletarianization thesis rests on the assumption that managers are *non-*'proletarian'. This would seem to be an entirely reasonable assumption. However, on examining the non-manual labour process (rather than just clerical work), our research indicates that many lower-level 'managerial' jobs are, in fact, almost entirely devoid of what would usually be thought of as 'managerial' content. Therefore, although progression to lower management certainly constitutes promotion, it is questionable whether the *class* position of these lower-level managers differs significantly from that of the 'clerks'.

Unfortunately, the mobility data available does not give us a clear indication of how much 'upward' male clerical mobility is eventually to what are unambiguously 'managerial' positions, and how much is to what we have described as 'skilled clerical' managerial positions. However, we would suggest that our findings should give rise to some scepticism as to the nature and extent of male mobility.

Female participation in the non-manual labour force (and indeed, more generally) is an important topic which has received insufficient sociological attention in the past. Our position here is very different from that of the critics of clerical proletarianization. We would regard the extensive recruitment of women, as proletarians, to clerical work as evidence *for* clerical proletarianization, not against.

Women's employment in non-manual work has always been concentrated at the lower end of the job hierarchy, and this feature is amply confirmed by our own research. However, this does not mean that women are confined to clerical occupations from which promotion is impossible. To the extent that women are in jobs where promotion opportunities exist, then the longer they are established in these positions, the more likely they may be to regard promotion as a real possibility. Recent figures indicate that women are delaying both marriage and childbearing; as a consequence, the (realistic) possibilities for at least short-range promotion must improve (*Social Trends* 11, pp. 35–7). If even only a minority of women do actively seek promotion, then male mobility – and its significance – will be further attenuated.

Our strategy in this paper has been to positively confront the complex issues raised by the clerical proletarianization debate. In particular, we recognize that critics of the proletarianization thesis are entirely correct in emphasizing the heterogeneity of the clerical workforce – it is indeed the case that:

> This curiously ageless, abstract creature, 'the clerical worker', serves to simplify the relationships between individuals and occupations by creating a false identity between them. (Stewart *et al.*, 1980, p. 112)

Nevertheless, it is equally the case that occupations cannot simply be characterized in terms of their occupants – as is implicitly suggested, for example, when female employment is treated as irrelevant to the 'proletarianization' debate simply because it *is* female.

Besides the heterogeneity of the clerical workforce, we would also emphasize the heterogeneity of clerical *work*. In fact, we would prefer to speak of the 'non-manual' workforce and 'non-manual' work. The terms 'clerical' and 'managerial' suggest more or less clearly defined work tasks and more or less identifiable personnel; in reality, as we have suggested, similar work content may be spread over a range of occupational labels.

Finally, we would reaffirm our belief that an examination of the labour process is central to both class theory and the more general understanding of the stratification system. In particular, this approach enables us to overcome some of the limitations of theorizing in this area imposed by the legacy of occupational classifications. As such, it may have important consequences for the analysis of the contemporary class structure.

Notes

The authors would wish to acknowledge the support of the SSRC who funded the research cited in this paper.

1   It has been argued that new skilled occupations such as computer programming and systems analysis emerge as a consequence of clerical deskilling, thus undermining the overall thrust of the deskilling thesis. It falls outside the scope of this paper to examine the validity of this position.

2   We would point out that we are only in the final stages of completing the fieldwork on this project. As we have not yet completed our data analysis, the evidence we offer in this paper will tend to be suggestive, rather than conclusive.

We anticipate being able to offer more substantial evidence once data analysis has been completed.

3   We are, of course, aware that chief clerks would not have been coded with routine clerical employees. Our present point is concerned with the instability of occupational titles.

4   Such distinctions have been given consideration by Gorz (1972), Marglin (1976) and others.

5   Many of these positions could plausibly be described as 'foreman clerical'. However, given their occupational titles, it is worth pondering where they would appear in occupational classifications.

References

AMSDEN, A. H., (ed.) (1980) *The Economics of Women and Work*, Harmondsworth, Penguin.

ANDERSON, G. (1986) *Victorian Clerks*, Harmondsworth, Penguin.

BECKER, J. F. (1973) 'Class structure and conflict in the managerial phase', I and II, in *Science and Society*, Vol. 37, Nos 3, 4.

BEECHEY, V. (1977) 'Some notes on female wage labour in capitalist production', *Capital and Class*, No. 3, Autumn.

BOWEN, W. G. and FINEGAN, T. A. (1969) *The Economics of Labour Force Participation*, Princeton University Press.

BRAVERMAN, H. (1974) *Labour and Monopoly Capital*, New York, Monthly Review Press.

CARCHEDI, G. (1975) 'On economic identification of the new middle class', *Economy and Society*, Vol. 4.

CROMPTON, R. (1976) 'Approaches to the study of white-collar unionism', *Sociology*, Vol. 10, No. 3.

CROMPTON, R. and GUBBAY, J. (1979) *Economy and Class Structure*, London and Basingstoke, Macmillan.

CROMPTON, R., JONES, G. and REID, S. (1982) in West, J. (ed.) *Women in the Labour Force*, London, Routledge and Kegan Paul.

CROMPTON, R. and REID, S. (1982) 'The deskilling of clerical work', in Wood, S. (ed.) *Degradation of Work?*, London, Hutchinson.

DALE, J. R. (1962) *The Clerk in Industry*, Liverpool University Press.

GIDDENS, A. (1973) *The Class Structure of the Advanced Societies*, London, Hutchinson.

GOLDTHORPE, J. H. *et al.* (1980) *Social Mobility and Class Structure in Modern Britain*, Oxford, Clarendon Press.

GREENHALGH, C. (1980) 'Participation and hours of work for married women in Great Britain', *Oxford Economic Papers*.

GRAHAM, S. and LLEWELLYN, C. (1976) 'Women in the occupational structure: a case study of banking', Oxford, Nuffield College Paper.

GORZ, A. (1972) 'Technical intelligence and the capitalist division of labour', *Telos*, No. 12.

HAKIM, C. (1980) 'Census reports as documentary evidence: the census commentaries 1801–1951', *Sociological Review*, Vol. 28, No. 3, August.

HERITAGE, J. C. (1977) 'The growth of trade unionism in the London clearing banks, 1960–1970: a sociological interpretation', University of Leeds PhD thesis.

HOOS, I. R. (1961) *Automation in the Office*, Washington.

HINTON, J. (1973) *The First Shop Stewards' Movement*, London, Allen and Unwin.

JAEGGI, U. and WEIDEMANN, H. (1965) 'The impact on managers and clerks in West German industry and commerce', in Scott, W. H. (ed.) *Office Automation: Administrative and Human Problems*, Paris, OECD.

KLINGENDER, F. D. (1935) *The Condition of Clerical Labour in Britain*, London, Martin Lawrence.

LARSON, M. S. (1980) 'Proletarianisation and educated labour', *Theory and Society*, No. 9.

LOCKWOOD, D. (1958) *The Blackcoated Worker*, London, Allen and Unwin.

MARX, K. and ENGELS, F. (1967) *The Communist Manifesto*, Harmondsworth, Penguin.

MANN, F. and WILLIAMS, L. (1960) 'Observations on the dynamics of a change to EDP', *Administrative Science Quarterly*, Vol. 5, September.

MARGLIN, S. A. (1976) 'What do bosses do?', in Gorz, A. (ed.) *The Division of Labour*, Brighton, Harvester Press.

MERCER, D. E. and WEIR, D. T. H. (1972) 'Attitudes to work and trade unionism among white-collar workers', *Industrial Relations Journal*, Vol. 3, Summer.

NICHOLS, T. (1979) 'Social class: official, sociological and Marxist', in Miles I. and Evans, J. (eds) *Demystifying Social Statistics*, London, Pluto Press.

POLLARD, S. (1968) *The Genesis of Modern Management*, Harmondsworth, Penguin.

POULANTZAS, N. (1975) *Classes in Contemporary Capitalism*, London, New Left Books.

ROUTH, G. (1980) *Occupation and Pay in Great Britain 1906–79*, London and Basingstoke, Macmillan.

SHEPARD, J. M. (1971) *Automation and Alienation*, Cambridge, Mass.

STEWART, A., PRANDY, K. and BLACKBURN, R. M. (1980) *Social Stratification and Occupations*, London and Basingstoke, Macmillan.

STYMNE, B. (1966) 'EDP and organisational structure: a case study of an insurance company', *The Swedish Journal of Economics*.

WEST, J. (1978) 'Women, sex and class', in *Feminism and Materialism*, Kuhn, A. and Wolpe, A. (eds) London, Routledge and Kegan Paul.

WESTERGAARD, J. and RESLER, H. (1975) *Class in Capitalist Society: a Study of Contemporary Britain*, London, Heinemann.

WHISLER, T. L. (1970) *The Impact of Computers on Organisations*, New York, Praeger.

WOOD, S. (ed.) (1982) *Degradation of Work? Deskilling and the Labour Process*, London, Hutchinson.

WRIGHT, E. O. (1976) 'Class boundaries in advanced capitalist societies', *New Left Review*, No. 98.

5 The corporation and the class structure

John Scott

One of the major arguments derived from the supposed 'separation of ownership from control' and the 'managerial revolution' is the view that wealth and power have become dissociated. The capitalist propertied class has been replaced by a managerial class, which is 'broad and diffuse . . . with several loosely integrated components', and which is based not on property ownership but on 'occupational status and occupational earnings' (Parsons, 1954a, p. 431; Lenski, 1966, p. 352). On the basis of his analysis of ownership and control, Berle drew very radical conclusions about the future of the propertied class: 'the transformation of property from an active role to passive wealth has so operated that the wealthy stratum no longer has power' (Berle, 1963, p. 53). The most sophisticated statement of this view from within the theory of industrial society is that of Bell in his paper 'The breakup of family capitalism' (1957). Bell argues that the series of economic crises at the beginning of the century led to the reconstruction of family enterprises by investment bankers, and that the consequence of this was the establishment of 'finance capitalism'. Gradually the power of the bankers declined, and the professional managers that they had installed in the major corporations became the new 'corporate organizers' (Bell, 1957, pp. 40–1). As inheritance through the family became less important and technical skill became more important, there was a 'break-up' of the old ruling class: the mere possession of wealth did not give access to economic power (Bell, 1958, pp. 50ff.).

Very similar conclusions to those of Bell have been arrived at by Burnham, who originated the notion of the 'managerial revolution'. Burnham begins from the position of the theory of capitalist society that economic power in the period after the First World War rested with the finance capitalists [. . .]

Burnham claimed, however, that the dominance of the financial oligarchy was a feature of the transition from capitalist society to managerial society. The managers are those who carry out the 'technical direction and coordination of the process of production and they are distinct from the finance executives and finance capitalists who are interested in the profitability of a company or group of companies' (Burnham, 1941, p. 70). Owing to their technical indispensability, the managers are destined to become the dominant class in the place of the finance capitalists. The managers are not dependent on private property and will base their dominance on their *de facto* access to the means of production: 'The position, role, and function of the managers are in no way dependent upon the maintenance of capitalist property and economic relations; . . . they

depend upon the technical nature of the process of modern production'
(ibid., p. 80).

This view of the rise of managers has not gone unchallenged: proponents
of the theory of capitalist society hold that ultimate economic power is still
vested in a financial oligarchy, and Zeitlin (1974, p. 46) has recently
claimed that: 'News of the demise of the capitalist classes . . . is, I suspect,
somewhat premature'. The aim of this chapter is to assess these rival
viewpoints in the light of the available evidence [. . .]

The managerial reorganization of the propertied class

Studies of the distribution of income and wealth in the USA and in Britain
have shown that both societies are highly inegalitarian. There is clear
evidence for the existence of a privileged social class. A study by Kuznets
(1953) has been used by Kolko (1962, pp. 15, 24 and 37) and others to show
that before-tax income in the USA was distributed in such a way that the
top 10 per cent of income recipients received a more or less constant share
of 30 per cent of all income throughout the first half of this century. The
share of the top 1 per cent declined from 14 per cent of income to 10 per
cent during the 1930s and 1940s (Birnbaum, 1971; Bottomore, 1965, p. 44).
Domhoff shows that by the late 1950s the share of the top 1 per cent of
families in total income stood at 8 per cent (1967, p. 41). It would appear
that the share of top income groups increased until 1929, decreased during
the Depression and the Second World War, and has remained constant
since then. This view is confirmed by Miller's findings that the 30 per cent
share of the top 5 per cent of families in 1929 had fallen to 21 per cent in
1944 and stood at 20 per cent in 1962 (Miller, 1966, p. 113). Kolko has
argued that the effect of taxation on this pattern has not been very great,
and the work of Lydall and Lansing (1959, p. 141) shows that during the
1950s taxation reduced the share of the top 10 per cent from 30 per cent to
26 per cent. The picture in Britain is remarkably similar. While the share of
the top 10 per cent of income recipients in before-tax income seems to have
remained in the region of one-third, the proportion received by the top 1
per cent has fallen in the post-war period from 11 per cent to between 6 and
8 per cent (Nicholson, 1967, p. 42; Lydall, 1959; Soltow, 1968; Blackburn,
1967). On the basis of their criticisms of the official statistics on income,
various writers have suggested that concentration may be somewhat higher
than this (Titmuss, 1962; Meade, 1964; Atkinson, 1975). The reduction in
the share of the top 1 per cent occurred primarily between 1949 and 1957,
the proportion remaining constant since then. The major cause of the
reduction was the fact that from 1949 to 1957 earned incomes rose faster
than income from other sources, while after 1957 the most rapidly growing
sources of income were rent, dividends and interest (Nicholson, 1967, p.
49). The trend in after-tax income has been slightly less marked, the share
of the top 1 per cent being 6 per cent in the 1940s and 5 per cent in the
1950s and 1960s. Even the conservative estimates of Polanyi and Wood

suggest that in 1970 the share of the top 1 per cent in after-tax income was 5 per cent (Polanyi and Wood, 1974, p. 64). Noble (1975, pp. 178 and 199) shows that, while the share of the top 1 per cent before tax fell from 9 per cent to 7 per cent, their share after tax fell from 5 per cent to 4 per cent. Allowing for minor variations in techniques, units and data, the basic pattern is clear. In Britain and in the USA as well as in France and Germany (Atkinson, 1973a; Babeau and Strauss-Kahn, 1977, pp. 41ff.), one-tenth of the population receives about one-third of total income, and has done for most of the century. One per cent of the population, about half a million families in the USA, receive between 5 and 8 per cent of total income and have received this proportion since the 1950s, having declined from an earlier position of greater concentration.

With respect to wealth distribution, a major study of the USA by Lampman (1959; 1962) shows that the share of the top 1 per cent in personal wealth fell over the period 1922–49 and then rose again through the 1950s to stand at between 25 and 30 per cent. It has since been suggested that this proportion continued to rise through the 1960s (Smith and Calvert, 1965; Domhoff, 1967; Lundberg, 1969). Lampman argues that much of the reduction in concentration in the period between the wars can be explained in terms of the redistribution of wealth *within* families and so does not represent a significant change in the social distribution of wealth. Nearly half of the wealth held by the top 1 per cent in 1953 was held by the top 0.11 per cent of the population, about 113300 people, and there is no evidence to suggest that the situation is different today. Data for Britain suggest a higher degree of inequality than in the USA, though wealth has gradually become more equally distributed. The share of the top 1 per cent fell from 69 per cent in 1911 to 56 per cent in 1936, 43 per cent in 1946, 42 per cent in the 1950s and 1960s, and to about 30 per cent in the 1970s (Lydall and Tipping, 1961, p. 253; Noble, 1975, p. 175; Atkinson, 1972, p. 21; Revell, 1965; Blackburn, 1967; Atkinson, 1975, p. 134). The proportion of wealth held by the top 5 per cent declined from 86 per cent to 55 per cent over the same period, and Atkinson shows that, while the share of the top 1 per cent has declined by a half, the proportion of wealth held by the next 4 per cent remained constant or actually increased over the period. Atkinson draws the conclusion that this reflects redistribution within families in order to avoid estate duty (Atkinson, 1972, pp. 22–3; Polanyi and Wood, 1974, p. 17). This view is confirmed by numerous studies pointing to the continued importance of inheritance in the accumulation of wealth (Harbury, 1962; Revell, 1960; Harbury and McMahon, 1974; Rubinstein, 1974). As in the USA, almost half of the wealth held by the top 1 per cent is held by the top 0.1 per cent, about 55000–60000 people today (Atkinson, 1975, p. 134).

It can be demonstrated not only that the top income recipients and the top wealth holders are the same people, but also that the major source of their income is that portion of their wealth which is held as company shares. The number of individual shareholders in US corporations increased rapidly from 1916 to 1921 and from 1927 to 1933, and by the early 1930s about 8 million people held company shares (Cox, 1963, p. 33; Means, 1930; Goldsmith and Parmelee, 1940, pp. 16–18; Perlo, 1958, p. 26). These people represented about 7 per cent of the population and held just over 60 per cent of all company shares, the remaining 40 per cent being held by other companies. This same group represented the top 20 per cent of income recipients, and it was found that the importance of stockholding increased with income. The higher the income within this group, the greater the contribution made by dividend income. Dividends accounted for 60 per cent of the income of individuals with incomes over $100000 (Goldsmith and Parmelee, 1940, pp. 10–13). Half of the 1937 shareholders held shares in one company only, but those with incomes over $100000 held shares in an average of twenty-five companies. The concentration was such that 0.1 per cent of shareholders, representing 0.02 per cent of income recipients, received a quarter of the dividend income accruing to individuals. Goldsmith and Parmelee claim that 'notwithstanding the wide dispersion of ownership indicated by the large number of stockholders, ownership of stock was highly concentrated in the hands of a relatively few persons' (ibid., p. 13). This is confirmed by the fact that only a third of shareholders held shares in the 200 largest companies. While the number of shareholders declined somewhat through the Depression and the Second World War, it began to rise again during the 1950s and had reached its 1937 level by 1959, although in proportional terms individual shareholdings were being overshadowed by 'institutional' holdings. However, the continuing concentration of individual shareholdings is shown in Lundberg's finding that 1.4 million families held 65 per cent of all investment assets in 1962, under a quarter of a million families holding 32 per cent (Lundberg, 1969, p. 28).

Atkinson has shown that the wealthiest groups in Britain have the highest rate of shareholding, the top 5 per cent of wealth holders in 1961 holding 96 per cent of all personally owned shares (Atkinson, 1972, p. 30; Atkinson, 1975, p. 135; Westergaard and Resler, 1975, pp. 107ff.). Shareholdings make an important contribution to income: the top 10 per cent of those in receipt of investment income in 1960 received 99 per cent of all income from this source (Blackburn, 1967), and the top 1 per cent of income recipients in 1970 received 7 per cent of all income but 17 per cent of investment income (Noble, 1975, p. 180). Noble argues that: 'About 500000 people, one per cent of the population, own just over a third of all private wealth in contemporary Britain and receive just over half of all the personal income derived from possession of wealth'. Within this stratum the very rich 50000, 0.1 per cent of the population, are the most important group (ibid., p. 182; Westergaard and Resler, 1975, p. 119).

The evidence which has been briefly reviewed here gives substantial support for the view that the class which is most privileged in relation to the distribution of income and wealth derives this privilege from property ownership. The propertied class remains a reality. But Berle and Bell have both argued that wealth has become dissociated from 'power' – that is, that the propertied class no longer monopolizes the control of business. In order to examine this claim it is necessary to analyse the composition of the propertied class in more detail. Considerable evidence has been amassed to show that the most important categories within the propertied class are company directors and executives [. . .]

Table 5.1 shows the actual percentage distribution of directors' share-holdings in their own companies [. . .] On the basis of [these] figures, Florence has argued that those who own company shares are a 'pool' from which directors are drawn, although holding a directorship in a particular company is not directly associated with holding shares in that company (Florence, 1961, pp. 93, 137; 1953, p. 200). That is, directors and major shareholders were one and the same people, though individual sharehold-ings were rarely large enough to ensure board representation in a specific company (Beed, 1966, p. 35; Klein *et al.*, 1956). Stanworth has analysed holdings by directors in the companies on which they sit and, as shown in Table 5.2, has documented the substantial monetary value which these holdings represent.

Table 5.1 Directors' holdings in 233 large British companies (1951)

% of shares held by directors	No. of companies in each category			
	Very large	Medium-large	Small-large	Totals
Less than 1%	44	16	19	79
1–5%	32	17	38	87
5–10%	4	8	13	25
10–20%	5	0	11	16
More than 20%	13	6	7	26
Totals	98	47	88	233

Source: Florence (1961) pp. 90–1, Table IVc

Table 5.2 Directors' holdings in the top seventy-five British companies (1971)

Market value of shares (£000)	% of directors
Less than 1	18.9
1–3	19.8
3–5	9.8
5–10	13.9
10–25	11.7
25–100	12.4
More than 100	13.5
Total	100.0

Note: Where a person sits on more than two boards, he will be counted twice in this table. The actual concen-tration of shares is, therefore, somewhat greater than the table suggests.

Source: Stanworth (1974) p. 255

It seems that directors in Britain and the USA comprise that very small proportion of the population who monopolize the ownership of company shares and derive a substantial part of their income from this source. They not only hold shares in the companies for which they work, but they own stock in other companies as well. They are not only the largest single shareholding group; they are the holders of the remaining large blocks of personally owned shares. The heart of the propertied class is the 'corporate rich'. The form taken by managerial remuneration is not a direct indication of changes in the relations of production. Banks has argued that the increasing number of salaried directors (Erickson, 1959, p. 50) indicates a move towards a 'collective mode of production' within which management is able to benefit itself through fees, salaries, bonuses, expense accounts and pensions at the expense of dividend payments (Banks, 1970, p. 168). However, if 'managers' and 'shareholders' are not distinct social categories, then the precise form in which managers are able to remunerate themselves becomes a reflection of such factors as the relative taxation advantages to be gained from 'earned' rather than 'unearned' income (Westergaard and Resler, 1975, p. 162; Baran and Sweezy, 1966, p. 47). The facts adduced here do suggest that important changes have occurred, but these changes are not those to which Banks has pointed.

Large personal stockholdings are monopolized by a propertied class which need no longer be tied to the particular enterprises in which it has a shareholding. While directors may not even hold a significant minority stake in the companies which they direct, they are, nevertheless, major shareholders in a large number of companies. Mills (1956, p. 147) has argued that this constitutes a 'managerial reorganization of the propertied class', a restructuring of the mediation of strategic control which does not alter the basic features of the system. He also maintains that:

> The growth and interconnections of corporations . . . have meant the rise of a more sophisticated executive elite which now possesses a certain autonomy from any specific property interest. Its power is the power of property, but that property is not always or even usually of one coherent and narrow type. It is, in operating fact, class-wide property. (ibid., p. 122)

Domhoff has shown very clearly what this involves: 'Family A does not own Company X while Family B owns Company Y, as it may have been in the past; instead, Family A and Family B both have large stockholdings in Companies X and Y, as does Family C, which used to be the sole owner of Company Z' (Domhoff, 1967, p. 40). Property has been 'depersonalized' (Birnbaum, 1969, p. 12), just as possession has become impersonal. The managerial stratum is now merely 'the most active and influential part of the propertied class' (Baran and Sweezy, 1966, p. 46; Sweezy, 1951). The basis of this process was discussed by Hilferding, who argued that the central feature of 'finance capitalism' was the growth of a reliable stock exchange. Hilferding holds that 'only through the securities market does the capitalist attain independence of the fate of the particular enterprise in which he has invested his money' (Hilferding, 1910, cited in Sweezy, 1942, p. 258). The consequence is that the propertied class has a common interest in the business system as a whole (Domhoff, 1967, p. 40).

The most forceful statement of the thesis of the managerial reorganization of the propertied class is that of Zeitlin, who argues that 'corporations are units in a class-controlled apparatus of appropriation; and the whole gamut of functionaries and owners of capital participate in varying degrees, and as members of the same social class, in its direction' (Zeitlin, 1974, p. 1079). That is,

> Although the largest banks and corporations might conceivably develop a relative autonomy from *particular* proprietary interests, they would be limited by the *general* proprietary interests of the principal owners of capital. To the extent that the largest banks and corporations constitute a new form of class property ... the 'inner group' ... of interlocking officers and directors, and particularly the finance capitalists, become the leading organizers of this class-wide property. (ibid., p. 901)

The trend towards management control and control through a constellation of interests is directly associated with this managerial reorganization of the propertied class. This is not to say that millionaires and wealthy families no longer exist – far from it. Rather, direct access to particular controlling positions by virtue of personal shareholdings is of declining importance in modern industrial capitalism [. . .]

The structuration of the propertied class

Structuration is the process through which structures are made to persist or become transformed. To study the structuration of a propertied class is to analyse the mechanisms through which its privileged position is reproduced over time. My concern here is with the mechanisms of 'mediate structuration', that is, the long-term processes through which closure and monopolization are achieved. The analysis will focus on the social institutions through which class structuration is mediated (Giddens, 1976, pp. 120–3). Giddens has argued that class structuration proceeds along two dimensions: integration and recruitment. That is, the solidarity and cohesion of a privileged class depends upon the quality and quantity of interactions between its members and upon the ability of the class to restrict entry to the privileged positions which it enjoys (Giddens, 1973, p. 120).

Integration is necessary because the propertied class has no monolithic unity; it comprises various 'segments'. The propertied class is internally differentiated into segments 'having a relatively distinct location in the social process of production and, consequently, its own specific political economic requirements and concrete interests which may be contradictory to those of other class segments with which, nonetheless, it shares essentially the same relationship to ownership of productive property' (Zeitlin *et al.*, 1974, p. 1009). In his original formulation of the thesis of the managerial revolution, Burnham had discussed the changing balance of power between 'managers', 'finance executives' and 'finance capitalists', and more recent studies have followed this lead. The most extensive study of this kind is that of Villarejo, who found three major categories of company directors: the 'propertied rich', 'executives' and 'outside' direc- tors. The latter group includes bankers, lawyers and other businessmen. More than half of the directors of top American companies were active or retired executives. About a fifth were major stockholders – the propertied rich – and about a third of these also held executive posts. Outside directors sit on the board as representatives of large holdings or because of their legal and financial skills (Villarejo, 1961, p. 52; Domhoff, 1967, pp. 58 ff.; Smigel, 1964; Smith, 1970, p. 48). A study by Soref found that outside directors came from a more 'exclusive' social background than executive directors and that they tended to hold a large number of directorships, giving them a broad interest in intercorporate affairs (Soref, 1976, p. 360). Useem calls these directors, following Zeitlin, the 'inner group' of the propertied class. The inner group is concerned mainly with integrating the activities of the business world and was found to sustain a class awareness – a sense of common identity and community (Useem, 1978, p. 238). This class awareness served as a diffuse mechanism of integration but did not involve specific political concerns or a consciousness of opposition. (See also: Seider 1974, 1977; Christ, 1970.)

Integration of the various segments of the propertied class, therefore, is brought about by a division of labour between the segments themselves. Full-time executives concern themselves with the management of particu- lar companies, while non-executive directors 'manage' the system as a whole. These non-executive directors are the core of the propertied class, which has its interests dispersed throughout the system which they manage. The major mechanism of integration pointed to in these studies is the informality and communication deriving from a common social back- ground. Indeed, this has been central to the whole discussion of social class so far. In Britain, this has been analysed in relation to the changing balance of power between landed, industrial and financial segments of the prop- ertied class. From within the theory of capitalist society Aaronovitch has stated the argument:

> The capitalist class itself, at first politically managed by the aristocracy and landed gentry, underwent a complex process by which the most powerful groups of industrial and trading capitalists married into and merged with the aristocracy and big landed gentry. . . . But the outcome of capitalist competi- tion and the fusion of banking and cognate capital with industrial capital has been, inevitably, the emergence of a small, oligarchic set of groupings who are the upper caste of the class which dominates capitalist society as a whole. (Aaronovitch, 1961, p. 70)

A number of studies have confirmed some aspects of this view. It is generally accepted that the fusion of industrial and financial interests with the older landed interests resulted in the creation of an 'establishment'. Rubinstein claims that in the early years of this century 'there took place the collapse of the three old elites and their merger into one elite, dominated by the South of England and finance' (Rubinstein, 1976, p. 124). Drawing on evidence from the Parker Tribunal (1957), Lupton and Wilson documented the high degree of integration characteristic of the City establishment (Lupton and Wilson, 1959; Sampson, 1962; Stanworth and Giddens, 1974a, pp. 99ff.). In this fusion, the values of the old landed class, the ideals of civilized gentlemanly behaviour, were fostered and maintained in the public schools and Oxbridge (Elias, 1939; Dunning, 1977; Coleman, 1973), and these values were passed on to the leaders of various institutions, whatever their social origins (Rex, 1974). A common background and pattern of socialization, reinforced through intermarriage, club memberships, etc., generated a community feeling among the members of the propertied class. This feeling could be articulated into a class awareness by the most active members of the class [. . .]

In Britain, a study of directors in large firms in the 1950s found that 58 per cent had been educated at public schools and that 57 per cent had some kind of high-level qualification. More than half of all the directors came from a business background, 44 per cent having fathers who had been directors. Just under one-fifth of the directors inherited their positions. The heirs were found to have the highest level of qualification of all directors. Nearly three-quarters had spent their whole career in business, a third having spent their career solely in large firms. In all, about three-quarters of the directors had some kind of 'commerical' training, while a quarter had a 'technical' training. Those directors trained in engineering or science tended to be single directors in engineering or chemical firms; those directors trained in law and accountancy tended to be multiple, outside directors (Copeman, 1955, pp. 89, 92–5, 120; Clements, 1958, pp. 173ff.). Nichols found that in the 1960s the situation was very similar: a large number of directors were unqualified, only a small number had science qualifications, and the most frequent single qualification was a training in accountancy. He did find, however, some evidence that professional management training was becoming more widespread (Nichols, 1969, pp. 81–3, 93; Marceau and Whitley, 1978). A study of company chairmen by Stanworth and Giddens suggested that, while recruitment in manufacturing industry had opened up a little, banking remained an exclusive occupation (Stanworth and Giddens, 1974a, p. 89). In view of the centrality of banks in corporate networks, it is important to investigate this more fully. Table 5.3 presents the results of a major investigation into the education of directors in British commercial banks.

Table 5.3 shows a clear and significant upward trend in both public school and university attendance. The clearing-bank directors were becoming more highly educated, but they were obtaining this education at the traditional privileged institutions. Examining the fathers of these directors, Boyd found that about half had appeared in *Who's Who* and that the directors who had not come directly from this privileged background had achieved their mobility through the public schools and Oxbridge (Boyd,

Table 5.3 Educational background of British commercial bank directors (1939–70)

Type of education	%			
	1939	1950	1960	1970
Major public schools	60.9	66.9	61.1	62.7
Other public schools	7.3	9.5	12.2	17.2
All public schools	68.2	76.4	73.3	79.9
Oxford and Cambridge	45.3	51.5	52.8	60.4
Other universities	4.5	1.8	4.5	8.2
All universities	49.8	53.3	57.3	68.6

Source: Boyd (1973), p. 84, Table 11, p. 92, Table 19

1973, pp. 96, 102, 110). Thus recruitment to the leadership of British business remained restrictive, though formal educational qualifications are becoming of greater importance [. . .]

Business leaders in the capitalist industrial societies are still drawn overwhelmingly from the propertied class, yet this class supplements direct inheritance with possession of educational diplomas. While technical expertise and education generally are increasingly prominent factors in executive recruitment, this does not preclude the continued dominance of propertied families. Stanworth and Giddens argue that:

> . . . the persistence of familial ties with the economic leadership of the very large companies is a notable phenomenon. This tends to be masked by the declining importance of 'inherited control' of the sort in which an entre-preneur passes on 'his' firm to his son. This obviously drops away among the giant corporations; but it does not signal the disappearance of less immediate forms of 'inheritance', whereby members of the same family continue to be prominently represented on the board. (Stanworth and Giddens, 1975, p. 24)

If the established families are able to monopolize access to the education system, they can ensure that those most qualified for controlling positions in the corporate system are none other than their own scions. The greater the monopolization of education, the greater the closure of the upper class and, therefore, the more secure will be the established families in the overall process of class reproduction.

The evidence I have presented suggests that, while class domination still persists, the mechanisms of this domination have changed. Although private ownership is of considerable importance, it is not always sufficient to ensure a leading position in the corporate world. Baran and Sweezy (1966, p. 29) have argued that 'stock ownership, wealth, connexions, etc., do not as a rule enable a man to control or to exercise great influence on a giant corporation from the outside. They are rather tickets of admission to the inside, where real corporate power is wielded'. Braverman has amplified this point and claims that severance of the direct personal link between capital and its individual owner has involved a transition from a 'personal' link between ownership and strategic control to a 'class' link.

Recruitment is based on technical expertise rather than on personal connections, and technical expertise is monopolized by the propertied class (Braverman, 1974, pp. 257–8). The link between legal ownership and control over capital has changed from a personal to an impersonal link and from a reliance on wealth to a reliance on 'cultural assets'.

Bourdieu, from whom the term 'cultural assets' is taken, expresses this transformation in terms of a move from the personal mode of class domination appropriate to the mechanical solidarity of the traditional market society, to the 'structural mode of class domination' characteristic of the organic solidarity of an administered oligopoly involving highly interdependent firms, complex networks of power, and bureaucratized enterprises. There has been a change in the mode of executive recruitment and, therefore, in the mode of reproduction of the system. Selection and promotion are now dependent on educational certificates rather than being directly dependent on personal property.

> The family enterprise run at least partially by its proprietors can overlook formal criteria in the recruitment of its leaders because the possession of property titles to the enterprise and/or its appurtenances by the proprietary family guarantees possession of the attributes and qualities considered socially necessary (for example, 'standing' or 'sense of authority') and the symbolic capital (notably personal relations) necessary for management of the enterprise; in assuring its own reproduction, the family assures at the same time the production of personnel endowed with the social competence (and often also the technical competence) necessary for running the enterprise. The tendential transformation of 'individual possessory holdings' within 'power systems' renders inoperative the means by which the enterprise can assure the managerial personnel endowed with the characteristics, and notably the class habitus, required. It is as if possession of an educational title, and particularly a diploma from a *Grande École*, which tends to become a necessary (though not sufficient) condition of access to positions of economic power, constitutes, like the possession of a property title in another stage of the system, a sort of syncretic index guaranteeing possession of most of the properties and qualities with which the leaders of the large integrated firms must be endowed in order to occupy positions of power in the apparatus of the enterprise. (Bourdieu *et al.*, 1973, p. 66)

The modern structural mode of domination requires agents with a high level of technical competence. The dominant class has transformed the institutions through which it reproduces itself and so is able to continue to control the economy; the reproduction of class domination operates through the mediation of the school (ibid., pp. 77, 80–2). Whereas the personal mode of domination involved the 'direct transmission of social positions between the holder and the inheritor designated by the holder himself', the structural mode of domination operates in an indirect way at the level of the class as a whole: transmission of social positions within the dominant class 'rests on the *statistical* aggregation of the isolated actions of individuals or collective agents who are subject to the same laws, those of the educational market' (ibid., p. 83).

This transition involves what Parkin sees as a move from collectivist rules of exclusion to individualist rules of exclusion. Increasingly, recruitment is based on rules which refer to the specific attributes of individuals which fit them for positions. In particular, this involves what Miller has called 'credentialism', 'reliance upon examination certificates as a means of controlling entry to valued positions in the division of labour' (Parkin, 1974a, p. 7). But this is not a straightforward transition from 'ascription' to 'achievement', although it may have the appearance of a meritocracy. Achievement of an educational title depends upon a person's cultural patrimony (*patrimoine culturel*). The new mode of domination

> . . . limits the powers of the family which, in the old mode of reproduction, controlled the totality of the mechanisms of reproduction from fertility and marriage to inheritance – by which the transmission of patrimony ensures the transmission of the social positions to which the patrimony gives access – and also, to a considerable extent, education. But this is only to restore them in another form, at the level of the class, through the intermediary of the better hidden mechanisms of social statistics which are capable, such is the logic of probability, of conferring on the class in its totality the properties which it refuses to its various elements taken separately. (Bourdieu *et al.*, pp. 83–4)

The inherited cultural assets of an upper-class background are amplified through the educational system, access to which is still dependent upon wealth. Thus wealth can be converted into cultural assets. Inheritance of cultural assets is possible only for those 'endowed with the means of appropriating it for themselves', and since these means are differentially distributed between social classes

> . . . it is sufficient to give free play to the laws of cultural transmission for cultural capital to be added to cultural capital and for the structure of the distribution of cultural capital between social classes to be thereby reproduced. (Bourdieu, 1971, p. 73; Bourdieu and Passeron, 1970)

Even if this form of closure is incomplete and a certain degree of social mobility occurs, this need not threaten the reproduction of the class structure, since 'the controlled mobility of a limited category of individuals, carefully selected and modified by and for individual ascent, is not incompatible with the permanence of structures' (Bourdieu, 1971, p. 71). Stability of class relations will occur so long as the occupants of dominant positions are endowed with the system of predispositions, the 'habitus', which generates actions that contribute to the reproduction of the structure.

Thus, to the extent that ownership and strategic control are no longer directly connected, the mechanisms of cultural patrimony and the educational market together ensure that the corporate economy remains under the control of the capitalist class as a whole. To the extent that ownership and strategic control are *not* actually separated, the mechanisms of personal domination will continue to operate. As Meynaud puts it:

> Without any doubt at all, modern capitalism has considerably modified its practices; but if the method of recruitment of the managerial circle has undergone any noticeable changes, it does not seem to me that either the

unity or even the homogeneity of this group is seriously compromised. (Meynaud, 1964, p. 175)

There is a privileged class of propertied families which are increasingly autonomous from particular proprietary interests. This class is able to secure a degree of closure sufficient to reproduce the positions of its members within the broader structure which it reproduces. Industrial capitalism shows a long-term tendency for the direct connection between private family property and strategic control to be broken. Nevertheless, it is also evident that propertied interests are still of central importance: a large number of companies are controlled by private owners, many executives are drawn from those who hold large blocks of shares in the corporation, and directors and executives are drawn from a pool of wealthy families.

The managerial reorganization of the propertied class has resulted in a structure of interdependent families and corporations. The families involved in this structure are the nucleus of a social class which reproduces itself over time. The propertied class is 'the social class formed around the core of interrelated principal owners of capital' (Zeitlin, 1974, p. 901). The most important mechanisms of class structuration are commonality of social background, the direct transmission of property, and the indirect transmission of cultural patrimony. Social class relations are reproduced on the basis of the 'resources' provided by the relations of possession with which they are associated. In class structuration, individuals are recruited in such a way that their actions reproduce the structure of class relations [. . .]

References

AARONOVITCH, S. (1961) *The Ruling Class*, London, Lawrence and Wishart.

ATKINSON, A. B. (1972) *Unequal Shares*, Harmondsworth, Penguin.

ATKINSON, A. B. (1973a) 'The distribution of income in Britain and the US', in Atkinson (1973b).

ATKINSON, A. B. (ed.) (1973b) *Wealth, Income and Inequality*, Harmondsworth, Penguin.

ATKINSON, A. B. (1975) *The Economics of Inequality*, Oxford University Press.

BABEAU, A. and STRAUSS-KAHN, D. (1977) *La Richesse des Français* ('The Wealth of the French'), Paris, Presses Universitaires de France.

BANKS, J. A. (1964) 'The structure of industrial enterprise in industrial society', in Halmos (1964).

BANKS, J. A. (1970) *Marxist Sociology in Action*, London, Faber and Faber.

BARAN, P. A. (1957) *The Political Economy of Growth*, Harmondsworth, Penguin.

BARAN, P. A. and SWEEZY, P. M. (1966) *Monopoly Capital*, Harmondsworth, Penguin.

BEED, C. S. (1966) 'The separation of ownership from control', *Journal of Economic Studies*, Vol. 7, No. 2.

BELL, D. (1957) 'The breakup of family capitalism', in Bell (1961).

BELL, D. (1958) 'Is there a ruling class in America?' in Bell (1961).

BELL, D. (1961) *The End of Ideology*, New York, Collier-Macmillan.

BERLE, A. A. (1963) *The American Economic Republic*, London, Sidgwick and Jackson.

BIRNBAUM, N. (1969) *The Crisis of Industrial Society*, Oxford University Press.

BIRNBAUM, P. (1971) *La Structure du pouvoir aux États-Unis* ('The Structure of Power in the United States'), Paris, Presses Universitaires de France.

BLACKBURN, R. (1967) 'The unequal society', in Blackburn and Cockburn (1967).

BLACKBURN, R. and COCKBURN, A. (eds) (1967) *The Incompatibles*, Harmondsworth, Penguin.

BOTTOMORE, T. B. (1965) *Classes in Modern Society*, London, Allen and Unwin.

BOURDIEU, P. (1971) 'Cultural reproduction and social reproduction', in Brown (1973).

BOURDIEU, P. and PASSERON, J. C. (1970) *Reproduction in Education, Society and Culture*, London, Sage.

BOURDIEU, P. *et al.* (1973) 'Les Stratégies de reconversion: Les classes sociales et le système d'enseignement' ('Reconversion strategies: social classes and the system of education'), *Social Science Information*, Vol. 12, No. 5.

BOYD, D. (1973) *Elites and their Education*, Windsor, NFER.

BRAVERMAN, H. (1974) *Labour and Monopoly Capital*, New York, Monthly Review Press.

BURNHAM, J. (1941) *The Managerial Revolution*, Harmondsworth, Penguin.

CHRIST, T. (1970) 'A thematic analysis of the American business creed', *Social Forces*, Vol. 49.

CLEMENTS, R. V. (1958) *Managers: A Study of their Careers in Industry*, London, Allen and Unwin.

COLEMAN, G. H. (1973) 'Gentlemen and players', *Economic History Review*, Vol. 26.

COPEMAN, G. H. (1955) *Leaders of British Industry*, London, Gee.

COX, E. B. (1963) *Trends in the Distribution of Stock Ownership*, University of Pennsylvania Press.

DOMHOFF, G. W. (1967) *Who Rules America?*, Engelwood Cliffs, NJ, Prentice-Hall.

DUNNING, E. G. (1977) 'Power and authority in the public schools', in Gleichmann *et al.* (1977)

ELIAS, N. (1939) *Über den Prozess der Zivilisation* ('On the Process of Civilization'), Volume 1, Frankfurt: Suhrkamp.

ERICKSON, C. (1959) *British Industrialists: Hosiery and Steel*, Cambridge University Press.

FLORENCE, P. S. (1961) *Ownership, Control, and Success of Large Companies*, London, Sweet and Maxwell.

GIDDENS, A. C. (1973) *The Class Structure of the Advanced Societies*, London, Hutchinson.

GIDDENS, A. C. (1976) *New Rules of Sociological Method*, London, Hutchinson.

GOLDSMITH, R. W. and PARMELEE, R. C. (1940) *The Distribution of Ownership in the 200 Largest Nonfinancial Corporations*, Monographs of the Temporary National Economic Committee, Number 29, Washington, Government Printing Office for the US Senate.

HILFERDING, R. (1910) *Das Finanzcapital* ('Finance capital'), Vienna, Ignez Brand.

HARBURY, C. D. (1962) 'Inheritance and the distribution of personal wealth in Britain', in Atkinson (1973b).

HARBURY, C. D. and McMAHON, P. C. (1974) 'Intergenerational wealth transmission and the characteristics of top wealth leavers in Britain', in Stanworth and Giddens (1974b).

KLEIN, L. R. *et al.* (1956) 'Savings and finances of the upper income classes', *Oxford Institute of Statistics Bulletin*, No. 18.

KOLKO, G. (1962) *Wealth and Power in America*, London, Thames and Hudson.

KUZNETS, S. (1953) *Shares of Upper Income Groups in Incomes and Savings*, New York, National Bureau of Economic Research.

LAMPMAN, B. (1959) 'The share of top wealth holders in the United States', in Atkinson (1973b).

LAMPMAN, R. (1962) *The Share of Top Wealth Holders in National Wealth*, Princeton University Press.

LENSKI, G. (1966) *Power and Privilege*, , New York, McGraw-Hill,

LUNDBERG, F. (1969) *The Rich and the Super Rich*, London, Nelson,

LUPTON, C. and WILSON, C. (1959) 'The social background and connections of top decision-makers', in Urry and Wakeford (1973).

LYDALL, H. F. (1959) 'The long-term trend in the size distribution of income', *Journal of the Royal Statistical Society*, Series A, 122/1.

LYDALL, H. F. and LANSING, J. B. (1959) 'A comparison of the distribution of personal income and wealth in the United States and Great Britain', in Atkinson (1973b).

LYDALL, H. F. and TIPPING, D. G. (1961) 'The distribution of personal wealth in Britain', in Atkinson (1973b).

MARCEAU, J. and WHITLEY, R. (1978) 'Management education in Britain and France', in Littlejohn *et al.* (1978).

MEADE, J. E. (1964) *Efficiency, Equality, and the Ownership of Property*, London, Allen and Unwin.

MEANS, G. C. (1930) 'The diffusion of stock ownership in the US', *Quarterly Journal of Economics*, Vol. 44.

MEYNAUD, J. (1964) *Technocracy*, London, Faber and Faber.

MILLER, H. P. (1966) 'Income distribution in the United States', in Atkinson (1973b).

MILLS, C. W. (1956) *The Power Elite*, New York, Oxford University Press.

NICHOLS, T. (1969) *Ownership, Control, and Ideology*, London, Allen and Unwin.

NICHOLSON, R. J. (1967) 'The distribution of personal income in the UK', in Urry and Wakeford (1973).

NOBLE, T. (1975) *Modern Britain*, London, Batsford.

PARKER TRIBUNAL (1957) *Proceedings of the Tribunal Appointed to Inquire into Allegations that Information about the Raising of the Bank Rate was Improperly Disclosed*, Cmnd 350, London, HMSO.

PARKIN, F. (1974a) 'Strategies of social closure in class formation', in Parkin (1974b).

PARKIN, F. (ed.) (1974b) *The Social Analysis of Class Structure*, London, Tavistock.

PARSONS, T. (1954a) 'A revised analytical approach to the theory of social stratification', in Parsons (1954b).

PARSONS, T. (1954b) *Essays in Sociological Theory*, Glencoe, Ill., Free Press.

PERLO, V. (1958) '"People's Capitalism" and stock ownership', *American Economic Review*, Vol. 48.

POLANYI, G. and WOOD, J. B. (1974) *How Much Inequality?*, London, Institute of Economic Affairs.

REVELL, J. R. (1960) 'An analysis of personal holders of wealth', *British Association for the Advancement of Science*, Vol. 17.

REVELL, J. R. (1965) 'Changes in the social distribution of property in Britain during the twentieth century,' *Actes du Troisième Congrès International d'Histoire Economique*, Munich.

REX, J. A. (1974) 'Capitalism, elites and the ruling class', in Stanworth and Giddens (1974b).

SAMPSON, A. (1962) *Anatomy of Britain*, London, Hodder and Stoughton.

SEIDER, M. S. (1974) 'American business ideology: a content analysis of executive speeches', *American Sociological Review*, Vol. 39.

SMIGEL, E. O. (1964) *The Wall Street Lawyer*, Glencoe, Ill., Free Press.

SMITH, E. P. (1970) 'Interlocking directorates among the "Fortune 500"', *Antitrust, Law and Economic Review*, Vol. 3.

SMITH, J. D. and CALVERT, S. K. (1965) 'Estimating the wealth of top wealth-holders from estate tax returns', *Proceedings of the American Statistical Association*.

SOLTOW, L. (1968) 'Long run changes in British income inequality', in Atkinson, (1973b).

SOREF, M. (1976) 'Social class and a division of labour within the corporate elite', *Sociological Quarterly*, Vol. 17, No. 3.

STANWORTH, P. (1974) 'Property, class and the corporate elite', in Crewe (1974).

STANWORTH, P. and GIDDENS, A. C. (1974a) 'An economic elite: a demographic profile of company chairmen', in Stanworth and Giddens (1974b).

STANWORTH, P. and GIDDENS, A. C. (eds) (1974b) *Elites and Power in British Society*, Cambridge University Press.

STANWORTH, P. and GIDDENS, A. C. (1975) 'The modern corporate economy', *Sociological Review*, Vol. 23, No. 1.

SWEEZY, P. M. (1942) *The Theory of Capitalist Development*, London, Dennis Dobson.

TITMUSS, R. (1962) *Income Distribution and Social Change*, London, Allen and Unwin.

USEEM, M. (1978) 'The inner group of the American capitalist class', *Social Problems*, Vol. 25.

VILLAREJO, D. (1961) 'Stock ownership and the control of corporations', Part III, *New University Thought*, Vol. 2, No. 2.

WESTERGAARD, J. H. and RESLER, H. (1975) *Class in a Capitalist Society*, London, Heinemann.

ZEITLIN, M. (1974) 'Corporate ownership and control: the large corporation and the capitalist class', *American Journal of Sociology*, Vol. 79, No. 5.

Section III   Race

Introduction

The settlement of substantial numbers of former citizens of the New Commonwealth in Britain since 1948 has created a significant new social division – race. Although the concept is used in ways which have almost nothing to do with scientific interpretations (Rose and Lewontin, 1983) social definitions of race do separate out people of West Indian and south Asian origin for different, often inferior, treatment. Although their numbers are not large, totalling less than five per cent of the population after forty years of highly publicized immigration, the 'black' groups have had major impacts on the British economy and on politics and could be seen as having brought about a restructuring of British society.

In line with our earlier recognition of different, though related debates about class position and class formation or structuration, the articles reproduced here throw light both on how the black minorities were fitted into previously existing British class and urban structures, and also on the way their presence and their cultures and aspirations have triggered off processes of struggle with effects well beyond their own circles. The articles set out to describe the position of black groups and to interpret the significances of differences in position in terms of social processes. In so doing, they begin to show that culture plays a central role in the interaction between black and white, a role with economic and political consequences. The presence of black people in British society, and especially of concentrations of black people in some towns and cities, has presented a serious challenge to the meanings attached to Britishness, a challenge which has brought into focus some of the least palatable features of national culture. Drawing on a wealth of evidence from previous studies, notably the three surveys conducted by PEP and PSI (Daniel, 1968; Smith, 1977; Brown, 1985), all three authors give a central role in their argument to racism, racial discrimination and disadvantage.

The extract by Miles (Chapter 6) addresses the question of the class position of post-war New Commonwealth immigrants. It reviews and criticizes a range of previous discussions of this question before moving on to present Miles' own position. Two of the earlier proposals came from Marxist authors: Westergaard and Resler (1976) saw immigrants as part of the working class, undifferentiated by racial factors, while Castles and Kosack (1973) saw them as working class, but separated into a lower stratum because of inferior incomes and conditions. Two others came from neo-Weberians: Rex and Tomlinson (1979) argued that discrimination in employment, labour and housing markets combined to relegate black immigrants to an underclass. Parkin (1979) went even further to stress that groups defined in racial terms could potentially be a more important factor than economic class, as more powerful groups worked to close opportunities to deprived groups. In so doing, he effectively allowed conscious collective action to take precedence over economic class position.

Miles' own position, which is developed from that stated in Phizacklea and Miles (1980), puts economic class position first but allows ideological and political factors a role in creating fractions of classes. In Miles' view, the concentration of New Commonwealth migrants in manual occupations and the central role of labour needs in drawing migrant workers into Britain (and also into other European countries) demonstrates that they are, in economic terms, working class. However, Miles recognizes that they are effectively separated from indigenous workers by socially defined race. Earlier in the book from which the extract is taken, he had shown that human variations are too complex to be categorized into different races and that there is no genetic separation between populations. The fact that society recognizes races, usually primarily on the basis of skin colour, is therefore an ideological process of 'racialization' rather than a scientific classification. However, it has real effects on allocation of resources, on subjective affiliations and on collective action. The tendency of racialization is to create divisions within economic classes, though its exact effects are historically and locationally contingent. The majority of blacks fall into a racialized fraction of the working class, but others are in fractions of the old or new petty bourgeoisie. The issues of racial disadvantage and discrimination and their variation in space and time are the starting point of the other two chapters.

The article by Ward (Chapter 7) extends the discussion of the way black minority groups have fitted into British society, particularly by showing how the amount and nature of Asian settlement relates to the availability of certain kinds of jobs in different localities, and creates four types of British city in terms of Asian involvement. However, it also shows that distinctive features of Asian culture and individual motivation have led to a move into self-employment, which makes black immigration more than just a process of labour migration, though in Britain as in most of Europe this was the dominant process in the labour shortage years of the 1950s and '60s. Some of the original migrants were looking for more than unskilled work, and in recent years they have been joined by redundant workers and British born blacks in seeing self-employment as a route to economic advancement which by-passes discrimination in getting jobs and promotion in existing organizations. The extent to which this strategy is succeeding is an open question: some commentators see Asian small business as economically marginal and wasteful of human resources, while others see it as having the potential to inject real dynamism into inner city economies.

The extract from Gilroy (Chapter 8) focuses on political disputes resulting from black settlement in Britain, and in particular on the different British allies of blacks in struggles against racism. There is a brief sketch of events in the 1960s when sympathetic liberals, notably Roy Jenkins while Home Secretary, argued for racial equality and integration. Gilroy's chief focus is on events in the 1970s and '80s when organized racist groups, notably the National Front, sought to capitalize on widespread hostility to inject an explicitly racist strand into British politics. Two strands of anti-racism appeared in the 1970s: Rock Against Racism sought to ally far left theory with youth culture to defeat the National Front on the grounds that it was 'no fun'. Its coincidence with the emergence of punk made this rather anarchic campaign somewhat ambiguous and involved it in ridiculing the central symbols of British culture during the Jubilee. The Anti-Nazi League identified the National Front with Nazism and drew in the strongly patriotic strand of the traditional Labour movement, but was so focused on this single issue that the electoral decline of the National Front in 1979 removed its *raison d'être*. Gilroy's next focus of analysis is the 'municipal anti-racism' which developed as a local government response to the riots in Britain in 1981 and in other cities in later years. Although these campaigns were conducted by elected bodies with considerable bureaucratic and economic resources, Gilroy criticizes them as ill thought out and ineffective, or even counter productive.

All three chapters indicate that the effect on British society of the new ethnic minorities is highly complex. It encompasses economic opportunities and resources, political demands and struggles, cultural influences from the ancient Hindu caste system to modern pop music, and ideological struggles to appropriate or redefine British nationalism. It is differentiated between localities and changes over time, sometimes with baffling speed. Later in the book from which Chapter 8 comes, Gilroy argues that the politics of race are part of a move from the national arena and traditional class basis to an oppositional politics based more on poor urban communities, in which struggles may be in effect class struggles, even though they are seen by their protagonists as territorial or racial. The mounting complexity of analysing such social divisions and struggles is further exacerbated by the fact that many discussions of racial divisions, like most discussions of class, neglect the additional effects of gender divisions. The interactions of class, race and gender are taken up in Chapter 10 in Section IV.

References

BROWN, C. (1985) *Black and White Britain: the Third PSI Survey*, Aldershot, Gower.

CASTLES, S. and KOSACK, G. (1973) *Immigrant Workers and Class Structure in Western Europe*, London, Oxford University Press.

DANIEL, W. W. (1968) *Racial Discrimination in England*, Harmondsworth, Penguin.

PARKIN, F. (1979) *Marxism and Class Theory: A Bourgeois Critique*, London, Tavistock.

PHIZACKLEA, A. and MILES, R. (1980) *Labour and Racism*, London, Routledge.

REX, J. and TOMLINSON, S. (1979) *Colonial Immigrants in a British City: A Class Analysis*, London, Routledge and Kegan Paul.

ROSE, S. and LEWONTIN, R. (1983) *Not In Our Genes*, Harmondsworth, Penguin.

SMITH, D. J. (1977) *Racial Disadvantage in Britain*, Harmondsworth, Penguin.

WESTERGAARD, J. and RESTLER, H. (1975) *Class in a Capitalist Society*, London, Heinemann.

6 Racism and class structure: migrant labour in contemporary capitalism

Robert Miles

Migration and class structure: some theories

Within both sociological and Marxist literature concerned with the class structure of Britain, recognition is given to the fact of migration to Britain from the New Commonwealth. Within this literature, the following distinct theses can be distinguished. The first and third of these arguments can be described as Marxist, while the second is sociological and is based upon Weberian premises and assumptions.

1 Unitary working class thesis

This claims that 'coloured immigrants' to Britain share with the indigenous working class the dependent conditions of exploited wage labour and that the practice of racial discrimination only serves to increase the impact upon these 'immigrants' of those otherwise common disadvantages. From this perspective, 'immigrants' are an integral part of the working class (Westergaard and Resler, 1976, pp. 356–60).

2 Underclass thesis

This claims that the impact of discrimination is crucial in allocating 'immigrants' to a specific class position apart from the working class. It is argued that 'immigrants' do not share the same experience as the working class because of the impact of discrimination upon their position in the employment, education and housing markets. Discrimination ensures that they occupy an inferior position in these three markets, with the consequence that they are not and cannot be assimilated into the working class. They therefore constitute a class beneath the working class by virtue of their inferior circumstances and life chances, an interpretation which is captured in the concept of 'underclass' (Rex and Tomlinson, 1979, pp. 275–6).

3 Divided working class thesis

This claims that class position is determined by the position in the relations of production and that, in Britain, this leads to the identification of two main classes, the bourgeoisie and the working class. Both 'immigrant' and indigenous workers, it is claimed, constitute the working class by virtue of their identical position in production relations. To this point in the argument, there is agreement with the unitary working class thesis. However, it is then argued that, because of their lower incomes and inferior social conditions, 'immigrants' occupy a distinct economic position within the working class and that this is paralleled by a subjective division within the same class. Consequently, the working class is conceived of as being divided into two distinct strata (Castles and Kosack, 1973, p. 477; cf. Moore, 1977).

These three theses are mutually exclusive by virtue of their different interpretations of the impact of racial discrimination upon the class structure. They are, therefore, unsatisfactory for different reasons. The unitary working class thesis is partly founded upon empirical claims which are contradicted by the available evidence (see Phizacklea and Miles, 1980, pp. 17–20) and is mistaken in claiming that discrimination creates no 'special disabilities' for 'immigrants'. For example, immigration law has placed New Commonwealth migrants in a quite distinct and disadvantaged position in political and legal relations (with the result, for example, that they are often required to produce their passports to demonstrate their right to live in Britain: see *The Guardian*, 30 May 1980; *Sunday Times*, 17 August 1980), while racial discrimination places specific economic constraints upon migrants which are not placed upon indigenous labour (for example, by limiting promotion opportunities: Smith, 1977, pp. 182–90). The underclass thesis mistakenly assumes that discrimination is the sole factor determining the position of migrants in what are defined as the three different markets which come to constitute the determinants of class position. It attributes no explanatory significance to the status of being migrants (Phizacklea and Miles, 1980, p. 227). Additionally, by defining class in subjectivist terms at the level of distribution of resources via markets, it rules out consideration of the significance of relations of production. Finally, the divided working class thesis makes the unwarranted assumption of there being a homogenous working class which is 'divided' only by 'immigration'. In fact, the working class is fractured by many political and ideological divisions, and these divisions existed prior to migration from the New Commonwealth. Moreover, it operates with an economistic definition of class, a position that is now largely rejected within Marxist analysis.

By rejecting the available theoretical positions, including those which would claim a Marxist parentage, it might seem that I am expressing sympathy with the arguments of Parkin who has claimed that traditional sociological theorizing and, even more particularly, Marxist theory, have proved themselves incapable of conceptualizing the class structure of contemporary capitalist societies because of their inability to take account of 'racial, ethnic and religious conflicts' (1979, pp. 4, 9, 29–31, 37). This is not so, and I want to examine critically Parkin's claim in order to outline and develop further the argument that migrant labour in Britain should be conceived of as constituting a racialized fraction of the working class (Phizacklea and Miles, 1980, pp. 1–25).

Parkin has developed a critique of Marxist theories of class primarily on the basis of an assertion that these theories cannot adequately take account of 'those complexities that arise when racial, religious, ethnic, and sexual divisions run at a tangent to formal class divisions' (1979, p. 4). This assertion is supported by the claim that Marxist theories place their emphasis upon structural factors, that is, upon the position occupied by persons in production relations. Parkin claims that these theories, because of this emphasis, are unable to take account of the significance of the social and cultural characteristics of the persons who occupy those positions in production relations (1979, pp. 37, 42). Parkin thereby locates the major analytical problem as being the need to specify the connection between class divisions and 'ethnic/communal' relations (1979, pp. 33, 42).

Parkin's solution to the problem originates in the notion of social closure, which refers to the process by which social groups attempt to maximize their rewards by restricting the access of other groups to resources and opportunities. He identifies two main forms of social closure (exclusion and usurpation), only the former being significant in this context. Exclusionary social closure, he continues, can operate by reference to individualist and to collectivist criteria, and the precise character and combination of these criteria determine the type and range of subordinate social collectivities. The use of individualist criteria excludes individuals from access to rewards and opportunities by reference to their ability to meet certain standards or qualities, while the use of collectivist criteria excludes individuals by reference to characteristics that are integral to their identification as a member of a group ('race, religion, ethnicity and so on . . .', 1979, p. 68) and that are negatively defined [. . .]

'Race' and class structure

Elsewhere, I have argued that one cannot utilize the concept of class and construct the notion of 'race' as equivalents; that is, they do not refer to two specific types of the same general phenomena (1980, p. 184). I now want to enlarge on that claim in order to pursue the argument initiated above. The primary emphasis of that analysis was that within Marxist theory, the concept of class is anchored in production relations, a structural feature of social formations. With reference to any particular social formation, one proceeds by first identifying its dominant mode of production because this constitutes the foundation for the subsequent identification of the primary classes. The existence of dependent modes of production entails the existence of additional classes. This structural identification of the primary antagonistic classes is but a first step in the direction of a specific, historical analysis of the social formation [. . .]

This first analytical step, the mapping of class positions, contains no space for a notion of 'race': this is simultaneously because this step is analytically prior to all other considerations and because there is no phenomenon which one can signify as 'race' [. . .] I have, however, accepted that phenotypical difference exists [i.e. surface appearances such as skin colour, hair type, bone structure, etc.] and that social significance and meaning has been and is attributed to certain aspects of such difference. I have suggested that this process can be grasped by the concept of racial categorization. This concept now requires some further elaboration. It is used to refer to a process of delineation of group boundaries and of allocation of persons within those boundaries by primary reference to (supposedly) inherent and/or biological (usually phenotypical) characteristics. It is therefore an ideological process, but it has effects at all three levels of a social formation: economic, political and ideological. These effects can, in combination, cohere to lead to the formation of fractions within classes. The process of categorization occurs at two analytically distinct but usually related levels: at the level of thought and at the level of action. The process can have as its object the identification and reproduction of groups which are self- or other-defined, while the criteria used to define the groups can be positively or negatively evaluated [. . .].

In order to conceive of the prime effect of racial categorization upon class structure, a further concept has to be introduced, that of class fraction (Poulantzas, 1973, pp. 77–84; 1978, pp. 14–24; Phizacklea and Miles, 1980, pp. 6–7, 24–5), which permits the conceptualization of the main lines of division within class boundaries. These lines of division result from the coincidence of different positions in economic, political and ideological relations within previously identified class relations. By virtue of these different positions, there develop different interests within classes which can be expressed in explicit struggles between class fractions. The process of racial categorization can then be viewed as affecting the allocation of persons to different positions in the production process and the allocation of material and other rewards and disadvantages to groups so categorized within the class boundaries established by the dominant mode of production. Such effects cannot and do not alter the ultimate structure of production relations because the resulting fractionalization occurs at the level of relations between persons occupying positions which share the same structural relationship with the other main class(es). But they do ensure that the structure of production relations takes a distinct form because of the real effect of racialization at all levels of the social formation: this entails recognizing that capital has specific interests deriving from the use of migrant labour and its racialization and that a new dimension is added to class struggle as a result of a creation of a racialized fraction within the working class.

In order to understand the impact of racial categorization upon class fractionalization within Western Europe since 1945, it is necessary to identify the primary dynamic within the capitalist mode of production which created the terrain for racial categorization, that is, labour migration. Labour migration is therefore a major dimension of the material and historical context for racial categorization in Britain (and much of the rest of Western Europe) since the Second World War.

Labour migration and class fractions

Now let me summarize the argument to this point. Parkin, in common with the sociology of 'race relations', begins his analysis with what appear as the 'facts' of 'race difference' and then attempts to analyse the 'effects' of this difference upon the distribution of resources and rewards (e.g. jobs, housing, education). The error is to ignore the processes by which 'race difference' is socially constructed and the processes by which 'resources and rewards' are first produced before they can be distributed. I now want to argue that it is by beginning the analysis with the production process and by simultaneously acknowledging racial categorization as an ideological process with its own determinate effects that one can identify one important dimension of class fractionalization in Britain. However, this dimension is not a specifically British phenomenon, as the political economy of labour migration since 1945 in Western Europe reveals (e.g. Nikolinakos, 1975; also Salt and Clout, 1976) [. . .]

The crucial stimulus for the actual migration of labour from [the] peripheries was the demand for labour in the 1950s and 1960s by capital in the metropolitan centres (Castles and Kosack, 1973).

This major labour migration did, however, have some specific characteristics which must be noted. First, in the majority of cases, the migration was not initiated and determined solely by the 'free play' of market forces (as in the cases of Irish migration to Britain and European migration to the USA in the nineteenth century), but involved the direct intervention of the state on behalf of capital (Carchedi, 1979). Labour is recruited by state agencies set up in the peripheral formations by means of a contract which mediates the wage labour/capital relationship (Corrigan, 1977): the individual is recruited to sell his or her labour power for a particular period of time, usually to a particular employer and under certain political/legal constraints (such as no right of permanent settlement, either as an individual or with a family) (e.g. Berger and Mohr, 1975). Secondly, this method of procuring labour power and bringing it into contact with capital by means of a time-specific contract was itself the result of a decision to obtain the greatest possible degree of control over the use of that labour power (although without appearing to break the ideological sanctity of the wage-labour relationship to capital) so that its utilization could be related to the cyclical nature of capitalist production. Thus, when the demand for labour at the 'centre' fell, the persons providing that labour power could be 'returned' to the 'periphery'. Thirdly, the use of contract migrant labour ensured that capital at the 'centre' did not have to meet the cost of its original production (the source of labour power, a human being, has to be fed, sheltered and educated), nor the cost of its reproduction when wage labour was not available at the 'centre'. This offsets the structural tendency for the rate of profit under capitalism to fall (Castells, 1975; Carchedi, 1979). Fourthly, because it constituted a solution to a particular problem at a particular point in time, one cannot assume that the migrant labour system will constitute a permanent characteristic, or at least not in terms of its earlier size and form (Paine, 1977, 1979).

It is at this point that we must acknowledge that the instance of Britain is historically distinct from that of Germany, France and Switzerland. I have argued this elsewhere (Phizacklea and Miles, 1980, pp. 10–23) and need only point out here that it was not until 1971 that British capital had made available to it the political/legal framework for a migrant labour system determined by contract (Sivanandan, 1976; Freeman and Spencer, 1979). Since 1971, British capital has not faced a major structural shortage of labour (but rather the opposite) and so has not had reason to utilize widely the framework established by the 1971 Immigration Act [. . .]

There are three major characteristics of the labour migration from the Caribbean and the Indian sub-continent which are relevant to the consequent class fractionalization. First, the demand was for wage labour, with the result that the majority of persons who migrated to Britain in the 1950s and 1960s were destined to enter production relations in a proletarian class position. It is therefore a nonsense to argue that 'immigrants' were prevented from 'entering' the working class by racial discrimination practised by employers and workers (e.g. Rex and Tomlinson, 1979): an analysis which determines class position by reference to the sphere of distribution alone makes the error of confusing human practice with the constraints set upon that practice by the need to reproduce production relations in a particular, historically determined form. In this case, our concern is with capitalist relations of production in Britain in the period after 1945. Rather, because the majority of migrants entered Britain to sell their labour power for a wage, they automatically became part of the working class.

Secondly, the demand for labour was not spread equally across all sections of the economy but was limited to certain sectors of production and distribution (e.g. Unit for Manpower Services, 1977). One of these was a group of industries which had been integral to the early domination of British capitalism but which had subsequently become less competitive on the world market and were consequently undergoing decline, for example, textiles, metal manufacture. Faced with tight profit margins and outdated technology (e.g. Cohen and Jenner, 1968), production could be maintained by low wages and this led to an outflow of 'indigenous' labour in a period of full employment. In these circumstances, migrant labour became replacement labour. In the case of metal foundries, the employment of migrant labour coincided with a process of de-skilling in combination with mechanization (cf. Braverman, 1974), reducing the number of skilled jobs and increasing the number of, comparatively, semi-skilled jobs (Unit for Manpower Services, 1977, p. 47). Another group consisted of more advanced, capital-intensive industries whose conditions of work also made labour supply problematic in a period of full employment, e.g. food and car manufacture. And finally there were those service industries which were also characterized by low wages and unsocial hours, for example hospitals, public transport. Hence, it is clear that within the structural position of wage labour, migrants were recruited to a particular position in production, that is, to manual labour, often (but not solely) semi- and unskilled, with low wages and poor working conditions (Smith, 1977).

The third factor was that migrant labour was recruited from colonial and ex-colonial social formations, and at a time when the retreat from empire and its repercussions was a matter underlying the political agenda (Nairn, 1977, ch. 5) [. . .] The interdependence of capital development and colonial exploitation were at least partly responsible for the articulation and reproduction of racism as an ideology within Britain. Racist images and beliefs were therefore an element of British national culture, shaped as it was by the need to explain and rationalize colonialism (cf. Lawrence, 1974, pp. 46–68). Consequently, migrants from the colonies and ex-colonies were not entering a neutral ideological context when they came to Britain to sell their labour power. There are two dimensions to this. The fact of the decline of British capitalism as an imperialist power is partly grasped by sections of all classes in Britain, and this fact can come to be measured and symbolized by the very presence of 'colonial subjects' in Britain (e.g. Pearson, 1976). In addition, the negative imagery of those 'colonial subjects', which is signified in the meaning attributed to phenotypical difference, was available for reinterpretation if the stimulus existed. The subsequent racial categorization of migrant labour will be discussed further below.

The result of these three characteristics, when combined with the previously mentioned political initiative to change the legal status of the migrants from one of Commonwealth and British citizen to that of alien, is that the migrants occupy a structurally distinct position in the economic, political and ideological relations of British capitalism, but within the boundary of the working class. They therefore constitute a fraction of the working class, one that can be identified as a racialized fraction (see Phizacklea and Miles, 1980, esp. pp. 20–5). This claim serves to locate my theoretical argument as a development of the divided working class thesis which I outlined at the beginning of this chapter.

At the earlier stage, I criticized the formulation of the divided working class thesis by Castles and Kosack (1973), partly on the grounds that they operated with an economistic definition of class. I want to emphasize that point here by further reference to the specificity of the British situation in comparison with the other labour-importing countries of Western Europe. Castles and Kosack's argument was directed against what they viewed as the failure of 'race relations' research to grasp the common political economy underlying both labour migration and the expression of racism throughout Western Europe. Their object of critical inquiry was correctly chosen, but their theoretical solution was shaped to too great an extent by their economistic Marxism. Their failure to take account of the impact of political and ideological relations upon class formation ensured not only that they ignored the extent to which the British working class was fractionalized prior to the post-1945 labour migration, but also that they failed to appreciate the significance of the impact of the political/legal framework for labour migration into Britain. That framework remained distinct from that in the rest of Western Europe until 1971, with the consequence that the process of migration more closely approximated the pattern and sequence identified as chain migration (MacDonald and MacDonald, 1964) [. . .] The fact that such a large proportion of migrants from the New Commonwealth to Britain have not only established families in Britain, but have also appeared to take up the right of settlement (despite the maintenance of the ideology of return to the 'home') has meant that British capital and the state has had to face the cost of the reproduction of those families to a much greater extent than other countries in Western Europe. Finally, they overstate the homogeneity of racism as an ideology in Western Europe by ignoring the specific impact of the colonial legacy in the case of Britain, a legacy which arguably means that there is much greater significance attached to phenotypical difference. It is a common error of much 'classic' Marxist analysis that it fails to appreciate that racist ideologies take different forms (cf. Hall, 1978, p. 26; 1980, pp. 336–7) and Western Europe is an important arena for demonstrating that [. . .]

Racial categorization of migrant labour: the British case

Although the material demands of British capital was the determinate factor in stimulating the labour migration from the New Commonwealth in the 1950s and 1960s, we cannot establish an equally clear and singularly determinate economic motive for the subsequent political and ideological reaction to the migration. It is important to try to establish by reference to historical analysis the sense in which this reaction (which I typify as racial categorization) was independent of directly economic pressures and the sense in which it was grounded in (but even then not necessarily directly determined by) such material factors.

As already indicated, the migrants from the Caribbean and the Indian subcontinent did not enter a neutral political and ideological context when they came to Britain. On the one hand, they entered a politico-legal context which defined them as British citizens while, on the other, they entered an ideological context shaped in part by the need to justify and rationalize the colonial exploitation of the previous three centuries. As we have seen, the ideology of racism was crucially structured (but not solely determined) by these processes. Herein lies one instance of the relative autonomy of racism as an element of the ideological process of racialization. Racist imagery was therefore available as an element of British national culture, available to be reproduced to categorize these migrants whose labour power was so urgently required on London Transport and in the textile mills of Lancashire. The interesting and decisive question concerns who it was who articulated that racist ideology, and for what reason. The former question is perhaps more easily answered than the second [. . .]

Much of the reaction does not seem to have been expressed in the form of the articulation of an explicitly racist ideology like that formulated by the amateur scientists of the nineteenth century, although the activities of the various fascist groups constitute a significant exception (e.g. Billig, 1978). Rather, racist images and beliefs are expressed in a piecemeal and often inconsistent form (Rex, 1970, p. 154; Phizacklea and Miles, 1980, pp. 131–2; Miles and Phizacklea, 1981). Nevertheless, the language of 'race' was and is used to refer to and describe these migrants, the object of much of the political agitation is to ensure that they are less favourably treated (or even 'repatriated') than the rest of the working class, and the practice of racial discrimination is widespread in the allocation of jobs and housing. The result has been a racialization of migrant labour. Migrants came to Britain to sell their labour power. They were met with an increasingly negative political and ideological reaction, particularly in the 1960s and 1970s, which succeeded in applying the label of 'race' to the migrants. Consequently, they were negatively racialized and were thereby assigned a special position in ideological relations (as well as simultaneously being assigned to a specific position in economic and political relations) [. . .]

This ideological process of racialization is not to be understood as an illusory process. As a social process, it is real not only in the sense that the label of 'race' is constructed and applied in the social world but also in the sense that its application has its own determinate effects. Those effects can decisively shape the form and direction of class struggles. The process of class fractionalization is paralleled by the production and reproduction of particular political interests which are expressed in a specific ideological form. The imposition of racist immigration controls stimulates resistance from those affected by them. Discrimination in employment, racist police practice and political attacks inspired by fascist political parties all similarly and necessarily bring about a distinct political consciousness and political practice from those subject to these processes. For Caribbean, Indian and Pakistani migrants, this constitutes the substance and reinforcement of fractionalization within the British working class. And, indeed, sections of the working class have had their own, independent effect on establishing and reinforcing this fractionalization because of the racial discrimination practised by trade union officials and members (e.g. Radin, 1966; Miles and Phizacklea, 1977, 1978) and because of working-class support for and membership of the National Front and British Movement (e.g. Walker, 1977; Miles and Phizacklea, 1979; Husbands, 1979; Fielding, 1981), etc. This economic and political division within the working class therefore spawns a set of distinct political interests and strategies which can take a multitude of forms, including everything from self-defence groups to English-language classes, from revolutionary sects to community associations (although the formation of many of these can also be encouraged by distinct cultural interests).

The emergence of these particular interests and the necessity for a distinct political practice by the class fraction so created mirrors the racial categorization. Indeed, the political and ideological boundary can be actively reinforced by the explicit utilization and re-evaluation of the notion of 'race', as illustrated in the formation of political organizations which have as one aim the developing of a positive identity for the 'black race' (e.g. Midgett, 1975; Miles, 1978). In this way, the language of 'race' (once having been positively re-defined), can come to be utilized as a solidaristic and unifying force (cf. Banton, 1977, pp. 136–55). But equally, if not more, likely is a decision not to become involved in the political organizations of the working class, or, if they are joined for pragmatic reasons, not to participate actively within them (cf. Lawrence, 1974, pp. 130–60; Phizacklea and Miles, 1980, pp. 189–223). Whichever strategy is 'chosen', it must always be analysed not in isolation, but in relation to the original expression of racism and the accompanying exclusionary activities. And although particular political interests are constructed which are specifically those of a racialized class fraction because of racism and racial discrimination, they are also general class interests because the fractionalization constitutes another obstruction to the emergence of that class as a more unitary political force.

To this point in this section, I have argued that those who migrated to Britain in the 1950s and 1960s were faced with a negative response which can be described as racialization because sections of all classes focused their ideological and political reaction upon the migrant's phenotypical characteristics. But this process occurred within certain material parameters and cannot be explained solely in terms of the simple reproduction of a racist ideology constructed in an earlier period as some have done (e.g. Sivanandan, 1973; Lawrence, 1974).

There are two senses in which racialization is anchored in material relations which I wish to mention here. The first is that the object of the process of racialization is not a group of people in the abstract, but a group of people who occupy a specific position in production relations. The migrants of the 1950s and early 1960s were, as we have seen, a replacement labour force, coming to Britain to occupy positions vacated by individuals who had moved into other sectors of wage-labour employment (e.g. Böhning, 1972, pp. 55–8). In this period, racial discrimination could not have been the major factor in allocating migrants to a position in production relations. Rather, employers were recruiting migrants primarily because there was no other source of labour available to them (e.g. Wright, 1968, pp. 41–7). But it soon became obvious that racial discrimination by employers served as a constraint when those migrants sought promotion or employment in sectors where there was no such shortage of labour (e.g. Daniel, 1967; Smith, 1977). Thus, racialization (in the form of direct discrimination) has served to reinforce and maintain the economic stratification of wage labour: the racialization of the migrants is simultaneously their confinement to certain ranks of wage labour, namely manual labour and often predominantly in semi- or unskilled jobs (see Figure 6.1).

Indeed, the extent of this confinement has encouraged some interest in the applicability or otherwise of the concept of dual labour market to describe this situation in Britain. The concept derives from research in the USA and refers to the existence of two distinct labour markets, one characterized by low wages, poor working conditions, unstable employment and few opportunities for advancement and the other by precisely the opposite characteristics. Moreover, the persons who occupy these two distinct markets tend to be distinguished by other characteristics; for example, those occupying the former labour market tend to be female

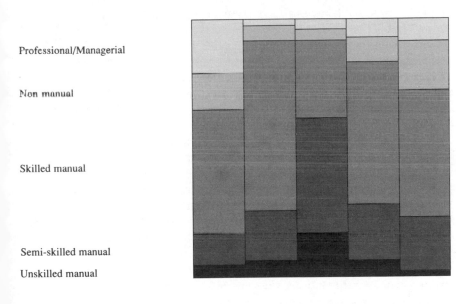

Figure 6.1   Male job level analysed by country of origin

Source: Smith (1977, p. 73).

and/or 'black' (Doeringer and Piore, 1971; Piore, 1979, pp. 35ff.). Bosan-quet and Doeringer (1973) concluded from British data that there was a close similarity with the situation in the USA.

Although it is unlikely that migrants constitute the sole source of labour in the 'disadvantaged market' in Britain, the fact that they are rarely employed outside it is testimony to the significance of racial discrimination. Moreover, the fact of this concentration has its own ideological effect in that it appears (i.e. can be interpreted) to demonstrate the 'suitability' of 'racialized' labour for only low skilled, low paid manual jobs. Thereby, phenotypical appearance can be equated with a disadvantaged position in production relations: the negative connotations of 'blackness' come to overlap with and reinforce the negative connotations of much semi- and unskilled manual work and so adds another level of meaning to the already existing fractionalization of wage labour.

The second concerns the ideological significance of the struggle over the distribution of scarce resources within the working class in the urban context, particularly in those areas undergoing material decline. With Annie Phizacklea, I have argued elsewhere that material decline consti-tutes an important underlying dynamic to the articulation of racism within the working class (Phizacklea and Miles, 1979, 1980; Miles and Phizacklea, 1981). In most of the major English conurbations there are areas of declining capitalist production which are also characterized by poor housing conditions, inadequate provision of social and other services and other measures of deprivation. These are also areas which for various reasons have often been chosen by migrant labourers and their families as areas of residential settlement. The coincidence of their settlement with material decline, combined with their demand for access to resources (especially housing) which are in short supply has, in the context of the racist legacy of colonialism, served as a direct stimulus to the articulation and reproduction of racism within the working-class resident in such areas. Such racism, born of the direct experience of material decline via 'com-monsense' reasoning (the coincidence of decline and residential settlement being interpreted causally, leading to the conclusion that 'the blacks cause decline') is arguably that which served as the initial current from within the working class in the late 1950s and early 1960s which resulted in the formation of immigration control associations (cf. Lee, 1980). This was a crucial stage in the racialization of British politics because British govern-ments interpreted their appearance with electoral significance and so set about appeasing this racism. Moreover, it is probably upon this form of racism that fascist political organizations subsequently developed in Eng-lish urban areas in the 1970s when Labour and Conservative governments failed to solve the 'inner city crisis' and baulked at following the racist policy of immigration control to the logical conclusion of compulsory 'repatriation'.

In both of these instances cited, the process of racialization is locked into and has its own effects upon the reproduction of material inequality and disadvantage within the working class. This process is simultaneously the reproduction of inequality *per se* and of the allocation of persons to different positions in the structure of inequality, with ideological and political significance coming to be attached to phenotypical differences. A consequence is that the material disadvantage of the migrant appears as disadvantage caused by 'race'. This appearance is misleading [. . .] The disadvantage results from the combination of positions of material inequality structured by capital (low wages result from an attempt to maintain profitability) with a particular process of allocation of persons to those positions, the process consisting in part of the reproduction of racism as an ideology and the practice of discrimination. The disadvantage and the ideological form in which it appears must therefore always be analysed and presented as a social (i.e. human) construction and not as a biological determinant [. . .]

Finally, we cannot assume that the British state serves as an automatic vehicle for the expression and implementation of the demands of the different factions of capital. The nature and role of the state in contemporary capitalism has been the focus of much debate recently and the direction of the debate has been influenced by the need to avoid economistic/ deterministic explanations and to identify the nature and extent of state autonomy (e.g. Poulantzas, 1973; Miliband, 1969; Holloway and Picciotto, 1978; Gough, 1979). Once having accepted this 'relative autonomy' of the state, it becomes necessary to demonstrate empirically the relationship between the role of the state in the process of racialization and the perhaps conflicting demands of the different fractions of capital. The former has been extensively documented and analysed, but the relationship with the conflicting demands of capital has not and there the matter must rest at present, unresolved [. . .]

In conclusion: a class divided

The process of racial categorization or racialization is simultaneously the historical consequence and the site of subsequent struggles between classes and of the formation and reproduction of class fractions. The ideology of racism and the practice of racial discrimination are central components of this process of racialization which has determinate effects on ideological, political and economic relations. These determinate effects, some of which I have mentioned in this chapter, are a measure of the relative autonomy of racialization as an ideological process. Consequently, although it is relevant, it is not sufficient to search for and 'measure' the extent of racist belief and the practice of discrimination. These should be analysed as moments in the reproduction of the mode of production, not least because they are integral to the process of allocation of persons to positions in production relations. But 'effects' cannot be understood solely in terms of the 'economic'. In contemporary Britain, following labour migration from the New Commonwealth, racialization has resulted in the articulation and reproduction of the idea of 'race relations'. It is important that this be recognized historically as a new ideological construction immediately within and often at the centre of British political and economic relations (although I have not denied that in the preceding centuries the racialization of 'colonial' subjects has had effects on British political relations).

The crucial point is that 'race relations' do not exist naturally or essentially by virtue of the existence of phenotypical variation: rather, certain forms of social relations are constructed as 'race relations' and this requires specific explanation. The notion of 'race' carries for a large proportion of all classes a certain set of negative meanings which attach to certain patterns of phenotypical variation. These meanings receive expression in a wide range of socio-economic contexts as a means of description and interpretation. But the effects of the social construction of 'race' differ according to class position. For example, the racialization of migrant labour from the New Commonwealth and its relative confinement to the position of manual wage labour in the context of scarcity of housing and social services, etc., has different implications for other fractions of the working class when compared with the ruling class for whom such scarcity is not a problem, except in so far as it becomes the focus for a political challenge to its position as a ruling class. Nevertheless, for both classes, the process of racialization (which occurs at the level of ideological relations) has effects on, but is also structured within and by, economic relations. By this I mean that although the process of racialization has an independent effect on production relations in so far as, for example, it directly assists in the allocation of persons to positions in those relations, it does not in itself determine the existence of the positions. The existence of the positions is determined by the mode of production.

Where racialization is an aspect of the fractionalization of classes, this has to be understood not only structurally but also as ongoing political and ideological struggle. Racialization, and the material and political disadvantages that are its consequence, produce a political and ideological response from those who are its object. The response is ideological in so far as those who are the object must construct a way of conceptualizing themselves and their circumstances. The response is political in so far as those who are the object negotiate a strategy by which to actively challenge their subordination. But in the instance of Britain, those responses take place within parameters set by the reproduction of a capitalist mode of production still undergoing the effects of a withdrawal from direct colonial exploitation. That sets limits not only to what can be achieved by that struggle but also to the form that the struggle can take. I purposely use the notion of 'setting limits' because I want to acknowledge that the struggle could take one of a number of different ideological and political forms (see Phizacklea and Miles, 1980, Ch. 2). Hence, in the 1960s and early 1970s, the predominant response (but not the only response: see Howe, 1973; Hall *et al.*, 1978) can be characterized as a form of political withdrawal (e.g. Lawrence, 1974; Pryce, 1979) but there are now clear indications that the response is taking a different form. Racism and racial discrimination are now more actively challenged and in a way that re-evaluates the negative connotations of racialization but which does not and cannot reject racialization *per se* because it is now expressed in a distinct set of disadvantaged, material circumstances. Hence, ideology remains the site of struggle between and within the classes [. . .]

An important consequence of the latter point is that divisions within the working class should not be assumed to be absolute and universal. Class fractions are historically constituted in circumstances that must always be spelled out. In the case of Britain, it is undeniable that the institutions of the labour movement have played a major role in the racialization of migrant labour: trade unions have actively practised and tacitly accepted racial discrimination while Labour governments have been as active as Conservative governments in enacting racist immigration controls. Nevertheless, a majority of these racialized migrants remain a working-class fraction and the institutions of the labour movement are not the sole source of class consciousness. The experience of wage labour and the fact of institutional attachment to the labour movement (by reason of trade union membership) constitute a foundation for the development of a political ideology and practice which expresses priority to class politics (Phizacklea and Miles, 1980, *passim*).

The emphasis of this chapter [. . .] results necessarily in the impression of a single division within the working class. It is, however, a false impression because I have made no attempt to locate the development and significance of this fractionalization in the context of additional bases of division. These include sex, level of skill, manual/non-manual labour, religious belief, country of birth, all of which can support the formation of class fractions as a consequence of their being actively constituted as objects of economic, political and ideological significance. These remain to be analysed in relation to the process of racialization in order to identify how and why each might overlap or coexist with others. What I have attempted is an analysis which outlines the main boundaries between and within the main classes in Britain following the labour migration of the 1950s. The process of racialization has been analysed as establishing both the further fractionalization of the working class and the basis for subsequent conflicts and struggles, some of which will be internal to the working class (as are those which arise from working-class racism and discrimination) and some of which will have a dual character as struggles of a racialized working class fraction, but as against capital (as are the struggles against racist immigration controls and policing motivated by racism). The continued existence of such struggles involves the reproduction of the class divisions that they first express. The outcome of those struggles will be determined by, *inter alia*, political practice and ideological struggle, and cannot be analysed in advance of the development of that practice and struggle.

References

BANTON, M. (1977) *The Idea of Race*, London, Tavistock.

BERGER, J. and MOHR, J. (1975) *A Seventh Man*, Harmondsworth, Penguin.

BILLIG, M. (1978) *Fascists*, London, Harcourt Brace Jovanovich.

BÖHNING, W. R. (1972) *The Migration of Workers in the United Kingdom and the European Community*, Oxford University Press.

BOSANQUET, N. and DOERINGER, P. B. (1973) 'Is there a dual labour market in Great Britain?', *Economic Journal*, Vol. 83, pp. 421–35.

BRAVERMAN, H. (1974) *Labour and Monopoly Capital: the Degradation of Work in the Twentieth Century*, New York, Monthly Review Press.

CARCHEDI, G. (1979) 'Authority and foreign labour: some notes on a late capitalist form of capital accumulation and state intervention', *Studies in Political Economy*, Vol. 2, pp. 37–74.

CASTELLS, M. (1975) 'Immigrant workers and class struggles in advanced capitalism: the Western European experience', *Politics and Society*, Vol. 5, No. 1, pp. 33–66.

CASTLES, S. and KOSACK, G. (1973) *Immigrant Workers and Class Struggle in Western Europe*, Oxford University Press.

COHEN, B. G. and JENNER, P. J. (1968) 'The employment of immigrants: a case study within the wool industry', *Race*, Vol. 10, No. 1, pp. 41–56.

CORRIGAN, P. (1977) 'Feudal relics or capitalist monuments? Notes on the sociology of unfree labour', *Sociology*, Vol. 11, No. 3, pp. 435–63.

DANIEL, W. W. (1967) *Racial Discrimination in England*, Harmondsworth, Penguin.

DOERINGER, P. B. and PIORE, M. J. (1971) *Internal Labour Markets and Manpower Adjustments*, Lexington, D.C., Heath.

FIELDING, N. (1981) *The National Front*, London, Routledge and Kegan Paul.

FREEMAN, M. D. A. and SPENCER, S. (1979) 'Immigration control, black workers and the economy', *British Journal of Law and Society*, Vol. 6, No. 1, pp. 53–81.

GOUGH, I. (1979) *The Political Economy of the Welfare State*, London, Macmillan.

HALL, S. (1978) 'Racism and reaction', in Commission for Racial Equality, *Five Views of Multi-Racial Britain*, London, CRE.

HALL, S., CRITCHER, C., JEFFERSON, T., CLARKE, J. and ROBERTS, B. (1978) *Policing the Crisis: Mugging, the State and Law and Order*, London, Macmillan.

HOLLOWAY, J. and PICCIOTTO, S. (eds) (1978) *State and Capital*, London, Edward Arnold.

HOWE, D. (1973) 'Fighting back: West Indian youth and the police in Notting Hill', *Race Today*, Vol. 5, pp. 333–7.

HUSBANDS, C. T. (1979) 'The National Front: what happens to it now?' *Marxism Today*, September, pp. 268–75.

LAWRENCE, D. (1974) *Black Migrants, White Natives*, Cambridge University Press.

LEE, A. (1980) 'Aspects of the working class response to the Jews in Britain, 1880–1914', in Lunn, K. (ed.), *Hosts, Immigrants and Minorities*, Folkestone, Dawson.

MacDONALD, J. S. and MacDONALD, L. D. (1964) 'Chain migration, ethnic neighbourhood formation and social networks', *Milbank Memorial Fund Quarterly*, Vol. 42, pp. 82–97.

MIDGETT, D. K. (1975) 'West Indian ethnicity in Britain', in Safa, H. I. and Dutoit, D. M. (eds) *Migration and Development*, The Hague, Mouton.

MILES, R. (1978) *Between Two Cultures? The Case of Rastafarianism*, SSRC Working Paper on Ethnic Relations, No. 10.

MILES, R. (1980) 'Class, race and ethnicity: a critique of Cox's theory', *Ethnic and Racial Studies*, Vol. 3, No. 2, pp. 169–87.

MILES, R. and PHIZACKLEA, A. (1977) *The TUC, Black Workers and New Commonwealth Immigration*, SSRC Working Paper on Ethnic Relations, No. 6.

MILES, R. and PHIZACKLEA, A. (1978) 'The TUC and black workers, 1974–1976', *British Journal of Industrial Relations*, Vol. 16, No. 2, pp. 195–207.

MILES, R. and PHIZACKLEA, A. (1981) 'Racism and capitalist decline', in Harloe, M. (ed.) *New Perspectives in Urban Change and Conflict*, London, Heinemann.

MILIBAND, R. (1969) *The State in Capitalist Society*, London, Weidenfeld and Nicolson.

MOORE, R. (1977) 'Migrants and the class structure of Western Europe', in Scase, R. (ed.) *Industrial Society: Class, Cleavage and Control*, London, George Allen and Unwin.

NAIRN, T. (1977) *The Break-up of Britain*, London, New Left Books.

NIKOLINAKOS, M. (1973) 'Notes on an economic theory of racism', *Race*, Vol 14, No. 4, pp. 365–81.

NIKOLINAKOS, M. (1975) 'Notes towards a general theory of migration in late capitalism', *Race and Class*, Vol. 17, No. 1, pp. 5 18.

PAINE, S. (1974) *Exporting Workers: the Turkish Case*, Cambridge University Press.

PAINE, S. (1977) 'The changing role of migrant labour in the advanced capitalist economies of Western Europe', in Griffiths, R. T. (ed.) *Government Business and Labour in European Capitalism*, London, Europotentials Press.

PAINE, S. (1979) 'Replacement of the West European migrant labour system by investment in the European periphery', in Seers, D. *et al.*, (eds) *Underdeveloped Europe: Studies in Core-Periphery Relations*, Brighton, Harvester Press.

PARKIN, F. (1979) *Marxism and Class Theory: A Bourgeois Critique*, London, Tavistock.

PEARSON, G. (1976) '"Paki-bashing" in a north-east Lancashire cotton town: a case study and its history', in Mungham, G. and Pearson, G. (eds) *Working Class Youth Culture*, London, Routledge and Kegan Paul.

PHIZACKLEA, A. and MILES, R. (1979) 'Working class racist beliefs in the inner city', in Miles, R. and Phizacklea, A. (eds) *Racism and Political Action in Britain*, London, Routledge and Kegan Paul.

PHIZACKLEA, A. and MILES, R. (1980) *Labour and Racism*, London, Routledge and Kegan Paul.

PIORE, M. (1979) *Birds of Paradise*, Cambridge University Press.

POULANTZAS, N. (1973) *Political Power and Social Classes*, London, New Left Books.

POULANTZAS, N. (1978) *Classes in Contemporary Capitalism*, London, Verso.

PRYCE, K. (1979) *Endless Pressure*, Harmondsworth, Penguin.

RADIN, B. (1966) 'Coloured workers and British trade unions', *Race*, Vol. 8, No. 2, pp. 157–73.

REX, J. (1970) *Race Relations in Sociological Theory*, London, Weidenfeld and Nicolson.

REX, J. and TOMLINSON, S. (1979) *Colonial Immigrants in a British City*, London, Routledge and Kegan Paul.

SALT, J. and CLOUT, H. (1976) *Migration in Post-War Europe*, Oxford University Press.

SIVANANDAN, A. (1973) 'Race, class and power: an outline for study', *Race*, Vol. 14, No. 4, pp. 383–91.

SIVANANDAN, A. (1976) 'Race, class and the state, the black experience in Britain', *Race and Class*, Vol. 17, No. 4, pp. 347–68.

SMITH, D. J. (1977) *Racial Discrimination in Britain*, Harmondsworth, Penguin.

UNIT FOR MANPOWER SERVICES (1977) *The Role of Immigrants in the Labour Market*, London, Department of Employment.

WALKER, M. (1977) *The National Front*, London, Fontana.

WESTERGAARD, J. and RESLER, H. (1976) *Class in a Capitalist Society*, Harmondsworth, Penguin.

WRIGHT, P. L. (1968) *The Coloured Worker in British Industry*, Oxford University Press.

7   Minority settlement and the local economy

Robin Ward

One of the consequences of the recession in Britain in the early 1980s has been to focus the attention of policy makers and academics on the extent to which ethnic minority business development can help to regenerate the economy, especially in inner urban areas marked by long term industrial and residential decline. The similarities between economic policy in Britain and the United States suggest that this structural pressure to maximize the contribution of minorities to economic activity may be more widely felt. Within the EEC countries in continental Europe, too, where the Gast-arbeiter system has been used to recruit workers during the period of post-war economic expansion, structural unemployment seems likely to create pressure for ethnic minorities to become more involved in entre-preneurial activities, especially where repatriation is not seen as a feasible solution. These developments give an added sense of urgency to the need to develop useful paradigms for understanding the role of ethnic business in Western capitalist economies. Indeed, a flurry of research activity in this area in America and in Britain has contributed substantially to this end (Cummings, 1980; Kim, 1981; Aldrich, Cater, Jones and McEvoy, 1981; Waldinger, 1983; Ward and Jenkins, 1984).

The conceptual frameworks employed in earlier studies of ethnic minorities in business drew extensively on the 'middleman minorities' model (Blalock, 1967; Bonacich, 1973); more recently the notion of the 'ethnic niche' or 'ethnic enclave' (Wilson and Portes, 1980) has been influential. There has been no real attempt, however, to establish in what circumstances such approaches can be used to explain the pattern of involvement of ethnic minorities in the economy in contrast to previous explanations which have stressed the role of immigrants as a 'replacement labour' force (Peach, 1968). Indeed, some studies of immigration to Britain (and to Western Europe as a whole) in the post-war period assume that all migrants have been employees (Grammenos, 1982). It is difficult to reconcile this with accounts which stress the preoccupation of particular immigrant communities with entrepreneurial activities (Tambs-Lyche, 1980).

At an aggregate level, statistics indicating the involvement of ethnic minorities in business in Britain are not revealing. The latest available national data showing the numbers and proportions of self-employed and employers (as opposed to those in the labour market) come from the National Dwelling and Housing Survey (NDHS), carried out in 1977–8.[1] Figures are given in Table 7.1.

Table 7.1 shows that while West Indians are significantly underrepre-

Table 7.1   Heads of households: self-employed in specified socio-economic groups by ethnic group for national sample (percentages)

	Employers		Self-employed professionals (SEG 3)	Own account workers (SEG 12)	Sum of SEGs 1, 2, 3 and 12	(no.)
	large firms (SEG 1)	small firms (SEG 2)				
White	0.3	3.8	1.0	4.9	10.0	1 101 181
West Indian	—	1.0	—	2.6	3.6	4 880
Indian	—	4.6	1.6	5.5	11.6	12 956
Pakistani/ Bangladeshi	—	2.4	0.4	5.1	7.9	4 372
Other non-white	0.8	5.7	0.5	6.0	13.0	23 036
Total	0.3	3.8	1.0	4.8	10.0	1 146 424

Note: Percentages read *across* the line and represent self-employed in designated SEGs as a proportion of all economically active household heads.

Source: National Dwelling and Housing Survey, special tabulation

sented among the self-employed, there is no major difference in this respect between Indian and Pakistani and white household heads. Furthermore, breaking down these figures into different types of self-employment does nothing to alter this conclusion. Aggregate statistics simply conceal the very substantial internal differences in the employment position of ethnic minorities in British cities (Ward, 1984, Ch. 7).

This chapter consists of a first step towards assessing the participation of ethnic minorities in business by classifying the settlement pattern and involvement in the local economy of members of ethnic minorities in urban areas in Britain. In so doing, it attempts to demonstrate the relevance of the main types of explanation of this phenomenon noted above. It posits five broad types of involvement in the local economy:

1   Some areas have been largely unaffected by immigration from the New Commonwealth in the post-war period. It is hypothesized that this will occur in two quite different contexts. First, where there has been a sharp contraction in the rate of economic activity over the last forty years, it is unlikely that there has been any real opportunity for an immigrant group to obtain employment. At the other extreme, where economic opportunities and the local lifestyle have been sufficiently attractive, it is equally unlikely that members of racial minorities would have found easy access to employment or business opportunities in the area. Where either of these sets of circumstances obtain, we should expect to find a *non-settlement* area.

2   In some districts a substantial number of local jobs have been abandoned by the traditional workforce, through migration either to other areas or to other places of work in the locality where terms and conditions have been more attractive. Thus, there has been a need for a *replacement labour* force to take over the jobs which have been abandoned. This thesis, set out by Peach (1968), has been widely adopted in other accounts of race and employment in Britain (see, for example, Rose *et al.*, 1969, Ch. 7). The main areas of employment at issue have included foundries, cotton and wool textiles, public transport, utilities and domestic work in hospitals.

3   In some situations where ethnic minorities have arrived to take over such jobs they have thereby created a market which can most easily be supplied by other members of the same minority. In particular, small businesses may thrive to the extent that such consumer demand constitutes a 'protected' market. Thus the more culturally alien the minority, the more the opportunities for self-employment within the community. That is, a pattern emerges of the *ethnic niche* or *enclave* which covers both a majority of wage workers and a minority of small businesses within the ethnic community.

4   In other contexts, however, there may be opportunities for ethnic minorities to develop businesses which rely on the established majority for custom. The *middlemam minority* model expounded by Bonacich was an attempt to conceptualize the circumstances in which this was likely to occur. Whether or not the explanation she puts forward as to which

minorities are likely to exemplify this pattern is validated in the British case, the self-evident presence of some minorities, most notably the Chinese, in areas of business where they are largely dependent on the majority community for patronage confirms that this is a further pattern of involvement in the local economy.

5   Lastly, while none of the above types will be found in a pure form, there are likely to be situations where more than one pattern is to be found. For while they are analytically separate, there is no reason to regard them as *alternative* forms of settlement. Thus, the final type could be described as a *general* settlement pattern.

Finally, it should be stressed that while each of these types is seen as distinctive, all derive from the particular structure of opportunities in the local economy, rather than the characteristics of the minority group members. Those migrating to a specific area may have distinctive characteristics (types of qualifications, for example, or business experience) but it is argued that this will only constitute an advantage where it relates to openings in the local economy.

In testing the utility of this classification scheme against data on the settlement of minorities in urban areas in Britain, it is desirable to select a minority group who are (a) culturally distinct (much of the theorizing in the area of ethnic business carries this assumption), (b) sufficiently numerous to allow the pattern of settlement in a wide range of areas to be examined and (c) sufficiently involved in business as well as the labour market to distinguish between the various alternatives set out. For these reasons, in this analysis we use data referring to Indian and Pakistani settlement in Britain, rather than that of West Indians or the Chinese, for both of which groups one or more of these conditions would not obtain.

Patterns of immigrant involvement in the local economy

Non-settlement

There are two types of economic conjunctures in which it was hypothesized that little or no Asian settlement would take place in an urban area. These consist of (a) a sufficiently sharp contraction in the local economy to discourage any immigration from outside and (b) economic or lifestyle opportunities sufficiently attractive to allow effective resistance towards any Asians trying to move in. For a crude measure of this we turn to a classification of British towns and cities in the period immediately preceding large scale immigration from India and Pakistan. Moser and Scott (1961) provide an analysis of 157 urban areas by economic and other variables based on the 1951 census which is most convenient for this purpose. Of these almost one-third (49) are within the London commuting area, and since London constitutes something of a special case in looking at immigration to Britain, they are ignored for the purposes of this paper, though the same broad trends apply in London too.

It was assumed that those areas experiencing the greatest decline in the economy could be identified by the proportion of men in semi-skilled and unskilled manual work. Of the twenty-six areas with the highest propor-tions only two had more than half of one per cent of their population of Indian or Pakistani ethnic origin in 1977–8, according to the NDHS, compared to a figure of 1.8 per cent for England as a whole. They consist almost entirely of long-established industrial areas dominated by heavy engineering, mining and docking. Many of them had as little as one in a thousand of their population of Indian or Pakistani origin – examples include Liverpool, Hull, Barnsley and Wigan. Some of these areas had received larger numbers of immigrants from Africa and Asia in earlier years (including Liverpool and ports in the north-east of England) but more recently there have been virtually no arrivals from South Asia.

Areas with the most attractive economic and lifestyle opportunities were identified by taking those places with the highest proportion of male jobs in professional and managerial positions. The top eighteen such areas had equally minute proportions of Indians and Pakistanis. Thus about 40 per cent (42 out of 108) of urban areas in Britain outside the London commuting region, those with the least and those with the most attractive opportunities, have been virtually unaffected by South Asian immigration. So while the conventional wisdom is that Asians have settled in those areas with the worst jobs, this analysis suggests that there are a substantial number of areas where there were no jobs, as well as where higher status jobs were available but monopolized by others. This fits in with Peach's conclusion that 'the main coloured groups form the highest proportion of the population mainly in the regions of moderate industrial attraction' (1968, p. 67).

Replacement labour

The classic explanation of the settlement pattern of New Commonwealth immigrants in Britain is, as noted above, that they came as a replacement labour force to take such jobs as were no longer attractive to local labour (Peach, 1968). Whether this refers to areas where workers turned to other jobs that were available locally and preferable or to areas which were losing their labour force as workers sought better jobs elsewhere, the central notion is that black people were *replacing* the local working population.

Where immigrants from the Caribbean have played this role, they have typically been drawn into the workforce in small units in sectors such as transport and public utilities. Where whole sections of an industry needed a replacement workforce, this is more likely to have come from Asia. In an attempt to define areas where replacement labour has been dominant in the settlement pattern of Asians, to the exclusion of ethnic business development, we looked for areas where there was (a) substantial Asian settlement (over 3 per cent of the population), (b) a heavy concentration of Asians in manual employment in local firms (over 75 per cent manual employees), (c) little small business (less than 3 per cent of Asians in business with no employees except members of their immediate family, i.e. SEG 12).

Data were available from the NDHS on the characteristics of Asian household heads in fifteen towns and cities in England outside London with over one per cent of their population of Asian origin (as well as two others, Liverpool and Salford, which were non-settlement areas). Figures from the NDHS used in categorizing Asian settlement patterns are contained in Table 7.2.

Five of these fitted the replacement labour form as defined above: Birmingham, Coventry, Wolverhampton, Sandwell and Walsall. All are in the West Midlands and in all of them metal manufacture and metal working are dominant in the economy. In each case at least twenty-five times as many household heads were manual employees as were running their own small businesses. Given this degree of dominance of manual labour in the employment profile of Asian workers, it is surely justifiable to refer to these areas as characterized by replacement labour, as far as Asian workers are concerned. Even if all the Asian household heads enumerated in the NDHS as working on their own account were in trade and commerce, there is no hint of middleman activities being any more than a minute adaptation among Asian settlers. Indeed, there is little sign of substantial numbers making a living by servicing members of their own ethnic groups, let alone acting as middlemen in businesses dependent on the host society for custom, which is presumably implicit in the middleman model. In fact, the replacement labour pattern found in the West Midlands well exemplifies Bonacich's recognition that 'many groups of sojourning migrant labourers do not enter small business' (1973, p. 588).

Ethnic niche

A recent study of Asian retailing in Britain has stressed the extent to which Indian and Pakistani shopkeepers are making a living by serving the 'protected' ethnic market (Aldrich, Cater, Jones and McEvoy, 1981; Cater, 1984). While this is not the only pattern observed (for cases where Asian retailers have mostly served the white market, see Aldrich, 1980 and Mullins, 1979), its existence suggests explanations of Asian retailing in terms of the dynamics of ethnic consumer demand at different stages of the process of residential succession. We noted that the presence of a concentrated body of Asian settlers in particular residential areas along with fellow countrymen making a living by selling or providing other services within the community has been described in terms of the 'ethnic niche' or 'ethnic enclave' (see also Auster and Aldrich, 1984). This represents the next of our types of settlement. Its main feature is a body of

	Asians in population	Socio-economic groups of Asian household heads							West Indians in population	West Indian h'hold heads in SEG 12
		1–2	3–4	5–6	9–11	12	Others	no.		
Non-settlement		(3)	(2)	(—)	(2)	(1)	(—)	8	0.3	(5.0)
Liverpool	0.1	(3)	(2)	(—)	(2)	(1)	(—)	8	0.3	(5.0)
Salford	0.5	(2)	(5)	(4)	(9)	(—)	(—)	20	0.1	(—)
Replacement Labour										
Birmingham	6.4	8.8	3.7	7.4	75.5	2.3	2.3	216	4.8	2.1
Coventry	6.2	4.3	2.9	4.8	79.5	2.9	5.7	210	1.1	
Wolverhampton	8.8	3.0	1.9	3.3	84.8	2.2	4.8	269	5.0	1.3
Sandwell	5.7	3.6	2.6	3.6	83.9	1.0	5.2	192	3.0	1.7
Walsall	4.2	5.2	0.6	4.5	83.9		5.8	155	1.0	(2.5)
(Dudley)	1.6	3.4	6.8	5.1	76.3	5.1	3.4	59	0.7	
Ethnic niche										
Bradford	7.8	5.0	1.5	3.8	80.1	5.4	4.2	261	0.6	(3.0)
Bolton	4.7	3.9	3.9	4.5	74.7	7.8	5.2	154	0.2	(9.1)
Rochdale	3.1	5.6	5.6	0.9	74.8	7.5	5.6	107	0.2	(—)
Middleman minority										
Manchester	3.1	17.0	10.6	12.8	38.3	14.9	6.4	94	2.5	3.0
Newcastle	1.3	26.2	2.4	16.7	21.4	31.0	2.4	42		(—)
General migration										
Leeds	2.5	9.1	3.0	7.6	68.2	9.1	3.0	66	1.0	—
Nottingham	2.4	10.0	2.9	11.4	54.3	10.0	11.4	70	3.4	0.7
Reading	2.2	16.9	7.0	8.5	64.8		2.8	71	3.6	5.4
Leicester	16.5	8.8	2.0	9.4	66.4	7.0	6.1	543	2.1	
London	4.1	12.6	9.8	22.2	42.3	6.5	6.6	4077	4.1	2.8

Notes: SEG 1–2 managers; 3–4 professionals; 5–6 other non-manual; 9–11 manual; 12 own account workers.
Others: Personal service, foremen, farm, armed forces, inadequately described. Actual numbers given for Liverpool and Salford because of small cell size.

Source: NDHS, special tabulations

migrant workers engaged in manual work, as in the previous type, but in association with a substantial number of community members running businesses heavily dependent on fellow ethnics for custom.

To qualify as examples of the 'ethnic niche' settlement pattern, we postulated that over 3 per cent of the population should be of Asian origin, as before, that over 70 per cent should be engaged in manual work as employees and that more than 5 per cent should be running small businesses on their own account which depended heavily on community support. Three of the fifteen urban areas for which data was available fulfilled the first three conditions (see Table 7.2). From the NDHS data it is not possible to deduce the extent to which businesses serve the protected ethnic market, the final condition, but from other sources it is clear that most Asian retailers in Bradford, a centre of the manufacture of wool textiles in Yorkshire, rely greatly on support from within the community (Aldrich, Cater, Jones and McEvoy, 1981; Aldrich, Jones and McEvoy, 1984). The other two examples, Bolton and Rochdale, are cotton textile towns in Lancashire, which seem to display the same pattern (Anwar, 1979; Hahlo, 1980).

In all three areas there are still ten to fifteen times as many manual workers as small businessmen. But trade and commerce, a key feature of middleman minority settlement, at least seem to provide a larger minority with a means of livelihood. However, this does not qualify as a middleman pattern of development, since the trade is largely within the ethnic community, and by implication would not exist if the majority of community members had not come to take jobs in local firms, i.e. it is a secondary adaptation. Perhaps the most interesting question that arises from a comparison between the replacement labour and ethnic niche adaptations is whether there are more small businesses in the latter because of some characteristic possessed by those who decide to go into business or whether it reflects the lack of jobs in the local labour market which are more attractive than petty retailing. The studies of Asian shopkeepers in Bradford contain little evidence that those going into retailing are particularly qualified to do so by virtue of their background, when compared to those who take jobs in industry. For example, only one-fifth had fathers who were self-employed (Aldrich, Cater, Jones and McEvoy, 1981, p. 177). On the other hand it may be no accident that in the West Midlands, where Asian retailing has been less widespread, half of the manual jobs taken by Asians in industry have been at the skilled level and are likely to carry higher wage rates than jobs in the mills, the majority of which are semi-skilled.

The suggestion for further research that emerges is that where the ethnic niche model best describes Asian involvement in the economy, rather than replacement labour, this says more about the lack of good opportunities for manual work in the ethnic niche areas than about the lack of qualifications for starting businesses among Asians in areas where replacement labour predominates. In both types of area, settlement has been largely by villagers, mostly peasant farmers, who have formed encapsulated 'ethnic villages' in new and strange urban surroundings.

Middleman minority

The main elements in the middleman minority model are concisely set out by Bonacich:

> A key variable is the orientation of immigrants towards their place of residence, with sojourning at first, and later a 'stranger' orientation affecting the solidarity and economic activity of the ethnic group. These in turn arouse the hostility of the host society, which perpetuates a reluctance to assimilate completely, or 'stranger' status. (1973, p. 583)

Central to this model is the notion that it is those who immigrate as 'sojourners', i.e. who have a clear intention of returning home, and thus see themselves as temporary migrants, who are predisposed both to become successful in business and in so doing to maintain their temporary status until they become *de facto* permanent settlers, while retaining a 'stranger' role comparable to that of recent migrants. Sojourners show a high degree of internal solidarity. This gives rise to business success, since along with the motivation to accumulate capital found among temporary migrants, it allows the efficient distribution of resources (capital, jobs, etc.) and the regulation of internal competition. It also leads to hostility against those who both live off and remain separate from the host society; and so to a reluctance to assimilate which perpetuates their stranger orientation in the society.

Bonacich recognizes that middleman roles extend beyond trade and commerce and include other ways of making a living, such as the independent professions, the practice of various skills and acting as agents, contractors or brokers in different sectors of the economy. But within the world of business where middleman minorities are mostly found they are concentrated in those activities which do not require large amounts of capital to be tied up. Thus she describes them as in 'portable' occupations which can easily be practised in new surroundings – a clear advantage for those who see themselves as temporary migrants.

The fifteen areas of Asian immigration outside London were further inspected with a view to identifying places where the middleman minority form was more dominant. Unfortunately, the four categories described in Table 7.1 which together make up the business population could not all be deduced from the available tabulations.[2] However, as a rough and ready way of categorizing areas displaying the middleman minority model, it was determined that at least 15 per cent of the heads of household should be working on their own account and that a minority of Asians should be employed as manual workers. Two areas satisfied these conditions, Manchester and Newcastle (see Table 7.2).

To find Manchester emerging as a middleman minority area was no surprise, since the Asian business community based on the clothing trade but extending into various other sectors has been well researched (Nowikowski, 1984; Nowikowski and Ward, 1979; Werbner, 1984). For Manchester, additional tables are available from the NDHS showing that a third of Indian heads of household and almost half (46 per cent) of the Pakistanis were engaged in some kind of business, with or without employees.

Little is known about the Asian community in Newcastle, an area of lesser Indian and Pakistani immigration, though Davies (1972) has shown that landlording was a favoured occupation among Pakistanis and that the Asian proletariat, whose housing careers in Britain have attracted considerable political as well as academic attention (Rex and Moore, 1967), were largely absent from the city. The NDHS figures show that 31 per cent of Asian household heads in Newcastle were working on their own account, to which would have to be added an unknown proportion running businesses with employees outside the family.

What has been said so far supports the middleman minority model as portrayed by Bonacich. But there are other features of Asian settlement to consider. For the explanation of this pattern that she gives to be substantiated, it would be necessary to show not only that trade and commerce was a major area of immigrant activity, but that those engaging in such activities saw themselves as sojourners and displayed the 'ethnic village' characteristics listed above. In fact, such evidence as is available points to the reverse.

First, the most distinctive sojourning group among Asians in Britain are the families of Indian and Pakistani ethnic origin who came to Britain following pressure to leave their adopted home in Uganda and Kenya. They could be said to be sojourning, certainly in relation to two homelands (India/Pakistan and Uganda/Kenya), possibly a third, i.e. Canada, where increasing numbers of community members have found a home. Further, many of them have come from a background of trading in East Africa and frequently they have transferred this to Britain. But neither Manchester nor Newcastle has been a centre of settlement for East African Asians, regardless of whatever business opportunities may be present here, and most Asian business is in the hands of Indians and Pakistanis who came direct from the subcontinent.

Secondly, while details of the personal characteristics and orientation to migration of Asians in Newcastle are not known, it is clear that members of the Asian business community in Manchester are much more anglicized than the ethnic villagers found in areas of replacement labour and ethnic niche. For example, they are much more residentially dispersed (Fenton, 1977; Ward and Nowikowski, 1981; Werbner, 1979) and more likely to have married outside the community and to be English-speaking (Nowikowski, 1980). They also show signs of the dilution of their cultural background, while retaining in most cases a strong sense of ethnicity (Nowikowski, *op. cit.*).

Thus, while they may be well established in business, it is difficult to attribute this to the sojourning outlook of immigrants who see their stay as temporary and seek to separate themselves from the host society wherever possible, arousing its hostility in so doing. Indeed, as Werbner (1984) shows, a familiarity with the English way of life, including a knowledge of English, is likely to be a considerable asset in carrying on business in the rag trade, and to be reinforced by the social situations thrown up in the course of trading. That is, empirically the middleman minority pattern of economic activity is well supported but much remains to be done to establish its theoretical basis.

General migration

The final item in this typology of Asian settlement patterns is frankly something of a catch-all. However, it is worth noting that only five of the fifteen areas we have been considering remain to be 'caught', so that while it may cover diverse situations, at least they constitute a minority. Labelling it 'general migration' is intended to distinguish it from the other types which all emphasize specific, collective adaptations, whether by manual workers or petty entrepreneurs. It is not suggested that in this final type migrants have come on a wholly different basis; rather, that they have been attracted by a *diversity* of economic opportunities. By implication it might be argued that these areas are characterized by a lack of opportunities for migrant workers to take over whole sections of manual employment in the locality or to become extensively involved in sectors of trade and commerce. The best examples of this among the remaining areas are probably Leeds and Nottingham, two regional centres where the basic industries have not drawn in large quantities of immigrant labour, but where various kinds of opportunities have arisen for Asians to make a living. In Nottingham, for example, Asians are more diverse in terms of the skill level required for their job and their employment status than in any of the other areas considered.

A third district, Dudley, is broadly comparable to the replacement labour areas which it adjoins, but contains rather more Asian small businessmen; it has a smaller Asian population a bit more scattered over the economy; this probably reflects the fact that it houses many of those working in better class jobs in surrounding areas. It should probably be treated as a replacement labour area.

The fourth area considered under this heading, Reading, could arguably have been excluded on the grounds that it is only forty miles from London and includes among its residents London commuters as well as those working in the locality. More of its Asian population are managers in small firms, or employed as professionals or clerical workers – a pattern found to a much greater extent in London, though even in Reading over three-fifths of the Asian household heads are engaged in manual work.

Leicester, the final area caught under this heading, is certainly the least easy to classify. It could be argued that it represents all of the types of adaptation considered except, by definition, non-settlement, since it had an estimated Indian and Pakistani population (mostly Indian) in 1978 of 45 000 (16.5 per cent of the population). Thus, (a) it includes a replacement labour force attracted particularly by jobs in the knitwear and hosiery industry; (b) there is an important business community (including a large element from East Africa) which is small in relation to the number of Asian employees in Leicester but large in comparison to the Asian business community in many other areas in Britain – some businesses depend on the protected market for custom, as in the ethnic niche areas, while others have developed a role as middlemen in the wider community (Clark and Rughani, 1983); (c) there are also quite large numbers of Indians scattered over the economy employed as managers or professionals or in a white-collar capacity, including some who have come to the city as individual households – a characteristic of general migration areas. Thus, examples of each type of adaptation could be found in Leicester, as in London, but in aggregate Asian settlement could not be categorized in terms of any of the three previous types. It may well contain the clearest example of the middleman minority adaptation as set out by Bonacich, but this is a minority element within the overall settlement pattern. It seems likely that it has grown as Indians have moved out of the manual employment which first drew them to the city, either because of the extra attractions of business openings or as a consequence of large scale contraction in local industry.

Discussion

We set out to assess the involvement of ethnic minorities in business by classifying urban areas in Britain according to the economic role played by Asian settlers. There were three distinctive patterns together with a residual category where a more diverse mode of settlement was evident, as well as other types of area where Asian immigration has not taken place. It is hardly a surprise that the places associated in each category turned out to have very similar local economies. *Non-settlement* districts (Liverpool, Salford) were traditional heavy engineering areas in an advanced state of economic decline. *Replacement labour* districts (Birmingham, Coventry, Wolverhampton, Sandwell, Walsall and to a lesser extent, Dudley) were all centres of engineering in the West Midlands and noted for the expansion of their economies over the post-war period. The three places displaying the *ethnic niche* pattern (Bradford, Bolton and Rochdale) were all textile centres in Lancashire and Yorkshire. Two districts (Manchester and Newcastle) showed a *middleman minority* model; both were regional commercial centres. This left what was described as a *general migration* pattern in Nottingham, Leeds, Reading and Leicester, to which London would have been added, given the opportunity to describe its complex immigration pattern. These are all urban industrial centres, though they have less in common than the places grouped in other categories.

The elements which singly or in combination made up the various types of Asian settlement were (1) replacing the white labour force in an area of manual work in the local economy, (2) running a business relying for custom on members of an Asian replacement labour force, (3) running a business oriented towards the wider, 'open' market and (4) taking advantage of job openings on a more individual basis wherever they arose. In practice these elements will be found to different extents and in different combinations and sequences.

Replacement labour and the immigration of individual families such as is likely to be found in the general migration pattern are typical initial modes of settlement, though the speed with which Chinese from Hong Kong took over large sections of the fish and chip business in post-war Britain (a better case of middleman minority adaptation than any of those considered in this chapter (Watson, 1977)) suggests that the middleman form may emerge early on in favourable circumstances. A natural progression from the replacement labour form is to the ethnic niche, though this assumes that making a living servicing community members is more attractive than manual employment. We have suggested that in the foundry industry this was probably untrue, but that in textiles the rewards of manual employment in the mills were insufficient to deter Asians from going into trade and commerce within the protected market. How far the rapid contraction of the foundry industry in recent years has pushed Asians in the West Midlands into shopkeeping and other areas of business is not known. It is to be expected that, in general, structural changes in the local economy will lead to a reorientation of Asian economic activity.

What are the implications of this analysis for academic enquiry into minority business development – an area which needs much more systematic examination if the questions raised at the beginning of this chapter are to be properly addressed?

Where Asians have gone into business, it can be argued that particular industries have been selected because they both have low barriers to entry and also offer a chance for immigrants from Asia to be competitive through efficient use of the resources of labour, capital and expertise available through the community network (where the ethnic niche pattern is followed the ethnic market is also a significant factor). Thus one area in which research might usefully develop is to consider the circumstances in which businesses are started and the *strategy* behind decisions taken at the start, as well as at subsequent phases of development, together with the barriers faced at each point. This would clarify the circumstances in which the ethnic niche pattern emerges or alternatively that of the middleman minority.

A second research priority concerns *business succession*. Presumably the considerations which are most salient change over the course of a business career. At the start, however, such research as has been carried out on Asian businessmen in Britain suggests that it is the availability of a business that is the chief consideration. It is unfortunate that so little work has been done so far outside retailing, but within this sector it is those types of business which come on the market because they are least attractive to white business people in which Asian retailers are overrepresented. They include those shops which are unattractive to whites because of their location in areas undergoing residential succession from white to Asian or West Indian. Indeed, it is a feature of the 'ethnic niche' explanation of Asian retailing patterns that residential succession is closely associated with business succession (Ward and Jenkins, 1984). It may be therefore that more of the conceptual apparatus used in analysing residential succession could be usefully applied in examining business succession, such as 'push' and 'pull' models of succession.

The second type of retail outlet typically taken over by Asians in Britain is the business which has little appeal because of the long and unsocial hours involved. Newsagents, tobacconists' shops and chemists are good examples, where late working is normal, as well as the corner shop which, if Asian owned, is likely to be open on Sunday morning as well as Monday to Saturday. Running a chemist's shop also gives a chance to use a professional training in pharmacy.

Finally, following the logic of the above discussion, we can conclude that research could usefully address itself to the notion of the *business career*. We have already suggested that a middleman role may emerge in the course of settlement in contexts where replacement labour or the ethnic niche or individual migration is dominant. The same applies to the careers of individual businesspeople as well as communities. The first venture into self-employment is quite likely to depend for success on the protected market, but relying on community members for custom on a permanent basis may be a recipe for remaining small. A second path is to graduate to selling (or making) the same product or providing the same service on the open market after an initial period of dependence on community support. Among the Afro-Caribbean community in Britain, for example, hairdressing is probably the best example of this process. A third possibility is to use the capital acquired in the first, intra-community phase of the business to branch out into a separate area which requires a higher initial capital investment but offers a higher rate of return. Others again will go straight into business on the open market, with varying degrees of success, usually offering goods or services with an ethnic aspect (e.g. restaurants). All these types of business career carry the prospect of success or failure or just an ability to hang on. A systematic classification of the business careers of a sample of migrants from different origins (e.g. Asians vs. West Indians), with different characteristics (e.g. urban vs. rural background) and approaches to migration (e.g. permanent vs. temporary settlement) would be of great value, not only in facilitating a clearer understanding of the processes underlying business success but in providing some guidance as to what steps can be taken in a period of economic crisis to assist in planning business success in the future.

While the burden of this paper has been to demonstrate that the structuring of the local economy in different kinds of urban areas has been substantially responsible for the broad pattern of Asian settlement, this does not mean that the characteristics and orientation of other immigrant groups are not powerful determinants of their situation. The concentration of the Chinese in middleman roles in Britain (Watson, 1977) as well as in the United States (Light, 1972) fits in well with the interpretation put forward by Bonacich – their involvement in the restaurant and fish and chips business seems to be largely independent of inter-urban differences in Britain, since the consumer market on which they depend is not differentiated in this way. By contrast, immigrants from the Caribbean are much more evenly distributed over different localities in Britain – and, contrary to their position in the United States (Foner, 1979), substantially underrepresented in business almost everywhere.

Thus, small business can be seen as an important, though usually subsidiary, element in the economic adaptation of Asian minorities in Britain. Reliance on the ethnic community and a middleman role are alternate strategies for business development. Some indication has been given of the uneven progress of those strategies in particular local economies. But much remains to be done by way of explaining the circumstances in which each pattern will flourish, anticipating likely trends and identifying implications for policy.

Notes

1 Most of the data from the NDHS referred to in this paper comes from special tabulations acquired by the ESRC Research Unit on Ethnic Relations.

2 In this paper 'small businesses' and people working 'on their own account' are defined by the number of 'own account workers', i.e. Socio-Economic Group (SEG) 12. This category includes all those working for themselves without using a professional skill, and with no employees outside the immediate family. SEGs 1 and 2 include both employers (i.e. those referred to in the first two columns in Table 7.1) and managers employed in large and small firms. Finally, SEG 3 consists of those using a professional skill while working for themselves. Figures on the whole business population for Asians in selected areas, as in Table 7.1, are contained in Ward and Reeves, 1980.

References

ALDRICH, H. (1980) 'Asian shopkeepers as a middleman minority: a study of small businesses in Wandsworth', in Evans, A. and Eversley, D. (eds) *The Inner City: Employment and Industry*, London, Heinemann, pp. 389–407.

ALDRICH, H., CATER, J., JONES, T. and McEVOY, D. (1981) 'Business development and self-segregation: Asian enterprise in three British cities', in Peach, C., Robinson, V. and Smith, S. (eds) *Ethnic Segregation in Cities*, London, Croom Helm, pp. 170–90.

ALDRICH, H., JONES, T. and McEVOY, D. (1984) 'Ethnic advantage and minority business', in Ward, R. and Jenkins, R. (eds).

ANWAR, M. (1979) *The Myth of Return: Pakistanis in Britain*, London, Heinemann.

AUSTER, E. and ALDRICH, H. (1984) 'Small business vulnerability, ethnic enclaves and ethnic enterprise', in Ward, R. and Jenkins, R. (eds).

BLALOCK, H. (1967) *Toward a Theory of Minority Group Relations*, Chichester, Wiley.

BONACICH, E. (1973) 'A theory of middleman minorities', *American Sociological Review*, Vol. 38, pp. 583–94.

CLARK, P. and RUGHANI, M. (1983) 'Asian entrepreneurs in wholesaling and manufacturing in Leicester', *New Community*, Vol. 11, pp. 23–33.

CUMMINGS, S. (ed.) (1980) *Self-help in Urban America: Patterns of Minority Business Enterprise*, New York, Kennikat.

DAVIES, J. (1972) *The Evangelistic Bureaucrat*, London, Tavistock.

FENTON, M. (1977) 'Asian households in owner-occupation: a study of the pattern, costs and experiences of households in Greater Manchester', *Working Papers on Ethnic Relations*, No. 2, ESRC, London Research Unit on Ethnic Relations.

FONER, N. (1979) 'West Indians in New York City and London: a comparative analysis', *International Migration Review*, Vol. 13, pp. 284–95.

GRAMMENOS, S. (1982) 'Migrant labour in western Europe', *Studies and Documents 3*, Maastricht, European Centre for Work and Society.

HAHLO, K. (1980) 'Profile of a Gujerati community in Bolton', *New Community*, Vol. 8, pp. 295–307.

KIM, I. (1981) *The New Urban Immigrants: Korean Immigrants in New York City*, Princeton University Press.

LIGHT, I. (1972) *Ethnic Enterprise in America*, University of California Press.

MOSER, C. and SCOTT, W. (1961) *British Towns*, London, Oliver and Boyd.

MULLINS, D. (1979) 'Asian retailing in Croydon', *New Community*, Vol. 7, pp. 403–5.

NOWIKOWSKI, S. (1980) 'The social situation of an Asian community in Manchester', unpublished PhD thesis, University of Manchester.

NOWIKOWSKI, S. (1984) 'Snakes and ladders: Asian business in Britain', in Ward, R. and Jenkins, R. (eds).

NOWIKOWSKI, S. and WARD, R. (1979) 'Middle class and British? An analysis of South Asians in suburbia', *New Community*, Vol. 7, pp. 1–10.

PEACH, C. (1968) *West Indian Migration to Britain*, Oxford University Press.

REX, J. and MOORE, R. (1967) *Race, Community and Conflict*, Oxford University Press.

ROSE, E. J. B. *et al.*, (1969) *Colour and Citizenship: A Report on British Race Relations*, Oxford University Press.

TAMBS-LYCHE, H. (1980) *London Patidars: A Case Study in Urban Ethnicity*, London, Routledge and Kegan Paul.

WALDINGER, R. (1983) 'Ethnic enterprise and industrial change: a case study of the New York garment industry', PhD dissertation, Department of Sociology, Harvard University.

WARD, R. (ed.) (1984) *Race and Residence in Britain*, Monographs on Ethnic Relations 2, ESRC, Research Unit on Ethnic Relations, University of Aston.

WARD, R. and JENKINS, R. (eds) (1984) *Ethnic Communities in Business*, Cambridge University Press.

WARD, R. and REEVES, F. (1980) 'West Indians in business in Britain'

(Memorandum submitted to the Home Affairs Committee Race Relations and Immigrations Sub-Committee, Session 1980–1), House of Commons, 15 December.

WATSON, J. (ed.) (1977) *Between Two Cultures: Migrants and Minorities in Britain*, Oxford, Basil Blackwell.

WERBNER, P. (1979) 'Avoiding the ghetto: Pakistani migrants and settlement shifts in Manchester', *New Community*, Vol. 7, pp. 376–89.

WERBNER, P. (1984) 'From rags to riches: Manchester Pakistanis in the textile trade', in Ward, R. and Jenkins, R. (eds).

WILSON, K. L. and PORTES, A. (1980) 'Immigrant enclaves: an analysis of the labor market experiences of Cubans in Miami', *American Journal of Sociology*, Vol. 86, No. 5, pp. 295–319.

8   Two sides of anti-racism

Paul Gilroy

This chapter examines recent political organizations and movements which have defined themselves as anti-racist. This is necessary for two main reasons. First, to show that the content of 'anti-racism' has not always been a direct response to the ideologies and practices of racism, and secondly, to look at the relationship between anti-racist politics and political formations more readily identifiably as expressions of class antagonism and consciousness.

This chapter will argue that the link between the language and practice of anti-racist politics and those of class politics is a tenuous one but that anti-racist politics have, at key points during the last ten years, articulated a means of representing class outside of the categories in which it has been constructed and reproduced by means of 'race' [. . .] To explore these arguments further, this chapter will address two periods in the recent history of anti-racism in Britain, comparing the different understandings of 'race' and anti-racism which have been expressed by organizations and movements which have declared themselves to be primarily anti-racist in their orientation.

Their political languages and some of the strategic and tactical questions raised by them and by the contrast between them will be examined. The more formal and institutionally-based politics of anti-racism which emerged in the interventions of Labour local authorities, particularly the Greater London Council (GLC) in the aftermath of the 1981 riots have been chosen to represent one pole of political activity. The anti-racist mass movement of the late 1970s, specifically Rock Against Racism (RAR) and the Anti Nazi League (ANL), comprises the other. These have been selected because each has a clear and substantial commitment to the cultural dimensions of struggle, moving beyond the confines of formal politics into the realm of popular discourses, and because each articulates in a different way with a class politics.

The first is associated with the institutions and agencies of socialist local governments and the second was directly influenced by the practice of far left groups, particularly the Socialist Workers' Party (SWP) which sought to incline the anti-racist movement in the direction of class consciousness and solidarity through developing a strategy guided by the slogan 'Black and White Unite and Fight'.

It is immediately necessary to emphasize that in looking at anti-racism as a political phenomenon, I will not be concerned with the self-organization and independent struggles of the black communities. The history of their struggles requires a broader and more detailed analysis than can be conducted under the heading of anti-racism. Political organization and struggle which have identified and promoted themselves as anti-racist are of more interest here not only because they have received virtually no attention from other writers, but because the commitment to a practical anti-racist politics necessarily generates an interesting commentary on and negotiation of actual relationships between black and white people [. . .]

Before we look at these struggles in detail it is necessary to grasp that black liberation and anti-racism are two quite distinct orientations which get regularly confused in British racial politics. They are not the same and may actively conflict. Tension may exist, for example, between an anti-racist pluralism which allocates 'race' the status of a substantive difference but seeks to detach it from the stigma of domination and subordination, and other anti-racist positions which deny that 'race' has any effectivity of its own. This is often part of a commitment to the idea that either or both class and gender are more profound and more important.

Anti-racism in the 1970s

Blacks have been actively organizing in defence of their lives and communities ever since they set foot in Britain. Several writers have looked at these patterns of self-organization in greater detail than is possible here (Hiro, 1971; Abdul-Malik, 1968; Pryer, 1984; Sivanandan, 1982). Their histories have also occasionally drawn attention to the anti-racist organizations and struggles created during the 1950s and 1960s, which brought black and white together and formed a significant counterpart to the movements for black liberation in Britain and in its colonized countries.

The rise and demise of organizations such as the Co-ordinating Committee Against Racial Discrimination (CCARD) formed to oppose the 1961 Commonwealth Immigrants Bill and the Campaign Against Racial Discrimination (CARD) inaugurated in February 1965 after a visit to London by Dr Martin Luther King and dedicated to campaigning for the elimination of discrimination in civil society and in the immigration legislation, are important subjects for further research (Glean, 1973). Yet the anti-racisms of the 1970s are even less well known. That decade contained a series of qualitative shifts in the racial politics of Britain. The 1971 Immigration Act brought an end to primary immigration and instituted a new pattern of internal control and surveillance of black settlers. It was paralleled by a new vocabulary of 'race' and crime which grew in the aftermath of the first panic over 'mugging'. These developments are two of the most important from the point of view of black self-organization. However, the expansion and consolidation of organizations of the extreme, neo-fascist right was also to transform decisively the meaning of anti-racism. Dilip Hiro points to the existence of street level harrassment and other activity by extreme racist groups including the British Ku Klux Klan as early as 1965, two years before the National Front (NF) was formed. Threatening letters to the London secretary of CARD had promised 'concerted efforts against West Indians, specially those living with white women' (1971). It was the entry of these groups into the process of electoral politics which acted as a catalyst for the creation of anti-fascist/anti-racist committees as an outgrowth of the organized labour movement in Britain's major towns and cities during the early and mid 1970s.

The NF had enjoyed its first party political broadcast during the February 1974 election and had fielded fifty-four candidates, a substantial increase from 1970 when only ten had stood. The party's journal, *Spearhead*, told its readers in January 1974 that 'It need hardly be said that our election campaign now takes absolute priority over everything else'.

In the second election of that year, the Front fielded ninety candidates who obtained 113844 votes. In the local government elections of May 1974, the NF averaged nearly 10 per cent of the poll in several districts of London (Fielding, 1981), and in a by-election at Newham South, beat the Conservative candidate and took 11.5 per cent of the total votes cast.

In June 1974 the anti-fascist forces organized a march and picket of a National Front meeting at Conway Hall in Red Lion Square. The resulting confrontation between demonstrators and the police ended with the death of one protester, Kevin Gately, who had been part of the International Marxist Group's contingent on the demonstration (Scarman, 1975; Clutterbuck, 1978). The fascists had been using the hall for meetings during the four years before 1974 and anti-fascist pickets of these meetings had begun in October 1973. Gately was claimed as something of a martyr to the re-born cause of anti-fascism. His death was seen as proof of the destructive nature of the extreme and anti-democratic forces which had been reconstituted on British streets, twenty-nine years after the war which had been fought to free Europe of fascist tyranny.

> Trades Unionists of the older generation were doubly shocked when reaching for their newspapers on the 16th June 1974. Firstly they learnt of the tragic death in a central London street of a young man, Kevin Gately. Then they read deeper to discover the circumstances of his death. They were to find that the ugliest and most brutal of twentieth century movements – fascism – which they had dearly hoped was buried forever in 1945, had returned to plague us anew. (Nicholson, 1974)

These words begin a pamphlet issued by the Transport and General Workers' Union which set out to alert its members and other trades unionists to the growing danger of British neo-fascism. Jack Jones's introduction to the pamphlet was clear about why the fascist groups should be opposed but the reasons he cites are unconnected with the experience of black settlers, make no mention of Britain's black population and contain no acknowledgement of the problem of racism as something distinct from, though connected to, fascism: 'Although they may deny it the "National Front" is the modern version of the Fascism of Hitler, Mussolini and Mosley'.

This definition of British neo-fascism exclusively in terms of the fascisms of the past against which the British had enjoyed their finest hours in battle, recurs again and again in the politics of anti-racism during the 1970s. Jones's words betray the central tension in the politics of the anti-racist struggle, namely the tendency to conceive of neo-fascism and racism as distinct and unrelated problems and to make the popular memory of the Second World War the dominant source of images with which to mobilize against the dangers of contemporary racism.

It is almost as though the activities of the National Front and similar groups only become a problem when they threaten democracy by their participation in its electoral system and only visible where a sham patriotism is invoked. Their record of racial violence against black individuals and communities remained either unseen or was not thought to have a place in the development of a socialist anti-fascist politics.

An informal and locally-based network of anti-fascist/anti-racist committees grew in the period between 1973 and 1976. It is during this period that the emergent anti-fascist movement began to express itself as a self-conscious political formation and to create its own organs for communication and debate. Though its primary audience lay in the black communities rather than among anti-racists, the journal *Race Today* (hijacked from the Institute of Race Relations and re-oriented by its activist editorial collective) had an important role in these discussions. The magazine's central place in the struggles between blacks and the police, around education and housing in the East End of London and in the attempt to build links between black political organizations in different parts of Britain as well as between British blacks and radical struggles elsewhere in the world, all made considerable input into what anti-racism was to mean.

Race Today posed a consistent challenge to the idea that black liberation was reducible to 'anti-racism' and to the related fallacy that the struggle against racism could be contained by the need to oppose the neo-fascist groups. At the opposite pole of the embryonic anti-racist movement was the anti-fascist magazine *Searchlight*. It had been founded in February 1975 with the aim of consolidating the anti-fascist forces so that they could challenge the electoral and the popular success of the NF. The magazine's first editorial took its cue from the slogan of the anti-fascist movement of the 1930s, 'They Shall Not Pass'. This motto was used as a caption for the magazine's front cover, a photograph of a young male neo-fascist with dark glasses, leather jacket and quiff, rather incongruously holding a Union Jack. The mandate for a new anti-fascism announced by the magazine derived from the need to defend democracy from the encroachments of the extreme right. *Searchlight* combined detailed information on the activities and histories of the extreme right groups with coverage of fascist violence and race related stories from mainstream and local press.

Though the network of local groups developed and the need to combat the growth of neo-fascist organizations was more widely accepted as the Nazi backgrounds of the NF leadership were gradually revealed, anti-fascist organizing remained locally-oriented and essentially small scale. A move towards anti-racist rather than anti-fascist politics was initiated by the conflict between blacks and the police which grew steadily after 1973 and culminated in the 'Long Hot Summer' of 1976 when London's young blacks defeated the Metropolitan Police at the Notting Hill Carnival and major confrontations with the police took place in Southall and in Birmingham. The neo-fascists had organized a 'March Against Mugging' in September 1975 under the slogan 'Stop The Muggers. 80% of muggers are black. 85% of victims are white'. This was significant not simply for its open defiance of the laws on incitement to racial hatred and the new tactic of provocative marches through black areas but for the convergence it represented between the official, respectable politics of race signalled by the authoritative official crime statistics and the street level appeal of the neo-fascist groups who had seized the issue of black crime and begun to refine it into a populist weapon which could prove the wisdom of their distinctive solution to Britain's race problems – repatriation.

The process in which anti-fascist and anti-racist activism became a movement rather than an aggregate of uneven and disparate local groups significantly had its origins outside the realm of politics. It relied for its development on networks of culture and communication in which the voice of the left was scarcely discernible and it drew its momentum from the informal and organic relationship between black and white youth which sprang up in the shadow of 1970s youth culture.

Rock Against Racism (RAR) was formed by a small group of activists in or around the Socialist Workers' Party (SWP) in August 1976. Its founders wrote to the music press inviting support for an anti-racist stance in answer to the racist pronouncements of rock stars like Eric Clapton,[1] who had expressed his admiration for Enoch Powell on several occasions, and David Bowie,[2] who had not only said that Britain was in need of a right-wing dictatorship but declared Hitler to be 'the first superstar'. The image of Bowie beside Hitler and Powell was to recur in RAR's visuals. The SWP had made anti-fascist organizing a major priority during the summer of 1976 and the original RAR letter was heavily derivative of their analysis and political style. It called for black and white to unite and fight along the fundamental lines of class. However, it deviated sharply from this traditional leftism in its insistence on the autonomous value of youth cultures and on the radical potential of 'rock' and its offshoots. This position seems to have been part of a wider argument about the value of populist struggle. 'Rock was and still can be a real progressive culture, not a packaged mail-order stick on nightmare of mediocre garbage. Keep the faith, black and white unite and fight'.[3] Following this intervention, the RAR group produced the first issue of its fanzine *Temporary Hoarding* for the 1977 Mayday celebrations at the Roundhouse in London (Huddle, 1978). The appearance of RAR coincided precisely with the growth of punk and the two developments were very closely intertwined, with punk supplying an oppositional language through which RAR anti-racism could speak a truly populist politics. The first issue of *Temporary Hoarding* made this relationship explicit and asserted the fundamental commitment to music which characterized the early RAR output. 'We want Rebel music, Street music. Music that breaks down peoples' fear of one another. Crisis music. Now music. Music that knows who the real enemy is. Rock against Racism. Love Music Hate Racism.' This kind of appeal was later to be expressed in slogans which made an even more overt plea for a non-sectarian transcendance of the various subcultural styles and identities and asserted a vision of the musics and the styles they had created in a pluralist coalition: 'Reggae Soul Rock and Roll Jazz-Funk and Punk Our music' read RAR's poster/broadsheet. The first issue coupled practical advice for the organizers of RAR gigs with some powerful photomontages and a short, didactic article 'What is racism?' by David Widgery. He coupled an overview of the development of racism in Britain's crisis with an important political argument which showed that from the start RAR was fighting for its corner in an anti-fascist/anti-racist movement which was reluctant to face the novelty of the forms in which racism was expressing itself.

The definition of racism proposed by Widgery and expanded in RAR's practice over the next three years stressed that racism linked the activity of the neo-fascists directly to the actions of state agencies, particularly the courts, police and immigration authorities.

> The problem is not just the new fascists from the old slime, a master race whose idea of heroism is ambushing single blacks in darkened streets. These private attacks whose intention, to cow and brutalise, won't work if the community they seek to terrorise instead organises itself. But when the state backs up racialism it's different. Outwardly respectable but inside fired with the same mentality and the same fears, the bigger danger is the racist magistrates with the cold sneering authority, the immigration men who mock an Asian mother as she gives birth to a dead child on their office floor, policemen for whom answering back is a crime and every black kid with pride is a challenge.

The strategic consequences of this position can be spelled out. Racism was there to be smashed, and the activity involved in smashing it was neatly counterposed to the passivity of sitting back and watching it unfold. The central problem perceived by this approach was the absence of adequate organization. The new structure which RAR was creating would fill the gap. Just as *Sniffin' Glue*, the punk fanzine, included a couple of chord diagrams and then told its readers 'now go and form a band', *Temporary Hoarding* included a blueprint for doing RAR's political work. It would be implemented with the guidance and assistance of experienced and sympathetic SWP members and supporters. Yet the defeat of racism was not to be accomplished in the name of youth or even of a common class position though both were implied. The hatred of racism and its organic counterpart – the love of music – were enough to hold together a dynamic anti-racist movement of young people. RAR's audience, the anti-racist crowd, was conceived not only as consumers of the various youth cultures and styles but as a powerful force for change which, in its diversity, created something more than the simple sum of its constitutive elements.

This anti-racism drew attention to the complex race politics of all white pop music and grasped the importance of the black origins of even the whitest rock as a political contradiction for those who were moving towards racist consciousness and explanations of the crisis. The third issue of *Temporary Hoarding*, published to coincide with the 1977 Notting Hill Carnival, contained an obituary for Elvis which, though seemingly at odds with the punk orientation of the rest of the magazine, made these very points:

> What Presley did in music was stunning. Everyone down in Memphis – which was the heart of the new South – 50% black population – stayed on their own side of the tracks or across the airwaves. Presley took the two and hurled them together. Black soul, hillbilly insistence. His fusion changed everything. It accelerated the Civil Rights movement. It jerked a dead generation alive. It changed the future. Sinatra symbolised a generation, Presley created one.[4] [. . .]

If the language and symbols of black culture provided the melody and harmony from which RAR would improvise its two-tone tunes, the key of its performances and the register of the movement was influenced by the general political mood of the period. Novel combinations of ethnicity, 'race' and national consciousness had emerged in popular celebrations of the Royal Silver Jubilee. This brought festivities – street parties, school holidays – and an explosion of monarchist memorabilia which pushed the icons and symbols of a royalist and patriotic definition of Britishness and the British nation to the fore.

The explosion of popular nationalism provided the punks with images of Britishness from which they could disassociate themselves and against which they could define their own, alternative definitions of the nation: past, present and future. No less than the upsurge of neo-fascist activity in the 1976–7 period, the Royal Jubilee formed the immediate context in which the relationship between racism and nationalism could be revealed and new forms of anti-racism created which were equally opposed to both [. . .]

Anti-Nazi or against racism?

The fourth issue of *Temporary Hoarding* came out in late 1977. The Anti-Nazi League (ANL) was launched on 10 November that year. It was to change and re-direct RAR's politics and orientation. The League was launched as a broad initiative, drawing together sponsors from right across the spectrum of radical politics with a variety of show business personalities, academics, writers and sports people. The League's founding statement drew attention to the electoral threat posed by the NF and their associates. The danger they represented was once again conveyed by reference to the Nazism of Hitler.

> Like Hitler with the Jews, the British Nazis seek to make scapegoats of black people. They exploit the real problems of unemployment, bad housing, cuts in education and in social and welfare services. . . . In these months before

the General Election the Nazis will seize every opportunity to spread their propaganda. During the election itself, National Front candidates might receive equal TV and radio time to the major parties. The British electorate will be exposed to Nazi propaganda on an unprecedented scale.

The League's sponsors sought to 'organize on the widest possible scale' and appealed to 'all those who oppose the growth of the Nazis in Britain [to unite] irrespective of other political differences'. As the League's name suggests, its aims were simpler and more straightforward than RAR's heterogeneous concerns. It was a single-issue campaign modelled on the Campaign for Nuclear Disarmament (CND) and centred on electoral politics whereas RAR's critique of Labour had fused with punk's anarchic and cynical analysis of parliamentarism [. . .]

The attempt to impose the elimination of Nazism as a priority on the diverse and complex political consciousness crystallized by RAR was a miscalculation. The narrow definition of the problem of 'race' – as a product of fascism – matched by a rapid broadening of the campaign against it drew on RAR's momentum, punk and the residues of anti-Jubilee sentiment. However, this shift imposed a shorter life and more limited aims on the movement. The goals of anti-racism were being redefined. The Rasta-inspired pursuit of 'Equal rights and Justice' was being foresaken, in the ANL if not RAR. It was replaced by the more modest aim of isolating and eliminating the fascist parties at the polls. The exposure of fascist leaders as Nazis was rapidly taken over into Fleet Street, broadening support still further and increasing popular hostility to those who would threaten democracy, but the exclusive identification of racism with Nazis was to create problems for anti-racism in the future [. . .]

The League emphasized the Nazi character of neo-fascist and racist politics to the exclusion of every other consideration. This may have led to the electoral defeat of the NF, British Movement and their allies but this was achieved ironically by reviving the very elements of nationalism and xenophobia which had seen Britannia through the darkest hours of the Second World War. This patriotism, temporarily articulated to the anti Nazi cause, was an unstable foundation. It could begin to detach itself from the anti-fascist forces as soon as the NF and the other similar groups began to shrug off accusations of Nazism and started to present themselves credibly as nothing more than concerned British patriots [. . .]

The first phase of the ANL mobilization drew to a close with the Conservative election victory of 1979 [. . .] The incoming Conservative administration had played the race card as part of its own populist electoral strategy. This altered the configurations of racial politics, further de-emphasizing the role of the neo-fascist parties. Anti-racism therefore acquired a party political connotation. The League's single issue orientation became harder to sustain and looked out of place when the Prime Minister elect made remarks about British people 'feeling rather swamped'. Destroyed at the polls, the neo-fascist groups adopted a lower profile, stepped up their work with youth using many of RAR's ideas and adopted what they called a strategy of tension which placed a greater stress on physical intimidation and harassment of blacks. As part of a belated answer to this, unsuccessful attempts were made to revive the League during the spring of 1981.[5]

Municipal anti-racism

The abortive attempt to revive the League preceded the first outbreak of street protests in Brixton by only a few wccks. It is to the after-effects of these events that we now turn. The riots of 1981 cannot be examined in detail here, but they are important to the history of anti-racism in Britain because they forced attention away from the marginal antics of the neo-fascists. The riots reasserted a definition of racism as something intrinsic to the political processes of Britain in crisis. Political debate about what anti-racism might be shifted and settled briefly on the systematic discrimination and disadvantage as well as the ruthless and coercive forms of policing to which the black areas where protest erupted had been subjected.

The subsequent racialization of the riots, which were labelled as black events expressive of the disorderly cultural and political traditions of their un-British protagonists, could provide raw material for an additional study of the languages of racial politics in contemporary Britain. The official explanation of the events was presented in the Scarman Report, and used the particular experience of Brixton to illuminate the national dimensions of the disorders, even where this was inappropriate. Less than a third of those arrested during the disorders had been 'of an ethnic appearance other than white'[6] yet the issue of 'race' dominated the popular memory of the events and cast the typical rioter as an unemployed, young Afro-Caribbean male living in an inner-city neighbourhood (Fielding and Southgate, 1982).

The extent to which these patterns of disorder actually grew out of the distinct experience of inner-city blacks is not important for the moment. Their capacity to represent the race problem being experienced by Britain as a whole is more important. The problem acquired substance in the account of black pathology which was given an official imprimatur by Scarman's report and 'race' duly emerged as a primary causal factor in his narrative of the riots. The Labour administrations elected in the metropolitan counties during the spring of 1981 were quick to institute a range of special agencies and programmes of work charged with the task of addressing the ethnic minority needs to which the burning and looting had given a supposedly inarticulate expression.

Scarman's clumsy denial that 'institutionalized racism' existed in Britain, however plausible within his own definitions, fuelled the anti-racist fervour of his new critics. They not only challenged his view but argued that the riots were proof that racism was not only endemic but a potent, corrosive force in society.

The initial strategy of the new Labour local authorities emphasized the need for them to put their own houses in order as a precondition for the credibility of broader campaigning around anti-racist objectives. This 'internal' struggle to transform or at least adapt local authorities required a distinct range of tactical manoeuvres tailored to the shape and character of local state bureaucracies. The anti-racist tactics which emerged inside these agencies and institutions have not been easily transferable to the struggle against racism outside their walls, on the streets and in popular politics. The attempt to apply what can be called the institutional/bureaucratic model of anti-racist strategy as if it were a general, universal blueprint rather than a specific plan adapted to the peculiarities of local government, forms the central contradiction in the discussion of municipal anti-racism which follows. However successful these initiatives have been in addressing the issue of black disadvantage inside the institutional structures of local authorities and the voluntary bodies they fund, the overall structure of the bureaucracies, their formal rationality, hierarchical mode of organization and the coercive powers they enjoy as a result of their role as providers of money, all point to the specificities of their anti-racist strategy and indeed to the narrow definitions of anti-racism being pursued [. . .]

Programmes for equality of opportunity for staff within the local authority structures were introduced. The bureaucracies which perpetuated a racial division of labour confining blacks to the lowest levels in the hierarchy came under official scrutiny from a new cadre of professional officers and advisers mandated for the elimination of racism. Committees were set up consistent with the formal structure of the local authorities which could highlight the needs of ethnic minority groups and organizations. Finally, new programmes for the financial support of ethnic minority cultural and political work were introduced. By April 1984 sixteen London boroughs, both Labour and Conservative, had taken at least some steps along this road. The hub of this municipal anti-racism was provided by the Labour Greater London Council (GLC). The leader of that authority, Ken Livingstone, signified the priority attached to the issue of 'race' by assuming the chairpersonship of the newly created Ethnic Minorities Committee himself. In 1982–3, the first year in which the committee had a budget for grants, over 300 applications were received for the annual budget of £850 000. The following year the committee's grants budget had risen to approximately £2.5 million (GLC, 1985).

The motives behind these developments were diverse. Pressure on the authority from specialized community relations agencies coincided with the growth of black political activism inside the Labour Party. The group of blacks, which also organized itself around the demand for a black caucus or section within the party, issued warnings that the electoral allegiance of black populations in urban areas could no longer be taken for granted by Labour. To other analysts who had suggested that the riots represented the formation of an alienated or dissident urban underclass, the growth of specialized anti-racist initiatives was a vehicle for the reincorporation of these marginal elements into the rituals of the political system.

The centrepiece of the GLC's anti-racist strategy was the declaration of London as an 'anti-racist zone' and the announcement that 1984 was to be an anti-racist year in which the struggle against racism would be a continual and primary focus of the council's work. These commitments took the council into the realm of popular politics, and relied on public awareness campaigning marshalled through billboards and press advertisements. Early in 1984 the Ethnic Minorities Committee approved an initial budget of £310000 for this purpose. Later in the year a further £552000 was approved in principle for an extension of the campaign until March 1985 (GLC, 1984).

Local counterparts to this strategy were supplied by borough councils which engaged in a parallel programme of popular anti-racist activity that included the same elements as the GLC along with more concrete popular initiatives such as the renaming of streets and estates to highlight the contribution made by blacks to world history as well as the multi-ethnic composition of neighbourhoods. Lambeth's Rhodesia Road was renamed Zimbabwe Road, and so on.[7]

It was, however, the GLC's billboard advertisements which formed the core of this campaign. The first posters produced in the campaign occupied large roadside hoardings and featured stark anti-racist slogans and exhortations against a plain white background. Typical of these was the following: 'Nearly a million Londoners are getting a raw deal – simply because the other 6 million let it happen. Let's kick racism out of town.' Another poster bearing the question 'Where would Mrs Thatcher have got to if she had been black?' was also distributed at this stage. No images were featured on these first posters and their textual form invited written comment. The question about Mrs Thatcher was answered by one graffito with the words, 'To the front of the housing queue'. This answer encapsulates a deeper problem which lay in the strategy that generated these posters, namely the tendency to assume that readers had a general perception of blacks as a disadvantaged group which could be drawn upon as the basis of an anti-racist sensibility. Related to this misplaced assumption was the idea that at this level of political communication, the concept of racism required no elaboration, but would be recognized immediately as a negative and unwholesome political trait. The poster provided no apparent link between the assertion that some Londoners were getting a bad deal and the political solution being suggested: 'Let's kick racism out of town'.

On one site in North London, the word racism was crossed out and the word 'blacks' written in its place. Leaving aside for the moment the issue of whether the effects of racism are felt 'simply because whites let it happen' (a proposition which either makes the struggle against racism appear facile or denies that whites have an active role in perpetuating the institutions and structures which reproduce it) the idea that racism adds up to a 'raw deal' for its victims suggests a fundamentally pluralist understanding of racial conflicts in which the structural aspects of racial politics are minimized. When the problems raised by racism are seen in this way, the solution to them becomes the provision of an unspecified 'better deal'. This can be seen counterproductively as a form of special treatment. Furthermore, by the manner in which the poster separates the discussion of interaction between people from the injunction 'Let's kick racism out of town' it creates a view of racism as an autonomous ideological force, readily extricable from other dimensions of social life. Who will do this kicking out? Where will those people or ideas thus kicked relocate themselves? The choice of the verb 'kick' raises obvious additional problems in that its connotations of physical brutality may not be wholly compatible with the task of winning broad popular support for the struggle against racism, particularly where blacks are already seen as a volatile and violent group. The stress on numbers of blacks and whites conveyed by the poster suggested that these numbers were, in themselves, significant when presumably an anti-racist position would be the same whether the number of oppressed blacks in London was 500000 or 50000 [. . .]

The problems of definition and strategy which arise from this brief discussion of the GLC anti-racist posters can be pursued further elsewhere in the council's anti-racist output. At every stage of the anti-racist campaign and the anti-racist year programme the council's underlying political and philosophical positions were spelled out in pamphlets and other supporting documents. For example, after the council ran a series of advertisements in national newspapers bearing the question, 'What is this thing called racism?'[8] readers were invited to write in to the Ethnic Minorities Unit for a booklet which would tell them the answer and suggest what might be done about it. The text of the ads continued:

> You may hear a lot about it [racism]. But you may not understand how it affects you and your life in London. So, send for our booklet 'What Can I Do To Challenge Racism?' It's surprising, it's alarming and helpful. And it's Free.

The sixteen-page booklet combined general definitions of racism and anti-racism with what was presented as practical advice as to what could be done about its particular manifestations of racism in discrete areas of social life – the church, employment, the arts, media, education, housing, the health service and policing. The first page asserts the political importance of racism and argues that it is a ubiquitous presence. This was one of the recurrent themes in GLC statements on 'race': 'Racism directly affects us all. We are either the victims or the perpetrators.' The formula which reduces the complexity of racism to these two positions seems to argue against the possibility of anti-racism at all. Where does anti-racism come from? How is it possible to cease being a perpetrator, and cease being a victim? Is there any traffic between groups? If so, how does it operate? The booklet does not tell us. Following on from this, it provides a definition of racism which presumably guided the GLC's own practice and anti-racist strategy.

> Racism is normally defined as prejudice plus power where prejudice is an unfavourable opinion or feeling formed beforehand or without knowledge, thought or reason, often unconsciously and on the grounds of race, colour, nationality, ethnic or national origins. Power is the ability to make things happen or prevent things from happening. Thus racism is having the power to put into effect one's prejudice to the detriment of particular racial groups.

Several critical points can be made about this definition. It appears to endorse the idea that racial groups are real in the sense of being fixed and exclusive. Race is presented as preceding racism and having the same status as 'national origins'. Race is differentiated from the question of colour (phenotype) but what it is remains unspecified. It is presented as an unproblematic commonsense category. Its existence can be taken for granted and the political problems which attend it are reduced to the issue of prejudice. This in turn ties the definition to observable human action denying implicitly the salience of structural and ideological factors which cannot be grasped through the concept of prejudice and its consequent behavioural focus. As an adjunct to this, power is seen as a possession rather than a relationship in the classic manner of the 'zero-sum game'. The basis on which this view of power is maintained is revealed once the discussion turns in the direction of strategy. 'In order to eliminate racism, there has to be a twin challenge aimed at the institution where power is located and at people's behaviour which is too often conditioned by racially prejudiced attitudes.' This is less of a definition than a justification for the GLC's own strategy which combined, as we have noted, an internal programme of equal opportunities policy with a public awareness campaign. One moment power is a property of individual relationships which involve prejudice between different races, the next it is located in institutions which have no discernable relationship to individual behaviour. How these two distinct objects of the GLC strategy relate to each other is not explained even though it is inferred that their relationship is functionally important in the reproduction of racism.

To its credit that booklet does, by comparison with the posters, emphasize that people can act against racism in all its diverse forms. Its definitional page ends with a prescription of how they can act and of the manner in which an anti-racist commitment comes into being: 'by being deeply aware of all forms of oppression and by taking action personally and collectively to end all oppression'. This vague, semi-religious language conveys a complete inability to locate what is specific to racial oppression and therefore to anti-racism.

Rather than tie the anti-racist project to a distinct and recognizable range of themes and political priorities as RAR had done (nationalism, fascism, policing, racial violence) this municipal anti-racism allows the concept of racism to ascend to rarified heights where, like a lost balloon, it becomes impossible to retrieve. This induces a strategic paralysis which is further encouraged by the allocation of a pre-eminent if not monopolistic role in the defeat of racism to the council's own agencies and activities. The council becomes the primary site of anti-racist struggle whether the racist object being kicked out of town is made up of the racist institutions which the council manages or the racist opinions of the public which only the council is equipped to challenge. The general task of advancing anti-racism is thereby collapsed into the specific strategic priorities of the GLC, a model which regardless of its in-house effectiveness, is not universally applicable to anti-racist politics in non-institutional settings but which is none the less offered up as a general blueprint. [. . .]

Towards a new anti-racism

Having explored contrasting definitions of anti-racist politics and drawn attention to some of their respective strengths and shortcomings, it is possible to identify some pointers towards what might be the basis of a more adequate conceptualization. Without adopting a programmatic tone or intent, I will now summarize what I think these might be.

The contradiction between understandings of racism based on the need to combat neo-fascism and those which have emphasized anti-racism of a more diffuse nature focused on state agencies and popular politics remains at the heart of racial politics today. We have seen that RAR and the ANL diverged around this point, setting different priorities for their work as a result. In the above discussion of their achievements I have tried to suggest why the second, primarily anti-racist rather than anti-fascist, orientation provided the more appropriate route [. . .]

The experience of the GLC campaigns examined above suggests that the pursuit of a general theory of anti-racist politics may itself be a misplaced and fruitless activity. Anti-racism will be deformed and discredited where it tries too rapidly to generalize a tactical or strategic orientation which has developed out of specific determinate conditions. Equal opportunities policies, for example, may be a necessary element in the formation of anti-racist initiatives inside the kind of bureaucratic agency in which an overall policy can be introduced and used as a baseline for political reform. However, these policies are not a sufficient precondition for the emergence of a substantive anti-racism in organizations of this type. The methods and strategy which they promote may be completely inappropriate in organizations which enjoy a less centralized or less rational structure. The abandonment of a general theory of anti-racist practice also requires the sacrifice of crude definitions of racism in the prejudice plus power formula quoted earlier. This may fit well into the rational bureaucratic conception of anti-racist politics but it is unable to account for expressions of racial classification and structuration which are not behavioural or attitudinal or which rely on a populist response from the white subjects they bring into being.

Races are political collectivities not ahistorical essences. 'Race' is, after all, not the property of powerful, prejudiced individuals but an effect of complex relationships between dominant and subordinate social groups. If whites have shared the same job centres, schools, police cells, parties and streets with blacks in what sense can we speak of them having additional power? The very complexity of these relations and the extent of difference which exists between the meanings and structures attached to 'race' in different social formations are additional factors which undermine the possibility of a general theory of race relations and the sociologically inspired attempt to elevate that concept into an analytical rather than merely descriptive term. Even within a single social formation at a particular phase of its development racism will not be an unbroken continuous presence. It will be unevenly developed. Even where it is diffuse it will never be uniform. The different forces which form 'races' in concrete political antagonisms will operate at differing tempos and in contrasting ways according to immediate circumstances. Racial attacks may be higher in one area than the next. The manner in which racist sentiment is expressed may vary, for example, according to the extent and character of black settlement; in relation to the composition of a black community, its position in the contradiction between capital and labour, its gender, age structure or even its ability to communicate with the dominant group and the degree of cultural overlap which exists between white and black.

If, as has been suggested, the 'race' issue has been seen from the vantage point of sympathetic liberalism as a matter of policy rather than politics (Hall, 1978), the tasks of a more sustained and thorough-going anti-racism must include an attempt to show how administration of institutional reforms (policy) can be articulated to a sound grasp of extra-institutional politics.

The development of anti-racist policy around which these reforms can cohere should be a cautious exercise. If they are to be credible outside the institutional settings in which they were dreamed up, anti-racist policies must not have the effect of appearing to reduce the complexity of black life to an effect of racism. This is a real danger when racism is presented sweeping all before it and the power relations involved are caricatured as an eternal tussle between victims and perpetrators. I have already argued in the introduction to this book that the role of victim is articulated into contemporary British racism. What anti-racism must do if it expects to be taken seriously by the black settlers in whose name it claims to act is to transcend this sociologism and move towards the longer-term aims of demonstrating the historical dimensions of 'race' and bringing blacks fully into historicity (Touraine, 1977), as actors capable of making complex choices in the furtherance of their own liberation. Finally anti-racism must negotiate, as RAR did, the political priorities which emanate from the defensive struggles and negotiations of racially subordinate groups. No meaningful anti-racism can ignore the content of these conflicts for it constitutes the raw material used to establish the meaning and limits of 'race'. These struggles may be both political and cultural and the manner in which these instances combine may result in new kinds of political practice which defy Eurocentric categorization.

Notes

1   *Melody Maker*, 9 December 1978.
2   *Evening News*, 29 December 1977.
3   *Sounds*, 28 August 1976.
4   Michael Gray, 'Elvis', *Temporary Hoarding*, No. 3, 1977.
5   *New Musical Express*, 7 March 1981.
6   Home Office Statistical Bulletin, 20/82, 13 October 1982.
7   *Daily Mail*, 1 July 1985.
8   1 April 1985.

References

ABDUL-MALIK, M. (1968) *From Michael de Freitas to Michael X*, London, Sphere.

CLUTTERBUCK, R. (1978) *Britain in Agony: the Growth of Political Violence*, Harmondsworth, Penguin.

FIELDING, N. (1981) *The National Front*, London, Routledge and Kegan Paul.

GLEAN, M. (1973) 'Whatever happened to CARD?' *Race Today*, January.

GLC (1984) *Ethnic Minorities and the abolition of the GLC*, London, Ethnic Minorities Movement.

GLC (1985) *Anti-racist programme 1984: review and assessment*, unpublished.

HALL, S. (1978) 'Race and moral panics in post war Britain', in *Five Views of Multi-racial Britain*, London, Campaign for Racial Equality.

HIRO, D. (1971) *Black British, White British*, London, Eyre and Spottiswoode.

NICHOLSON, B. (1974) *Racialism, Fascism and the Trade Unions*, London, Transport and General Workers Union.

SCARMAN, LORD JUSTICE (1975) *The Red Lion Square Disorders of 15 June 1974*, Cmnd 5919, London, HMSO.

SIVANANDAN, A. (1982) *A Different Hunger*, London, Pluto Press.

TOURAINE, A. (1977) *The Self-production of Society*, London, University of Chicago Press.

Section IV   Gender relations

Introduction

One of the key social transformations of post-war Britain has been the large-scale entry of women into capitalist wage relations. For many women in Britain in the 1980s, the experience of waged work is no longer a temporary one but a permanent part of their lives, albeit broken for a few years in their twenties or early thirties. Despite the numerical rise in labour force participation rates, women remain on the whole concentrated in particular areas of the labour market. They are on average in less skilled and lower paid jobs than the majority of men, have less security and fewer promotion prospects. These inequalities do not appear to be reducing. Indeed the differential between men's and women's average wages widened again in the 1980s after a period of reduction in the mid-1970s.

In other areas of social life, it is even more questionable whether gender relations and the relative positions and responsibilities of women and men have changed in recent decades. Women's responsibility for domestic work, child care and the care of other dependants remains untouched. Indeed, cut-backs in state provision in the 1980s have tended to increase women's responsibilities. Women's ownership of wealth and income and their access to goods and services, such as housing, have not fundamentally changed in the post-war period, although younger women are increasingly gaining educational credentials and narrowing differentials in educational achievement. The tax and social security systems continue to be based on assumptions of women's economic dependence on men. There have, however, been changes in legislation (the Equal Pay Act 1975; the Sex Discrimination Act 1975 and the Equal Pay for Equal Value Work Amendment 1985) that despite limited effects have raised awareness of women's disadvantaged position and made continued discrimination in several areas illegal. In addition, the rebirth of the Women's Movement in the late 1960s has affected the attitudes and lives of many women.

If material changes in gender relations and women's subordination have been relatively insignificant, the way in which these structures of gender inequalities are theorized has changed fundamentally in the last decade. Economic restructuring and women's entry into waged labour has transformed the way in which social scientists think about gender. Until the mid-1970s, issues concerning gender tended to be subsumed under the heading of the 'sociology of the family'. In studies of the workplace, the gender of workers was seldom seen as significant, partly because most of the studies dealt only with male workers. The ways in which particular occupations or shop-floor cultures fostered a particular conception of masculinity and appropriate role behaviour tended to be taken for granted. The links between waged labour and home life, between the public and private spheres were seldom theorized or empirically examined, except perhaps in that genre of community studies that dealt with social and community life in single industry towns. Typically the heavy and often dangerous work of men led to a shared male camaraderie and clearly defined gender divisions that extended beyond work into social relations at home and in the community.

The entry of women into the labour market, however, forced a re-examination of the empirical and theoretical validity of examining the worlds of waged work and the family in isolation. For women's position in waged labour is inextricably bound up with the rest of their lives. In the absence of other changes, women workers' domestic responsibilities have to be accommodated and renegotiated to fit into the routines of the factory floor or the office. The expansion of part-time employment in recent years has been a key part of economic restructuring, reflecting the continuing acceptance of the idea that domestic tasks are women's alone. Waged work has changed to facilitate the entry of women into the 'public' sphere, rather than changes occurring in the nature of domestic work or state provision for dependants being expanded. Feminist scholars, impatient with conventional analyses, have challenged commonplace distinctions between productive and unproductive work, between waged and unwaged labour and between the public and the private. They have argued that gender relations – conventional assumptions about the nature of femininity, for example, or the structure of male power and control over women – must be an integral part of the analysis of changing social divisions in Britain. In the area of waged work, concepts of skill, the nature of job responsibilities, and the impact of restructuring on the nature of the labour process have all been subjected to a rigorous critique. By taking gender into account, the analysis of these changes is altered, and strengthened. The extracts in Section IV illustrate how this may be done.

In Chapter 9, Juliet Webster develops an argument about the gendered nature of skills, and subjects Braverman's thesis of deskilling to an empirically-based critique. She shows in a detailed investigation of the secretarial labour process how the introduction of word-processors has both deskilled and reskilled particular types of work.

Webster is a feminist, but in her chapter she leaves implicit her theoretical assumptions about the causes of women's oppression. By example, she shows that an understanding of the structure of gender relations strengthens analyses of changes in the labour market. She refers to male power over women and to the social relations between the sexes in the office within capitalist organizations. She does not, however, develop an argument about how patriarchal gender relations and capitalist social relations are related to each other. This is taken up in the first of the three extracts in Chapter 10 from a book by Sallie Westwood.

Sallie Westwood's book is a study of gender relations on the shop-floor in an East Midlands clothing firm. The author spent almost a year observing the labour process and social relations within the StitchCo factory, and she includes a wealth of fascinating detail about the ritual of everyday life. She also developed at some length her own theoretical position in the debate about the relationship between capitalism and patriarchy as social structures and about the interconnections between class position, race and gender of these hosiery workers in determining the lives they lead and their restricted opportunities.

The first of the three extracts included in Chapter 10 focuses on the relationship between capitalism and patriarchy. Westwood's own position is that they are two separate, but interdependent, systems, which together structure women's lives in contemporary Britain. The two are not easily divided – patriarchal relations are created and reproduced in the workplace as well as in the home. And capitalism is not a gender-blind system. Gender as well as class divisions are a fundamental part of capitalist development.

Britain is also a racist society. Discrimination against black workers is an institutional part of the operation of the labour market, as well as being enshrined in the culture and practices of society at large (see Section III). Many of the workers in StitchCo were black women and Westwood shows how race and gender both divide and unite the women workers.

The second of the three extracts considers everyday social relations on the factory floor. One of the strengths of Westwood's book is that it is not at all pessimistic, despite dealing with inequality, oppression and subordination. The women have developed a set of rituals and practices that celebrate their position as women and subvert the authority of the factory management, as well as enabling them to cope with the daily grind of monotonous work. Significant events in the women's lives such as birthdays, but particularly engagements and weddings, are used to structure and punctuate the industrial routine. Women's role in reproduction is used as a form of resistance to the organization of production. But it is a double-edged sword. The particular view of womanhood and femininity that is celebrated reinforces women's subordination.

Westwood's book is about strength and resistance, about sisterhood as well as a realistic assessment of the limited prospects that face most working-class women in Britain today. The contradictions are clear and the book evokes rage and delight in equal proportions.

In the final extract, Westwood returns to the question of the inter-relationship of class, gender and race. Feminist scholarship has been in the lead in the development of more theoretically-sophisticated studies of the relationship between these key social divisions in contemporary Britain. Although, as Westwood emphasizes, and the earlier extract from Ward illustrates, these are not only academic questions. Working against racism and sexism means entering the political arena too.

9 Word-processing and the secretarial labour process

Juliet Webster

Theoretical background

Social concern with the effects of technological change is by no means new. The topic first became a matter of public debate during the Industrial Revolution, when new machinery and working methods were the subject of both eulogy and criticism, and were simultaneously held responsible for all human progress and all social evil. Today, in the face of what has been described as 'the most remarkable technology ever to confront mankind' (Forester, 1980, p. xiii), and which is regarded in some quarters as constituting another industrial revolution, reactions to the latest micro-electronic technology are no less ambivalent [. . .]

New technology in the office

In the office, new technology has been seen as the means by which capital reorganizes the labour process along the same lines as factory work, doing away with managerial control based solely on patriarchy and replacing it by watertight, machine-based forms of control (Downing, 1981). Deskilling, the elimination of mental labour, and complete loss of control by the worker over the labour process, in other words, the 'proletarianization' of office workers as a result of the application of the new technology, is forecast:

> Word processing and auxiliary office equipment are intended to increase productivity by an average of 100% by radically changing the relation between capital and labour due to the conscious application of science and technology to office work. Capital is attempting to gain greater control over the relationship between labour and the means of production leading to *de-skilling and the subsequent cheapening of labour*. (Barker and Downing, 1980, p. 90; my emphasis)

The word-processing machine enables the techniques of the assembly line to be introduced into the office (Harman, 1979, p. 10).

The research evidence

What validity do such arguments have? In my research I set out to re-examine the elements of the secretarial labour process (using the category 'secretarial' in its loosest sense because I looked at typing work as well) to try to ascertain how far word-processing (WP) has the impact that is presumed. I therefore looked for certain features or elements, drawn from concepts utilized in labour process theory. I wanted to find out whether word-processing had brought about fragmentation of tasks, deskilling, the separation of conception from execution, intensification of work, physical and social isolation and tight managerial control of the labour process coupled with a loss of control by the secretarial worker. I therefore conducted eight case studies of organizations in Bradford, representing a cross-section of employers: a small structural engineering firm, a university department, a mail order catalogue company, a firm of solicitors, a large knitting yarn manufacturer, a replacement engine parts supplier, a division of the local council, and the headquarters of a building society. The studies covered a range of different WP installations – large and small, 'shared logic' and 'stand alone' as well as looking at the jobs of private secretaries, typists working in small groups and those in large typing pools. I interviewed over 100 office workers and their managerial superiors – the latter, about their objectives in implementing WP, and the former about their perceptions of changes in the organization of work and their responses to change; observations of the women at work provided more detailed information on the characteristics of their jobs and their working patterns.

What principally emerged from my work at the outset was the essential difference between the job content of secretaries and of typists – although the two obviously have features in common. On the basis of the largely theoretical evidence advanced so far, it would seem that WP would have the effect of reducing both jobs to one and the same level. Counter Information Services (CIS), for example, have pronounced that

> From being a member of a social office, responsible for all stages of document preparation bar its organisation, *office workers* become little more than skilled machine minders. And those skills that the typist once needed are lessened. (CIS, 1979, p. 12; my emphasis)

My findings suggest, however, that there is no uniform effect attributable to WP. Therefore, when dealing with jobs that are very differently structured, one cannot make blanket formulations about its impact on skill levels, for example, without examining the skills in question and differentiating between those present or absent in different jobs [. . .]

The job of secretary

Generalizing, one can say that secretarial work is characterized by a relative variety of tasks, both mechanical (for example, typing, shorthand, filing) and social (such as dealing with visitors and calls, performing general administrative duties, and performing that class of duties whose function is to 'service' the boss in a variety of ways and which has led certain writers to refer to secretarial work as being that of an 'office wife' (Benet, 1972; Barker and Downing, 1980) – anticipating their bosses' every need, shielding them from unwelcome callers and providing psychological and emotional support). This variety of tasks, coupled with the fact that supervision tends to be extremely loose, affords the secretary a comparatively high degree of discretion over her working day. Generally, she (and virtually all secretaries *are* female in Britain) organizes her own work around what she considers to be the most 'efficient' lines (Vinnicombe, 1980, p. 25). Since the work often involves responding to matters as they arise, much of it is neither standard nor repetitive. Some judgement and initiative is required. Even the purely manual typing tasks are usually far from standard, often quite involved and generally call for an ability to conceptualize how the completed document ought to look, before beginning to lay it out on paper. In the case of particularly complicated work, there is some satisfaction to be gained from producing neat, well set out copy. Generally the secretary paces her typing according to her own judgement of the time she has available to spend on it and it is not unusual for secretaries to 'batch' their work themselves, dealing with all filing, all typing, all photocopying and so on, in one go. The job usually also involves a relatively high degree of social contact – it demands communication with other workers – and physical mobility about the office.

The job of typist

The labour process of the typist possesses few of these qualities. It is not characterized by the same variety of tasks as secretarial work; as its title suggests, it is concerned purely with the reproduction of text in typewritten form, the only change being from one kind or format of document to another. A typist simply sits and types all day, either from manuscript copy or from dictation on audio machine. Many of the typists I spoke to in the course of my research were therefore able to tell me exactly what each working day would consist of, it being dominated by the routine of performing this one particular task. Within this routine there is consequently little or no discretion open to the typist as to how to organize her working day, which is governed by the division of labour in the entire office. The nature of the documents she types may well demand the exercise of all the manual skills she will have learnt at college, such as layout, tabulation and accuracy with speed, but all too often the work a typist does on the typewriter is the more mundane, simplified or standardized work that bypasses the secretarial staff. Often a large pile of typing (or audio-cassettes) are simply placed before her and she must spend all day working through them. Consequently, the work is intensified and the typist is 'paced' by the repetitive rhythm. One typist remarked: 'You're just like a battery hen, you know, just sitting there typing.'

The existence in many organizations of typing pools, often managed by a typing supervisor, makes typists a physically and socially isolated category of workers. Work is brought to the pool from outside, sorted and allocated by the supervisor or a senior typist, typed, collected from the typist's desk again by the supervisor and put in an out-tray to be collected and distributed through internal mail. Many typists therefore have little or no direct contact with the people whose work they type, whilst being closely monitored by what is effectively a process supervisor, exactly analogous to industrial supervision. There is little need for them to move from their seats and certainly no need for them to leave the office. As a result, typists in pools have no idea who they are working for, recognizing the author only by a set of initials or a disembodied voice. Nor is there any opportunity for them to mix with other staff in the organization, or build any conception of its overall functioning. Their existence in a closed-off unit permits little awareness of where their work comes from, where it goes, or how it fits into the overall labour process. Often even the very limited contact they might have with one another is prevented, either by having to work with earphones on (which makes their work by definition a very solitary business) or by very strict supervision which does not permit talking [. . .]

It is evident that WP has a completely different effect on them, both being governed by the structure of the work in question rather than by the technology. Generalizations about 'the effects of new technology' are potentially misleading, since they focus upon the assumed characteristics of the technology to the exclusion of the features present in the jobs affected. As Arnold *et al.* (1982) have noted:

> The distinction between secretarial and typing work is crucial to analysis of the likely effects of WP in offices . . . female typists – essentially machine operators – have existed as long as the machines themselves. As specialist machine operators, typists can be managed like factory shopfloor workers; this may not be true for secretaries, who perform a range of other duties in addition to typing. (p. 60)

I found little evidence of fragmentation, deskilling and heightened managerial control supposedly brought about by the introduction of new technology in the jobs where these characteristics had not already been long since endemic.

The effect of new technology on the secretaries

The secretaries whom I studied, who now worked with WP, had lost few of the skills and work patterns which made their work comparatively interesting and controllable. In all cases, the WP had been brought into the office quite simply to replace the typewriter, and no reorganization of the labour process had taken place. Therefore, far from being fragmented, their jobs still contained a variety of tasks both on and off the WP. They were in no sense tied to the machine, and still had to attend to the whole gamut of administrative and ancillary secretarial tasks:

> . . . it is not 100% typing; I would say about 50% is typing. The rest is running around, making arrangements, quite a lot of administrative work . . . couldn't really say what takes up most of my time because every day is so different.

The implication of having a variety of tasks was that these secretaries had an overview of the whole of the office labour process, and understood the role and function of each constituent task they performed within it. They were therefore able to take decisions as to how and when to perform tasks based on their knowledge of the office routine and practice and their judgement of how their own working day might develop. For Marilyn, a university professor's secretary, this judgement extended to assuming responsibility for some of her boss's administrative tasks as well as her own. For example, she dealt with some examinations problems in his absence, her very ability to do so deriving from her understanding of all aspects of the work that passed through her office. Similar instances of secretaries deputizing for their bosses were present in solicitors' practices. In fact, in some offices, I found that most routine legal work such as conveyancing is handled, not by a qualified solicitor, but by his 'unqualified' secretary. The lack of the technical division of labour in these secretarial jobs also dictated all the other features of the labour process. Owing to their responsibility for aspects of virtually all work that passes through the office, often for whole tasks as opposed to fragments of them, for all stages of a particular project, there was a consequent diversity of movements and operations, external stimuli and social contact which gave the job variety and interest. Furthermore, work that consists of a variety of activities is harder for management to control and intensify, and consequently such workers are neither 'placed' by a repetitive rhythm of motions nor easy to supervise.

In fact, WP was considered to be of some considerable help by these secretaries. Many of them were vastly overworked and found it hard to cope with the quantity of typing that often came from more than one boss, all of whom invariably wanted their work to be given highest priority. Such competing claims put many secretaries under continuous pressure. They were in no doubt that the speed of working at a WP helped them to cope with a volume of work which before had made them work flat out, often into evenings and weekends (usually unpaid since office workers can rarely claim for overtime). The secretary to a financial director of a small structural engineering company remarked, 'I don't think the processor has changed this job. It has just made it easier, that's all'.

From the employers' point of view, of course, it is likely to mean that a greater volume of work is processed and the unit cost labour is reduced. It was noted earlier that secretarial work is difficult to standardize as long as it contains its various ancillary tasks. Although it has been suggested that WP may bring about a division of secretarial labour into typing jobs and administrative jobs (*Women's Voice Word Processor Pamphlet*, 1979, pp. 10–11), this had not (as yet) occurred in any of the organizations I studied. First, individual managements were often far less aware of the possibilities for rationalization of work than is often assumed. In a knitting yarn manufacturing company, management demonstrated a positive irrationality in its application of WP. It bought one machine as an addition to its four typewriters in a pool, restructured the labour process not at all, and continued to use the typewriters at full output, allowing each typist to use the WP only occasionally for odd tasks. Consequently, the WP stood idle for the majority of the time.

A second explanation for such lack of work rationalization around the new technology may lie in the price of the labour-power and the sexual division of labour. Marglin (1976, p. 23) has suggested that the specialization of tasks was not necessarily technologically superior as a method of organizing production, but simply a device employed by capital to ensure that only it had an overall conception and therefore total control over the production process. Secretarial labour, particularly in the Yorkshire area, is very cheap. One woman interviewed in January 1983 was earning only £40 per week gross, and this was by no means uncharacteristic. Many of the companies I studied paid their typists and secretaries very low wages. Female office labour has generally been cheap precisely because it has been seen as 'women's work' (Leghorn and Parker, 1981). How far this principle applies to secretarial work must be an important consideration. From management's viewpoint, why bother to go to the trouble and expense of embarking on total reorganization and standardization of work if the savings are not potentially very great and managerial control is already assured by traditional methods. In addition, there is a degree to which secretaries' value to their bosses and to the organization is irrationally raised because of the 'conspicuous consumption' value (Veblen, 1964). It is clear that having one's own 'office wife' is one of the perks of a managerial career and few bosses would be willing to trade in this status symbol for increased efficiency, in the unlikely event that rationalization or new technology could guarantee it.

Standard letters or routine typing work are not the norm for the secretary; most documents are one-off jobs so there is little repetition even in the typing part of the job [. . .]

Since many of the secretaries' typing tasks were based and dependent upon their administrative duties, they too could not be easily standardized. Marilyn, for example, regularly received instructions to arrange meetings between professors and then send out notices confirming them. Consequently, areas of discretion as to how to lay out work on the WP remained and she was often still in a position to make use of the manual skills she once used on a typewriter. Secretarial work still involved conceptualizing the finished article and the best way to tackle it, before beginning to type it; some women were also able to use the machine to experiment with different layouts, using their judgement and initiative to decide on the best one, something that is simply not possible on a typewriter without an enormous amount of extra work. Janet described this process:

> I'll set something out and think 'I'll just see what it looks like that way'. It's a very little thing to do on a processor, but to try different things on a typewriter you've got to do it again.

This hardly squares with Harman's claim that:

> The new technology can be so designed as to reduce complex tasks to quite simple tasks, to take away from the operators their old skills, and to enable management to put pressure on for much more work. (1979, p. 10)

The complexity of the tasks depends more on the structure of the work than on the technology, and secretaries have for the most part retained the discretionary side of their skills, a point illustrated by Janet's comment:

> If you've got two ideas you can open one page for that idea and one for another, and at the end you can compare it and *decide which you like the best.* (my emphasis)

It is true that a WP indents, justifies and shuffles text, and removes the need to count spaces when laying out a document. However, many secretaries welcome this; counting spaces is regarded as a 'chore', and not by any means an interesting feature of the work. One woman remarked, 'Things like that never interest me much anyway. You always had to do it but you wouldn't put it down to a thrilling experience!' Yet just as Braverman romanticized craft skills, so commentators on new technology have romanticized this kind of typing skill as affording the secretary 'control' over her machine. As such, it is a very limited form of control. For secretaries there are other, more fundamental, ways of controlling their labour process, allied to taking decisions as to how and in what order and manner to organize their working day. These forms of control were still present in the secretaries' jobs I studied. By the same token, it is the structure of the job which dictates the existence and range of skills employed rather than the machine, which merely alters the manner in which those skills are deployed [. . .]

The effect of new technology on typists

If we turn to the experience of typists working with WPs, we again discover that in fact the labour process has been little altered by the presence of the new technology. As I showed earlier, the work of a typist is indeed in some ways comparable to production line work. It is largely repetitive, routine and fragmented, isolated, often tightly controlled and supervised and affords the typist little discretion or power in determining the quality of her working day. The comparison of a typist with a battery hen is indeed apt, and the typist who made it was one of many who drew similar analogies. In all the interviews, the typists were under no illusions as to what their jobs amounted to. They had a realistic recognition of the limitations of typing work, which they felt had never afforded them much opportunity to use their skills. *Women's Voice*, however, has this to say about WP:

> . . . the typist does not just lose her typing skills to the machines, the job itself becomes fragmented. Tasks such as filing, photocopying, even putting letters into envelopes, are all taken away. Since the word processor can store information the typist need never leave her seat to look something up in the

filing cabinet because it's all there, contained within the memory of her word processor. (*Women's Voice Word Processor Pamphlet*, 1979, p. 14)

Both before and after the introduction of WP, the tasks of the typists I spoke to were limited and standardized, restricted to typing routine documents such as forms, standard letters, labels and envelopes. In the building society typing pool, the division of labour was carried to such an extreme that certain women did only audio typing, others did copy typing, and a third group typed standard letters on magnetic card typewriters. Even the putting of letters into envelopes was split from the typing function and carried out by authors, who also checked over the completed work. By the time the word-processing system was introduced in late 1979, the complaints of boredom from the typists had reached such a pitch that the society's Organization and Methods (O & M) Manager now felt compelled to look at ways of injecting variety into the work. The technical division of labour, albeit highly 'productive', was beginning to yield 'diminishing returns'. His solution, however, was piecemeal, involving job rotation. When WP came in, each typist was to spend a couple of hours a week operating the printers, an activity carried out physically and organizationally separately. This involved feeding the machines with the correct stationery and batching output. This of course merely added a different source of repetition to the job; as West (1982) points out:

> ... rotation between several routine jobs is itself often routinized (printing with WP one day a week say, keyboarding the rest) and such *systems* may well be little different from those on factory production lines. (p. 77; my emphasis)

The contention that WP leads to standard documents being created, where the only task is filling in the variables, was simply not borne out by investigation. Many firms, building societies, mail order firms and large manufacturing companies with routine correspondence in particular, had been using standard letters for years. They were either duplicated on paper, leaving the typist to type the name and address directly onto the paper, or printed through magnetic card typewriters (a precursor of the WP whose 'memory' was on cards rather than discs). Thus, the work had long since been fragmented and routinized, and the mental involvement demanded of the worker was minimal. Little skill is required to type names and addresses into standard letters, nor does the continual copy typing of orders, a frequent task of the motor parts distribution company I studied, require either the layout skills or the discretion that the critics of the new technology suppose. This is perhaps one of the greatest sources of boredom in a job, where the mind must be engaged but not involved. Some factory workers are perhaps better off in this respect, for it is well known that routine manual workers have their minds free to do such things as mental crosswords (Beynon, 1973, p. 117), perfecting what Pollert (1981, p. 131) aptly refers to as 'robotic dexterity' [. . .]

In addition, because the work was structured and routinized, each typist was able to say in advance exactly what each working day would consist of:

> You know exactly what you are going to be doing in the morning, and at a certain time of day. You know you will be getting furthers (a kind of standard letter) in the afternoon, and you'll be doing audio. You know exactly what you are going to be doing, and it is the same thing every day of the week, just the same work all the time.
>
> It is the same thing day in, day out. Nothing really changes except the letters are different, but you are still doing letters and audio typing. It is the same in a factory I suppose – packing, you are still packing things all day every day, aren't you?

Since there is for the typist no choice of tasks other than typing, she is completely unable to structure her working day for herself, or to choose when and how she wants to perform each task. She is simply part of a continuous flow process in which the object is to turn out as much of her constituent pieces of work in as short a time as possible. Unlike secretaries, the typists were not responsible for laying out their own documents, either because the layout was specified by the organization in advance (often in the form of a standard letter), or more usually because the typing work was of the most straightforward kind, the more complicated work being retained by secretarial staff or typing supervisors. In the building society, the choice of WP system that was easy to operate merely reflected this simplicity. The typing pool supervisor admitted this when she said,

> This is a very simple system *for the type of work of the operator*. . . . The thing is that all the time they work on the whole is very very boring. If you got a very intelligent girl she would not tolerate it. (my emphasis)

Few layout skills were therefore required:

> We just do letters; there is no tables to do, except for just setting out statements which are in paragraphs anyway. . . . It is just letters all day.

It has been alleged that WP has deskilled these workers:

> Since the machine can perform all the tasks of a skilled typist, such as indenting, centring, tabulating, justifying margins, etc., all essential components of a basic RSA typing examination, *the typist effectively loses important areas of control*, not only choosing how to set out work, but over her typewriter itself. The typist is in control when she chooses to lay out [a] particular document and guides the machine through its various functions. *Word processing means the typist is now controlled by the machine*. (*Women's Voice Word Processor Pamphlet*, p. 14, my emphasis)

This displays a romanticized notion of a typist's job prior to the introduction of WP, as one which combined technical craft-type skills with control over the labour process and its instruments, which the WP then eliminates. For many typists this has never been a reality. Few typists I studied ever had any significant degree of control over either their work on their machine to lose. When it was suggested to them that WP might have deprived them of skill and control, they seemed amazed that anyone could be naïve enough to imagine that there was ever anything remotely resembling discretion, choice or control in a purely typing job, whether performed on a WP or a typewriter [. . .]

Similarly, the physical and social isolation to which many of them were subject derived, not from the WP automatically performing all ancillary tasks such as filing, and therefore allowing them no movement out of their seats, but from the organization of the job which had already removed these elements by fractionalizing the office labour process and reallocating ancillary tasks elsewhere, coupled often with strict supervision.

Similarly, devotion to audio typing eliminates personal contact with the boss or author and the chance for mobility, as do typing pools. Even queries about the work they were given were often taken up by the supervisor who relayed the question to the author and the answer back to the typist. Consequent upon their isolation, the typists' work appears doubly monotonous. Like manual workers in mechanized jobs, they are prevented from making conversation with their workmates by the noise of the machinery (Friedman, 1955; Beynon, 1973), although in this case it is the sound of audio dictation which demands their senses. In the building society, the typists turned the machinery to their own advantage by listening to music cassettes on their playback machines when copy typing! Whilst this may be seen as an attempt by the typist to exert control over the work environment, it might more accurately be seen as merely a demand for one of the ameliorating aspects of routine, alienating work long established in factories and, as such, an acquiescence in the deskilling process. Employers are not unaware of the productive utility of 'music while you work' and it is perhaps only a matter of time before typists are routinely issued with up-tempo, undemanding cassettes whose potential as instruments of intensification has been researched by the ergonomics department. So typists are appendages to machines not because of the features of the machine itself, but because they are like cogs in a divided labour process, the effectiveness of which is ensured by strict managerial domination. The technology may *appear* to be the main instrument of subordination, but it is the use to which it is put and the organization of work which determines the pace and conditions of work, in clerical as in manual work.

Braverman's (1974) critique of technological determinism is incisive on this point. He argues that because it is not an 'independent participant in human social arrangements', while machinery is neither the 'servant of humanity', nor it is the enemy of mankind; 'it has become fashionable to attribute to machinery the powers over humanity which in fact arise from human social relations' (p. 229). Theories which view technology as 'negative' in its objective structure are, in Braverman's estimation, 'constructed on every level to exonerate capitalism' (ibid.). They can only be upheld by a total neglect of the dynamics and class relations of capitalist society, and border on technological determinism.

Conclusion

In drawing out the contrast between the different types of office work I do not intend to glorify secretarial work. There is plenty of evidence demonstrating that it is riddled with monotonous tasks (Vinnicombe, 1980) and exploitative features, most notably deriving from the presence of patriarchal relations within the office (Downing, 1981). But office work varies, as has been discussed, and is aptly illustrated by a comment from one of the secretaries I spoke to:

> It all depends on the environment that you're in. I'm not sure that I'd like to be in a building society just being set at a word processor churning letters and statements out, just pressing a few keys. I did use to work in a building society and I know what we had to do on a typewriter, so I can imagine what you'd be doing on a word processor . . . I don't think I'd be very keen on just sitting for eight hours a day just having the typewriter spewing out the same letters and things.

The lesson to be drawn from this is that there is a desperate need for empirical investigation of the effects of new technology. Just as Braverman failed to examine the specific requirements of capital in different situations and has therefore been accused of offering an over-simplified conception of the deskilling process (More, 1982), so certain commentators propound an analysis which ignores the particular situations of the different office workers and is in effect ahistorical. It takes no account of the social and historical factors within which new technology is introduced in different instances.

The organizations which I studied showed a massive diversity in both the technology already adopted and in their organizations of work around the new technology. Some firms, such as the building society and mail order firm, already had highly automated, highly structured labour processes. They regarded themselves therefore as already having an organizational system of word-processing. WP machinery merely represented what the building society's O & M Manager referred to as 'an accumulation of what had gone on before'. The advance of technology merely 'offers to management the opportunity to do by wholly mechanical means that which it previously attempted to do by organizational and disciplinary means' (Braverman, 1974, p. 195). Crompton and Jones (1984) note that the rationalization and fragmentation of clerical work long predated the advent of computer technology. Furthermore, WP by no means represents the apotheosis of such rationalization processes. At the mail order firm, the WPs were ironically regarded as obsolescent and correspondence was handled by the firm's powerful mainframe computer, eliminating altogether this part of the typing function. Indeed, office computer systems are likely to be far more threatening to employment levels than to skill levels, because of the great mass of work performed wholly by automation.

The smaller organizations, conversely, showed a still great preponderance of old office equipment and working practices. Despite the advent of the new technology (which was generally regarded as merely a replacement for typewriters), there was no evidence of consequent work restructuring and the traditional boss/secretary relationship persisted. It was clear from the interviews I conducted with management that they regarded the increased productivity enabled by the machinery as constituting sufficient cost saving, without any work rationalization scheme. A similar diversity in work organization and its impact of skill levels is apparent in the other chapters in this book which discuss technological innovation. Littek and Jones and Rose, in particular, show how management style and the dynamics of custom and practice have crucial impacts on how technological potential is accommodated in a given organization.

It is the organization of new technology into a *system*, based upon the technical division of labour, as opposed to the implementation of single mechanisms, that has the crucial impact on the labour process. It is capitalism which imparts to the production process its specific character, not the discrete mechanical components – that is, the mode rather than the means of production [. . .]

References

ARNOLD, E. *et al.* (1982) *Microelectronics and Women's Employment in Britain*, Science Policy Research Unit Occasional Paper, Series 17.

BARKER, J. and DOWNING, H. (1980) 'Word processing and the transformation of the patriarchal relations of control in the office', *Capital and Class*, No. 10, pp. 64–99.

BENET, M. K. (1972) *Secretary: An Enquiry into the Female Ghetto*, London, Sidgwick and Jackson.

BEYNON, H. (1973) *Working for Ford*, London, Allen Lane.

BRAVERMAN, H. (1974) *Labour and Monopoly Capital: The Degradation of Work in the Twentieth Century*, New York, Monthly Review Press.

COUNTER INFORMATION SERVICES (CIS) (1979) *The New Technology*, London, CIS.

CROMPTON, R. and JONES, G. (1984) *White Collar Proletariat: Deskilling and Gender in Clerical Work*, London and Basingstoke, Macmillan.

DOWNING, H. (1981) 'Developments in Secretarial Labour: Resistance, Office Automation and the Transformation of Patriarchal Relations of Control', PhD. thesis, University of Birmingham, unpublished.

FORESTER, T. (ed.) (1980) *The Microelectronics Revolution*, Oxford, Basil Blackwell.

FRIEDMAN, G. (1955) *The Anatomy of Work*, New York, Free Press of Glencoe.

HARMAN, C. (1979) *Is a Machine After Your Job? New Technology and the Struggle for Socialism*, London, Socialist Worker Pamphlet.

LEGHORN, L. and PARKER, K. (1981) *Women's Worth*, Boston, Routledge and Kegan Paul.

MARGLIN, S. A. (1976) 'What do bosses do? the origins and functions of hierarchy in capitalist production', in Gorz, A. (ed.) *The Division of Labour*, Brighton, Harvester Press.

MORE, C. (1982) 'Skill and the survival of apprenticeship', in Wood, S. (ed.) *The Degradation of Work?*, London, Hutchinson.

POLLERT, A. (1981) *Girls, Wives, Factory Lives*, London, Macmillan.

VEBLEN, T. (1964) 'Conspicuous consumption', in Coser, L. and Rosenberg, B. (eds) *Sociological Theory*, 2nd edition, New York, Collier Macmillan.

VINNICOMBE, S. (1980) *Secretaries, Management and Organisations*, London, Heinemann.

WEST, J. (1982) 'New technology and women's office work', in West, J. (ed.) *Work, Women and the Labour Market*, London, Routledge and Kegan Paul.

WOMEN'S VOICE WORD PROCESSOR PAMPHLET (1979) *Job Massacre at the Office*, London, Women's Voice.

10   All Day, Every Day

Sallie Westwood

10.1   Introduction

[The extracts that follow are part of a study of a hosiery firm in the East
Midlands. As the author of the study explains, StitchCo (a pseudonym to
ensure confidentiality) is] a reputable and paternalistic firm which recruits
in a way which is often mediated by the family, rather than the job centres
or careers officers in schools. Management saw this as a continuity between
the present and the past – when whole families moved out of the house and
into the factory together. The intervention of familial ties in the labour
market illustrates clearly the case upon which this study is founded: that
home and work are part of one world [. . .]

The setting for this story is a city I have called Needletown which has a
population of over a quarter of a million and which is ethnically and
racially diverse. Since the Second World War the city has become home to
refugees and migrants from Poland and other Eastern European states that
were absorbed into the USSR. It has a thriving Irish community and since
the 1950s it has had a black population which has grown in the last decade
with the arrival of many Asians from East Africa. The city has a long
history as a centre for the hosiery industry, and many of the more recent
immigrants have come to work in this sector [. . .]

I hoped that my year on the shop-floor would enable me to illuminate
the lived experiences of women workers who come together to generate
and sustain a culture, a world of symbols and meanings which has to be
unravelled. But there is an important caution: lived experience, everyday
life, the 'real' world, are not simple unambiguous phenomena which can be
easily caught and reproduced in the pages of books. Life does not lie
around like leaves in autumn waiting to be swept up, ordered and put into
boxes. The drama of everyday life is richly textured, multifaceted and
dense and we cannot hope to make sense of our world and, more, interpret
it, without a coherent theoretical understanding. We need theories to
explain the world in which we struggle, to inform our practice and our
politics, but this does not mean that we necessarily need a spectacular set
of mental acrobatics, or a fencing match with all that has gone before. In
this book, theoretical issues arise at every turn and they inform the
understanding that I have brought to the world of the factory, but it is not
my purpose to fetishize theories. My hope is that the world presented here
will contribute to the development of feminist theory because it draws
attention to the complexities of women's subordination, but in a way that is

rooted in the experiences of women's lives, just as our politics has been and must remain.

It is the capitalist mode of production that concerns us and this is a system in which formally free labourers sell their labour power to employers for wages and thereby enter the world of social production and relations of exploitation in the workplace which give them a class position. But women are also workers in the home and within this setting they are exploited through the gift of unpaid labour to the men who are their husbands and fathers. Both these situations are oppressive and conceptually we might want to distinguish two systems, to analyse two modes of oppression. But it is becoming increasingly clear that patriarchy and capitalism are not so easily divided between the home and the workplace. I have always been uneasy with the division and in an effort to look at it anew I went first to the workplace to seek out patriarchy, rather than start from the home. I am not alone in sensing that the terrain in which women's subordination is generated and reproduced cannot be so easily divided [. . .] Lucy Bland and her co-writers have argued convincingly that:

> It is incorrect to see the nature of women's subordination as either determined solely by the economic and political needs of capitalism or the results of class struggle; women's subordination under capitalism lies in the articulation between patriarchal relations and capitalist development.[1] [. . .]

Veronica Beechey has usefully reviewed the history of the concept of patriarchy as it has been used in feminist debates and the problems that surround it.[2] I support her call for a more historically specific understanding of patriarchy and endorse her conclusion that we have to find a way of bringing together the worlds of production and reproduction in a feminist account of women's oppression. I do not think that the concept of patriarchy should be abandoned, not least because it allows us to think our way through 'the woman question' in ways other than those offered to us by sociology, for example, or Marxism which has so enriched the study of capitalist formations. To seek out and analyse the articulation between patriarchy and capitalism is to move on to political questions about the nature of the relationship between feminism and Marxism. Heidi Hartmann has pointed out that this relationship is an unequal one with a deep tension because class relations and the forms of exploitation on which they are premised are given pre-eminence by Marxists.[3]

The concept of patriarchy has been criticized, for example, by Sheila Rowbotham, for its lack of explanatory power because it concentrates attention upon biology and the universal condition of female subordination.[4] But this view ignores the important attempts that have been made to provide an historicized and contextual understanding of patriarchy by feminists like Roisin McDonough and Rachel Harrison[5] [. . .] who argue for a materialist understanding of patriarchy grounded in both sexual and economic exploitation which does not alter the power of patriarchy to 'infest' other aspects of the social formation. They concentrate upon the workplace and the family as the crucial sites for patriarchal relations, an emphasis shared by this study and reproduced in Heidi Hartmann's work. The latter provides a definition of patriarchy that I have used to guide my own analysis because it includes a materialist understanding of male power:

> We can usefully define patriarchy as a set of social relations between men, which have a material base, and which, though hierarchical, establish or create interdependence and solidarity among men that enable them to dominate women . . .
> The material base upon which patriarchy rests lies most fundamentally in men's control over women's labour power. Men maintain this control by excluding women from access to some essential productive resources (in capitalist societies, for example, jobs that pay living wages) and by restricting women's sexuality. Monogamous heterosexual marriage is one relatively recent and efficient form that seems to allow men to control both these areas.[6]

By basing an analysis on this understanding of patriarchy it is quite clear that the lives of the women I studied were encompassed by patriarchal relations, which are one part of 'patriarchal capitalism'. Consequently, neither capitalism nor patriarchy are wholly autonomous in their actions and effects, nor are they reducible one to the other. Rather, patriarchy and mode of production are simultaneously one world and two, relatively autonomous parts of a whole which has to be fought on both fronts [. . .]

One of the most important recent developments in Marxism has been the reassessment of the role of ideologies in the social formation. My analysis takes seriously the claim that the economic level is also affected by the ideological and the political and that because of this patriarchy has a material base not only in the way in which men control and exploit women's labour power, but in the way in which patriarchal ideologies intervene at the economic level. Ideologies are both outside and within individual subjectivities, and they play a vital part in calling forth a sense of self linked to class and gender as well as race. Thus, a patriarchal ideology intervenes on the shop-floor and subverts the creative potential of shop-floor culture to make anew the conditions of work under capitalism.

This is a complex notion and one which, I am acutely aware, is more easily illuminated in relation to the actual practices of shop-floor culture which are explored later in this book. What I am suggesting is that, within the setting of capitalist production, we have not only the reproduction of capitalist exploitation through the way that women are positioned in the production process as workers, but through patriarchal ideologies we have the reproduction of gendered subjects and the social construction of masculinity and femininity on the shop-floor. Consequently, this book examines the way in which women who enter into waged employment become workers and, therefore, classed subjects. But working outside the home is not only about becoming a worker; it is most crucially about becoming a woman. Shop-floor culture offers to women at work a version of woman and they take upon themselves elements of this in ways which tie them more firmly to a 'feminine' destiny and the culture of femininity.

However, it is a deeply contradictory culture which the women fashion: it reveals a resistant and creative attempt to overcome the stultifying aspects of the capitalist labour process – only to find that this creativity has bound itself securely to an oppressive version of womanhood. This book provides glimpses of shop-floor life and culture as both oppositional and resistant in form and as a site in which patriarchal ideologies and therefore the materiality of patriarchy is reproduced. The contradiction is in creativity and sisterhood and its subversion by the commonsense world which makes of all women wives and mothers.

This book is suggesting that gender identities are not produced and reproduced simply in the home or through schooling and the mass media (although they all play a part), but centrally through the workplace – both the capitalist labour process, which enshrines the subordination of women, and the culture that is produced in opposition to it by the women. The move from the home into the factory simultaneously opens and closes doors. The liberating potential moves women together to take on a collective struggle, but it is also in the workplace that young women are encouraged to embrace domesticity, become brides and have children. When Paul Willis studied 'lads' in school they showed just how much they wanted to leave school and rush in through the factory gates, viewing this as a moment of choice and freedom; young women rush out of the factory in the opposite direction, into domesticity, with the same sense of a decision freely made, a choice exercised.[7]

Before I embark upon the world of the factory more has to be said about the post-colonial setting for the interaction of patriarchy and capitalism. We live in Britain in a society which, as a colonial power, exploited the riches and the labour power of women and men in Africa, Asia and the Caribbean and which then brought this labour power to Britain to work in unskilled, poorly paid jobs. And, if their economic privations were not enough, the British state and society confounded the pain of black workers by racism, institutionalized in the laws and practices of Britain and internalized within the cultures of all sections of British society [. . .]

Immigrants, from what the statistics call the New Commonwealth countries, have been arriving in Britain since the 1950s. Asian women are the most recent arrivals, often coming after male family members, or as brides, following the expulsion of the Asians from East Africa. They are faced with a multiplicity of contradictory demands upon them [. . .] It is important to reflect upon the issue of racism in relation to both the class structure and patriarchal relations. The women in this study all share the same relationship to the means of production: they are all 'free' labourers selling their labour power for wages. But because they are women their position in the labour market is always affected by their domestic lives; being a woman counts. Nevertheless, not all women are white: women of colour are faced with an additional ideological hurdle – racism – and this affects the class position of black workers generally and black women in particular, giving them a specific place in the working class. They are, in the view of Annie Phizacklea and Robert Miles, a class fraction because the position they occupy is 'determined by both economic and politico-ideological relations'.[8] They adopt this position as a way of understanding both the links between race and class and the specific situation of black workers and other migrant workers. Racism is an ideology which, when reconstructed and analysed, exhibits an internal coherence [. . .]

My purpose in this study was not to take a detailed predetermined position on the crucial question of what black and white women share beyond their membership of an already stratified working class. Of course, I set out with the view that patriarchal relations oppress all women, but I was conscious of the need to be sensitive to the specificities surrounding the position of black women.

In so far as this study concentrates attention upon the generation and reproduction of shop-floor culture by women and sees this as both oppositional and collusive and, moreover, as contributing to the processes whereby gender identities are formed, what are the implications for black women of a culture formed in a specific cultural and historical setting? This raises important and complex questions because shop-floor culture promotes sisterhood and makes appeals to the universal woman through the symbols of the bride, and the mother and yet we must recognize that the idea of universal woman is a problem. I think it important to be aware that the abstracted woman is an inadequate beginning for our analysis. We cannot use a simple unity 'woman' as the basis of our understanding; instead, we have to posit real women, human beings formed and sustained materially in a specific social formation who may, nevertheless, have come from other cultures and another part of the global economic system. To find out what unites these women, who come together as workers on the shop-floor, and what divides them is part of the reason for undertaking a study such as this [. . .]

This book gives a central role to patriarchal relations in defining and elaborating the lives of both black and white women while acknowledging that they share a class position within contemporary capitalism. This is, however, a post-colonial capitalism and in its institutions and its populace it is deeply racist; thus I recognize that black women share a triple, not just a double, burden of oppression through class, gender and race. But as white women struggle against class and gender oppressions so black women fight to overcome the constraints upon their own lives. Yet in their very struggles these constraints are made anew, through the family and the workplace. Relations in both areas are deeply contradictory: they offer the possibilities of free spaces within the lives of women whereby they can enact their own cultural creations, but cultures are not simply lived experiences. They are shot through with ideological components, or manifest ideological consequences. There is a deep tension born of this contradiction and the women of the factory live this out with consummate skill. Given these material circumstances, how and in what ways are the individuals that come to understand themselves as women produced? I am suggesting that it is not just class identities that are forged at work, but gender identities. Girls arrive in the factory and they become women on the shop-floor. This process encompasses the same contradictions as those that are found in the culture of the shop-floor itself. The family and school have a major part to play, but it is at work that adulthood is acknowledged and made through the wage that itself generates a class identity and through the way that women workers are always subordinated in the capitalist labour process and the labour market.

The women in the factory were workers in a declining industry and many of the jobs that were lost in the hosiery industry during 1980 and 1981 were women's jobs. Of the women who work in manufacturing, half of them work in only four areas: food and drink, clothing and footwear, textiles, and electrical engineering and they do so in the low paid sectors of these industries.[9] Black women are over-represented in all low-paid sectors, including low-paid manual work in the state sector.[10] Of the 10.4 million women (over 40 per cent of the workforce) who were working in 1980, an estimated 45 per cent worked in totally segregated jobs.[11] [*All Day Every Day*] provides a case study of this situation of low-paid, segregated work, commonly known as 'women's work' [. . .]

The organization of work has major implications for sisterhood and worker resistance [. . .] The women resist both management imperatives and union manipulations, turning their energies instead to the generation of an elaborate shop-floor culture which celebrates everything from birthdays to babies. It is the ritual and the celebration which surrounds the life-cycle events of women's lives – such as marriage and motherhood – which are elaborated [below . . .]

10.2   You sink into his arms

Marriage was booming in [StitchCo]. If there was one area of excitement which never seemed to wane, it was the glamour of a white wedding. Everyone was excited by the prospect of a wedding because it kept romance and sex alive through the boredom of sewing side-seams day after day. It made real the world of Hindi films and Mills and Boon romances with their gallant heroes and beautiful women who sailed off into the sunset together. The heroes and the brides were an essential part of the culture of femininity on the shop-floor and this [section] follows the fortunes of some of the young white women who married during my year at StitchCo. With them I shared some of the experience, while I struggled to understand the sense of liberation they felt as they walked down the aisle. Prior to this, there were complex ritual processes to be undergone which transformed girls into women – 'women' being defined in relation to domesticity and biology, as wives and mothers [. . .] Whether the bride wore a white dress and a veil or a red-and-green sari shimmering with gold, the patriarchal assumptions about the bride–woman were the same [. . .]

Getting it together

Girls coming into the factory as trainees arrived starry-eyed, bringing dreams of their latest heart-throb into an environment already heavily saturated with the themes of romance and sexuality [. . .] I tried to coax from them their vision of the future and they presented me with a picture of the next ten years of their lives: they could see an engagement at 17, marriage at 19 or 20, followed by two children – a boy and then a girl. The future, in fact, looked like the past. It is easy, of course, to judge the visions presented here as myopic and restricted, but it is more important to try to understand the nature of the constraints within which the next generation of wives plot a course or conceive a future. I came slowly to appreciate, as they did, that the ideological and material parameters of their lives presented marriage and children not as burdensome and oppressive, but as liberating events – part of the great adventure of life. In taking hold of these moments, young women locked themselves into domesticity and subordination in just the same way that young men, taking hold of manual labour as their moment of liberation from boyhood, locked themselves into dead-end jobs with low wages.[12] For the women, there were very good reasons why they should embrace both marriage and men.

Nikki and Trish, like their older sisters and friends, lived at home as daughters and it was not economically possible for them to do anything else. They did not earn a living wage nor could they expect to; instead, they paid £10–£12 a week to their mums for their 'keep' and dreamed of the day when they would be able to leave home. The only way out of the family and into a house or a flat of their own was to join hands with a male wage and, therefore, with the man who went with the wage packet. The contradictions in this situation were very clear: on the one hand, the possibility of independence from family and home; on the other, the actuality of dependence, of being 'tied down'. The contradictions deepened because the young women felt that, in choosing a boyfriend and getting married, they were exercising some control over their lives and joining the adult world. In addition, they suggested to me that, as women in a society controlled by men, the possibility of being linked to one man offered at least a chance of exercising some power in the world. So engagements and weddings were emphasized.

This meant that sexual relations were invariably taken to mean relations between men and women. Sex in all its aspects on the shop-floor – from 'smutty' jokes to discussions which expressed fears and joys – was invoked in a heterosexual context and thus women's sexuality was bound to be explored in relation to men. Gay women were quiet and hidden: to be thought 'queer' and discussed as though you were was to be insulted and stigmatized [. . .]

Romance and realism

Although romance breathed life and energy into shop-floor culture it was not a simple notion, but a complex and contradictory element in women's lives. Their commitment to love and marriage and their insistence upon heterosexuality were underpinned by the economic constraints which necessitated an 'alliance' between men and women if they were to enjoy a reasonable standard of living and some of the freedoms of being away from their parents. Marriage was part of a strategy adopted by women to realize some of the benefits of our society. It was not, however, simply material benefits that were at issue. Womanhood, as it was understood on the shop-floor, was realized through marriage and motherhood; the celebration of engagements and weddings was part of the confirmation of this. Alongside marriage was the network of friends and relatives who provided a system of support for women, and these relationships among women were not denied or diminished by the emphasis upon romance and weddings. On the contrary, relations between men and women, womanhood realized through marriage and motherhood, were validated by friends, sisters, mothers and aunts who provided a vital cultural context. The tensions between romance and realism existed and were skilfully lived out on a day-to-day basis and when women looked to the future. The effect of all this was, of course, to reinforce the importance of the family and all the attendant inequalities that go with it [. . .]

If you were young enough to stand the pace and had money in your pocket, Friday and Saturday nights were nights spent in town at the pubs and discos, dancing, flirting and getting 'pissed up'.[13] Friends went together to the clubs in town and danced in groups until they were divided by the men who, it was hoped, would finance drinking for the night and not prove too troublesome at the end when the group would reform to go home in shared taxis by twos and threes [. . .] Meeting new men was part of the fun of being around town. Men, however, were classified: 'yobs' were avoided even for free drinks and a quick dance and my friends were quick to spot them. Getting drunk was part of the fun. Although parents disapproved, on the whole they were fairly indulgent towards their daughters [. . .]

A diamond is for ever

The energy and enthusiasm with which Lisa, Tessa and others pursued engagement rings made me wonder if they really did believe that 'a diamond is for ever'. I was reassured by my friends that nothing so simple was at work. The importance of the ring was not so much the diamond, although its design and value were discussed at length, but the way in which becoming engaged marked another point along the road to adult status [. . .] Womanhood was clearly defined [. . .] as being a wife and mother, a view accepted by most of the women and celebrated on the shop-floor through the rituals which surrounded engagements, marriages and motherhood [. . .]

An engagement signals the arrival of a woman's sexuality because she is linked to a man. Being engaged allowed young couples to become lovers, legitimately, in the eyes of parents. Although often engaged couples slept together on family holidays or at each other's homes, this did not mean licensed promiscuity. On the contrary, it was one way in which working-class families and communities regulated the sexual behaviour of their daughters. In principle, an engagement tied a man and woman together. The continuity of life with your mates, holidays with 'girlfriends', away from both families and fiancés, meant that this regulation could be disrupted by the discos of Skeggie and Blackpool.

I was fascinated by the clear passion for engagements exhibited by young women throughout the department so I spent a long time talking to women of all ages about the meanings that they attached to engagement parties, diamond rings and having a fiancé. Despite my persistent questioning, however, none of them clearly articulated the role engagements played in their lives. Most of the fiancées in the department were still in their teens and did not expect to marry for several years unless they were pregnant. They didn't seem to be anxious to rush into marriage and it was this reluctance, amid the general interest in weddings, flowers, confetti, and the like, which initially baffled me. It was only by getting to know the women that I gradually built up a picture of the importance of being engaged and how this changed not only the status of young people, but, most important, the economic relations between them.

The common pattern among engaged couples was to pool their income and to save one wage packet and live on the other, as described by Lisa: 'After we get engaged, we're gonna open a joint account and save his wages and live on mine. Then we'll be able to get a house and the things we need for it. It will take a long time, but it's worth it. I don't want to get married in a rush like the twins.' [. . .]

Angie [was also engaged and her story] was not unusual. She had left school at 16 and a year later was locked into a relationship which left her virtually no control over her own earnings. Angie had few clothes and spent very little money on anything else. Her boyfriend behaved towards her as he would when they were married, taking on the role of breadwinner and providing for her basic needs. This relationship reproduced the ideal pattern of working-class family life as it was constructed in the minds of men. In this case, though, the family wage was a combination of Pete and Angie's wages, the most common economic basis for family life.[14] Angie was waiting for Pete to pay for his bike before they could marry, but she didn't wait long. By the time she was 19, Angie was proudly and happily pushing her baby son through the city market with her mum and told me she didn't expect to be going back to work in the factory for a long time.

Engagements, then, allowed young couples to plan a future and to put money aside for it. Saving was a way of trying to deal with the material limitations of working-class life; for those involved, it meant that hedonism gave way to a much more restricted life. Engaged couples seemed to spend most of their time at home in front of the telly, at the house of one family or the other. They carefully rationed nights out in the pub or at the discos in town and these soon became part of a routine. So the excitement of the engagement ring very soon gave way to the rigours of saving and the constraints that this imposed. It was not surprising that this situation generated resentment and regrets [. . .]

From girl to woman: the bride's ritual

Engagements were often celebrated with a party which brought friends and relatives together to toast the new couple, and possibly the eighteenth birthday of the bride, as well. At work, sweets and cakes were passed around while everyone admired the ring and the wearer became a celebrity for a day, recounting the details surrounding the choice of the ring, its cost and where it was bought. The real event was still to come. The wedding was the centrepiece which brought the women in the department together in the most complex and creative drama in the life of the shop-floor, the event I have called the bride's ritual. The pattern for this event was set way back in history and no one was able to tell me when or why it began in the hosiery industry, whether it was similar or different in other areas of the country or if it was part of shop-floor culture among women in other industries.[15] It was so much a part of life in 'the hosiery' that everyone took it for granted. Though the celebration of the bride corresponded to the passing-out ceremonies and celebrations used to announce the arrival of a new craftsworker, the bride's ritual celebrated neither a craft nor a skilled worker, but womanhood. It was a rite of passage for the move from girl to woman, from daughter to wife; the symbolism used not only celebrated the bride, it also pointed to the subordination of women in marriage.[16]

The bride's ritual, which was staged many times during my year in the factory, is best described in relation to the twins, Tessa and Julie, who married in the summer of 1980. They were the source of special excitement because they were planning a double wedding. By concentrating on young white women, I do not want to give the impression that Indian women were not involved; they were, but in ways which were tempered to suit them. For example, it was well known on the shop-floor that few Indian women drank alcohol and so they were not expected to come to the pub in the lunch-hour. White women also felt that too many bawdy references to sex were not welcomed, by the older Indian women, especially, so they cut this out and concentrated instead on romance and hearts and flowers in an effort to be sensitive to the needs of their Indian friends.

When the date of the twins' wedding was fixed, the women on their respective units set to work to make appropriate costumes for them using company materials and time. This was the first part of the ritual and one which emphasized the creative skills and abilities of the women on the units in making forms of fancy dress. Some of the units were well known for producing very elaborate and inventive costumes, which they tried to relate to the kind of person the bride was [. . .] It was well known that Tessa was pregnant and already living with Carl. Julie, although not pregnant, was also living with Dave – something, it must be said, she was not very happy about. What this meant was that their costumes could be very suggestive without any possibility of offending either of them; it was on this basis that they were created.

On the day of their celebration (a Thursday, the day normally chosen), the twins arrived at work grinning and looking a little wary as they waited for their units to unveil their handiwork. Both units had excelled themselves and, amid roars of laughter, Julie was dressed in a St Trinian's outfit with a short gymslip, black suspenders and stockings, her tie askew; the ensemble was topped off by a large black top-hat made of crêpe paper and cardboard and decked with gaudy pink tinsel that flowed around the brim and trailed down the side. On the back of the gymslip was an 'L' plate with a contraceptive pill stuck to the side of it. The suggestion that Julie might be a Learner was greeted with total disbelief. ' "Learner" – that's a joke Julie!' said her friends. Her sister, who also pointed to her suspenders and short skirt and made jokes about Julie's lack of ability in school, prompted another set of innuendoes about Julie's sexual experiences. Julie responded by telling Tessa that she was in for a shock, and we set off to see Tessa dressed in her costume.

Julie's gymslip paled into respectability when it was confronted with Tessa's costume, described by Avril as 'a pornographic Andy Pandy suit'. Hands covered smiles, heads rolled and everyone stared at Tessa almost in disbelief before they burst into raucous laughter which degenerated into a prolonged fit of the giggles. Tessa's dress was outrageous. It was an oversize Babygro, a fairly loose fit on Tessa, with two large pink cloth breasts attached to the front and two hands appliquéd on the seat of the suit across Tessa's bottom. Over one of the hands the words 'It feels good' had been embroidered. To set off this creation – it did look like a piece of soft sculpture from a distance – the women on the unit had made a large black-cloth penis and testicles which Tessa wore around her neck, when she was not pushing them into everyone's faces; 'Nice innit, Sal? I'm gonna give it to you as a memento,' Tessa said wickedly, grinning at her friends and tilting her new acquisition in the direction of the managers. She took on the mantle of the suggestive clown as it was given to her by the costume, and clearly thoroughly enjoyed it. To crown her clothes, she wore a lopsided mobcap with 'the pill' stuck to it and cotton reels dangling from it. As Lisa summed it up: 'Gawd, you look a sight, Tess.' [. . .]

Stuffed with cakes and pop and still giggling at the sight of Tessa, at lunch-time we headed for the nearest pub where the twins' mum, Rita, and one of their older sisters, Gina, were waiting for us. Management had given the twins an extra ten minutes on their lunch-break. Although it was not intended, this extra ten minutes was also taken by a number of the twins' friends [. . .] We pushed our way towards the bar and ordered drinks for each other. Julie and Tessa were plied with rum and coke, although Tessa protested mildly and tried to drink only coke; instead, others drank vodka and lime, gin and orange, and some, like Sally, drank everything in sight. While Rita laughed and encouraged her daughters to drink, bundles of binding were being passed between hands, unknown to Tessa and Julie, ready for the next stage of the celebration [. . .]

We were all pretty pleased with things and preparing for the next step although, by now, Julie and Tessa knew what was coming and looked at each one of us and asked us not to tie them to the railings outside the factory. But tradition demanded that this be done and a few drinks later we were all outside the tiny pub a few steps away from the pedestrian bridge over the dual carriageway next to the factory. It was pouring with rain. Lisa and Marie grabbed Julie, while Tracey and Jo made a dash for Tessa as she tried to run back to the factory. As the twins struggled, Jo tried to wind some binding around them and the support for the pedestrian bridge so they were at least a little sheltered, but the cars threw up spray from the road and the twins struggled harder. Reinforcements managed to make secure the binding: yards and yards of it wound round and round the two women, their legs and arms tied to the concrete bridge [. . .]

They struggled with the binding, cursing and swearing and promising revenge on their friends. It eventually gave way under their constant pulling and tugging; they were bruised in the effort, their ankles cut and their clothes soaking wet. Tessa and Julie re-emerged in the department a sorry sight, Julie's black stockings were torn and muddy and Tessa's red outfit was soggy with the rain. They were greeted with hoots of laughter and shouts as they staggered in, Julie looking very green and complaining that she was about to throw up [. . .]

This [. . .] ritual was enacted again and again throughout the summer and in each case the drama was the same, although the costumes varied [. . .] It was an opportunity for the women on the units to use their creativity and technical skills for each other and everyone enjoyed the excitement which surrounded each new creation [. . .]

All of [the] versions of the ritual share in the powerful sexual imagery which saturated the events at StitchCo and which amplified the jokes, sexual innuendoes and ribaldry of the shop-floor. It was bawdy and everyone enjoyed it. The emphasis upon sexuality must be viewed in the light of the comments I have already made on the privileged position of heterosexuality; women became sexually active as wives following their weddings and this meant that their sexuality was crucially mediated by men. The pill found its way onto all the outfits, suggesting a clear change in status between the sexually unavailable girl and the sexually experienced woman. Womanhood was defined in the ritual in relation to becoming a wife and therefore becoming a woman was located within the context of marriage and being joined to a man.

It was also abundantly clear that marriage was equated with bondage and the binding of a woman to a man – the notion of capture and plunder lingers on in the ritual. While the young women were bound, they also sought to struggle free – thereby securing for the bride a new freedom. This struggle was enacted in public as though the whole exercise was a shaming experience, a way of showing women as harlots and witches symbolized in the costumes worn by the brides. The scarlet woman, the vamp and the sexually alert schoolgirl were all part of the ritual, just like they are part of the enduring myths which surround women's sexuality. Such myths are not, of course, simply benign. They are part of the subordination of women, clearly expressed in the ritual and cheerfully emphasized by the women involved in the drama. It was, in all its parts, a deeply contradictory event – not because the symbolism was ambiguous, but because it involved women in a celebration of their own oppression in marriage. And it was this oppression that the young brides came, all too quickly, to know and articulate [. . .]

10.3   Conclusion: race and class are feminist issues, too

[. . .] In looking at the texture of women's lives across racial and cultural boundaries, it is important to hold both similarity and difference in one's mind's eye. Only in this way can we hope to grasp the contradictions which mark women's lives, giving rise to strength and sisterhood alongside weakness and division. I want to try to hold on to this mosaic of understanding and to relate this to feminist politics [. . .] There are no prescriptions for action here and no single, clear route through the complexities. Instead, there are cross-cutting layers, sometimes in coalescence and sometimes in contradiction with one another, shifting and forming in struggle not unlike patterns in a kaleidoscope.

[My study has] shown the interaction of patriarchy and capitalism in the factory and the home, and the response the women make to this by generating and sustaining a shop-floor culture which structures the way that becoming a worker, through a woman's role in production, and becoming a woman, through her role in reproduction, are brought together and reinforced. It is an oppositional culture, providing a focus for resistance to managerial authority and demands, while forging solidarity and sisterhood. It is also an ambiguous resistance because it so clearly colludes in promoting a specific version of womanhood. That version of womanhood is tied to Western, romantic idealizations of love, marriage and motherhood, which promote a subordinate definition of woman founded upon weakness and division. The celebrations surrounding the bride and the mother on the shop-floor offer these as universal representations to all women in the department, but they are located in a culture which has been historically generated and sustained by white working-class women. Yet it is possible for the symbols of the bride and the mother to have a resonance beyond race and class – but only when the symbols are rooted in an essentialist understanding of woman that concentrates on the biological capacity to reproduce that all women share. Is this the crucial issue?

Feminists have long debated the inadequacies of a politics founded upon biology and the universal 'woman' who automatically has common cause with all women. It is, in effect, a romantic fiction to treat 'woman' as an *a priori*, or natural, category which does not need to be theorized. On the contrary, the task is to theorize difference *and* unity and it is not surprising if, despite our best efforts, we have stumbled in relation to this knotty problem. But it has now been given a new impetus by black women who have attacked the racist assumptions of feminist discourses and demanded that the experiences of black women inform a reconstructed feminism[17] [. . .] Feminism has to engage in a work of excavation and reconstruction which integrates the insights provided by black women [. . .] It is the case, of course, that feminism is not a simple unified whole. Nevertheless, feminisms do coalesce around a fundamental concern with explaining and overcoming the oppression of women and we cannot have an adequate account of either unless we have an understanding of racism and a commitment to fight it.

Most black women, I have suggested, are part of a stratified working class and [. . .] feminist socialists have consistently tried to bring gender and class together in an effort to hold on to the complexities of both. But rather than adding race on as a further complication and considering the triple oppressions that exist through class relations, patriarchal structures and racism, it is more illuminating, if more complicated, to try to see contradictory and complementary relationships between these areas as they relate to ongoing struggles. The issues cannot be simply theoretical ones because, as Jenny Bourne has reminded us, 'Working against racism means tackling political issues,' and Anna Coote and Beatrix Campbell have emphasized the need for feminists to take issues into the arena of conventional politics and power struggles[18] [. . .]

In so far as this book has provided an analysis of women's lives within patriarchal capitalism, it has shown that women do two jobs, but still do not earn living wages. The nature of this 'rip off' cannot be explained simply by the mechanisms of class oppression located in the economics of capitalism. Jean Gardiner has pointed to the duality of women's relationship to class.[19] Women are class members because, as workers, they have a relationship to the means of production which, on the whole, gives them non-living wages and makes them an impoverished section of the working class; it is because of this that they look to marriage as a means to higher wages and access to resources controlled by men. This means that women have a second relationship to class through their relationship to the male wage which reinforces their dependence and subordination in relation to men. Although the relevance of this can be seen in this book, it is not the whole story.

First of all, it is important to ask why there is this duality. Second, black workers and immigrant workers are also impoverished; and, third, women may not have access to the male wage because its place may have been taken by state benefits. Consequently, in seeking answers to the question of why women have a dual relationship to class, the reasons must be sought outside the crude economism of 'cheap labour' arguments. Rather, they must be found in the power of sexist and racist ideologies to affect employers and unions and the way that people are positioned in labour markets.

This means that the issues surrounding women's wages and the struggles that have to be fought to secure living wages for women cannot be encompassed in a call for 'equal pay now' because this leaves out the vital question: equal to whom? Attempts to promote equal pay have been tried and they have foundered. Instead, we have to work on a number of fronts: against the ghettoization of low-paid work in general and white male privileges in highly paid skilled work and, at the same time, against low pay and for living wages sufficient to the needs of women.[20] Such a strategy presents black and white women with a powerful common cause. Although low pay affects men as well (black men and other immigrants, predominantly) women, too, have to fight to raise their own wages because raising male wages has shown itself to be false strategy for women and no guarantee against female impoverishment.

The women in the department came together to fight targets and rates they considered unfair and it was often Indian women who were in the forefront of these struggles. Similarly, in the discussions surrounding the recession and lay-offs the women emphasized that 'an injury to one was an injury to all' and they insisted that whatever work was available should be shared among all the women. Solidarity and sisterhood marked the struggles around economic issues on the shop-floor. Away from the department, however, wages were negotiated by the recognized organs of the labour movement – the trade unions – and, in this case, the union supported large differentials between male and female wage rates, defending their decision on the basis that men's work was skilled work while women's work was not. This illustrates that the fight against low pay is crucially bound up with a struggle against sexist ideologies in the trade union movement. This book has shown that this is one battle that black and white women fight already. This common struggle does not mean that black women are not also a part of an autonomous black struggle against racism in the trade union movement, or an autonomous black women's struggle against sexism and racism. The struggles overlap because racism is not confined to the trade unions, but extends to the whole British working class [. . .]

This is the contradiction: black and white women workers share in the experience of exploitation under patriarchal capitalism, yet racism cuts through and across a potential unity. It does so not simply because management used racism as a strategy to divide the working class as a whole (such conspiratorial simplicities do not advance our understanding of racism among the working class). Management can only use racism effectively if workers are racist [. . .]

The women at StitchCo worked with and against racism at the same time, reproducing it and undermining it through their lives on the shop-floor and beyond, in the city. These dualities were part of the contradictory and complex whole which made up their lives and which were marked, for me, by the extraordinarily powerful creativity that they possessed and the determination they showed in making out of necessity a work of art – a huge landscape into which they insisted they would paint some of the landmarks. This meant that their lives were committed to struggle and the insistence upon a different and better world, predicated not simply upon higher wages or more consumption and, therefore, not located within capitalist imperatives. The complexities of women's lives and the struggles they waged encouraged them to take on a wider vision which was, nevertheless, located in their experiences as black and white working-class women. The view the women expressed incorporated an understanding that the quality of life was badly in need of revision and that this should form an essential part of any programme to change the lives of working people. Much of what the women wanted to promote was connected to the creative and collective response they made to women's issues. They shared with the women's movement an insistence upon a larger set of options for women, and better and more resources for health care, childcare and education; in addition, the issue of control was central. Women wanted more control over their own fertility and sexuality, and they fiercely defended their rights to have children. Their sense of control was vitally important in a situation where they feared ideological and medical attacks on their reproductive rights. Their fears are well grounded as the use of the contraceptive Depo-Provera on black women in Britain and elsewhere demonstrates. These attacks are rooted deep in the Eugenics Movement and bring together the issues of race and class as Angela Davis's writing has shown in relation to the USA.[21] The Eugenics Movement in Britain also had a part to play in locking Empire and Motherhood into an embrace which made 'motherhood' the prerogative of white middle-class women.[22] The issue of sexuality raises further complexities which also need to be uncovered to show the ways in which it became enmeshed with racial stereotypes and a key plank in racist discourses [. . .]

Women celebrated babies and part of their vision of the future was bound up with their commitment to their children. Black and white women wanted their daughters to have the opportunity to pursue education and training as a means to a life which would be more autonomous. There was a strong sense from the women that they did not want their daughters to be undervalued or wasted in the way that they had been. Women struggled to make sense of their lives and to invent a future for their children while, at the same time, they looked at the lives they led and analysed marriage and the family in ways that enabled them to see the oppressive elements. Yet, to ask that working-class women on non-living wages should break out of family life and opt for alternatives is to misunderstand the very real constraints that economics places on women and to overlook the meaning of family life for both black and white women. They can see the alternatives, because circumstances often force them into situations where they are single parents trying to provide a home for children without adequate material support. It is hardly surprising (given their relative economic positions) that some working-class women try to insist upon a male commitment to mothers and children which allows them to stay at home. Apart from the ideological push they receive in this direction, it is quite clear that working-class women are committed to the family because it is an experience and a space which offers them some degree of autonomy over their lives and the warmth, support and affection from a group of people who matter and who in turn make a woman feel that she is important and valued. It is not that they do not know about the underside of family life or the way that unemployment affects the contributions that members of families can make. Young men, black and white, can no longer hold out the hope of a family wage or of being a breadwinner [. . .]

Commitment to family does not mean that friends, 'mates' or sisters are ignored. For many women, the nexus of relationships that makes up family life offers them sisters and friends who provide the essential support for their lives. Women give their energies and their creativity to their families, especially their children, because this is one area where they feel that their strength and competence counts and is exercised to satisfy real needs. Many of the women I knew, despite an already overworked life, wanted to contribute to other aspects of community or cultural life, become involved with campaigns or local issues. However, there never seemed to be a way into these activities for the women, which meant that their abilities and ideas were locked up, and away from society.

It is also quite clear [. . .] that the trade union made no effort to connect with or use the women's power and skills. The world of the trade union presented itself, instead, as a frustrating irrelevance which seemed, from the women's point of view, to promote ignorance and powerlessness rather than knowledge and control. What the relations between the women, their culture and the union show with abundant clarity is the way in which current union practices reproduce the subordination of women by ignoring them and their expertise, and by writing out issues that are crucial to women's lives. And this will continue until the trade unions dump their identikit picture of the worker as white, male and skilled. It is simply not enough to produce glossy booklets on women workers or to order leaflets on sexual harassment. Women and black people are waiting to see changes made in the ideologies and practices that make up the trade union movement so that unions can be effective campaigning organizations committed to the anti-racist, anti-sexist struggle. Thus far, it is fairly clear that in relation to both feminist and black struggles the union movement, with all its potential power, has shown itself to be not a champion, but a quaint, outmoded movement that has ossified around issues that are located in the past. Can it change? We have to believe so and work for change because the collective strength of the trade union movement could be *for* us, rather than *against* us. First of all the movement has to engage seriously with feminism, the world of women and black people and take upon itself a future which gives a central role to these struggles. Without this kind of vision, the trade unions seem destined to go on fighting defensive struggles around workplace issues connected to craft privilege. While such action relates to one part of the working class, it cannot pretend to speak for the working class as a whole – let alone the struggles of women and black people.

The women also stayed away from party politics because it looked, and sounded, dreary and alien just like the union – a world of ageing grey men, despite Margaret Thatcher's powerful presence. They were impressed neither by Thatcherism or the calls from the new right, nor by the Labour Party. The Labour Party has neglected both women and the black communities at its peril. It now finds that black people and women do not owe any simple party loyalty to Labour; instead, the black communities are using their energies and skills to forge a black politics outside the Labour Party, and have given notice to the Labour Party that black people now come from a position of strength, not weakness.

The yawning gaps in our cultural life are being made over by black people because they understand that politics is not simply about production, the factory, the union, the party and parliament; it is also about theatre and poetry, the streets and protest. The early black struggle in the United States showed that an autonomous movement could be generated with its roots in the experience of racial exploitation. The women's movement has used this insight and its success has been to establish the terrain of politics as part of everyday life. But if it is to grow and develop, it has to connect with the struggles of working-class women around material issues. Working-class women are proud of their tradition of self-help and this has an important connection with the autonomous politics of the women's movement. We cannot allow self-help to be hijacked by the right and given back to us in ways that deride the power and pride associated with this.

Currently, the women in the factory use their expertise to help one another through pregnancy, death, illness, marriage breakdown and sadness. There was no doubt that the women were engrossed in a personal and practical world which they claimed as their own; it was a sisterhood and a culture which had clear parallels with the women's movement's calls for sisterhood and to make the personal political. Black and white women inhabit largely separate worlds outside the factory; both sets of women, however, inhabit their own women's culture because of the divisions between the world of men and the space that is the women's world. The sense the women have that they control their own part of this world sits uneasily with an analysis from feminism that tells them they are powerless, subordinate and dependent. The call for women to develop their sister-hood also seems strange to women who spend most of their lives with other women, who depend on each other, and whose kinship relations are mediated by mothers and sisters, daughters and aunts. Nevertheless, the language of the women's movement has had an impact on women beyond it and, consequently, women have new ways of thinking about their relations with men and work.

The commitment that women have towards their children means that childcare facilities are a major issue in their lives. Women are both forced to work and work because they want to do so; too many of them spent their days worrying about their children. Lack of facilities are, as Prathibha Parmar has pointed out, a major impediment to Asian women joining waged work outside the home and this contributes towards many of them being confined to the super-exploitation of homeworking.[23] But childcare is an immensely complex issue. When I talked to the women about it, many were wary of a suggestion that there should be 24-hour nurseries, or even 10-hour nurseries. The reason for their lack of enthusiasm was that nurseries conjured up pictures of other state institutions – such as schools and hospitals – which were beyond their control and which were marked, in their eyes, by repression and sterility. Consequently, to hand a child into a nursery was to relinquish control over her, just as schools took over from parents and hospitals undermined the power of mothers. Far from regarding the state as a societal benefactor, the women saw the state much more starkly in predatory terms, as powerful and authoritarian. The women who did support nurseries [. . .] already had contacts with local facilities and the women who ran them and this mediation altered their view. Nurseries did not seem to them like places outside their control and influence; on the contrary, they found that the women who ran them became their friends. It is clear from this that the discussion of nurseries cannot confine itself to provision of childcare in a society where people have so few opportunities to exercise control over the institutions and organizations which provide a major part of the material base of their lives.

There was also another aspect to the response that the women made to nurseries. Both black and white women saw the state as anti-family, not as a set of practices and ideologies which constructed the family, but as one which controlled it. Black women saw in the immigration laws, perpetrated and managed by the state, a set of regulations which destroyed families by separating parents and children, brothers and sisters, and which they regarded as far more pernicious and repressive than the calls to stop new immigrants. And white women saw in the agencies of schooling, health, social work and the police sets of practices designed to deny them control over their own bodies, their own lives, houses or their children. Black women saw this, too, and added the institutional racism of these agencies to their disaffection and their conception of the state. It is important that we try to understand the politics of this situation because the interaction between gender, race and class in relation to the state is a very complex one.

Black people are in the front line in relation to the power of the state, facing racist immigration laws which have culminated in the physical abuse of black women – and that is just the beginning. They face the police, in what is coming to be an almost daily harassment, in their streets and in their homes, and their racial and cultural differences are defined negatively in relation to schools, hospitals, and state benefits. In addition, many black people are employed by the state, in health or transport, and they face the state as an employer. They are both inside and outside the state, producers and consumers of services.[24] As producers they constitute many of the low paid and as consumers they are harassed by the control agents that surround state benefits. However, black people are not simply the victims of this iron mountain; they have fought back and have organized both independently and as members of the working class in common struggle with others who are also 'up against the state'. The struggle around the health services demonstrates a coalescence of issues which simultaneously involve race, class and gender.

The patriarchal assumptions of the British state mean that both black and white women face harassment from social security agents if they are single parents or the heads of households. State benefits in relation to women and children are a crucial factor in promoting the feminization of poverty in Britain. It is also the case that both black and white working-class women often encounter white middle-class women as teachers, social workers, health visitors and doctors or as state officials, and their relations with them can often be fraught, as this book showed. Feminism has been quick to spot that while the state offers careers and salaries to some women (which provide a material base unknown to most working-class women, black or white), the patriarchal relations of state power have not been changed by the arrival of numbers of women in the so-called 'people-working professions'. Usually, women in these professions are placed in the situation of gate-keepers to state resources and many of those who want access to these resources are women. Or they are placed in a situation where they have power over working-class women through their certificated knowledge as teachers, doctors and paramedics or social workers. Yet [. . .] there are contradictions in this situation: all teachers are not racists and women in education have played a major part in the struggle against sexism in schools and education generally, insisting upon more opportunities for girls and promoting new practices and new knowledge. It is not surprising, therefore, that feminists working in the state sector should call not simply for more resources, but for a change in working practices and power relations which will not simply give the poor, women and black people, more access to state resources, but will do this in ways which do not deny their own competences and their ability to take hold of their own lives.

As we saw, health issues and childcare are a high priority for all women. Many do not support state nurseries because they see in these another attempt to wrest control from them, and to diminish their power in an area which they insist is theirs. Instead, they were sympathetic to a system of state-subsidized childminders who would be properly trained and paid according to a new status associated with the care of children. It was also clear that education mattered enormously to all the women; even though they knew its limitations and failings, they still felt that it held out a real possibility of something better for their children. And both black and white women were prepared to fight for the kind of education they saw as relevant for their children. It was, in fact, the struggle for women's education in America that prompted Angela Davis to write: 'Sisterhood between black and white women was indeed possible, and as long as it stood on a firm foundation it could give birth to earthshaking accomplishments.'[25]

Perhaps, more now than at any other time, we need 'earthshaking accomplishments'. Despite the ideological and economic climate which seeks to marginalize black struggles, women's issues and socialist alternatives, there are indeed powerful contradictory forces at work. The complexities surrounding the issues of gender, race and class remain, not surprisingly, unresolved. Nonetheless, what is clear is that both the black struggle and feminism have given a new impetus to politics in Britain, which has meant that now at least race and gender issues are on the agenda – for some of us. We must support and protect the efforts being made by those working at the local level, in the unions and left Labour councils, who are trying to forge meaningful alternatives. Generally, though, we are still waiting to see how far our 'brothers' in the trade union movement and our 'comrades' in the Labour Party and on the left can actually move in the direction of a new politics.

I am conscious that in concluding I have concentrated upon strength and struggle. I make no apology for this; I have taken my cue from the lives of the women at StitchCo. We have to believe that we can change the world we live in, in small and large ways that have real effects. This does not mean that I am any less conscious of the deprivation, pain and waste that black and white working-class women live with on a daily basis. For many of them, though, this was a spur to action rather than defeat. The lives of the women at StitchCo were a powerful indictment of the type of society of which we are a part. Their celebration and sisterhood was a vindication of their creativity and resourcefulness in an increasingly bleak world.

Notes

1   Lucy Bland, Charlotte Brunsdon, Dorothy Hobson, Janice Winship, 'Women inside and outside the relations of production', in Women's Studies Group, Centre

for Contemporary Cultural Studies (eds), *Women Take Issue: Aspects of Women's Subordination* (Hutchinson: 1978), p. 48.

2   Carol Smart, 'Law and the control of women's sexuality', in Bridget Hutter and Gillian Williams (eds), *Controlling Women* (Croom Helm: 1981), p. 41.
Veronica Beechey, 'On patriarchy', *Feminist Review*, No. 3, 1979, pp. 66–82.

3   Heidi Hartmann, 'The unhappy marriage of marxism and feminism', in Lydia Sargent (ed.), *Women and Revolution: A Discussion of the Unhappy Marriage of Marxism and Feminism* (Pluto Press: 1981), pp. 1–42.

4   Sheila Rowbotham, 'The trouble with "patriarchy",' and Sally Alexander and Barbara Taylor, 'In defence of "patriarchy"' were first published in the *New Statesman* as a debate and are now reprinted in Mary Evans (ed.), *The Woman Question* (Fontana: 1982), pp. 73–83.

5   Roisin McDonough and Rachel Harrison, 'Patriarchy and relations of production', in Annette Kuhn and AnnMarie Wolpe (eds), *Feminism and Materialism* (Routledge: 1978), pp. 11–41.

6   Heide Hartmann, 'The unhappy marriage of marxism and feminism', pp. 14–15.

7   Paul Willis, *Learning to Labour: How Working-Class Kids Get Working-Class Jobs* (Saxon House: 1977).

8   Annie Phizacklea and Robert Miles, *Labour and Racism* (Routledge: 1980), p. 6.

9   Anna Coote and Beatrix Campbell, *Sweet Freedom: The Struggle for Women's Liberation* (Picador: 1982), p. 51. The rest of this chapter provides a discussion of both waged work and unemployment among women.

10   Ibid., pp. 49–52.

11   D. J. Smith, *Racial Disadvantage in Britain: The PEP Report* (Penguin: 1977), p. 77, showed that in the 1970s 29 per cent of all working women were involved in semi- and unskilled manual work; the figures for black women were much higher – 47 per cent of West Indian women, 48 per cent of Asian women from East Africa and 58 per cent of Indian women.

12   See Paul Willis, *Learning to Labour: How Working-Class Kids Get Working-Class Jobs* (Saxon House: 1977).

13   This suggests that, like their male counterparts, young working-class women also compensate for the tedium of work through their weekend activities. The literature on youth sub-cultures has been dominated by accounts of boys and young men, but there is a growing recognition of the specificity of sub-cultural styles among girls at school and young women at work. The elements of these cultures, with their emphasis upon romance and domesticity, show a marked continuity with shop-floor culture among women which also emphasizes the culture of femininity.
For an overview see, M. Brake, *The Sociology of Youth Culture and Youth Subcultures* (Routledge: 1980); Angela McRobbie and Jenny Garber, 'Girls and subcultures', in S. Hall and T. Jefferson (eds), *Resistance Through Rituals: Youth Subcultures in Post-War Britain* (Hutchinson: 1976), pp. 209–22; Angela McRobbie, 'Working-class girls and the culture of femininity', in Women's Studies Group, Centre for Contemporary Cultural Studies (eds), *Women Take Issue; Aspects of Women's Subordination* (Hutchinson: 1978), pp. 96–108. Earlier studies also suggest a historical continuity in the lives of young working-class women, both Pearl Jephcott and F. Zweig, writing in the late 1940s and early 1950s emphasized romance in the lives of young working-class women and the way in which dancing, films and boyfriends compensate for the monotony of factory life. See Pearl Jephcott, *Rising Twenty: Notes on some Ordinary Girls* (Faber and Faber: n.d. but it appears to be 1947), and F. Zweig, *Women's Life and Labour* (Gollancz: 1952), pp. 57–62.

14   As the General Household Survey Statistics (1979) show, only 5 per cent of households are based on a male breadwinner who supports a woman and two children.

15   Diana Leonard's study of courtship and wedding did mention jokes played on the bride which included confetti stuffed into clothes and bags and carrots given to young women, but this is at some distance from the elaborate ritual played out at StitchCo. See Diana Leonard, *Sex and Generation: A Study of Courtship and Weddings* (Tavistock: 1980), pp. 145–7.

16   Marriage was discussed as *the* trade for women in Cicely Hamilton's famous book, *Marriage as a Trade*, first published in 1909 and reprinted by the Women's Press in 1981.

17   See the full discussion by Gloria Joseph, 'The incompatible menage a trois: marxism, feminism and racism', in Lydia Sargent (ed.), *Women and Revolution: The Unhappy Marriage of Marxism and Feminism* (Pluto Press: 1981), pp. 91–107; Cherríe Moraga and Gloria Anzaldúa (eds), *This Bridge Called My Back: Writings By Radical Women of Colour* (Watertown Mass., Persephone Press: 1981); Angela Davis, *Women, Race and Class* (The Women's Press: 1982); *Spare Rib*, No. 132, July 1983.

18   Jenny Bourne, 'Towards an anti-racist feminism', *Race and Class*, Vol. 25, summer 1983, pp. 16; Anna Coote and Beatrix Campbell, *Sweet Freedom: The Struggle For Women's Liberation* (Picador: 1982), p. 238.

19   Jean Gardiner, 'Women in the labour process and class structure', in Alan Hunt (ed.), *Class and Class Structure* (Lawrence and Wishart: 1977), pp. 155–63.

20   For the feminist case on women's wages, cogently argued, see, Anne Phillips, *Hidden Hands: Women and Economic Politics* (Pluto: 1983), pp. 102–6.

21   Angela Davis, *Women, Race and Class*, chapter 12.

22   For a more extended discussion of the Eugenics Movement in Britain, see Lorna Duffin, 'Prisoners of progress: women and evolution', in Sara Delamont and Lorna Duffin (eds) *The Nineteenth-Century Woman: Her Cultural and Physical World* (Croom Helm: 1978), pp. 57–91, and Brian Easlea, *Science and Sexual Oppression: Patriarchy's Confrontation with Woman and Nature* (Weidenfeld and Nicholson: 1981), pp. 157–69. The continuity of Eugenicist views is shown in the 1942 *Beveridge Report*, p. 52, where it notes: 'In the next thirty years housewives as mothers have vital work to do in ensuring the adequate continuance of the British race and British ideals.'

23   Pratibha Parmar, 'Gender, race and class: Asian women in resistance', in Centre for Contemporary Cultural Studies (eds), *The Empire Strikes Back: Race and racism in 1970s Britain* (Hutchinson: 1982), p. 253.

24   See the London Weekend Return Group, A Working Group of the CSE, *In and Against the State* (Pluto: 1980).

25   Angela Davis, *Women, Race and Class*, p. 104.

Section V Changes in the distribution of income, wealth and consumption

Introduction

The preceding sections outlined some of the major changes which have taken place in the structure of class, race and gender relations in Britain over the last 30 years and their relationship to changes in the structure of the labour market. In addition, there have been marked changes in the distribution of income and wealth and in the structure of consumption. In the aftermath of the Second World War, the welfare state was firmly established in Britain and housing, education and health became available on the basis of need rather than ability to pay. But real incomes have risen considerably since the 1950s, and it has been argued that they have permitted a growing number of people to afford private provision of key items of consumption. The changes in income and wealth distribution have not been uniform or equally distributed across all social groups, however.

In Chapter 11, Pond shows that, whereas wealth inequality declined in the immediate post-war years, largely as a result of progressive taxation, this was generally confined to the top 20 per cent of individuals. It reflects both redistribution of wealth within wealthy families and the impact of growing home ownership. The share of the bottom 50 per cent of wealth owners was little changed, and between 1938 and 1972 the share of wealth owned by the top 20 per cent fell from 91 to 85 per cent. As Pond points out, such a decline can hardly be described as cataclysmic. The degree of wealth inequality stabilized in the 1960s and '70s but in the 1980s it began to increase again, partly as a result of a fall in income and wealth taxation at the higher levels, and partly as a result of the stock market boom in the first half of the 1980s and the rise of the so-called 'enterprise culture'. But, although privatization and 'popular capitalism' in the 1980s has widened the base of share ownership, the concentration of share ownership in the hands of the insurance and pension funds has continued to grow. And, while many new fortunes have been made during the 1980s, inheritance is still the key to wealth inequalities and the sharp reductions in income and inheritance taxation in 1988 suggest further widening of wealth inequalities in the future.

If the changes in the distribution of wealth have been fairly small scale, the distribution of income altered even less during the 1950s, '60s and '70s. Pond shows elsewhere (Pond, 1989) that the degree of income inequality (both before and after tax) declined only very marginally during this period. This reflects continuing inequality in the distribution of earned income, the limited redistributive impact of income taxes on higher income earners, the extension of income taxes down the income scale and the limitations on welfare benefits. Thirty years of redistributive policies therefore made little impact on the distribution of income. But, given that the degree of income inequality increased again during the 1980s, as the Government reduced taxes and social benefits it may be that redistributive policies reduced income inequality to lower levels than would have otherwise prevailed.

In recent years there appears to have been something of a shift away from state provided or collective forms of social provision towards the growth of private forms of provision and consumption. Not only has home ownership grown from just over a quarter of all households immediately post-war to nearly two-thirds of households in the late 1980s, but 10 per cent of children are educated privately and 8 per cent of the population are members of private health care schemes.

This has led some theorists, notably Peter Saunders (Chapter 12), to argue that we are witnessing a *restratification* of the population based on 'different relationships to the means of consumption'. He sees the social and economic divisions arising from this process as a 'new major fault-line in British society' between those who own (in the case of housing), or have access to private forms of consumption, and those who are reliant on state provision. According to Saunders the fault-line between public and private consumption has implications for both individual life chances and, in the case of housing, for the possibility of equity accumulation and wealth which are not open to non-owners. He further argues that the privatization of welfare provision is intensifying this cleavage to the point where consumption may be becoming more important than class.

This is a radical claim which, if correct, must dramatically reshape our ideas about class and social stratification in Britain. (The argument is discussed in detail in *The Changing Social Structure*, 1989, Chapter 6.) The issue taken up in Chapter 12 below is the related one that it is possible to identify a sequence of three distinct *phases* (not evolutionary stages) in the structure of provision and consumption in Britain over the last 150 years. Saunders labels these the 'market', 'socialized' and 'privatized' modes of consumption and he argues that in the first phase consumption was organized primarily through the market on the basis of ability to pay. But, because working-class incomes were low, this generated major problems over working-class education, health and housing conditions which forced the state into growing intervention in the market. At first this took the form of regulation to ensure certain minimum standards, but during the latter part of the nineteenth century, a second phase developed in which direct state intervention in key items of consumption came to supplement and replace market provision. Saunders suggests that this new socialized form of provision reached maturity in the wake of the Second World War in the form of the welfare state. But he argues that, while it overcame the contradictions inherent in the market mode between low wages and an adequate standard of provision, it did so only at the cost of another contradiction – that between the costs of welfare provision and the state's ability to fund them. This contradiction became increasingly marked in the 1970s in the form of a fiscal crisis of the state. The response has been a shift towards a third phase of privatized consumption in which the costs of provision are shifted towards individuals and away from the state. Saunders sees this not just as a short-term phenomenon but as an 'established and enduring' one.

This is an important argument because it explicitly contradicts the argument put forward by some Marxist theoreticians that state provision of collective consumption is necessary for reproduction of labour power in all advanced capitalist societies. Saunders argues, on the contrary, that while private provision is often underpinned by the state in some instances (tax relief on mortgage interest and company subscriptions to private medical schemes), universal direct provision by the state is no longer functionally necessary for the reproduction of labour power, and is proving to be historically specific rather than a permanent phenomenon.

This is a radical claim, but Saunders is not alone in arguing this thesis. A number of neo-Marxists would also accept that we are witnessing 'the decollectivization of consumption' as Harloe and Paris (Chapter 13) term it. They argue that the cuts in collective consumption, via cuts in local government expenditure and housing expenditure have been a result of Britain's economic problems and the international economic crisis rather than political ideology and that cuts have taken place under Labour and Conservative governments since the mid-1970s. While they accept that cuts have been pushed further under the Conservatives than under Labour, they reject the idea of a sharp political break in 1979.

Where they differ from Saunders is in the mechanisms they identify for bringing about this phenomenon. They agree that the fiscal crisis of the state has been a key determinant of privatization. They also agree that privatization has been underpinned by rising real incomes which have given a growing proportion of the population the resources to purchase forms of private consumption such as houses and cars. However, Saunders stresses individual preference for personal autonomy and control as being central to the growth of privatized consumption, whereas Harloe and Paris reject this and stress fiscal austerity.

This economistic interpretation of events is also open to challenge. Forrest and Murie (Chapter 14) accept that large cuts have taken place in state spending on council housing in Britain since the mid-1970s, particularly since 1979, and that these have often been linked to notions of fiscal crisis and arguments about what the country can afford. They argue however that these cuts should be examined in the context of other shifts in the pattern of housing expenditure, notably the emergence of housing benefits (which count as social security spending) and the tax subsidies to owner occupation. When these are taken into account, they argue there has *not* been an overall cut in housing spending but a *reorientation* away from council housing and towards owner occupation. As a result, they suggest that it is misleading to see the changes in housing policy as the inevitable outcomes of fiscal constraint. Instead they argue that the reorientation of housing expenditure can best be explained in terms of

Conservative political and ideological antipathy towards council housing and the desire to foster the growth of owner occupation.

The detailed empirical analysis of Forrest and Murie casts doubt on the notion that the fiscal crisis of the state has been responsible for the cuts in social expenditure. Instead, they point to the role of wider political and ideological considerations. Thus, while there has been a major shift towards the decollectivization of consumption as Saunders and Harloe and Paris suggest, this appears to have occurred for political rather than economic and fiscal reasons; which suggests that the shift towards privatization of consumption is not necessarily a permanent or inevitable phenomenon but one which can be reversed.

Reference

POND, C. (1989) 'The changing distribution of income, wealth and poverty', in Hamnett, C., McDowell, L. and Sarre, P. (eds) *The Changing Social Structure* (Restructuring Britain), London, Sage/The Open University.

11 Wealth and the two nations

Chris Pond

Britain is a deeply divided society, and the deepest division of all is the inequality in the ownership of wealth. That the inequalities have persisted for so long helps in itself to legitimate them, to make them more acceptable; the status quo is an influential public relations officer for the rich. And the very extremities of wealth inequalities somehow deprive the statistics of credibility or meaning. They defy comprehension, let alone challenge. Yet the truth is that inequality feeds upon itself. Wealth begets income and opportunity, status and power; and from each of these springs wealth. The inequalities are circular and self-perpetuating.

In the first part of this chapter we examine the changes that have taken place in the distribution of personal wealth [during] this century. We then examine the nature of wealth inequalities as they manifest themselves today, and explore the explanations that have been offered for their persistence [. . .] We begin by looking back to the 1920s, the years of Gatsby and Bloomsbury. How much more equal is Britain today?

The gallop towards equality?

Measurement of the size and nature of a problem, without the intention even when the information is available to do very much about it, is an exercise which lacks a sense of purpose. It is perhaps unsurprising, therefore, that official statistics are still unable to describe conclusively the true extent of wealth inequalities. The statistics, like those on the distribution of income, are a by-product of the administrative process of tax collection. Wealth in Britain, for most of this century, has only been taxed when its owner dies, so that estimates of total wealth holdings are based on a relatively small sample each year. And since wealth-holders have to be either very rich, or very careless, or both, for their wealth to pass through the estate duty office at all, estimates of the true magnitude of wealth inequalities require some elaborate, and not always wholly reliable, adjustments. Partly for this reason [. . .] the Royal Commission on the Distribution of Income and Wealth, established as part of the last Labour government's commitment 'to shift the balance of wealth and power in favour of working people and their families', spent most of its time working out what the current balance of wealth and power actually was. The Commission was left with little time to consider what should be done about the situation, even if it had wished to do so.

For the most part it has been left to independent academics and researchers to estimate the distribution of wealth, and how it has changed. Prominent amongst these are A. B. Atkinson and A. J. Harrison. It is their

Table 11.1   Distribution of wealth in England and Wales 1923–72

	Top 1%	Top 5%	Top 10%	Top 20%	Bottom 80%
1923	60.9	82.0	89.1	94.2	5.8
1928	57.0	79.6	87.2	93.1	6.9
1938	55.0	76.9	85.0	91.2	8.8
1950	47.2	74.3	—	—	—
1953	43.6	71.1	—	—	—
1958	41.4	67.8	—	—	—
1960	33.9	59.4	71.5	83.1	16.9
1965	33.0	58.1	71.7	85.5	14.5
1968	33.6	58.3	71.6	85.1	14.9
1970	29.7	53.6	68.7	84.5	15.5
1971	28.4	52.3	67.6	84.2	15.8
1972	31.7	56.0	70.4	84.9	15.1

Source: Table 6.5, Atkinson and Harrison (1978)

work which has provided us, very recently, with the most consistent statistics on wealth inequalities stretching back over half a century, from the early 1920s to the early 1970s. Although, as the authors make clear, the series is still subject to certain discontinuities, and the actual magnitude of the figures should be treated with caution, these are the most reliable statistics yet made available. They suggest that, although the share of the top 1 per cent of wealth-holders has declined, the rate of decline has been very much less than previous estimates, including those used by the Royal Commission, would lead us to believe. The estimates are given in Table 11.1.

The Royal Commission's figures had suggested that the share of the richest 1 per cent of wealth-holders had fallen over this period at a rate of 0.7 per cent a year – hardly a gallop. But the more consistent series compiled by Atkinson and Harrison show that the rate of decline was little more than half that suggested by the orthodox presentation. Over the entire period 1923 to 1972, the share of the richest 1 per cent declined at an annual rate of only 0.4 per cent, subject to a once-and-for-all jump in 1959 and 1960. Contrary to the established view, there has been no apparent acceleration in the arithmetic rate of decline. It follows that, by the end of this century, if change continues at this rate, the top 1 per cent can still look forward to owning almost a fifth of all the personal wealth. Even in the year 2020 they will still enjoy a tenth of the nation's wealth.

The more wealthy of our readers may still be alarmed at this prospect, and we should point out that, on the basis of the more recent figures, the share of the richest groups is unlikely to continue falling at even this pedestrian pace. The estimates suggest that, by the mid-1960s, the rate of decline had evaporated altogether. The authors calculate that the downward trend in their estimates between 1966 and 1972 was not significantly different from zero when statistical tests of significance are applied. As one of the authors reported in the first edition of 'The Wealth Report':

the errors introduced as a consequence of estimating the distribution of wealth from a sample could alone explain all the variations observed in the share of the top one per cent over the period. Overall, the safest conclusion is that the distribution of wealth in the early 1970s was little different from that observed in the early 1960s. (Harrison, 1979, p. 40)

The rate of decline in the share of wealth monopolized by the very richest individuals appears to have been much slower than had previously been assumed. Moreover, while the share of the top 1 per cent has been slowly declining, that of the richest four per cent immediately below them has remained constant. In other words, the decline has been confined to the share of the richest one per cent. As Atkinson explained in an earlier work 'what redistribution there has been is not between the rich and the poor, but between the very rich and the rich' (Atkinson, 1972, p. 22). We will return to an explanation of this phenomenon in a moment.

Overall, therefore, the share of wealth enjoyed by the richest 1 per cent has almost halved over the period of half a century considered. But the rest of the top 5 per cent apparently increased their share marginally from just over 21 per cent to just over 24 per cent. This change is unlikely to be statistically significant but the direction of change is clear. Taking the lower half of the richest 10 per cent (the top 6–10 per cent), their share apparently doubled, from 7 per cent to over 14 per cent; and the share of the next richest 10 per cent (the top 11–20 per cent) almost trebled their proportionate wealth-holding from 5 per cent to 14½ per cent. In 1923 the top fifth of the adult population enjoyed 94 per cent of the personal wealth; in 1972 they still retained 85 per cent of the total. Such a decline may hardly be described as cataclysmic.

One explanation for this pattern of change in the relative shares of the top groups might be that the redistribution had taken place, not from the richest families, but within them. In other words, heads of household (likely to fall into the richest 1 per cent) were passing their wealth on to other members of the family (who were also numbered within the top 5 per cent) (see Atkinson, 1972, p. 23). This explanation received considerable support from an examination of a sample of estates receiving probate in 1973, carried out by the Royal Commission. Not surprisingly, the great majority of bequests were made to relatives of the deceased. The Commission concluded that: 'The fragmentation of large wealth holdings at death reduces the share of the top one per cent, but to the benefit of the groups immediately below as a number of beneficiaries each receives a sizeable bequest' (Royal Commission Report No. 5, 1977, para. 399). This, of course, is redistribution of a rather special kind, representing little more than the re-ordering of affairs within the richest families, possibly to minimize the impact of death duties. The poor gained nothing; for them, changes in the distribution of wealth between the 1920s and 1970s was little more than a spectator sport, with no prizes for the crowd.

Wealth shares in the 1970s

The Atkinson/Harrison series presents us with a picture of changes in the distribution of wealth up until the early 1970s. Since then official estimates have become available on a much improved basis. The share of half the population was so small that the Inland Revenue previously found it difficult to measure it at all, and presented estimates on the assumption that they owned no wealth. The exclusion of half the population left the statistics open to criticism (especially from such as the Institute of Economic Affairs) that the figures dramatically overstated inequality. The adjustment of the figures yielded estimates remarkably similar to the old series. The wealth of half the population was indeed negligible.

Part (a) of Table 11.2 shows the distribution of personal wealth amongst the adult members of the UK population in the 1970s.

The distribution changed very little after 1974. In each year, the richest 1 per cent of the adult population enjoyed almost one-quarter of the nation's personal wealth. We should put this in perspective. One per cent of the adult population represents slightly more than 400 000 people – the turnout normally expected at Epsom on Derby Day! This tiny handful of people owned four or five times as much wealth as the least privileged half of the population had to share between them. Two per cent of adults owned

Table 11.2   Distribution of wealth 1971–9

	United Kingdom 1971	1974	1975	1976	1977	Percentages 1978	1979
(a) Marketable wealth							
Percentage of wealth owned by:							
Most wealthy 1 per cent of population[1]	31	23	24	24	23	23	24
Most wealthy 2 per cent of population	39	30	31	32	30	30	32
Most wealthy 5 per cent of population	52	43	44	46	44	44	45
Most wealthy 10 per cent of population	65	57	58	61	58	58	59
Most wealthy 25 per cent of population	86	84	83	84	82	83	82
Most wealthy 50 per cent of population	97	93	93	95	95	95	95
Total marketable wealth (£ thousand million)[2]	164	236	272	296	345	401	488
(b) Marketable wealth plus occupational pension rights							
Percentage of wealth owned by:							
Most wealthy 1 per cent of population	27	19	20	21	19	19	20
Most wealthy 2 per cent of population	34	26	26	27	25	26	26
Most wealthy 5 per cent of population	46	38	38	40	38	39	38
Most wealthy 10 per cent of population	59	52	52	53	51	52	51
Most wealthy 25 per cent of population[3]	78–83	76–82	75–81	75–81	74–78	75–79	75–79
Most wealthy 50 per cent of population[3]	90–96	88–92	88–92	89–93	88–92	89–93	89–93
(c) Marketable wealth plus occupational and state pension rights							
Percentage of wealth owned by:							
Most wealthy 1 per cent of population	21	15	13	14	12	13	13
Most wealthy 2 per cent of population	27	21	18	18	17	17	18
Most wealthy 5 per cent of population	37	31	27	27	25	25	27
Most wealthy 10 per cent of population	49	43	37	37	35	36	37
Most wealthy 25 per cent of population[3]	69–72	64–67	58–61	58–61	55–58	57–60	58–61
Most wealthy 50 per cent of population[3]	85–89	85–89	81–85	80–85	78–82	79–83	79–83

Notes: 1. Aged 18 and over. 2. End year. 3. Estimates vary with assumptions.
Source: 'Social Trends' 12 (1982), London, HMSO

almost one-third of the wealth; 5 per cent owned almost half; and 10 per cent owned almost two-thirds.

Such figures are still difficult to comprehend. Indeed, as we suggested above, this may be one reason why the persistence of wealth inequalities is not subjected to more rigorous public enquiry. The figures are so extreme that, for most of the population, they have little meaning. There is an old saying: 'What you've never had, you never miss.' And since half the population has never had more than a negligible amount of wealth, the concept defies comprehension, let alone challenge.

The scale of the inequality becomes clearer if we consider the actual amounts of wealth involved. In 1979, total marketable wealth was estimated at just under £500 billion. If equally distributed, each member of the population aged over eighteen would have had average net wealth (after paying off their mortgages, debts and other liabilities) of around £12000 at 1979 prices. Each household would have net wealth, on average, of over £30000 in 1979. The actual situation was rather different. Those in the bottom half of the distribution had average wealth of only £1200 each or £3000 per household – less than a tenth as much as if wealth had been equally shared. Meanwhile, those in the top half of the distribution had an average wealth-holding of £23000 each (almost £60000 per household). A sharper illustration of Disraeli's 'two nations' would be difficult to contemplate. Half the population had an average twenty times as much wealth as the other half.

These are, of course, only averages based on the assumption of 2.6 adults per household; we are not suggesting that all households conform to the average composition. Nor do we assume that the assets which make up the wealth could be easily divided in this way. Furthermore, even amongst the richest half of the population wealth is extremely unequally divided. As Tony Atkinson has explained, 'the gap between Mr X who just qualifies for the top one per cent and the millionaire with a household name is much larger than that between Mr X and the average wealth-holder' (Atkinson, 1975, p. 131). The richest 1 per cent of adults owned an average of almost a third of a million pounds or nearly £800000 per household – 250 times as much as the average wealth-holding amongst the least privileged half of the populace.

Explaining wealth inequalities

The magnitude and persistence of these inequalities requires some explanation. Recent years have seen substantial growth of various forms of 'popular' wealth: housing, pensions, insurance policies, national savings. Certainly, these have had some impact. But their effect has, to a large extent, been offset by influences operating in the opposite direction. We should begin by examining the effect of the growth of pensions. The analysis we have presented so far has been concerned primarily with 'marketable' wealth – that which could be sold and realized as cash without very much difficulty. Now it may be argued that this definition of wealth is too narrow. We should be concerned with an individual's 'command over economic resources', and this goes beyond the value of his goods and chattels. A young man, assured of a good job or future inheritance, may well be able to persuade his bank manager to advance him a loan now in anticipation of the day when his ship comes in. His command over economic resources is well in excess of his current wealth. Using similar reasoning, the Royal Commission on the Distribution of Income and Wealth argued that the present (capitalized) value of the future incomes assured by an occupational or state pension should be included in calculations of the value of wealth. Table 11.2(b) shows estimates of the distribution including occupational provisions, while Table 11.2(c) includes state pensions rights. Because the estimates of the effect of this on the wealth of the least privileged vary according to the assumptions used about their allocation, a range of estimates is given.

The inclusion of such assets in the estimates makes a significant difference, to the actual shares, if not to trends in the distribution during the 1970s. Including occupational pensions reduces the overall share of the top 1 per cent from 24 to 20 per cent, and, if state pension rights are also included, this falls again to 13 per cent. The 'poorest' half of the population are seen to gain a bigger share of wealth defined in this way.

We have to ask whether this adjustment to the figures improves our understanding or simply helps to numb us to the harsh facts about the distribution of marketable wealth. It is quite correct to say that a more comprehensive definition of wealth is desirable; but if only a small part of the additional elements of wealth can be calculated, their inclusion may serve only to distort the picture. For if we are to include a future rights to pensions why not also prospective inheritances, rights to education, and to future earnings? Since rights and opportunities normally go hand in hand with wealth and privilege, it is not at all clear that estimates based on a truly comprehensive definition of wealth, even if they could be calculated, would yield a distribution more equal than that of normally defined marketable wealth.

Moreover, as Louie Burghes pointed out in the first edition of *The Wealth Report*, there is an important difference between occupational and state pension rights. Entitlement to a state pension promises a flow of income at some date in the future. The size of this flow will depend on the individual's contribution during his/her lifetime and the length of time they live to enjoy it. Since many manual workers live only a short time into retirement, they may be excused for scepticism about their inclusion amongst the wealthy. But even those who have entitlement to a full state pension will be unable either to cash in this entitlement or to use it as security on a loan. Those with occupational pension rights may enjoy both these options. Even so, only about one third of the population have any form of occupational pensions (Burghes, 1979, pp. 27–8). There is no doubt, however, that other forms of 'popular' wealth should be included –

housing, insurance policies, national savings – as indeed they are in Table 11.2(a). These are unequivocally elements of the total stock of wealth. And, of these, housing is, of course, the most important.

The growth in home ownership this century has been quite dramatic. At the turn of the century only 10 per cent of dwellings were owner occupied. By the early 1960s this had increased to over 40 per cent, rising again to 54 per cent by the late 1970s. The growth in owner occupation in itself need not have had a major impact on the inequalities we recorded above. We are dealing in net wealth, after taking account of debts and liabilities, including mortgages. So the average family can only count in its 'wealth' the amount of its home that it actually owns – what it has 'paid off'. However, this growth in owner occupation has been accompanied by a very considerable growth in house prices. Between 1960 and 1976 the price of housing rose six-fold, with a large part of this rise occurring between 1970 and 1973. No other form of wealth increased in value so dramatically. (Royal Commission Report No. 8, 1979, p. 125).

As house prices increased, 'home owners' found the value of their wealth (net of liabilities) increasing and with it their share of total wealth. The very poorest, who are less likely to be amongst the owner-occupying classes, probably gained little but the increase in owner occupation was undoubtedly an important social change. What is perhaps more remarkable is the fact that this change together with the growth in other forms of popular wealth had such a limited impact on the overall distribution. To understand why, we need to look more carefully at the nature of wealth inequalities.

Our discussions earlier in this chapter have been in terms of aggregate wealth, boiling all assets down to their money value. The top 1 per cent of the population, as we noted above, overall owned about one-quarter of the personal wealth. But they also owned almost 70 per cent of the personal wealth held in the form of land, and almost half that in the form of buildings (other than dwellings). The same 1 per cent of the population owned 70 per cent of the listed ordinary shares and 77 per cent of the other company securities, and two-thirds of all UK government securities.

The concentration is still more remarkable when one considers the wealth-holdings of the richest 0.1 per cent of the population. There were little more than 40000 people in this group. But between them they owned over 40 per cent of the private land, a quarter of the listed ordinary shares and a third of other company securities in private hands plus a third of UK government securities.

Now we are in a position to examine why the growth in owner occupation (and other forms of 'popular wealth') have not had more impact, why the 1950s Conservative dream of 'every man a capitalist' has not been realized. The elements of 'popular wealth' which are most important to those with relatively small wealth holdings are of little significance to the very richest.

For example, those who had net wealth of less than £5000 in 1976 held virtually all of it in the form of dwellings, household goods, life policies, building society deposits, cash and bank deposits, and national savings. By contrast, those with net wealth exceeding £200000 held less than a third of its gross value in these forms. It follows from this that an increase in house prices, for instance, will have a considerable impact on the wealth of the least wealthy, but little on that of the very richest. Rapid changes in the price of land or shares will have the opposite effect. The first will tend to equalize the distribution of wealth; the second to increase the degree of inequality.

An illustration of how this can effect the degree of measured inequality was provided by the Royal Commission who calculated the impact of the changing importance of different types of assets as well as their changes in price. Over the period 1960 to 1972, for instance, the growth of owner occupation and mortgages as well as increasing home prices resulted in a decline in the relative share of the top 1 per cent by 6 percentage points. But the increase in the quantity and price of stocks and shares increased their share by $7\frac{1}{2}$ percentage points. The two effects cancelled each other out. The net decline in the wealth-holdings of the richest groups was attributed to an increase in the importance of cash assets, insurance policies and household goods.

Look again at table 11.2(a). At first glance the table is puzzling. Between 1971 and 1974, a period of conservative rule, the share of the richest 1 per cent fell significantly, from 31 per cent to 23 per cent of the total. After 1974, with the election of a Labour government committed to 'a redistribution of wealth and power in favour of working people and their families', we would have expected a further fall. Instead, the richest wealth-holders recovered somewhat from the unnerving decline in their share under the previous administration. The explanation is to be found in the asset composition of wealth and relative price changes. The early 1970s saw a virtual collapse of the stock market, with the result that the book value of shares was reduced 'at a stroke' (to borrow a phrase rather popular at that time). The redistribution which we witnessed in the 1970s was therefore of a rather special kind. Once again the poor gained nothing from the declining fortunes of the rich, except perhaps a little smug satisfaction.

Readers may be surprised that, in considering changes in the distribution of wealth, we have as yet made no mention of wealth taxation. [However, . . .] wealth taxes have been largely irrelevant, certainly in the most recent past. In the previous volume of *The Wealth Report* Alan Harrison summarized the results of his work with Tony Atkinson attempting to assess the causes of the change in the distribution of wealth between 1923 and 1972. Two possible conclusions emerged from this analysis: one was that the decline in the share of the top 1 per cent was due to an increase in the importance of 'popular wealth', offset by an increase in share prices working in the opposite direction; the other, perhaps less plausible, explanation was that estate duty taxation had been most important in reducing wealth inequalities, offset again by the increase in share prices.

Harrison's own assessment was that 'Estate Duty, if it has had any influence, has conducted a "holding operation", preventing an increase in concentration' (Harrison, 1979, p. 42).

Wealth and power

An analysis of the types of asset that make up the wealth of different groups, as shown in the [. . .] tables, helps us to explain why there has not been a more dramatic equalization of wealth during the post-war period. Certainly, there has been an increase in the importance, and value, of 'popular wealth' – houses, insurance policies and pensions. But these have always been of relatively little importance in the portfolios of the very rich, and the equalization that has taken place has to a large extent been offset by movements in the opposite direction.

This type of analysis also helps us to understand the true nature of wealth, and its importance as a social and political, as well as economic, concept. In the earlier edition of *The Wealth Report*, Louie Burghes drew attention to an important distinction between different types of wealth which Professor Halsey had identified as the distinguishing division of society:

> property for power by which I mean property which carries control over the lives of other people, and property for use – possessions that free a man from other people's control A tiny minority has monopolized wealth, and an even tinier minority has monopolized property for power. (Halsey, 1978, p. 80)

What Halsey meant by this distinction becomes clear from our discussion on the types of assets which make up wealth. Those forms of wealth that yield an improvement in living standards and security – houses, consumer durables, pensions, insurance policies – all have grown. But the wealth that confers social and political power – land, shares and company securities – remains heavily concentrated in the hands of the few. All these provide their owners with an ability to control not only their own lives, but the lives of others as well. If one is to take issue with Professor Halsey's distinction, it may be in his assertion that the ownership of 'property for use' frees its owner from other people's control. Such property may provide improved living standards or security; but in itself it is unlikely to free him or her from the need to work for their living, remaining under the control of others.

An alternative distinction between different types of wealth has been offered by Chris Hird who argues that capital (similar to Halsey's 'wealth for power') is the most important element in social inequality:

> Capital . . . is different from other forms of wealth: shares in an industrial company, for example, will typically grow in value over time, produce a regular dividend, confer legal ownership over part of the company's material assets, and are, moreover, easily marketable when necessary. Other forms of wealth are quite different: consumer goods generally depreciate and have

low second-hand value; the value of houses may in the main appreciate, but they are often difficult to sell and the owner generally needs to buy another as replacement; pensions provide an entitlement to a future income only as long as the pensioner lives, are not transferable, and often depreciate in value; and cash, although it confers immediate economic power through its purchasing power, generally depreciates. It is changes in the ownership and control of the means of production that need to be treated as the central criterion in assessing the distribution of wealth, for changes in other forms of wealth are intimately related to these. (Hird, 1979, p. 202)

Hird goes on to argue that the Royal Commission's preoccupation with the distribution of personal wealth, and its failure to distinguish between different types of personal wealth, had caused it to overlook the major concentrations of power in society. It is often argued, for instance, that the growth of institutionalized wealth – in companies, pension funds, insurance institutions and the banks – has led us nearer to the 'property-owning democracy' by breaking the hold on the nation's wealth of a few powerful individuals. On the contrary, the evidence suggests that control of institutionalized wealth is still more heavily concentrated than personal wealth. Hird cites Department of Trade evidence to show that, even by the late 1960s, just thirty insurance companies controlled 85 per cent of all insurance company assets, while the biggest five companies controlled 38 per cent (Hird, 1979, p. 203). And in these companies perhaps a handful of people have real control.

The wealth owned by the pension funds is also heavily concentrated. It has been calculated that 40 institutions control three-quarters of all pension fund money and that, within these funds, perhaps just 200 people have investment authority and control. The banks, too, represent enormous concentrations of wealth: the 'big four' banks between them account for 70 per cent of bank deposits (Cripps *et al.*, 1981).

In all these cases ownership and control of this wealth has been sieved and separated; and in the process the power attaching to the wealth, that is (nominally) owned by many millions of ordinary people, is transferred to those who have control of it in its concentrated and institutionalized form. The pension contributions and entitlements of workers, the building society deposits and mortgages, the bank deposits and insurance policies, none of these confer on those who 'own' them any measure of control or power. This lies in the hands of what have been described as 'small oligarchies of power' – the chief executives, boards of directors, and investment managers who determine how such wealth shall be used. While the Royal Commission busied itself allocating the nominal ownership of this wealth in terms of owner-occupation, pension entitlements, insurance policies and bank deposits, it overlooked the control of the building societies, the pension funds, the insurance companies and the banks.

In no area is the importance of control, irrespective of ownership, more effectively illustrated than in the area of corporate wealth. In 1979 it is estimated that the six largest industrial concerns listed on the London Stock Exchange accounted for over one-quarter of the turnover, while the top 180 accounted for 80 per cent. Just over 150 industrial concerns accounted for 30 per cent of the output and for the same proportion of net tangible assets (quoted in Aaronovitch, 1981, p. 7).

As Sir Arthur Knight, Chairman of the National Enterprise Board and formerly of Courtaulds, has reminded us:

> It is too often forgotten that 80 per cent of our manufacturing industry is run by 400 firms, in each of which three or four people are responsible for the key strategic decisions – say 1500 at most. And in the investing industry (pension funds, insurance companies, etc.) I would guess that the number of key individuals is even smaller. (Quoted in Cripps *et al.*, 1981)

The 'institutionalization' of personal wealth in recent years has therefore brought with it an increased concentration of power and not, as might have been expected, a democratization of wealth. 'Popular' wealth has certainly grown, but the control of that wealth has been transferred to the individuals who administer and control it. Meanwhile, those forms of personal wealth that continue to confer power on those who own them remain heavily concentrated.

This vital link between wealth and power helps us, in turn, to explain the persistence of wealth inequalities. At the outset we suggested that this was due to the circular and self-perpetuating nature of wealth. Those who have wealth have not only the income and the opportunity to generate and replenish their wealth-holding, but also the power with which to defend their position from challenge. Only when we have grasped the interlocking nature of wealth and power can we understand the persistence of both.

Accumulation and inheritance

Some may argue that this association between wealth and power presents no cause for alarm. There is an enduring belief that differences in wealth represent differences in individual attributes and abilities. The wealthy may enjoy more of the fruits of society; but they have also contributed more to their propagation. The argument was put most forcefully by William Sumner, the prominent American economist, writing towards the end of the last century. He explained:

> The millionaires are a product of natural selection . . . It is because they are thus selected that wealth – both their own and that entrusted to them – aggregates under their hands . . . They may be fairly regarded as the naturally selected agents of society for certain work. They get high wages and live in luxury, but the bargain is a good one for society. (Quoted in Galbraith, 1977, p. 46)

Such crude 'Social Darwinism' is rarely expressed nowadays. In its place an elaborate body of economic theory has developed to provide justification and legitimization for the rewards of the rich. The belief that wealth and ability go hand in hand retains a powerful grasp on the public imagination. Now if such a belief is justified, we need not concern ourselves that power is vested in the wealthy; we are in good hands. We must choose our rulers somehow; how better than to leave the choice to 'natural' or 'economic' selection.

Of course, it takes little more than simple observation to shake us out of this cosy mythology. As Robert Heller, financial journalist with 'Management Today', has explained:

> It is often only when the rich man has been incautious that the private and public images suddenly coincide and the realities emerge – that riches and true achievement bear only a tenuous relationship to each other: but that, if only you are rich enough, nobody will ever notice the truth. (Heller, 1974, p. ii)

Some of the rich, of course, are people of outstanding ability; so, as history reminds us, are some of the poor. But there is no systematic relationship. We need to look more closely, then, at the sources of wealth. We have already examined the factors influencing the change in relative shares of the rich, but we still need to know how different groups acquired their wealth in the first place. There is fairly general agreement that, luck and fortune aside, people's wealth-holdings are attributable to two main factors: inheritance and accumulation out of savings. Accumulation itself depends, of course, on age as well as the level of an individual's income. The relative importance attributed to each of these factors varies greatly. *The Times*, for instance, has argued that:

> in the most egalitarian of societies one would not expect the new born babe and the man on the point of retirement to have identical savings . . . and there must therefore be a concentration of wealth in a minority of hands in any society one can conceive of. Where inheritance is not allowed, only the old can be rich. (*The Times*, September 1968 quoted in A. B. Atkinson, 1972)

There is clearly considerable validity in this explanation. Those who have been continuously employed for several years obviously have more of an opportunity to accumulate wealth than those who have just left school. But age is not the only factor. A preliminary examination of wealth-holdings by age, by the Royal Commission, though subject to some deficiences, suggested that 'the distribution of wealth within age groups was generally similar to that of the population as a whole' (Royal Commission Report No. 7, 1979, p. 96). Also important are differences in the level of earnings from which different groups have to save: inequalities in wealth reflect in part the inequalities in incomes, and vice versa.

One way of taking account of this is to build a 'model' of the amount that people could save during their lifetime, using different assumptions about earnings and savings [. . .]

In [1974], the top 1 per cent of wealth-holders owned 22.5 per cent of all the personal wealth. How much of that could be explained by savings over the life cycle? The answer depends on the assumptions used, but the models would lead us to expect this group to have only between 3 and 7 per cent of the total, if their wealth was accumulated during their lifetime.

Savings help to explain a larger proportion of the share of the next richest group, the top 2–5 per cent, but still account for only one-half to two-thirds of their actual share. At the other end of the scale, the savings of the bottom 80 per cent would have been rewarded with a rather larger share of total wealth than was actually the case. Thrift and hard work may put you on the road to wealth, but will not take you very far along it. The extreme of the distribution cannot adequately be explained by savings out of earnings. Where, then, do the very rich acquire their wealth? There are three other main possibilities: financial windfalls, entrepreneurial fortunes or inheritances. The Royal Commission calculated that approximately 40 per cent of all wealth was derived from these sources. But they accounted for three-quarters of the wealth of the top 1 per cent and for over half of that of the rest of the top 5 per cent. Their importance diminished with the size of the total wealth-holding. Inheritance and entrepreneurial fortunes do not fall randomly. The Royal Commission noted: 'a marked tendency for transmitted wealth and entrepreneurial fortunes to be concentrated heavily amongst the top wealth groups' (Royal Commission Report No. 7, 1979, p. 98).

A more comprehensive picture of the pattern of inheritance has been provided by work carried out by Professor Colin Harbury and David Hitchens. They undertook the laborious, but rewarding, exercise of tracing the transmission of wealth from one branch of the family tree to the next, adapting the method used by Josiah Wedgewood as long ago as 1929. The researchers examined the wealth which had been left by the fathers of the very rich – the top 0.1 per cent who owned about one-sixth of all personal wealth. These people left the equivalent (at today's prices) of about £500000. Of these, about half the men and three-quarters of the women had fathers who left more than the equivalent of £250000. At a compound annual rate of interest of 7 per cent, this sum might be expected to double (to the amount left by the heirs themselves) in just a decade. Three-fifths of the rich men and three-quarters of the rich women (those who left £500000) had fathers who had left the equivalent of £125000. Compound interest of 7 per cent would have converted that sum into £500000 (the amount the heirs were worth) in just twenty years.

Harbury and Hitchens put the importance of inheritance into perspective by pointing out that, if there was no systematic relationship between the wealth of fathers and sons – if, for instance, inheritance was prevented by taxation or other means – it would be a matter of chance whether one had a rich father or not. In this lottery of wealth, the probability of having a rich father (worth more than £250000) is less than one per cent. As we have seen, the odds were rather better for some people: rich men had a fifty-fifty chance of having had rich fathers; rich women had a better than even chance (3:1). The authors concluded that 'without question, the firmest conclusion to emerge from this study is that inheritance is the major determinant of wealth inequality' (Harbury and Hitchens, 1980, p. 239).

What also becomes clear from this type of analysis is the link between accumulation and inheritance. The inheritance of a substantial sum makes it very much easier to accumulate more. As Robert Heller explained to those aspiring to wealth 'time and the magic of compound interest' can help to turn even a modest inheritance into a substantial estate:

> It has never been especially difficult to achieve 7 per cent growth tax-free, which doubles your money every ten years. . . . And in half a century turns that million into 32 millions. You have to be especially inspired in your choice of investment or adviser (and remember with a million you can afford advice) to do worse, although it is not impossible. (Heller, 1974, pp. 15–16)

There are many tales of self-made men and women who have travelled the journey from rags to riches. But what makes such stories worth the telling is that their subjects are the exception, not the rule. Many people have acquired for themselves a comfortable enough standard of living through their own efforts, but they are rarely to be found amongst the very wealthy. It is inheritance that generates and perpetuates the largest concentrations of wealth and power [. . .]

References

AARONOVITCH, S. (1981) *The Road from Thatcherism*, London, Lawrence and Wishart.

ATKINSON, A. B. (1972) *Unequal Shares: Wealth in Britain*, London, Allen Lane.

ATKINSON, A. B. (1975) *Economics of Inequality*, Oxford, Oxford University Press.

ATKINSON, A. B. and HARRISON, A. J. (1978) *Distribution of Personal Wealth in Britain*, Cambridge, Cambridge University Press.

BURGHES, L. (1979) 'The old order', in Field, F. (ed.) (1979).

CRIPPS, F. *et al.* (1981) *Manifesto*, London, Pan Books.

FIELD, F. (ed.) (1979) *The Wealth Report*, 1st edition, London, Routledge and Kegan Paul.

GALBRAITH, J. K. (1977) *The Age of Uncertainty*, London, BBC/Andre Deutsch.

HARBURY, C. and HITCHINS, D. (1980) 'The myth of the self-made man', *New Statesman*, 15 February.

HARRISON, A. (1979) 'Recent changes in the distribution of personal wealth in Britain', in Field, F. (ed.) (1979).

HELLER, R. (1974) *The Common Millionaire*, London, Weidenfeld and Nicolson.

HIRD, C. (1979) 'The poverty of wealth statistics', in Irvine and Evans (eds), *Demystifying Social Statistics*, London, Pluto Press.

ROYAL COMMISSION ON THE DISTRIBUTION OF INCOME AND WEALTH (1977) Report No. 5, Cmnd 6999, London, HMSO.

ROYAL COMMISSION ON THE DISTRIBUTION OF INCOME AND WEALTH (1979) Report No. 7, Cmnd 7595, London, HMSO.

ROYAL COMMISSION ON THE DISTRIBUTION OF INCOME AND WEALTH (1979) Report No. 8, Cmnd 7679, London, HMSO.

12   Beyond housing classes: the sociological significance of private property rights in means of consumption

Peter Saunders

The significance of domestic property ownership for the distribution of wealth, the structuration of classes and the mobilization of political conflicts has in recent years been the subject of widespread academic debate and political argument. In academic circles there is now general agreement that housing tenure should be seen neither as the basis for a distinct system of 'housing classes' (as was originally proposed by Rex and Moore, 1967), nor as the source of merely ideological divisions and interests (as was suggested in some of the cruder Marxist analyses of this question), but intense disagreements still remain over the way in which housing tenure in general, and owner occupancy in particular, should be analysed in relation to wider class relations and political struggles. Similarly in political circles, there is much confusion and dispute among socialists over whether and how private home ownership can be reconciled with socialist principles of equity and collectivism, and this confusion has been exacerbated in Britain by the problem of how to respond to the Thatcher government's undeniably popular move to sell off desirable parts of the public housing stock to working-class tenants who seem all too eager to buy it.

I have addressed some of these issues in earlier work (Saunders, 1978; 1979) and in this paper I begin by critically reviewing my earlier arguments concerning the sociological significance of house ownership in the light of more recent work (and more recent developments in Britain) which has called some of them into question. In particular, I would now wish to abandon the attempt to theorize home ownership as a determinant of class structuration and instead to view the division between privatized and collectivized modes of housing as one factor which is contributing to what one recent writer has termed 'a process of restratification' (Mingione, 1981, p. 18) based on differing relationships to the means of consumption. I suggest, in other words, that social and economic divisions arising out of ownership of key means of consumption such as housing are now coming to represent a new major fault-line in British society (and perhaps in others too), that privatization of welfare provisions is intensifying this cleavage to the point where sectoral alignments in regard to consumption may come to outweigh class alignments in respect of production, and that housing tenure remains the most important single aspect of such alignments because of the accumulative potential of house ownership and the significance of private housing as an expression of personal identity and as a source of ontological security. Such an argument has obvious implications for current socialist thought and practice, and some of these are considered in the concluding section of the paper.

Domestic property and social class

In earlier work on the sociological significance of housing tenure, I sought to demonstrate that house ownership represents a crucial material resource giving rise to interests which cut across lines of class cleavage originating in the social organization of production. Central to this argument was the view that, in post-war Britain as in a number of other Western countries, ownership of housing has increasingly provided access to a significant means of wealth accumulation. Three principal sources of accumulation were identified: house price inflation (which has tended to outstrip inflation of other commodity prices), favourable rates of interest on housing loans (which have often been negative in real terms) and government subsidies on house purchase (which in Britain take the form mainly of tax relief on mortgage interest repayments, but also include various grants to owner occupiers for house improvements).

The importance of domestic property ownership as a means of wealth accumulation lay in the fact that the division between owners and non-owners provided a basis for distinct patterns of political alignment, both locally (as in conflicts over land use) and nationally (over questions of housing policy and housing finance). Arguments which attempted to represent this division as in some way 'false' or 'ideological' were therefore rejected on the grounds that housing tenure is both a material as well as an ideal basis for political mobilization, and it was concluded that we should consider the ways in which domestic property ownership may be contributing to a restructuring of class relations in advanced capitalist societies.

There have been three main lines of criticism in response to this argument. One questions whether owner occupation really does represent a significant and enduring source of wealth accumulation. A second argues that owner occupiers cannot be treated as an homogeneous interest group since they have not all been in a position to secure real economic gains. A third argues that the significance of tenure as a basis for social and political alignments has been grossly exaggerated. I shall briefly consider each of these points in turn [. . .]

If we accept that domestic property ownership is in the contemporary period an important source of wealth accumulation for individual owners, and that owner occupiers as a whole share common material interests which are likely to become manifest in distinct forms of political alignment, there still remains the question of whether home ownership can therefore be seen as a significant factor in class restructuration. Views expressed in the recent literature range from those of Geraldine Pratt (1982), who argues strongly for a theory of home ownership as the basis for a middle property class, through those of David Thorns (1981; 1982), who endorses a theory of home owners as a middle property class while emphasizing the internal fragmentation of this class, to those of Peter Williams (1982) and Michael Ball (1982), both of whom reject house ownership as a factor in class structuration and detect in the current housing crisis a fusion between owners and tenants as both groups come to exert pressure on governments for reform of the housing system.

All three positions must be rejected. The problem with a conception of home owners as a property class, whether or not it is seen as internally fragmented, is that it overextends class theory and ultimately fails to relate class relations generated around ownership of domestic property to those generated around ownership of means of production. The attempt to integrate housing tenure divisions into class analysis, as in the work of Pratt and Thorns and my earlier conceptualization, is fundamentally flawed (e.g. see Hooper, 1982), the reason being that it elides the analytically distinct spheres of consumption and production. Class relations are constituted only through the social organization of production. It is confusing and unhelpful to use the same theoretical and conceptual tools to analyse relations constituted in the sphere of production around ownership and control of the means of production, and relations constituted through processes of consumption, even where (as in the case of house ownership) private ownership of the means of consumption may function as a source of revenue.

The recognition that housing tenure cannot be a factor in class structuration does not, however, necessitate agreement with writers such as Ball and Williams who seek to expel the question of tenure from the analysis of social stratification. Rather, we need to recognize that class is not the only major basis of social cleavage in contemporary capitalist societies, for increasingly people find themselves involved in political struggles which emanate not from their class location but from their location in what Dunleavy (1979) terms 'consumption sectors'. Seen in this context, home ownership does not alter people's class interest, but it is a major factor which helps to define their consumption sector interests. Consumption sectors, which are constituted through the division between owners and non-owners of crucial means of consumption such as housing, crosscut class boundaries, are grounded in non-class-based material interests and represent an increasingly significant form of social cleavage which may in certain circumstances come to outweigh class membership in their economic and political effects.

As a prelude to developing this argument further, it is important to emphasize that sectoral cleavages arising out of property rights in means of consumption are not merely ideological or status divisions but reflect real divisions of material interest. Owner occupiers, for example, form a distinct sectoral interest not because as property owners they naïvely *believe* that they have some sort of stake in the capitalist system, nor because their lifestyle (e.g. suburbanism) leads them to *claim* a superior status to that of non-owners, but because the objective conditions of their material existence are such as to drive a wedge between their interests and life chances and those of non-owners. Unlike Dunleavy, therefore, who sees such cleavages as primarily ideological, I am using the concept of consumption sectors to refer to material divisions which are every bit as 'real' and every bit as pertinent as those which arise out of the relations between classes.

It is also important to stress that interests represented in private ownership of crucial means of consumption such as housing cannot be dismissed as secondary to class interests arising out of ownership and non-ownership of means of production. One's class location does of course set limits upon one's consumption location (Ball, for example, shows that 86 per cent of British mortgagors are drawn from the Registrar-General's classes I, II and III) but it does not determine it, and consumption-based interests must therefore be taken seriously in their own right as the foundation for sectoral alignments which bear no necessary correspondence to class alignments. As I have argued elsewhere with Alan Cawson in respect of the theorization of the state, consumption is constrained but not determined by production, and processes of consumption have their own specificity (see Cawson and Saunders, 1983; also Cawson, 1982; and Saunders, 1981, Chapter 8). Thus, the fact that there is likely to be an empirical overlap between class and sectoral alignments (most council tenants in Britain, for example, are working class) does not lead to the conclusion that sectoral struggles can 'therefore' be seen merely as an expression of deeper class struggles. Consumption-based material interests are no less 'basic' or 'fundamental' than production-based (class) ones; which is primary at any one time and place cannot be determined on the basis of an appeal to the logical primacy of production over consumption (to consume we must first produce), but will depend entirely on the issue at hand.

To summarize, housing tenure, as one expression of the division between privatized and collectivized means of consumption, is analytically distinct from the question of class; it is neither the basis of class formations (as in the neo-Weberian tradition) nor the expression of them (as in the neo-Marxist tradition), but is rather the single most pertinent factor in the determination of consumption sector cleavages. Because such cleavages are in principle no less important than class divisions in understanding contemporary social stratification, and because housing plays such a key role in affecting life chances, in expressing social identity and (by virtue of the capital gains accruing to owner occupiers) in modifying patterns of resource distribution and economic inequality, it follows that the question of home ownership must remain as central to the analysis of social divisions and political conflicts.

Private ownership of the means of consumption and the process of social restratification

Just as the main social division arising out of the organization of production in capitalist societies is that between those who own and control the means of production and those who do not, so the main division arising out of the process of consumption in such societies is that between those who satisfy their main consumption needs through personal ownership (e.g. through home ownership, personal means of transportation, private medical insurance and private schooling) and those who rely on collective provision through the state. In both cases, therefore, the main cleavage is that between property owners and non-owners, for while the principal classes are distinguished according to ownership and non-ownership of production resources, the principal consumption sectors are distinguished by ownership or non-ownership of consumption resources.

Clearly, however, we are dealing here with very different types of property rights, and ownership in one sphere has little correspondence to ownership in the other (few house owners, for example, also own the factories or offices in which they work). As Williams points out, private ownership in means of consumption does not generally confer the social and economic power associated with property rights in the means of production:

> . . . the legal institution of property covers a wide range of situations . . . But clearly not all property has the same significance . . . The spread of home ownership does not confer economic power in the sense of the rights to those properties giving a say in the direction of the British economy. (1982, pp. 19–20)

Leaving on one side the observation that most of those who today enjoy property rights in the means of production (small business owners, shareholders, contributors to pension funds, etc.) do not enjoy the power to give direction to the British economy either, we may nevertheless agree with Williams that the legal category of ownership needs unpacking. However, to argue from the fact that ownership of consumption goods such as housing is different from ownership of production goods such as factories to the conclusion that private ownership in the sphere of consumption is thus unimportant (or even, as in Forrest *et al.*, [1985], that it does not represent property ownership in a sociological sense at all) is clearly fallacious. What such arguments do is to focus entirely on one dimension of property relations (the question of economic power) to the neglect of another which is equally important (the question of exclusivity in rights of control, benefit and disposal).

This point may be made clearer by reproducing the typology of property rights developed by Newby, Bell, Rose and myself in our study of agricultural landownership (see Table 12.1). It is clear from this that an exclusive focus on the significance of the difference between types (1) and (2) (e.g. in the argument that house ownership is different from ownership

Table 12.1   A typology of property

| | | Degree of exclusivity | |
		HIGH	LOW
Degree of potential for accumulation	HIGH	Individual means of production (1)	Collective means of production (3)
	LOW	Individual means of consumption (2)	Collective means of consumption (4)

Source: Newby *et al.*, 1978, p. 339

of capital) fails to take into account the equally important distinctions between types (2) and (4). Just as important for an understanding of the sociological significance of property ownership as the distinction between production and consumption property is that between personal and collective property. Put another way, consumption sector cleavages between individual and collective modes of ownership are no less significant than production-based class divisions between ownership and non-ownership of accumulative forms of property, for increasingly today, ownership rights in crucial means of consumption such as housing, transportation, education and health care provide not only a degree of personal autonomy and control which is denied to non-owners, but also privileged access to key determinants of life chances (shelter, mobility, cultural capital and even life itself).

I take up the issue of personal autonomy and control in the final section of this paper, and shall concentrate here on the growing importance of individual ownership in the means of consumption as a determinant of life chances.

If we were to develop an historical analysis of the changing 'modes of consumption' in a country such as Britain over the last 150 years, then we could begin by identifying a succession of three phases (I avoid the theoretically contaminated notion of 'stages' for no necessary evolutionary model is intended) which may be termed 'market', 'socialized' and 'privatized' modes of consumption.

In the first of these phases, consumption was organized primarily through the market. The contradiction between low wages (a condition of capitalist profitability *at that time* given the low productivity of labour characteristic of labour-intensive production methods) and a market-based mode of consumption was manifest throughout this period, not only in the form of periodic cycles of 'over-production' (due, as Marx argued, to the necessarily restricted purchasing power of workers in their role as consumers) but also in the material conditions of life endured by the working class (slum housing, disease, ignorance and so on). In this first phase, however, the role of the state in respect of consumption was generally limited to regulation (e.g. through the establishment of the municipal boards of health) and to maintenance of the Benthamite subsistence principle (e.g. through the Poor Law), and material provision on any scale beyond this was left to private charities and benevolent employers.

Gradually, as a result of a number of factors including paternalistic concern from one section of the dominant class, fear of insurrection from another, economic self-interest from a third and diverse pressures for improved living standards on the part of some working-class people and working-class organizations, a second phase developed during the latter part of the nineteenth century in which direct state provision of key items of consumption – health, housing, education – whose cost was still prohibitive for most working people, came to supplement and eventually largely to replace the subsistence provisions of the Poor Law Guardians and the handouts of private charities. In Britain, this new mode of consumption became firmly established before the First World War and reached its final maturity in the wake of the Second.

This new socialized mode of consumption to a large extent overcame the contradiction which had lain at the heart of the market mode between low wages and adequate provision of consumption, but as many writers have recently pointed out, it achieved this at the expense of another – that between the socialized costs of welfare provision and the availability of government revenues. It is this contradiction which became increasingly manifest through the 1970s in the form of a 'fiscal crisis', and the response has been a marked shift in recent years towards a new third phase in the form of a privatized mode of consumption.

In retrospect, it can be seen that the foundations for this third phase were in fact laid much earlier than the 1970s, however. For the last 30 years or more, we have arguably been witnessing the transition from socialized to privatized consumption. The first steps, taken very early on, involved the abandonment of the universalistic welfare principle (thus acceptance of and even support for the private sectors in medicine, education and housing) and the introduction of user charges, and the shift in emphasis from 'citizenship rights' to 'private property rights' which these steps entailed has continued with a few breaks and minor reversals ever since.

Now there is no doubt that a major factor in explaining the development of a privatized mode of consumption has been the growing strain placed on government budgets by welfare spending. Much more important than this in the long term, however, has been the growth in real incomes experienced by a large proportion of households (due both to rising real wages during periods of economic growth, and to increasing numbers of dual-earner households), for it is this which represents the necessary condition of privatization. Since the 1950s, an increasingly large proportion of working families have come to be able to afford private modes of provision – first (in the 1950s), in personal transportation, then (through the 1960s and 1970s) in housing (where the privatized mode is, of course, still subsidized by the state), and increasingly today in health care (the recent decision of the Electrical Trades Union to subscribe on behalf of its members to private health insurance represents an extension of private medicine from the professional to the skilled manual sectors of the workforce, just as house ownership spread across the same class boundary a decade or so earlier) and in education (e.g. in the growth of private tuition in subjects like music, in the increased fees for adult education, and so on).

The way in which this transition to a privatized mode of consumption has been, and continues to be, accomplished is through first, the introduction of user charges, second, the raising of user charges to notional market levels, and third, the transfer from state to private sector ownership. The clearest example of this in Britain relates to housing (where the process is now well developed), for having raised public sector rents to private sector levels, it is now a simple matter to transfer ownership from the state to the individual tenant. The same process is also now clearly visible in the fields of health and education, as is apparent in a report of the Central Policy Review Staff to the Thatcher Cabinet in September 1982 which outlined proposals for replacing the NHS with a new system of public and private health insurance, and for replacing free entitlement to higher education with a limited number of state scholarships. In virtually every area of consumption, the same process of transition is occurring, and once set in motion, the move to privatization seems to take on a momentum of its own. Thus, the raising of public transport fares to market levels serves to encourage private car ownership; the raising of school meal charges to market levels serves to encourage private forms of catering; increased charges in the National Health Service serve to encourage private health insurance – and in all of these cases, the more users who opt for a private solution, the poorer becomes the quality and the higher the price for those who remain dependent upon the dwindling socialized mode (see Hirschmann, 1970 on the 'exit phenomenon').

We are then, moving towards a dominant mode of consumption in which the majority will satisfy their requirements through market purchases (subsidized, where necessary, by the state) while the minority remain directly dependent on state provision. As Rose observes: 'Collective consumption is proving to be not a permanent feature of advanced capitalism but an historically specific phenomenon' (1979, p. 23) and the period of collective provision (phase two above) may come to be seen in retrospect as a temporary 'holding operation' or period of transition between the decline of the old market mode and the emergence of a new mode of private sector provision which has today become both possible and attractive for an increasingly large proportion of the population. If this is the case, then the division between the privatized majority and the marginalized minority (which is already evident in respect of housing – see Forrest and Williams, 1980, p. 16) is likely to create an increasingly visible fault-line in British society, not along the lines of class but on the basis of private ownership in the means of consumption.

In arguing thus, I am explicitly denying the claims of those, like Szelenyi, who continue to argue that state provision in the sphere of consumption (i.e. phase two) is 'necessary for the whole reproduction process and more specifically to the reproduction of labour power in modern capitalism' (1981, p. 579). Such arguments ignore both the rise in real incomes of many middle- and working-class households which has made privatization possible, and the widespread desire for personal control in the sphere of consumption which has made privatization politically feasible. While it remains the case that private provision is still underpinned in some instances by the state (e.g. through mortgage interest subsidies, pay beds in National Health hospitals, tax benefits for private schools, and so on), and that the shift to a privatized mode of consumption does not therefore represent a return to the market mode of the nineteenth century, it is also clearly the case that universal direct provision by the state is in no sense functionally necessary in advanced capitalist societies and is now in a process of decline.

It is important to emphasize that my argument does not rest merely on the extrapolation of a current trend which may soon be reversed, for I see the shift to privatization as both established and enduring. Apart from Szelenyi's argument about the necessity of socialized provision for reproduction of labour power, an argument which ignores the crucial significance of the rise in real household incomes, two main arguments have been advanced in the recent literature to suggest that privatization may turn out to be a temporary phenomenon. Neither is convincing.

The first suggests that, like the earlier market and socialized modes of consumption, a new privatized mode gives rise to a fundamental contradiction which now takes the form of that between support for private ownership of consumption provisions and the requirements of capital for what Miller (1978) terms 'recapitalization'. Applying this argument to housing provision, for example, Harloe suggests that the level of government subsidy required to support further owner occupation represents a degree of drain on state revenues, and hence on capitalist profits, which is likely to provoke intense pressure from private industry (apart from the building industry) for a reversal of policy:

> Perhaps the continued development of the private market in housing, at the very time when it seemed as if its dominance was generally established, is becoming ever more problematic. (1981, p. 46)

Similarly, Ball has argued that, 'The present structure of owner-occupied housing provision is increasingly coming into contradiction with the needs of capital' (1982, p. 72).

This economic argument is then reinforced by a political one to the effect that loss of electoral support, together with incoherent but threatening outbreaks of civil unrest (as in the British inner-city riots of 1981) is likely to check any further attempts at decollectivizing consumption. Harloe and Paris, for example, suggest that in Britain 'The political base for the policy of reducing collective consumption . . . seems to have largely disintegrated' (1982, p. 6), that the Thatcher government is almost certain to fall at the next election, and that no future administration is likely to continue reducing collective consumption provisions in the light of this experience.

Neither of these two arguments against the likelihood of a continuing spiral of 'decollectivization' or privatization of consumption is compelling, however. While accepting that high levels of subsidy to encourage home ownership represent a deflection of revenues away from investment-starved industrial capital, there is no reason to suppose that such subsidies must therefore be reduced in the future. Pressure on government by corporate capital is by no means always successful, nor are subsidies to owner occupiers the only area of state spending which could be cut in response to such pressures. Furthermore, privatization in other areas of consumption such as health and education need not necessitate increased subsidies but on the contrary probably represents a reduction in state spending and is thus entirely consistent with a strategy of recapitalization. Harloe's argument can in this sense be turned on its head, for demands from the private sector for recapitalization may be seen as one factor likely to encourage further privatization of consumption provisions. The main economic limitation on such a process is not so much the investment requirements of private capital as the level of effective demand on the part of consumers, and here, as we have seen, the level of real incomes and of popular aspirations is now such as to suggest that the scope for further privatization (even at a time of economic recession) may be considerable.

This leads us to consider the political argument that further substantial cuts in the provision of collective consumption are unlikely since the support base for such a policy is small and is becoming yet smaller. As Harloe and Paris put it 'It is hard to see what basis of political support will eventually remain for such policies' (1982, p. 37).

This is a curious argument for it overlooks the widespread popularity of the private ownership solution in areas such as housing where most people have for many years aspired to owner occupation. As I have argued elsewhere, British political culture is founded on a dichotomy of principles – citizenship rights on the one hand, rights of private property on the other. If the erosion of citizenship rights is coupled with an extension of private property rights (as, for example, in a policy of reducing the public housing sector while supporting the extension of individual home ownership), then the basis of political support is likely to be as large as the potential number of new owners. To argue that decollectivization is unpopular is to ignore the fact that privatization (the reverse side of the same coin) may be highly popular. Indeed, the further privatization extends, the greater becomes its momentum. The more council tenants who buy their houses, the greater will be the pressures on government to support and generalize the home ownership option and the stronger will be the desire on the part of the remaining tenants to escape the increasingly marginal and inadequate state sector. Similarly, the more trade unions that cover their members by private health insurance, the more parents who withdraw their children from the state education system and the more people who resort to private car ownership in order to ensure personal mobility, the greater will be the tendency for privatization of health, education and transport to continue. Far from having reached the limits of decollectivized consumption, all the signs are that the scope for further privatization, especially in health and education, is considerable.

If this is the case, then we may see developing in British society a major new fault-line drawn not on the basis of class (ownership of means of production) but on the basis of sectoral alignment (ownership of means of consumption). A fundamental division is already beginning to open up between those (the majority) who are or will be in a position to enjoy market access to good quality services and those (the increasingly marginalized minority) who are not. The contrast between owner occupiers and public sector tenants (a division which takes on additional significance given the accumulative potential of house ownership) is merely the most developed form of this sectoral cleavage.

My argument here has something in common with Mingione's discussion of 'social disgregation' and the process of 'social restratification' in advanced capitalist societies. Thus Mingione argues that traditional class boundaries have become fragmented as new divisions have emerged around questions, not of production, but of reproduction (i.e. consumption):

> The main axis of the contradictions of modern societies is progressively shifting from the economic sphere of production relationships to the social sphere of complex reproduction relationships. (1981, p. 11)

While he insists that this shift has not significantly modified the division of capitalist societies into the two main antagonistic classes (those who manage capitalism and those who are oppressed by it), he does recognize that these two principal classes have become internally differentiated with respect to conflicts arising out of the process of reproduction, and in this sense his argument is consistent with my suggestion that divisions in the sphere of consumption do not restructure class relations but do crosscut them.

Where I differ from Mingione is in his attempt to reduce consumption cleavages to a class analysis even in the face of his own recognition that the main axis of conflict has now shifted from production to consumption. In his attempt to reconcile his observations that consumption may be becoming the primary basis of social cleavages with his theoretical commitment to a Marxist class theory in which the struggle between capital and labour must remain paramount, Mingione is forced to the conclusion that struggles in the sphere of consumption are just one part of a broader movement aimed at the overthrow of capitalism:

> Urban conflicts to get better housing or transport are only part of a much more comprehensive conflictual movement to establish an alternative social system. (ibid., p. 24)

This empirically implausible conclusion is justified in theoretical terms by the extension of the Marxist concept of exploitation to include reproduction (consumption) as well as production relationships:

> Class struggles are fundamentally originated by capitalist exploitation relationships – mainly the direct extraction of surplus value from the immediately productive part of the working class. But . . . exploitative capitalist social relations do not occur only in the strict production area but also and necessarily within the general social reproduction process which is formed to reproduce the very possibility of exploitation. In this sense, exploitation not only strikes the productive workers in social relations other than the immediate production of surplus value, but it also involves various social groups, which cannot be considered productive workers, in different aspects of their everyday life. (ibid., pp. 30–31)

In this way Mingione is able to argue that 'the large majority of the population' is today 'exploited' in the realm of consumption since consumption is organized in order to facilitate continued exploitation in the realm of production.

The argument is, however, fallacious because of its assumption that any process which directly or indirectly enables capitalist production to continue must be part of the exploitative relationships on which such production is founded. Further, it also assumes that patterns of exploitation in production are directly mirrored in patterns of exploitation in other spheres of social activity (an assertion which is likely to be hotly contested by feminists among others). It simply does not make sense to argue that, because the great majority of the population is 'exploited' (in the Marxist sense) at work, they must also be exploited in every other aspect of their lives, for it is a very curious notion of exploitation which allows us to see home owners, car drivers, private patients and the like as 'exploited' in the realm of consumption.

If the concept of exploitation is to retain any meaning or analytical value when applied outside of production relationships, then it can only be in the sense of the denial by one group of another's access to crucial social resources. A relationship of exploitation thus involves the *generation* of unequal life chances. This is the sense in which Giddens (1973) uses the concept, and it is also the basis of Parkin's theory of exploitation as social exclusion (Parkin, 1979). But seen in these terms, exploitation in the process of consumption takes place, not between big capital and everybody else, but between those who can claim exclusive access to crucial consumption resources, and those who are excluded from such resources. Thus, superimposed upon class relations of exploitation (in which a very small number of people exploit a large majority) are new sectoral relations of exploitation (in which a relatively large number of people exploit an increasingly marginalized minority for whom collective provision remains the only, and strictly second-best, option). This means that if, as Mingione argues, consumption divisions are today replacing production divisions as the major axis of social stratification, then the implications for future patterns of social conflict and cohesion are enormous, for in a 'them-and-us' society, the 'them' is assuming a majority position of exclusive access to crucial life chances, while the 'us' – composed almost entirely of those who, by virtue of race, gender, religion, age or education cannot achieve market access to basic consumption resources – is becoming a small, isolated and fragmented minority.

The response of this marginalized minority to a progressive process of exclusion – from personal mobility and personal housing today, and in the future from prompt and high-quality health care and perhaps from decent education for their children – remains to be seen, but already there are indications that it may range from relatively coherent communal self-help strategies on the part of those who enjoy cohesive social networks (i.e. what Pahl, 1980, has termed the development of an 'informal economy') to sporadic and relatively unorganized outbreaks of civil unrest and attacks on private property on the part of those who lack either the patience or the resources necessary for the development of such a compensatory strategy.

Private property, consumption and socialism

The increasing significance of the division between ownership and non-ownership of key means of consumption in advanced capitalist societies has recently begun to pose some significant dilemmas for socialists, largely because socialist thought has hitherto lacked a theory or an ethics of personal (consumption-oriented) property ownership.

In Marxist theory, consumption has always been analysed as secondary to and derivative of production. Marx himself provided the logic for this:

> Production, distribution, exchange and consumption . . all form the members of a totality, distinctions within a unity. Production predominates not only over itself, in the antithetical definition of production, but over the other moments as well. The process always returns to production to begin anew. That exchange and consumption cannot be predominant is self-evident . . . A definite production therefore determines a definite consumption. (1973, p. 99)

It is this logic that has led subsequent Marxist theory to view divisions and interests arising out of the process of consumption as merely phenomenal expressions of deeper and more fundamental (because logically prior) divisions between those who own and control the means of production and those who do not. Thus struggles over access to or control of resources such as housing or health care are treated simply as 'displaced' class struggles, and the division between production-based movements (e.g. trade unions) and consumption-based movements (e.g. community groups) is analysed as 'at best a surficial estrangement, an apparent tearing asunder of what can never be kept apart' (Harvey, 1978, p. 34). Even where Marxist theory has focused particularly on the politics of consumption (as in the work of Castells), the argument has been that consumption-based social movements only become theoretically and politically significant insofar as they feed back into and are subordinated to class movements in the sphere of production (e.g. by facilitating new popular class alliances in opposition to monopoly capital).

Now it is of course the case, as Marx argues, that production is logically prior to consumption, for we cannot consume what has not first been produced and consumption thus marks the end point of the production-exchange-distribution-consumption cycle. It is also the case that the ability to consume is to some extent dependent upon location in the social organization of production, for those who are unemployed or are in low-paid and insecure employment cannot generally gain access to private modes of provision of key consumption resources. Nevertheless, as Acton (1955) among others has argued, the logical primacy of production does not itself demonstrate its social determinacy. For example, the fact of being an owner of capital or a wage earner does not itself determine whether or not one is in a position to gain access to particular private modes of consumption, for lines of class cleavage do not correspond to lines of sectoral cleavage in the sphere of consumption, and those who are exploited in one sphere may occupy an exploitative location in another. It is therefore quite misleading to argue, as Harvey and others have done, that there is an 'underlying unity' between the two, for although consumption location is to a large extent dependent upon production location, it does not correspond to it, and it generates new and independent effects which may prove more significant (e.g. in structuring material life chances and in stimulating political mobilization) than the simple division between those who sell their labour power and those who purchase it.

The failure of Marxist theory[1] to recognize the independent significance of the sphere of consumption is today reflected in widespread confusion and argument in socialist circles concerning the appropriate response to the privatization of key areas of consumption. The failure of theory to distinguish consumption and production cleavages (through the constant reduction of the former to the latter; consumption is seen simply in functional terms as reproduction) has resulted in the surprising failure of socialist practice to distinguish two very different forms of property (namely, individual means of production and individual means of consumption). Thus, despite the insistence of Williams and others that corporate ownership of capital is a very different form of property from, say, individual ownership of housing, socialist writing still continues to argue against the latter through an extension of arguments relevant only to the former. Because Marxist theory establishes the case for common ownership and control of the means of production and because Marxist analysis reduces consumption to production, Marxist practice finds itself opposing any extension of individual property rights in the sphere of consumption, even when the majority of working-class people appear to aspire to such rights.

An obvious case in point concerns recent British housing policy which has deliberately set out to support the extension of private home ownership and to reduce reliance on welfare (collective) provision. For the remainder of this paper I shall concentrate on owner occupation as an example of private ownership of means of consumption, for this illustration demonstrates clearly the need for fresh thought by socialists on the whole question of property rights and collectivism in the sphere of consumption.

The Labour Party in Britain has, at least since 1964, been a reluctant champion of owner occupation while at the same time attempting when in government to safeguard the welfare sector (although as Harloe and Paris, 1982, point out, the 1974–79 administration in fact initiated the current cutbacks in public-sector housing investment). The Marxist literature over this period has tended to be highly critical of such a position and has argued firmly against further extension of home ownership among the working class despite the fact that about 40 per cent of manual worker households already own the houses they live in. These criticisms have come to a head since the election of a Conservative government in 1979 which has pursued an energetic policy of selling council houses to sitting tenants at substantial discounts. Although there has been some disagreement among Marxist intellectuals over the appropriate response to such a policy (see, for example, the debate in volumes one and two of *Critical Social Policy*), this has tended to revolve around the question of tactics (is it wise for socialist-controlled local authorities to attempt to block sales when many tenants wish to buy?) rather than the principle, on which all parties to the debate are agreed, that socialized provision is the only appropriate mode of housing provision, and that owner occupation is thus to be discouraged if not actually abolished (cf. Cowley, 1979, p. 146).

The question raised by, but rarely addressed in, this whole debate is why collective provision of a resource such as housing is to be upheld against individual ownership. The only coherent attempt to answer this question has taken the form of an economic argument relating to the pooled historic cost of public housing and the costs incurred in home ownership through interest payments to financial institutions and charges levied by exchange professionals. Public provision, in other words, is seen as being in the interests of all householders because it is, or in principle could be, cheaper. Cheapness, however, does not establish the case for socialism, nor does it provide a conclusive case for restricting or even preventing individual choice in the matter of housing provision. As we shall see in a moment, the case for socialism rests on the case for abolishing relations of exploitation, and any attempt to restrict market choice in the sphere of consumption should be weighed against this rather than on what will inevitably be a paternalistic judgement about the individual costs incurred in market provision.

Such economic arguments do not, however, generally lie at the heart of the socialist 'gut reaction' against home ownership. Two other factors are more pertinent in explaining it.

The first is the historical legacy of anti-landlordism bequeathed by radical thought of the nineteenth and early twentieth centuries (the period of the market mode of consumption referred to earlier). Landlord ownership clearly was and is incompatible with socialist principles since housing here takes the form of private capital which is used to lay claim to a portion of the surplus value extracted from workers at the point of production. Since, 80 years ago in Britain, the only effective alternative to private landlordism was state landlordism, public provision came to be championed in opposition to the capitalist form of housing provision, and today it is still championed even though the principal alternative is now owner occupation which has transcended the problem of tenant-landlord relations. It is in this sense that we may agree with Stretton when he observes:

> It was a tragedy that socialism had to be born between the first industrial revolution and the second, when working families had scarcely any private resources and an appalling proportion of all private property was used by the few who owned it to exploit the labour of the many who didn't . . . It is a terrible mistake to let the abuse of capitalist property discredit the idea of family property or to confuse commercial capital with the home capital which really has opposite possibilities. (1974, p. 76)

This is, however, a 'terrible mistake' which continues to be made in socialist writing on housing tenure.

The second factor, also historical in origin, is the traditional intellectual distaste for all forms of 'petty property' and the ways of thinking and acting which have been associated with it. Owner occupiers are for socialists today what the French peasantry was for Marx in the mid-nineteenth century – a hopelessly conservative section of the population which is too easily seduced into supporting the status quo by virtue of its vested interest in a small holding of land. Every display of personal attachment to this land and property on the part of owner occupiers – the gnomes in the garden, the name on the garden gate, the classical door chimes inside the personally erected front door porch – is for socialist critics a further wincing reminder of the 'petty bourgeois' mentality and aspirations which are apparently unleashed by a 'home of one's own'. Private ownership is attacked because individualism – the private realm – is deeply distrusted.

The socialist case against owner occupation thus boils down to little more than an ill thought-out commitment to the ultimate value of collectivism coupled with an implicit fear of individualism. As Keat has noted, 'For many socialists, capitalism is to be condemned not only as a system based on the exploitation of one class by another . . . but also for the individualistic character of its social relationships' (1981, p. 127). Yet it is clear that socialism must be reconciled with individualism, and that common ownership of the means of production cannot imply collective ownership of *all* property. What Lafargue calls property of personal appropriation (a subcategory of individual ownership of means of consumption which relates to 'the food one eats . . . and the articles of clothing and objects of luxury – rings, jewels, etc. – with which one covers and decks oneself' – Lafargue, no date, p. 4) will presumably remain individual private property even under socialism. Indeed, it can plausibly be argued that such intensely personal forms of ownership perform important psychological functions for the individual, whether in socialist, capitalist or precapitalist societies [. . .]

Notes

1 Although not central to my argument here, it should be noted that Marxist theory is not alone in this failure, for Weber too inadequately theorizes the sociological significance of consumption in the modern period (not surprisingly, perhaps, since both he and Marx were writing at a time before the division between privatized and collectivized consumption became pertinent).

In contrast to Marx, Weber does of course explicitly recognize that consumption may generate social cleavages which are distinct from, and may even be more fundamental than, divisions arising out of the social organization of production (i.e. ownership and non-ownership of productive property). However, for Weber, consumption forms the basis of status stratification in which different social groups are distinguished, not in terms of their life chances, but in respect of their differentially valued life styles. This distinction between class and status stratification seems to have most salience for Weber in the analysis of precapitalist societies where the principal basis of social differentiation may reflect differences of social honour rather than economic (market) power. In the context of modern capitalist societies, however, it is clear that for Weber, as for Marx, domination rests firmly on economic power rather than social prestige, in which case status divisions arising out of consumption are very much secondary to class divisions. Indeed, as Parkin (1971) suggests, status allocation in capitalist societies may more usefully be understood as an emergent function of class relations than as an independent basis of social stratification.

While accepting Weber's observation that mode of consumption is closely associated with the attribution of prestige, it has been my concern in this paper to show that it is also increasingly associated with the distribution of life chances. Those who can afford to buy private medical treatment, for example, are not simply engaged in a process of conspicuous consumption, but are laying exclusive claim to privileged treatment which has a crucial bearing on their future life chances. Consumption location is thus a source of material as well as ideal interests and cannot be analysed merely in terms of status any more than it can be reduced to class. Weber is in this sense no more useful for developing a theory of consumption-oriented ownership than is Marx.

References

ACTON, H. (1955) *The Illusion of the Epoch*, London, Routledge and Kegan Paul.

BALL, M. (1982) 'Housing provision and the economic crisis', *Capital and Class*, No. 17, pp. 60–77.

CAWSON, A. (1982) *Corporatism and Welfare*, London, Heinemann.

CAWSON, A. and SAUNDERS, P. (1983) 'Corporatism competitive politics and class struggle', in King, A. (ed.), *Capital and Politics*, London, Routledge and Kegan Paul.

COWLEY, J. (1979) *Housing for People or Profits?*, London, Stage I.

DUNLEAVY, P. (1979) 'The urban bases of political alignment', *British Journal of Political Science*, Vol. 9, pp. 409–443.

FORREST, R., MURIE, A. and WILLIAMS, P. (1985) *Bulwark against Bolshevism*, London, Hutchinson.

FORREST, R. and WILLIAMS, P. (1980) *The Commodification of Housing: Emerging Issues and Contradictions*, University of Birmingham, Centre for Urban and Regional Studies Working Papers, No. 73.

GIDDENS, A. (1973) *The Class Structure of the Advanced Societies*, London, Hutchinson.

GIDDENS, A. (1981) *A Contemporary Critique of Historical Materialism. Volume I: Power, Property and the State*, London, Macmillan.

HARLOE, M. (1981) 'The recommodification of housing', in Harloe, M. and Lebas, E. (eds) *City, Class and Capital*, London, Edward Arnold.

HARLOE, M. and PARIS, C. (1982) *The Decollectivization of Consumption: Housing and Local Government Finance in Britain, 1979–81*. Paper presented at the Tenth World Congress of Sociology, Mexico City, August.

HARVEY, D. (1978) 'Labour, capital and class struggle around the built environment in advanced capitalist societies', in Cox, K. (ed.) *Urbanization and Conflict in Market Societies*, London, Methuen.

HIRSCHMANN, A. (1970) *Exit, Voice and Loyalty*, Cambridge, Mass., Harvard University Press.

HOOPER, A. (1982) Review essay, *Political Geography Quarterly*, Vol. 1, pp. 97–107.

KEAT, R. (1981) 'Individualism and community in socialist thought', in Mepham, J. and Ruben, D. (eds) *Issues in Marxist Philosophy. Volume 4: Social and Political Philosophy*, Brighton, Harvester Press.

LAFARGUE, P. (no date) *Evolution of Property from Savagery to Civilization*, Calcutta, Sreekali Prakasalaya.

MARX, K. (1973) *Grundrisse*, Harmondsworth, Penguin.

MILLER, S. (1978) 'The recapitalization of capital', *International Journal of Urban and Regional Research*, Vol. 2, pp. 202–212.

MINGIONE, E. (1981) *Social Conflict and the City*, Oxford, Basil Blackwell.

NEWBY, H., BELL, C., ROSE, D. and SAUNDERS, P. (1978) *Property, Paternalism and Power: Class and Control in Rural England*, London, Hutchinson.

PAHL, R. (1980) 'Employment, work and the domestic division of labour', *International Journal of Urban and Regional Research*, Vol. 4, pp. 1–20.

PARKIN, F. (1971) *Class, Inequality and Political Order*, London, MacGibbon and Kee.

PARKIN, F. (1979) *Marxism and Class Theory: A Bourgeois Critique*, London, Tavistock.

PRATT, G. (1982) 'Class analysis and urban domestic property: a critical reexamination', *International Journal of Urban and Regional Research*, Vol. 6, pp. 481–502.

REX, J. and MOORE, R. (1967) *Race, Community and Conflict*, London, Oxford University Press.

ROSE, D. (1979) *Toward a Reevaluation of the Political Significance of Home Ownership in Britain*, Paper presented at the Conference of Socialist Economists Political Economy of Housing Workshop, Manchester, February.

SAUNDERS, P. (1978) 'Domestic property and social class', *International Journal of Urban and Regional Research*, Vol. 2, pp. 233–51.

SAUNDERS, P. (1979) *Urban Politics: A Sociological Interpretation*, London, Hutchinson.

SAUNDERS, P. (1981) *Social Theory and the Urban Question*, London, Hutchinson.

STRETTON, H. (1974) *Housing and Government*, Sydney, Australian Broadcasting Commission.

SZELENYI, I. (1981) 'The relative autonomy of the state or state mode of production?', in Dear, M. and Scott, A. (eds) *Urbanization and Urban Planning in Capitalist Society*, London, Methuen.

THORNS, D. (1981) 'Owner occupation: its significance for wealth transfer and class formation, *Sociological Review*, Vol. 29, pp. 705–728.

THORNS, D. (1982) *Owner Occupation, the State and Class Relations in New Zealand*, Paper presented at the Sociological Association of Australia and New Zealand Annual Conference, University of New South Wales, August.

WILLIAMS, P. (1982) *Property, Power and Politics: Home Ownership and Social Relations*, Paper presented at the Association of American Geographers Annual Conference, San Antonio, Texas, April.

13   The decollectivization of consumption: housing and local government finance in England and Wales, 1979–1981

Michael Harloe and Chris Paris

Introduction

Szelenyi (1981) has suggested that the 'new urban sociology' of the 1970s is gravely deficient in the present economic and political circumstances of much of the advanced capitalist world. Among its faults is a kind of determinism about the nature of advanced capitalism, the role of the state and, more particularly, the role of urban policies. Broadly speaking, this involves the view that there is an almost inevitable, if crisis-ridden, extension of the means of collective consumption via the state, in order to underpin the profitable development of large-scale ('monopoly'/multinational) capital. Local government is central to this process because it delivers and partly finances many of the specific goods and services concerned – housing, roads, social services, etc. Despite criticism of state intervention and the ways in which collective consumption has developed, however, the assumption has usually been that, whatever the problems, collective consumption will continue to expand.

Events in countries such as Britain, the United States and (until recently) Australia, where governments have been attempting to abandon the Keynesian economic orthodoxies that were the foundation stone for the expansion of state-provided collective consumption, seem to have involved a retreat from collective consumption. This is necessary if monetarist policies – tax cuts, reductions in public expenditure, the diminution of the state's role and the 'freeing up' of the market – are to be achieved. Many theories of the growth of state intervention and of collective consumption were based on the view that Keynesian economic management was *the* way forward for capitalism. How, then, could they cope with this new challenge? [. . .]

The aim of New Right governments to reduce state intervention and the provision of the means of collective consumption fits into the broader economic and social changes. But Szelenyi warns against too readily accepting a new form of determinism in which current attempts to withdraw from the provision of the means of collective consumption are seen as an unproblematic and functional response to deindustrialization [. . .]

This paper was written as a tentative contribution to the examination of attempted withdrawal by the state from intervention in urban processes.

We focus on two developments, both initiated by the Conservative government elected in Britain in 1979. The first was the attempt to reduce local government expenditure generally and, in the process, greatly to increase central government control. The second involved reduced state provision of housing in favour of provision through the market. Before discussing these policies in detail, we outline the relevant economic and political background and note that this paper examines developments only up to the end of 1981 [. . .]

The economic and political context

While it may be popularly supposed that the coming into power of Mrs Thatcher in Britain marked a dramatic change in the political policy climate, this is to some extent an illusion. Monetarist policies had already been applied by the preceding Labour government and, more generally, had had a growing significance in the debates of economists for some years previously (Bonnett, 1981; Townsend and Bosanquet, 1980). Nor should attention be focused solely on the personalities involved, as Thatcher's assumption of the Conservative leadership after Edward Heath had lost the 1974 election was something of an accident (Butler and Kavanagh, 1980). Any new Conservative leader probably would have adopted some form of monetarist stance, for Thatcher's rise to power was a result of political reaction to the failure of Keynesian policies to solve the twin problems of unemployment and economic decline. Hence the defeat of Labour was less a result of popular support for the Conservatives and more a negative reaction to Labour's failures [. . .]

The Conservatives promised that reductions in public expenditure and taxes and the withdrawal of the state from allegedly excessive intervention in everyday life would lead to the rebirth of a vigorous private enterprise economy. Most people, they claimed, would soon have rising disposable real incomes and so would be able to purchase goods and services previously provided by the state.

The failure of this strategy resulted in a considerable loss of political support for Conservative policies by the end of 1981. Several ministers who had opposed monetarist policies were sacked by Mrs Thatcher. There was growing opposition to some government policies among leading Conservative back-benchers; and above all, there was a loss of popular support as registered by opinion polls and in parliamentary by-elections. While the rapid rise of the new Social Democratic Party was essentially the product of the split between Right and Left in the Labour Party, it seemed that electorally it might do as much or even more damage to the Conservatives. The prospects for the survival of the Thatcher government beyond the next general election (in 1983 or 1984) did not look good (although subsequent events [. . .] overturned expectations held widely during 1981).

By the end of 1981, too, the economic strategy of cuts in taxes and public expenditure and a renaissance of the private economy was in ruins.

Unemployment had accelerated; output had slumped; inflation had continued above the level bequeathed to the Conservatives by the previous Labour government (by 1983 it had fallen to a lower level because of the massive deflation of the economy that had occurred).

Much of what has occurred in Britain is a product of the international economic crisis. But the scale and speed of, for example, the rise in unemployment (up by about 1/2 million during 1980 and by a further 1 million in 1981, with no decline in sight even in early 1983) has been a product of the attempted imposition of highly deflationary monetary policies, including the cuts in public sector spending (especially in capital investment in housing, roads, schools, etc.) (Coutts *et al.*, 1981). Britain tried to move much more rapidly to the free market state than any of its European neighbours, with disastrous results in terms of output and employment. The attack on pay, especially in the public sector, and the lead taken – in Europe, as least – in cutting social welfare, added to a general policy that sought to restrict state aid to the very neediest, while shifting the burden of support for the rest from the social wage and sphere of collective consumption to private, wage-financed consumption and unpaid domestic work. The failure of these policies to achieve resurrection of the British economy and the accompanying growth of mass unemployment resulted in the government's strategy being reduced to incoherence.

In 1980 Britain had the highest rise in unemployment (+66 per cent) and the worst growth record of all the EEC countries. There was no growth at all in 1980 as GDP fell below the 1979 level (EEC, 1980). Manufacturing production by mid-1980 was 15 per cent below the 1973 level and company profits had slumped. Company liquidations numbered 5000 in the first nine months of 1980, 20 per cent higher than the previous peak, and many areas experienced the total collapse of major employers (Coutts *et al.*, 1981). At the end of 1981 the deterioration was still continuing, with unemployment touching 3 million (actually considerably over this figure if the effect of short-term government programmes to provide work experience to young people was discounted) and no end of the upward movement in sight.

The general features of economic policy – the (failed) attempt to control the money supply and the accompanying high interest rates and overvalued pound, the cuts in public expenditure involving reductions in capital spending and redundancies, the control of public sector pay rises and the effects of unemployment on 'disciplining' private sector wage demands – need only be noted in this paper. Instead of economic growth and a fall in unemployment, there was economic decline and rising unemployment. Despite massive and repeated cuts in public expenditure, the overall total of such expenditure had risen (Chancellor of the Exchequer, 1981, Tables 1.1 and 4.5).

Put in crude terms, the reason for this state of affairs is that the government's economic requirements – reductions in public expenditure – have been in conflict with the political impossibility of withdrawing state benefits from the unemployed (although there is a continuing attempt to chip away at benefit levels). So, as unemployment has risen, the government has had to find more and more money for benefits. This has had to be achieved by abandoning the policy of tax cuts, which in the end have benefited only the very rich, in favour of tax increases, and by cutting less politically untouchable areas of public expenditure even harder. All this has served to deflate the economy even more, thus creating more unemployment, more demand for public expenditure and a further round of deflation.

The apparently ceaseless and senseless pursuit of this self-defeating strategy became the major focus of vocal criticism of the government by some of its own supporters (including two ex-Cabinet ministers) as well as by other political parties, most reputable economists, the financial press and other media. Ironically, the Treasury provided evidence that showed the self-defeating effects of government policies (HM Treasury, 1981). This calculated that a decline in economic activity increased the demands on the public sector borrowing requirement (PSBR) in several ways, including higher unemployment and welfare payments and more payments from the government's redundancy fund. The cost of unemployment-related expenditures alone was estimated to increase by £340 million for every extra 100 000 people out of work. At this rate, in the two years 1980–81, given the rise of approximately 2 million in the unemployed, public expenditure increased by about £6.8 billion; and public expenditure was used increasingly to support the workless while publicly financed investment, which would stimulate and support private enterprise slumped.

The government failed to deliver its promised economic miracle. Instead of alleviating the impact of the world recession on the British economy, government policy accentuated it and contributed to rapid deindustrialization. Public expenditure cuts had bitten deeply into key areas of collective consumption. Instead of stimulating private sector provision, public expenditure cuts added to economic decline and any benefits have been swallowed up by the rising costs of unemployment. While aspects of government policy have been of undoubted value to British capital, especially the effects of unemployment on moderating working-class demands and allowing the imposition of measures to raise productivity without raising wages, their general impact has been disastrous. We can now examine the impact of the Conservative government's policies on housing and local government. These two areas of state intervention have been of crucial significance for the whole Conservative strategy. An examination of them is therefore of central rather than peripheral interest to any assessment of the ability of the British 'New Right' to decollectivize consumption.

The significance of local government finance and housing

Local government expenditure accounts for approximately 25 per cent of all government expenditure in Britain. In recent years about 60 per cent of this total has been met by central government grants, the rest coming from local property taxes (rates) and charges for locally provided services (especially rents paid for public housing). Local government itself, while financially very dependent on central government, is independently elected and has a certain degree of autonomy and separate legitimacy as a result. It is not simply a tool of the centre, and within limits may be expected to resist central government incursions on its autonomy.

Despite this, local autonomy has become progressively more limited. While local government still has major responsibility for key areas of collective consumption, including housing and education, it has lost others, such as water. Despite the growth of services provided under each main service area, local government has increasingly been subjected to central controls concerning how services are supplied. The key to this control is the increasing proportion of local government expenditure that is met by the centre. Since central government began financing local government in the nineteenth century, there have been measures to limit the size of this commitment. Over the last 20 years or so, however, as government became ever more closely concerned with the overall management of the economy, there have been increasing attempts to limit *all* local government expenditure. This objective is in immediate and obvious conflict with the claim, based on notions of local democracy, that local government has, within limits, its own sovereignty, and that local councillors have the right to determine local needs and expenditure, raising the revenue required – beyond that provided by the centre – via whatever levels of local taxation and charges they deem necessary.

The strategic importance of imposing tight control on local government expenditure becomes clear when the past and projected growth of public expenditure as a whole is examined. The government's 1981 public expenditure plans showed total public expenditure falling in real terms between 1975/76 and 1981/82, by about $2\frac{1}{2}$ per cent. Interestingly, public expenditure fell further than this under the previous Labour government (i.e. from 1975/76 to 1978/79), so, despite the aim of cutting expenditure, it rose under the Conservatives – although not to the 1975/76 level (Chancellor of the Exchequer, 1981). Between 1975/76 and 1981/82, central government expenditure rose by almost 8 per cent; hence, cutting local government expenditure became a key central government objective. Between 1975/76 and 1981/82 local government expenditure declined by almost 21 per cent (though a substantial part of this decline was initiated by Labour).

Whereas Labour managed to reduce both central and local expenditure, the Conservatives had to concentrate much more on reducing local government expenditure because of their inability to cut aggregate central government expenditure. Services provided by local authorities therefore bore much of the burden of the overall attack on public expenditure.

Most public housing expenditure is incurred by local authorities, mainly for building new public housing and improving existing public and private sector housing. In addition, central government provides subsidies for these activities and to meet the costs of rent allowances and direct subsidies to lower-income owner occupiers. While central government housing expenditure is a relatively modest proportion of all central government expenditure, it was until recently second only to education in its share of local government expenditure. The strategic significance of cuts in local housing expenditure would in any event have been considerable. Its significance has been heightened because it is a sector involving largely capital expenditure, whereas education, for example, involves mainly current expenditure, i.e. staff salaries and other running expenses of schools and colleges. There are often greater political difficulties when current rather than capital expenditure is cut; not only are jobs directly and immediately lost in the service concerned, with all possibilities for trade union resistance that this gives rise to, but existing services rapidly and visibly deteriorate. Education cuts affect most voters, whereas cuts in expenditure on council housing affect only a minority (who rarely vote Conservative anyway). It is thus easier for governments to cut capital and not current expenditure, and for the present Conservative government, which has also attacked current expenditure, to have as a relatively easy first option the cutting of housing expenditure in particular.

Housing expenditure cuts have been of central importance to the overall public expenditure strategy. Overall government housing expenditure fell by an extraordinary 52 per cent between 1975/76 and 1981/82, by far the largest cut of any major programme. The strategic significance of cuts in housing for the future plans of the government was revealed in a report of a House of Commons Committee published in 1980. This stated that they were equivalent to no less than 92 per cent of the government's total planned expenditure cuts for the period 1980/82–1983/84 (House of Common's Environment Committee, 1981a, p. v).

Almost the entire burden of these housing cuts fell on the working class, those already in public housing and for whom such housing provides the only real chance they have for decent accommodation. Planned capital expenditure on new social housing in 1981/82 was only one-third of what was spent in 1975/76 (and down by 50 per cent from the level at which it was left after previous Labour cuts). A large-scale programme of enforced council house sales was being used to offset other housing expenditure and, in the process, reducing the stock available for letting to low-income households. Social housing rents have been raised sharply, to levels where in many areas a majority of tenants are now eligible to receive rent allowances (therefore being, in public expenditure terms, less cost-cutting than it would at first seem). In contrast, subsidies to owner occupiers, many of whom are Conservative voters, remained untouched and in aggregate actually rose. By 1980/81 the two main tax subsidies to owner occupiers amounted to about £4.5 billion, the third largest item in all direct tax allowances and reliefs (after income tax allowances and tax reliefs for business). In this same year total central and local government direct housing expenditure (some of which also went to owner occupiers) amounted to only £3.1 billion.

To summarize, reductions in collective consumption, via cuts in overall local government expenditure and in capital and local government housing expenditure, have been a key element in monetarist policies in Britain. These policies have not been solely products of the 'New Right' Conservative government that has been in power since 1979. However, the failure of this government's economic strategy has given an added importance to the struggle to cut local government expenditure, and, to a degree that would be unlikely under Labour, public housing has been most severely affected.

These conclusions must make us very cautious about suggesting that a sharp political break occurred in 1979. Rather, it seems that the attack on collective consumption has gathered pace under both right-wing Conservative and right-wing Labour governments since the mid-1970s. Essentially, this is a result of economic circumstances and a common acceptance by both Labour and Conservatives of the need for, *inter alia*, reductions in public expenditure. There was also some degree of common acceptance that certain items of public expenditure cannot so easily be cut; principal among these are social security benefits and also, to a very large degree, defence and 'law and order' expenditures. The reasons why these have not been cut are principally to do with social integration. A return to the nineteenth-century state, with its almost total lack of responsibility for education and income maintenance, might result in such massive protest, conflict and disorder that there are few signs, as yet at least, that even a 'New Right' government would contemplate such developments as a practical political possibility, although for some it exists as a longer-term political aim.

We may conclude, on the one hand, that the exclusive identification of the New Right with the attack on collective consumption is misleading. On the other hand, it may reasonably be argued that in Britain under the Conservatives the attack has been pushed further and in directions less politically possible for Labour. Even so, the attempt to impose even more severe cuts has run into many difficulties [. . .]

Housing, 1979–81

We have already explained some elements in the Conservative government's housing policies and its approach to housing expenditure. Housing policies have been affected by the general approach to public expenditure and also by successive Conservative and Labour governments' support for owner occupation.

The Conservatives have campaigned for decades on the ideal of a 'property-owning democracy'. But the drift in the 1960s and 1970s towards this policy by Labour, which had traditionally supported social rented housing as the major alternative to the private landlord for the working class, needs explanation. One of the authors of this paper has recently argued that Labour never really challenged the domination of the housing market by private enterprise, because social rented housing was provided in ways that made it less desirable tenure than owner occupation. He concluded that electoral considerations played an important role in changing the party's attitude to owner occupation (Harloe, 1981). As increasing numbers of working-class households were able to buy their own houses, Labour came to view opposition to owner occupation as a political liability. So in 1965 the Labour government stated that support for extension of owner occupation was at the heart of its housing policy. The role of social rented housing began to change, too, during the 1960s. The introduction of a new subsidy system (by Labour) in 1967 was accompanied by cost and quality controls. The return of a Conservative government in 1970, committed to boosting owner occupation and reducing social rental housing to a residual role, marked the end of local autonomy in housing. That government sought radically to reduce direct subsidies for social rented housing (while leaving the indirect tax subsidies for owner occupation intact), to raise rents and to reduce new social rented building. In 1972 it passed a controversial Housing Act giving it the powers to achieve these ends. For the first time local authorities had rent determination taken out of their hands, and rents were to be set at levels that would mean that some councils would make a profit on their housing accounts, thus breaching the non-profit principle maintained until then. The Act was opposed by the Labour Party and there was considerable local opposition to it. It was one of the most unpopular measures of the 1970–74 Conservative government and was a contributory factor to their election defeat in 1974.

The Act was repealed by the new Labour government, which embarked on a programme of expanding housing expenditure including expenditure on public and private sector improvement and on new social housing. At the same time, an inquiry into housing finance was set up with a brief to devise an overall system of housing subsidies that would be more equitable and efficient than previous systems.

As the economic crisis grew, the Labour government began to adopt monetarist policies of high interest rates and cuts in public expenditure. Housing expenditure was reduced, and there was a progressive restriction of local autonomy in housing. When Labour's Housing Policy Review (Secretary of State for the Environment, 1977) was eventually published, the chief Conservative spokesman (who became Secretary of State for the Environment in 1979) congratulated the Labour government on much of its contents (Harloe, 1978, 1980). The document saw owner occupation as the 'normal' tenure for most households. It refused to make any changes in the highly regressive system of tax subsidies to this sector. Under the guise of achieving a more rational system by which capital expenditure could be related to local needs, it introduced a system of Housing Investment Plans (HIP). Under this system, local authorities had to make annual bids for capital investment and central government would then make allocations from the global sum available for housing. The HIP system was accompanied by a complex set of procedures whose stated aim was to enable housing investment to be adequate for housing needs, but which in practice was no more than a device for allocating a predetermined sum and which, like the RSG, could be politically 'bent' to favour some areas rather than others.

Accompanying this was a new system of general housing subsidy. Although this did not actually control how much local authority housing expenditure should be met by rents and local taxes, it gave government the power to determine what these *should* be. Subsidy would be paid only to cover the gap between, on the one hand, 'allowable' expenditure and, on the other hand, rents and local taxes.

Although local authority housing expenditure remained a significant domestic priority for Labour up to its general election defeat in 1979, this did not prevent successive expenditure cuts and increasing tightening of the strategic controls exerted through the new planning system. In short, by the late 1970s Labour had radically changed the nature of central-local relationships in housing in pursuit of greater control over public expenditure. This system was taken up and developed by the new Conservative government from 1979 onwards.

The Conservatives came into office with a radical housing policy which aimed to reduce social rented housing drastically while promoting owner occupation even more vigorously than previous governments. A central feature of their strategy was the 'the right to buy', with the sale of council houses to sitting tenants at well below market valuation. They also set about sharply raising rents in the remaining stock and cutting back on new investment. By 1980 these changes had been enacted; despite considerable resistance, including some from Conservative-controlled local authorities, local councils were required to sell off their social housing.

Housing activity, having briefly risen in 1974/75, was rapidly cut back under Labour. In the three years from 1974/75–1976/77, housing expenditure fell by 22 per cent whereas other public expenditure had been cut by only 8 per cent (Lansley, 1979). The new Conservative government soon cut still further. More reductions were made in November 1979 and again early in 1980. In the autumn of 1980 all local authority building was stopped, allegedly because some authorities were 'overspending', but with the effect of depressing new investment still further. More cuts followed in 1981. Some of the hardest-pressed inner-city authorities lost even more than the average authority in cuts, whereas other less hard-pressed areas, mainly outside the big cities, did less badly. Public tenants' rents, meanwhile, were increased, but subsidies to local authorities for housing were strictly controlled. The government calculated subsidy entitlement on the basis that certain target levels of rent increases would contribute to local authority expenditure, and local authorities lost grant if they refused to increase rents sufficiently. If they put up local taxes to compensate they faced grant penalties too. The overall strategy was to cut direct housing subsidies and to raise the revenue coming from the sector by selling off social housing and by increasing the rents of the remaining tenants. Rent increases also have the effect of increasing the pressure on tenants to buy their own homes if at all possible.

This policy of limiting support for social rented housing to those who are unable to afford private housing is presented in ways that stress the need for housing subsidies to be more effective and efficient than in the past. This might be more convincing if the grossly inefficient and inequitable system of indirect tax subsidies for owner occupation had also been altered, but nothing would be more likely to alienate the suburban Conservative voter (or for that matter the suburban Labour voter). It has been calculated that in 1981/82 the average tenant in social rented housing would receive £153 per annum in subsidies compared with the £360 per annum received by the average owner occupier with a mortgage. Further changes proposed for 1982/83 were likely to make this disparity even more extreme (Wilcox, 1981), hence increasing inequality and focusing state support on the private market.

So far, despite the protests of housing pressure groups and Labour local authorities, the attack on social housing has not led to nearly as much political conflict as the attack on local government finance. There are several reasons for this, including the fact that housing is one of the issues on which local government splits on party lines. But also, the effects of the collapse in new building and improvement resulting from cuts takes some time to filter through the system and result in dramatically falling housing opportunities. Finally, those worst affected by the cuts are the poor, and they are rarely a coherent or effective political force.

The impact on the housing market, however, has been immense. The social rented housing programme has collapsed. This began with Labour's cuts, but by 1980/81 only about 39 000 new social rented dwellings per annum were being started, the lowest since the 1930s. Recession, mass unemployment and high interest rates have resulted in the collapse of private housebuilding, too; thus, only about 100 000 new private houses were started in 1980 and the same approximately in 1981 (House of Commons Environment Committee, 1981a, pp. vii–viii). The total output of new and improved housing had by 1981 fallen far below the levels necessary to maintain, let alone improve, housing standards. At the same time, both social rented tenants and owner occupiers (the latter as a result of the general policy of high interest rates) faced rapidly rising housing costs – including, as a direct result of government policies, increasing local property taxes and payments for utilities. New entrants to the housing market – mostly young, on relatively low incomes and frequently unemployed and dependent on state benefits – are finding decent and affordable accommodation more and more difficult to obtain.

Overall, the impact of government policies on housing is perhaps second in severity only to the impact of government policies on employment. Moreover, the case of housing illustrates one of the central confusions of the New Right, i.e. the notion that the market can be 'set free' by the reduction of state involvement. In fact, the market in housing is crucially dependent on continued state support. For those who are unable, even with state subsidies, to buy their own homes, direct state provision is the only alternative to a return to nineteenth-century standards.

By the end of 1981 the extent to which housing policies had become hostages to the central imperatives of monetarism was clear. The protests of housing pressure groups about the disastrous effects of government policies on the housing market had been accompanied by others. In September 1981 the House-builders Federation (the main national body of private house builders) warned that the housing shortage threatened to reach 'crisis proportions' in the next four years (*Roof*, November/December 1981). The Association of Metropolitan Authorities produced a report prophesying a new era of mass demolition and slum clearance (*Guardian*, 15 December 1981). The House of Commons Environment Committee, with a majority of Conservative back-bench members, also brought out their third highly critical examination of government policies in a year. In evidence to the Committee, the Secretary of State claimed that housing forecasts could never be accurate and thus were not worth making. His main priority of reducing public expenditure determined the parameters of housing policy. The Committee concluded that housing was being treated as a ' "residual" item of public expenditure receiving what is left after other expenditure programmes have been met' (House of Commons Environment Committee, 1981b, pp. vi, xi).

By the end of 1981, the government largely had failed to substitute the private market for public provision in housing. Public sector activity was greatly reduced, but general economic policies had devastated the private sector too. The re-emergence of a large-scale housing problem by the mid 1980s seemed inevitable, and even some Conservatives and representatives of construction capital were fiercely critical of government policy.

Conclusion

It is both difficult and dangerous to predict the likely course of Britain's New Right government while it is still in power, especially bearing in mind Szelenyi's criticisms of the rigidities of thought concerning the supposed lack of adaptability of capitalist development which pervaded much of the new urban sociology in the late 1960s and 1970s. Even so, the New Right's policies of reducing state expenditure, 'setting the market free' and decollectivizing consumption faced many difficulties.

First, though, what was 'new' about the policies of the Thatcher government? Many policies since 1979 represented further development and intensification of trends that stretch back many years and have become particularly apparent in the last 10–20 years. Broadly speaking, the state management of the economy and society has become ever more problematic as British capitalism has declined. Pressure to cut the burden of 'unproductive' state expenditure; pressure to maintain a minimum of welfare for those who cannot earn a living wage; pressure to cut taxes, especially on capital and on the better off; pressure to provide more state support for private capital – all these have faced successive Conservative and Labour governments and, ultimately, destroyed them. The room for manoeuvre, for distinctively different policies – ranging from 'reformism' to the 'New Right' – is actually less than conventional political rhetoric would lead one to believe. The record of the last few years shows that, whether Labour has come to power with some commitment to reducing inequality and improving working-class standards of life, or the Conservatives have come to power promising to set the private market free to grow and protect middle-class standards, neither party has had great success in achieving these ends; and both have been riven with internal conflicts as a result of their failures.

Much of what local government provides is required whether in a middle-class suburb or an inner city. Any government that wishes to cut back local expenditure regardless of these needs will face conflict with some of its own supporters. In housing, a strategy of decollectivization of consumption and the return to the private market, when taken in conjunction with other aspects of economic policy, has resulted in the collapse of both public and private sector provision [. . .]

References

BONNET, K. (1981) *Classes, Class Fractions and Monetarism*, paper delivered at the BSA Annual Conference, Aberystwyth (mimeo).

BUTLER, D. and KAVANAGH, D. (1980) *The British General Election of 1979*, London, Macmillan.

CHANCELLOR OF THE EXCHEQUER (1981) *The Government's Expenditure Plans 1981–2 to 1983–4*, London, HMSO.

COUTTS, K., TARLING, R., WARD, T. and WILKINSON, F. (1981) 'The economic consequences of Mrs Thatcher', *Cambridge Journal of Economics*, Vol. 5, 81–93.

EUROPEAN ECONOMIC COMMUNITY (1980) *Social Report 1980*, Brussels, EEC.

HM TREASURY (1981) 'The impact of recession on the PSBR', *Economic Progress Report*, No. 130, London, HMSO, pp. 1–4.

HARLOE, M. H. (1978) 'The housing policy review', in Baldwin, S. and Brown, M. (eds) *Year Book of Social Policy in Britain 1978*, London, Routledge and Kegan Paul.

HARLOE, M. H. (1980) 'Housing and the state: recent British developments', in Ungerson, C. and Karn, V. (eds) *The Consumer Experience of Housing*, Farnborough, Hants, Gower Press.

HARLOE, M. H. (1981) 'The recommodification of housing', in Harloe, M. and Lebas, E. (eds) *City, Class and Capital*, London, Edward Arnold.

HOUSE OF COMMONS ENVIRONMENT COMMITTEE (1981a) *Enquiry into Implications of Government's Expenditure Plans 1980–1 to 1983–4 for the Housing Policies of the Department of the Environment*, London, HMSO.

HOUSE OF COMMONS ENVIRONMENT COMMITTEE (1981b) *DoE's Housing Policies: Enquiry into Government's Expenditure Plans 1981/82 to 1983/84 and the Updating of the Committee's First Report for the Session 1979/80*, London, HMSO.

LANSLEY, S. (1979) 'Black marks for White Paper', *Roof*, November, p. 172.

SECRETARY OF STATE FOR THE ENVIRONMENT (1977) *Housing Policy. A Consultative Document*, London, HMSO.

SZELENYI, I. (1981) 'Structural changes of and alternatives to capitalist development in the contemporary urban and regional system', *International Journal of Urban and Regional Research*, Vol. 5, No. 1, March, pp. 1–14.

TOWNSEND, P. and BOSANQUET, N. (1980) *Labour and Equality*, London, Heinemann.

WILCOX, S. (1981) 'Subsidies out of balance', *Roof*, May/June, p. 9.

14 Fiscal reorientation, centralization, and the privatization of council housing

Ray Forrest and Alan Murie

Introduction

British housing policy since the mid-1970s and especially the election of the Thatcher government in 1979 has been dominated by two factors: the need to reduce public expenditure and more pervasive support for the further growth of home ownership. Notions of fiscal crisis and fiscal austerity have permeated the policy debates. Ministers have frequently referred to 'what the country can afford' as the background to public policy and public expenditure decisions (Murie, 1985). Home ownership would transfer social and financial responsibilities from the state to the individual. Both ideological and fiscal objectives would be neatly achieved in one package. The depressed British economy could no longer afford the scale of public provision of the past. Collectivism would give way to privatized, individual solutions in housing, education, health, and transport. Subsidies would be drastically reduced and more narrowly concentrated on those in real need, leaving the majority to compete in a competitive free market.

Judged against the monetarist, free-market rhetoric of the New Right, what has been achieved falls far short of expectations and aspirations. The key institutions of the welfare state, such as National Health Service and state education, may be facing financial stringency but they remain largely intact. If inroads have been made it has been in the contraction of the state housing sector through privatization and reduced investment. It is in the housing sector where we should find the greatest contraction of the state in both its fiscal and regulatory roles. This chapter explores these assumptions and argues that what has occurred can be more accurately described as a reorientation in state housing expenditure and greater central control. While there have been significant changes in the pattern of public expenditure, it would be misleading to attribute changes in housing policy as logical and inevitable outcomes of fiscal constraint.

Fiscal reorientation and the attack on council housing

The present government's stated policy priorities for housing are: to increase the level of home ownership; to encourage the repair and improvement of the existing stock; and to concentrate public resources within the housing programme on capital provision for those in greatest housing need (HM Treasury, 1985). For the Thatcher government one of the key policies designed to achieve these objectives has been the privatization of council housing. The further extension of home ownership, most notably through the sale of public sector dwellings, has formed part of a broader restructuring of the welfare state (Forrest and Murie, 1985a). With one-third of all British households in the public sector in 1979 there was seen to be opportunity for a significant transformation of the tenure structure. This has involved not only boosting levels of home ownership through encouraging tenant purchase but also reducing the role of council housing (housing provided by local government authorities) to a residual service for those in special and exceptional need. In 1986 the Conservative government achieved these objectives to only a limited extent. The council housing sector accounts for a significantly smaller proportion of households in both absolute and relative terms (for the United Kingdom as a whole less than 29 per cent in 1983 compared with over 32 per cent in 1979). However, in spite of unprecedented encouragement to buy, over one-quarter of households remains as tenants. Perhaps of greater importance, and contrary to the philosophy of the New Right, these changes have not meant a disengagement of government from the housing sphere. A plethora of special policies as well as continuation of existing measures to assist home ownership signify a shift in the nature, direction, and methods of state intervention in housing rather than a simple withdrawal or abandonment of the tradition of state intervention in housing through the general provision of council housing.

In simple terms, public expenditure on housing has experienced a series of cuts. The Labour government made major cuts in housing expenditure in 1976 and since the election of the Conservative government in 1979 further major cuts have been implemented. The severity of the cuts has relegated the housing programme from a major to a minor one. As set out in the annual Public Expenditure Survey Committee White Papers, spending has fallen in real terms from £6.6 billion in 1979/80 to £3.0 billion in 1983/84 and a planned £2.4 billion in 1988/89 (at 1983/84 prices). This represents a reduction of 64 per cent. Housing's share of total public spending has fallen from 7.6 per cent in 1978–79 to an anticipated 3.7 per cent in 1988/89. No other welfare programme has been cut so substantially. The housing programme has borne the lion's share of public expenditure cutbacks. In 1980 the House of Commons Environment Committee noted that housing cutbacks planned for the period up to 1983/84 accounted for 75 per cent or more of all public spending reductions (Environment Committee, 1980). O'Higgins (1983, pp. 167–68) noted that 'housing is not only the welfare programme suffering the largest cuts, it is also the only programme where cuts have been overachieved: by 1981/82 the estimated outturn cut was one-and-a-half times the size the government had planned in 1980.'

The result, in terms of investment and subsidy, can be briefly summarized. Public sector dwelling starts and completions have fallen dramatically. Council house building has declined to its lowest peacetime level since 1925; the availability of council housing to rent has declined for the first time in peace time since 1919; exchequer (treasury) subsidies benefiting council tenants in general have been drastically cut and council rents have risen substantially. In 1978/79 average unrebated local authority rents were

£5.90 per week and this represented 6.6 per cent of average weekly earnings for adult males working full time. In 1982/83 rents were £13.58, representing 8.8 per cent of earnings. Provisional figures for 1985/86 put average rents at £15.66 (8.1 per cent of earnings). The reduction in general assistance subsidy for council housing and in housing capital expenditure generally has been achieved partly by switching housing subsidy expenditure into the social security budget. As rents have risen, so the costs of means-tested assistance with housing costs have increased. Because of changes in the administration of these benefits it is difficult to provide an accurate measure of increase. However, the best estimate shows almost a tripling of cash cost between 1979/80 and 1985/86 during which period housing capital expenditure (in cash terms) remained static. By 1985/86 housing benefit costs stood at £3056 million and this figure exceeded the total housing expenditure programme. This represents a rapid growth in individual, means-tested assistance with housing consumption costs. The change is partly associated with the impact of unemployment and recession and partly with the characteristics of those living in council housing. Over recent years the sector has catered to an increasing proportion of supplementary benefit recipients (Forrest and Murie, 1983). The growth of means-tested subsidy amounts to a significant *switch* in method of subsidy and does not involve as substantial a *reduction* in subsidy as appears from looking at housing expenditure alone.

Crucial to all these assessments, however, is the inclusion or exclusion of items as public expenditure for housing. There are two significant categories of public expenditure on housing that do not appear in the housing expenditure programme. First, items counted as public spending but incorporated in other programmes, the most important item being housing benefits, which appear in the social security programme; and second, 'tax expenditure' items, which are not defined as public spending at all, the most important of which include tax foregone as a result of mortgage interest relief, exemptions from capital gains tax of capital gains made on sale of main residence, and discounts to purchasers of council housing.

It is relevant to bear in mind that the structure of tax relief and other 'subsidies' to home owners has not been reviewed. The cost of mortgage interest relief increased by almost five times in real terms between 1963/64 and 1983/84. In 1983/84, official estimates put the cost of mortgage interest tax relief at £2750 million. This almost equalled the cost of the total housing programme (£2760 million) and compares with total capital expenditure (net of capital receipts) of £1650 million (HM Treasury, 1985). For 1985/86 the estimated cost of mortgage interest tax relief is, at £4750 million, well in excess of the total housing programme (£2742 million) (HM Treasury, 1986). The value of exemption from capital gains tax in each of these years is tentatively estimated at a further £2500 million. Discounts for council house sales under the 'right to buy' involved a new set of subsidies (with a new set of inequities). In 1983/84 the value of these discounts was £940 million (House of Commons Debates, 1985). The limit on mortgages qualifying for tax relief has been raised at a cost of some £60 million in revenue foregone. Expressed in these ways, it would seem that either there has been little systematic application of notions of what the country can afford, or the view is that the country can afford substantial support for home owners but not for housing investment or other housing subsidies. There is, of course, considerable debate as to whether these items should be counted as subsidies to home ownership and hence as public spending, even though they are essentially income foregone rather than moneys paid out (see, for example, Ermisch, 1984). Such debates, however, often proceed as if the exercise were merely technical, resting on accounting conventions. Balance sheets may not be politically constructed but they certainly have political implications and effects.

If the items referred to above are included in the public expenditure calculus then the impact of public expenditure and taxation decisions affecting housing is somewhat different from the official picture. As Tables 14.1 and 14.2 show, in 1985/86, for example, while expected outturn expenditure on the housing programme is £2.7 billion, £3.2 billion will be spent on housing benefit. In addition, mortgage interest tax relief will cost some £4.7 billion. Capital gains tax exemption for 1985/86 is estimated at £2.5 billion. Public spending on mortgage tax relief was about one-third of the level of spending on the housing programme in 1979/80, but in 1985/86 it has exceeded it. High interest rates have contributed to this, but tax relief continues to rise as house prices increase. Over the same period spending on housing benefit has also grown to a level where it exceeds the housing programme. Discount on sales of council houses in England and Wales between 1979/80 and 1984/85 amounted to £4.7 billion.

Tables 14.2 and 14.3 illustrate the switch in housing expenditure when mortgage interest tax relief and housing benefit are added to the 'conventional' picture of housing expenditure.

Even if we confine our analysis to include only housing benefit and mortgage interest tax relief, the total of the 'other' housing expenditure after falling slightly in *cash terms* between 1980/81 and 1982/83 rose sharply in 1983/84 and has continued to rise since. What we have seen is a major transfer of resources from those programmes conventionally included in the housing programme (mainly subsidies to public sector housing and new capital investment) towards other expenditure (housing benefit and support to home owners), rather than a simple cut in spending. In the government's own terms this must count as a major failure in public expenditure policy; but on the other hand the transfer – from support of the public sector to support of the private sector, from investment to subsidy, and from the subsidization of the production of public housing to the subsidization of individual consumption – reflects the priorities of the government.

In addition, within the official housing programme not all expenditure is on council housing. In the period of reduced expenditure since 1979, a striking feature is that both the voluntary sector (housing associations) and

Table 14.1 An alternative housing programme (£ million cash)

	1979/80 outturn	1980/81 outturn	1981/82 outturn	1982/83 outturn	1983/84 outturn	1984/85 outturn	1985/86 estimated outturn	1986/87 plans	1987/88 plans	1988/89 plans
Public sector[1] housing expenditure										
Gross capital expenditure	3152	2933	2563	3301	3981	3914	3283	3253	3210	3110
Net capital expenditure (i.e. gross expenditure less value of capital receipts from the housing programme)	2680	2330	1517	1424	2026	2131	1632	1652	1730	1770
Total current expenditure	1842	2123	1601	1228	1076	1073	1110	1100	1100	1100
Total housing expenditure (capital and revenue)	4522	4452	3118	2652	3102	3204	2742	2752	2830	2880
'Other' housing expenditure										
Housing benefit	932[2]	1039[2]	1395[2]	1663[2]	2624	2954	3214	3277	3320	3420
Tax relief on mortgage interest	1639	2188	2292	2456	2767[3]	3500	4750			
Total 'other' expenditure	2571	3227	3687	4119	5391	6454	7964			

[1]Local authorities, new towns, Housing Corporation, and home loan scheme.
[2]Estimated figures. Payments of housing costs to supplementary benefit applicants not included in housing benefit for 1979–83.
[3]Excludes £55 million (mortgage interest relief at source).
Source: Annual Public Expenditure Survey Committee White Papers 1979/30 to 1986/87 and *Hansard* 49 (November 11, 1983)

Table 14.2   An alternative housing programme (percentage shares)

	1979/80	1980/81	1981/82	1982/83	1983/84	1984/85	1985/86
Total housing programme (£m)[1]	7093	7679	6805	6771	8493	9658	10 700
Public sector housing expenditure							
Net capital expenditure	38	30	22	21	24	22	15
Current expenditure	26	28	24	18	13	11	10
Total capital and revenue	64	58	46	39	37	33	20
'Other' housing expenditure							
Housing benefit	13	14	20	25	31	31	30
Tax relief on mortgage interest	23	28	34	36	33	36	44
Total 'other' expenditure	36	42	54	61	63	67	74

[1] As in table 14.1.
Source: HM Treasury, 1986

Table 14.3   An index of housing activity, 1979/80 to 1988/89 (1979/80 = 100)

Public sector housing expenditure	1980–81	1981–82	1982–83	1983–84	1984–85	1985–86	1986–87	1987–88	1988–89
Gross capital expenditure	93	81	105	126	124	104	103	102	99
Net capital expenditure	87	60	53	76	80	61	62	66	66
Current expenditure	115	87	67	58	58	60	60	60	60
Total housing expenditure	98	69	59	69	71	61	61	63	64
'Other' housing expenditure									
Housing benefit	111	150	178	282	317	345	352	356	367
Tax relief on mortgage interest	133	140	150	169	214	290			
Total 'other' expenditure	126	143	160	210	251	310			

Source: HM Treasury, 1986

home owners have obtained an increased share of this expenditure. In 1979/80 the housing association sector accounted for some 15 per cent of net spending; by 1982/83 this had risen to 48 per cent and it is expected that it will remain near that level in the foreseeable future. New dwellings completed by local authorities in England fell from 70 000 in 1979/80 to 27 000 in 1984/85; in the same period completions by new towns fell from 7 000 to 1600 and those of housing associations fell from 16 700 to 12 800.

For home owners the most significant development has been the sixfold increase in improvement grant expenditure between 1979/80 and 1983/84. In 1983/84, improvement and thermal insulation grants, most of which are paid to home owners, accounted for some 28 per cent of local authority gross capital expenditure. The 1986 public expenditure White Paper shows gross capital expenditure support to the private sector as £413 million in 1980/81 rising to £1345 million in 1983/84 and falling back to £840 million in 1985/86.

Fiscal opportunism

The picture of fluctuations in *gross* capital expenditure understates what has been achieved. The results of the 'right to buy' for council tenants and other measures have been to produce an enormous increase in the level of capital receipts, especially for local authorities. These rose fourfold between 1979/80 and 1982/83. As a result the level of *net expenditure* by local authorities has been reduced much more significantly than has gross expenditure. In real terms, new net capital expenditure by local authorities in 1982/83 was only about 25 per cent of its 1979/80 level and in 1985/86 is planned to approach 20 per cent. Although gross spending increased during 1983/85, the continuing high level of capital receipts reduced the rate of increase of net spending, which even in 1983/84 reached only 40 per cent of its 1979/80 level.

The government has used the level of capital receipts to permit the reduction of net new investment on a dramatic scale. In 1982/83 net capital expenditure by local authorities (£729 million) barely exceeded the net level of funding of housing associations by the Housing Corporation (£680 million). This raises major issues in relation to the use of capital assets. First, the real value of assets disposed of is far higher as a result of discounts. Second, the disposal of assets will lead in the medium or long term to additional and greater expenditure (if any attempt is made to replace lost relets or meet demand) – for example, on the acquisition of sites to replace those previously sold or the construction or acquisition of new housing. Finally, whatever view is taken of these longer-term arguments, and of the view that proceeds (however discounted) should be used for *additional investment*, the prospect of *declining receipts* poses a real threat to the maintenance of even the reduced housing programme that capital receipts have facilitated.

Capital receipts associated with the housing programme have been more substantial than those from any other programme despite the publicity that some sales (such as British Telecom) have received. Sales of local authority dwellings have represented the most significant act of privatization or sale of assets carried out in the period since 1979 (for a more general assessment see Le Grand and Robinson, 1984; Shackleton, 1984; Whitfield, 1983; Thompson, 1984). In 1979/80 total receipts from sales of other public assets were £370 million; in 1980/81, £405 million; in 1981/82, £494 million; in 1982/83, £488 million; and in 1983/84, £1142 million. Total sales and repayments from the housing programme for these years were £448 million, £568 million, £976 million, £1739 million, and £1789 million, respectively. The actual market value of council houses sold over this period exceeds £11 billion and discount exceeded £4.6 billion.

Table 14.4 details the composition of housing capital receipts since 1978/79. The volume of receipts has risen dramatically since 1979/80 with increasing levels of council house sales, and initial receipts from the sale of dwellings have supplanted repayments of loans as the principal source of receipts.

Council house sales in the period 1979/84 were more than double those in the previous 40 years combined and have exceeded those completed in the whole history of council housing. Neither sales nor capital receipts are a totally new phenomenon. The main difference in recent times, however, is in the relationship of the volume of capital receipts to capital expenditure. The local authority housing capital programme has become substantially self-financing and the call of housing on the public sector borrowing requirement has been considerably reduced because of the volume of capital receipts.

A number of arguments could be advanced over whether capital receipts 'should' be reinvested in housing. Without entering into such a debate at length it is apparent that the housing sector's demands on 'non-housing' funds have been more substantially cut than is compatible with the level of gross capital expenditure. Without housing capital receipts in recent years either the housing programme would have been even more severely cut or housing would have come into sharper conflict with other expenditure programmes in resource demands.

At present, it seems likely that capital receipts from the sale of council houses will diminish unless there are new measures to stimulate them. Interest in purchase by tenants has shown a steady decline despite more generous incentives. Many tenants who remain in the public sector may be too old or too young to consider buying, may be occupying an unattractive dwelling, or may simply be too poor, unemployed, or insecurely employed. Emergent government policy suggests a shift from incentives for individuals to purchase towards a greater emphasis on the wholesale transfer of local authority estates to private or quasi-public organizations. While the accumulated backlog of receipts could serve as a cushion for some years, any significant reduction in the longer term will require substantial new investment or more dramatic cutbacks.

Table 14.4   Sources of local authority housing capital receipts (£ million cash)

	1978–79		1979–80		1980–81		1981–82		1982–83		1983–84		1984–85	
	£m	%	£m	%	£m	%	£m	%	£m	%	£m	%	£m	%
Sales of land and other assets	24	5	38	8	95	17	99	10	135	8	103	6	105	7
Initial receipts from sales of dwellings	138	28	122	27	186	33	532	55	1017	58	970	54	830	57
Repayments of sums outstanding on sales of dwellings	40	8	43	10	53	9	89	9	282	16	445	25	315	21
Repayments of loans by private persons	293	58	241	54	216	38	240	25	287	17	246	14	185	13
Repayment of loans by Housing Associations	7	1	4	1	16	3	15	2	18	1	25	1	30	2
Total	501	100	448	100	568	100	976	100	1739	100	1789	100	1465	100

Source: Cmnd 9143 II and 9428 II and *Hansard* 49 (November 23, 1983), cols. 212–13.

In all of these changes, the government's attitude to council housing occupies a prominent position. Not only has its historical development represented a major and very visible ideological irritation for the Conservative party but its management and allocation has been one of the major areas in which locally elected councils could exert influence on the local social and economic structure. With the extension of home ownership high on the political agenda (with its symbolic value as the extension of citizenship rights) the disposal of council houses has been in the forefront of a broader ideological crusade. These ideological considerations have, however, progressively taken second place to more pressing fiscal imperatives. Council housing, unlike the National Health Service, has always been a minority provision for the working classes. Moreover, unlike cuts in education and health, disinvestment in council housing has less immediate consequences. Representing, as it has, the soft underbelly of the welfare state, it has been caught in a pincer movement between ideological commitments to individualism and to monetarism. The consequences of these commitments have increasingly fallen on local government expenditure given the failure of central government's macro-economic strategies.

Increasing central control of local provision

In Britain, the responsibility for planning and meeting local housing needs has rested with local government. It is local government that has been blamed for failure to house the homeless or to build the right houses in the right places at the right time. While central government has provided the framework for local policy, it has always been able to argue that it is local decisions and local councils that should be reviewed when local shortcomings are apparent. In this way local government in housing has provided a convenient buffer for central government between itself and political action in relation to housing; but the 'right to buy' has involved more direct central government intervention to secure the sale of local authority houses and contribute to the changing levels and priorities in central government's expenditure plans. This direct intervention has involved central government in taking more responsibility for housing and housing circumstances.

Central government from the outset took an active part in implementing the 'right to buy'. The political and financial importance of this legislation meant that the task was not completed with the passage of legislation. The expectation of local obstruction, the desire to appeal over the heads of local administrations, and the desire to publicize the 'right to buy' involved the central department with a substantial continuing role. Initially the government appears to have been satisfied to concentrate on publicity. In 1980/81, £655000 was spent on advertisements on television and in national newspapers telling and reminding public sector tenants of their new rights including the 'right to buy'. In 1981/82, £239000 was spent on publicizing the 'right to buy'.

In this same initial period, considerable press coverage was given to local housing authorities that expressed an intention not to implement the act. The minister of housing was at the same time making it clear that the government would use its powers of intervention. He was reported as saying these powers would be used to ensure that tenants in areas controlled by the Labour party were not denied the right to buy (House of Commons, 1980).

Although the Department of the Environment has not been concerned to monitor the 'right to buy' in terms of social or financial impact, it has from the outset obtained sales figures in the statistical returns made to it by local authorities. In addition, the department has obtained impressions on progress or delay through letters of complaint from or on behalf of tenants, from press reports, or from informal discussions between the department and the authorities. Where the secretary of state received information suggesting that significant delays were occurring or likely to occur he normally made a formal approach to the local authority concerned on the question of current and future progress. In such formal approaches the secretary of state usually sought overall statistical information on the number of 'right to buy' applications received, the numbers at various stages in the sales process, and estimates of future progress. Where the information given in reply to such approaches indicated to the secretary of state the possibility that tenants were having difficulty in exercising their right to buy, further information and assurances were sought. In typical cases this involved meetings between the central department and the local authority. Following such further correspondence or meetings the secretary of state either stated that he would take no further action in light of assurances, undertakings, or indications of future progress (but usually requiring monthly progress statistics); or, where satisfactory assurances had not been forthcoming, gave a formal warning that he was contemplating using his powers of intervention under the act and requesting, within a specified time, further information on future progress. Where such formal warning was given and the information supplied still appeared unsatisfactory, local councillors were invited to a meeting with a minister. After that stage the formal warning could be withdrawn but monthly progress information is still required. This formal scrutiny and pressure has been widely used. Indeed in December 1983 the government was in contact with about 200 local authorities, most of which were Labour-controlled, about aspects of their performance in implementing the 'right to buy'. This represented a much more active and interventionist stance than had generally applied in the housing area in the past.

The extreme example of intervention arose when the secretary of state was not satisfied by the progress and undertakings offered by Norwich City Council in respect of the implementation of the 'right to buy'. Norwich was not refusing to implement the law but argued other priorities and issues of staff and costs in response to complaints about progress. The secretary of state used his powers under the Housing Act of 1980 to send in his representative to take over the administration of the 'right to buy'. Such intervention was resisted in the courts by Norwich but the secretary of state's action was supported by the judiciary (Forrest and Murie, 1985b).

The Housing and Building Control Act of 1984 was not introduced because of the Norwich intervention. Nevertheless there are aspects of the new legislation that represent a response to the kind of circumstances that led to the conflict and litigation involving Norwich. Some parts of the act can be seen as steps to close loopholes in the original legislation. For example, the new act provided a power for the secretary of state to give directions on covenants and conditions included in grants or conveyances, and to serve a notice requiring the landlord to produce documents or supply information. At the same time the legislation of 1984 required the landlord to meet a more stringent timetable in acknowledging the 'right to buy'.

These sections of the 1984 legislation provide the central government with a more varied armoury of mechanisms for intervention. In the event of future conflicts the long-drawn-out, public, and heavy-handed procedure culminating in the introduction of a 'commissioner' could be avoided. Instead the secretary of state could carry out legal processes on behalf of individuals – and be seen to be acting on behalf of the powerless individual rather than basking in the arrogant exercise of power on behalf of a centralized bureaucracy. The consequence seems likely to be an even greater shift of real power to the centre.

The 'right to buy' has been a major element in pursuing the *ideology* of individualism and property ownership and in reducing the intrusiveness of the state. Ironically, in implementing this policy the central government has, in fact, become more rather than less involved. This has come about in two ways. First, the responsibility of central government for specific local patterns of housing tenure and opportunity has been greatly increased. While the central government in other areas, notably housing benefits, has sought to identify local administrations with responsibility for service delivery, the opposite has happened in relation to tenure mobility and housing choice. Second, the central government has increasingly become involved in the details of day-to-day policy implementation. This is apparent in the extent of monitoring and in the increasing detail of scrutiny. Whereas the Department of the Environment had little practical knowledge or experience of issues in conveyancing it has become involved in a detailed way and the Housing and Building Control Act provides powers to intervene over this and other areas.

These developments relate to a favourite theme of the New Right: that of the overburdened state. This notion derives from two main contentions. First, government at central and local levels has increased its role to a degree where its failings and lack of competence have become apparent. Second, the libertarian strand of the New Right's critique of the growth of government would point to the intrusiveness of state control and regulation of people's everyday lives. The growth of government has involved increasing failures to deliver what was intended and has been marked by an overextended bureaucracy that proves inefficient, unresponsive, and ineffective. It is argued that the development of local government and of various quasi-nongovernment organizations is evidence of this. Historically the central government has found it more effective to use other organizations than to try to do everything itself. Whether the central government uses such agencies (including local government) or becomes more involved in local service delivery and day-to-day policy implementation itself (for fiscal or any other reasons), the problems of an overextended bureaucracy become apparent. The 'right to buy' represents a response to this situation. It is presented as part of the process of reducing the role of the state and transferring control and ownership to individual citizens. However, in order to deregulate or demunicipalize services the central government has become more enmeshed in local housing provision. Legislation, publicity, scrutiny, and subsidy have all been necessary elements in demunicipalization. The establishment of a Norwich Office of the Department of Environment sounds more like a further extension of the state than a disengagement. The questions pursued by that office and the contents of the legislative step that followed – the Housing and Building Control Act of 1984 – involved more and more detail rather than withdrawal. The most obvious conclusion is that greater intervention was needed to secure disengagement.

As in other areas of state involvement the consequence, if not the intention, of recent policy development has been to strengthen the central levels of government at the expense of the local levels. Arguably, therefore, the state is not so much 'rolled back' as withdrawn into a centralist shell less open to democratic demands and public scrutiny. As the central government becomes more obviously directly responsible for local circumstances and living conditions so it becomes the target for criticism and complaint. It becomes more directly and obviously responsible and is less able to shelter behind other organizations. Thus, in achieving one set of objectives, the central government could be diminishing the mechanisms that strengthen and legitimate its role. By changing the established structure of responsibility the central government risks upsetting these mechanisms. The increased concentration of power through legislation and other policy action has political implications *beyond* those of the individual policies themselves. Problems of legitimacy are more likely to arise when the failure to deliver services effectively is unavoidably the responsibility of central government and the failure cannot easily be attributed to other organizations.

Emerging issues

The policy of privatization through council house sales did not emerge because of some financial calculation. Rather it was presented as a means of extending home ownership, redistributing wealth, and reducing the power and control of the state. However, as the policy has emerged since

1979 it has increasingly contributed to the relief of fiscal problems. Large capital receipts have helped the government meet its spending plans without raising taxation. Without such receipts either spending programmes would have had to be cut further or policies on taxation and borrowing revised. But the appeal and apparent success of the policy raises important issues about the future development of privatization and the emergence of a crisis in housing supply and condition.

Dilemmas in relation to the future of privatization are already emerging. The sale of council houses to sitting tenants has a declining appeal as tenants in the best position to buy and in the best properties complete their purchases. But what of the very large (by international standards) remaining state housing sector? And how can the level of capital receipts generated by this asset be maintained? The emerging solution appears to involve alternative forms of privatization.

The Housing and Planning Bill of 1986 is designed to facilitate the sale of estates or portfolios of properties to privately financed housing trusts and approved landlord bodies and to generate capital receipts. Unlike sales to sitting tenants, however, such sales obviously do not also meet the tenure or other housing aspirations of households. A large number of council tenants may have expressed a desire for home ownership. There is little evidence, however, that any wish to become private tenants.

After six years of obsessive concern with privatization and the extension of home ownership there is considerable evidence of a coming housing crisis in the United Kingdom. An official government report estimated the need for expenditure of £19 billion on the existing council stock (Department of the Environment 1985). New building is still at minimal levels. Damning criticisms of current housing policy have been made in recent well-publicized reports by the Church of England (1985) and an Inquiry chaired by the Duke of Edinburgh (National Federation of Housing Associations, 1985), hardly traditional critics of a Conservative government.

In housing opportunities and conditions as in other areas, the gap between rich and poor has widened over the past six years. Some groups have experienced a deterioration in their living conditions and life chances (Central Statistical Office, 1985). Yet in 1983 the combined cost of mortgage tax relief, central and local government subsidies, benefits, and improvements grants amounted to over £10 billion, around two-thirds higher than in 1979. Political and legislative energies and fiscal resources have been directed at the emasculation of local government and local housing provision with greater central control and allocation of subsidy. As the figures referred to earlier illustrate, despite the rhetoric of austerity, the reality has been profligacy in subsidizing consumption for the relatively privileged at the expense of much-needed new investment in housing production for lower-income groups.

References

CENTRAL STATISTICAL OFFICE (1985) *Social Trends* 15, London, HMSO.

CHURCH OF ENGLAND (1985) *Faith in the City*, London, Church House Publishing.

DEPARTMENT OF THE ENVIRONMENT (1985) *An Inquiry into the Condition of the Local Authority Stock in England*, London, HMSO.

ENVIRONMENT COMMITTEE (1980) *Enquiry into the Implications of the Government's Expenditure Plans 1980–81 to 1983–84 for the Housing Policies of the Department of the Environment*, HC 714, London, HMSO.

ERMISCH, J. (1984) *Housing Finance: Who Gains?*, London, Policy Studies Institute.

FORREST, R. and MURIE, A. (1983) 'Residualisation and council housing: aspects of the changing social relations of housing tenure', *Journal of Social Policy*, Vol. 12. No. 4, pp. 453–68.

FORREST, R. and MURIE, A. (1985a) 'Restructuring the welfare state: privatization and public housing in the UK', in van Vliet, W., Huttman, E. and Fava, S. (eds) *Housing Needs and Policy Approaches & Trends in Thirteen Countries*, Durham, N.C., Duke University Press.

FORREST, R. and MURIE, A. (1985b) *An Unreasonable Act? Central-Local Government Conflict and the Housing Act 1980*, School for Advanced Urban Studies, No. 1, University of Bristol.

HM TREASURY (1985) *The Government's Expenditure Plans 1985–86 to 1987–88*, Cmnd 9428, London, HMSO.

HM TREASURY (1986) *The Government's Expenditure Plans 1986–87 to 1988–89*, Cmnd 9702, London, HMSO.

HOUSE OF COMMONS (1980) House of Commons *Parliamentary Debates*, 16.04.80 cols 1983–4.

LE GRAND, J. and ROBINSON, R. (eds) (1984) *Privatization and the Welfare State*, London, Allen and Unwin.

MURIE, A. (1985) 'What the country can afford? Housing under the Conservatives in 1979–83', in Jackson, P. (ed.) *Implementing Government Policy Initiatives: The Thatcher Administration 1979–1983*, London, Royal Institute of Public Administration.

NATIONAL FEDERATION OF HOUSING ASSOCIATIONS (1985) *Inquiry into British Housing (chaired by HRH the Duke of Edinburgh) Report*, London, National Federations of Housing Associations.

O'HIGGINS, M. (1983) 'Rolling back the welfare state: the rhetoric and reality of public expenditure and social policy under the Conservative government', in Jones, C. and Stevenson, J. (eds) *The Year Book of Social Policy in Britain 1982*, London, Routledge and Kegan Paul.

SHACKLETON, J. (1984) 'Privatization: the case examined', *National Westminster Bank Quarterly Review*, May, pp. 59–73.

THOMPSON, G. (1984) 'Rolling back the state? Economic intervention 1975–82', in McLennan, G., Held, D. and Hall, S. *State and Society in Contemporary Britain*, Cambridge, Polity Press.

WHITFIELD, D. (1983) *Making it Public*, London, Pluto Press.

Section VI   Images of social change

Introduction

Each of the extracts that follow provides different but related insights into the cultural state of modern Britain, that is into the various meanings that people attach to all the economic and social transformations that are currently taking place. Each of the extracts addresses, in its different way, the three chief themes brought out in *The Changing Social Structure* (Hamnett *et al.*, 1989). These themes are, first of all, the importance of seeing culture as contested, as a political process in which certain interpretations of events are adopted at the expense of others; secondly, the rise of the middle classes and its accompanying cultural correlates in the growth of feeling for the countryside and the national heritage; and, thirdly, the importance of other cultural traditions, especially those connected with Scotland, Northern Ireland and Wales and the various ethnic communities. Each of the extracts has been chosen to reflect different aspects of these three themes.

The article by Urry (Chapter 15) is concerned with the current condition of British working-class culture. Working-class culture no longer has quite the hold on the British imagination that it had in the 1950s and '60s when northern working-class culture, in particular, was celebrated in a variety of media, whether on record in the shape of the Beatles and other rock groups, on television in programmes like *Z-Cars*, or in the novels of writers like Stan Barstow, John Braine, Alan Sillitoe and David Storey (Laing, 1985). The reasons for this decline in cultural influence are not hard to find. Most especially they include: widespread deindustrialization (especially of the north) and the resulting unemployment; the increasing affluence of segments of the working class and the corresponding take-up of consumer-orientated values; and the rise of the middle class to a new status and confidence. Certainly, the old working-class culture, based in manufacturing industry, a particular kind of male domination and the lack of more than a few consumer goods, is dying away.

Ian Jack (1987, pp. 2–3) provides a lament for his late Scottish working-class father and his way of life which could equally well be applied to other parts of the UK:

> He ended his working life only a few miles from where he had begun it, and in much the same way; in overalls and over a lathe and waiting for the dispensation of the evening hooter when he would stick his leg over his bike and cycle home. He never owned a house and he never drove a car, and today there is very little public evidence that he ever lived ... Few of his workplaces survive. The cargo steamer went to the scrap yard long ago, of course, but even the shipping line it belonged to has vanished. The coal pit is a field. Urban grassland and car parks have buried the foundations of the mills. The house he grew up in has been demolished and replaced with a traffic island. The school which taught him ... has made way for a supermarket. In its way, deindustrialisation has disinherited the sons and

daughters of the manufacturing classes; a benign disinheritance in many respects, because many of the places my father worked were hell-holes, but also one so sudden and complete that it bewilders me.

Urry fixes on one aspect of the decline of this old manufacturing-based working class, the way that its sons and daughters have turned away from the traditional working-class seaside resorts like Blackpool and More-cambe that people that Ian Jack's father frequented. Urry's argument is that in these days of mass tourism/consumption going to the seaside has simply moved outside of the cultural frame of reference of many members of the current working class (and other classes too) as a pleasurable activity. An increasingly white-collar, privatized and consumption-orientated working class now has values nearer to those of the middle classes (Clarke and Critcher, 1985). Traditional seaside resorts do not fit these values. Instead, they tend to fall between two stools. They are not 'modern' enough. That is, they do not offer competition with high-tech pleasure parks of the kind typified nowadays by places like Alton Towers. But nor do they have enough buildings of the type which would allow them to be thought of as 'historic'. Places like Blackpool and Morecambe are making determined efforts to re-present themselves as places which can take on the meanings of modernity and heritage but at present they often seem stranded by a cultural tide which has now gone out.

Mention of heritage brings us to the study of the dominant meanings currently circulating in British society. These meanings appeal particularly to the growing middle classes (especially those located in the south of England). The articles by Hewison and Wright (Chapters 16 and 17) each investigate these meanings in their different ways.

It is important to note how often the countryside tradition is found harnessed to the heritage tradition, that is to an appreciation of and enthusiasm for the past which is now so widespread in Britain that Urry and others can describe Britain as a 'museum culture'. Hewison's paper relates the history of how the country house has become an icon of middle-class life, powerfully mixing together images and meanings from the countryside and the heritage tradition. At the end of the Second World War, many country houses were in varying states of neglect, perceived by the population as relics of a bygone age. But now they are seen, by members of the middle classes in particular, as not only the ultimate in consumer objects to aspire to own but also as emblematic of the world in which they want to live.

> On one side stands Brideshead – a countervailing and predominantly rural world based on private values and culturally sanctioned hierarchy, where history is venerated as traditions and society is based on ancestry and descent. On the other side, and piled up in a heap under the sign of the urban tower block, lies the wreckage of 1945; the commitment to public as opposed to private values, the anti-hierarchical egalitarianism, the hope that history could be made through the progressive works of an expert and newly enlightened state, the idea of a society based on consent rather than descent. (Wright, 1988, p. 7)

Hewison documents this shift in the meaning of the country house by examining the various groups who support the country house and the tradition of historic Britain it stands for. He is very sceptical of the 'heritage industry' he describes, in which the country house is a vital cog. For him it shows that England, in particular, has become 'like an actor who has played one character for so long that every other role he plays resembles the role for which he is famous' (Bragg, 1976, p. 13).

This sceptism is echoed by Wright in his paper. Wright is concerned to show that the process of gentrification, by which the middle class colonize working-class areas of inner cities is not just economic and social, it is also cultural. It involves appeals to the idea of heritage to legitimate the whole process – the middle classes are the only appropriate curators of the past that inner city areas like Stoke Newington represent in the present. Wright writes with anger and commitment of the way in which Stoke Newington has become a whole set of different mental worlds, a 'cultural oscillation' between the physical reality and how different groups of people perceive it. Thus, there is the world of the middle-class gentrifier, reading the *Guardian* or *The Times* or the *Independent*, working in a white-collar professional job in London, and much concerned with the architectural merits of the Victorian villas he or she inhabits. That world contrasts with the world of the harder-pressed working class of the area which tends to be more bounded by circumstance. Think only of the Asian homeworkers Wright mentions, eking out a living.

Hewison and Wright tend to be very critical of the heritage industry, partly for polemical purposes. But it is important to remember that not all conservation of the past is necessarily 'bad'. The growing number of museums may sometimes have an ersatz quality but they present a way of life which certainly deserves as much remembrance as that eulogized by various country houses. Ian Jack's father (1987, p. 3) left behind a kind of cultural treasure trove:

> There were books, suits from Burtons, long underpants, cuff-links, shirt armbands, pipes which continued to smell of Walnut Plug, the polished black boots he always preferred to shoes, half-empty bottles of Bay Rum, tools in tool boxes, shaving brushes, cigarette cards, photograph albums, photographs loose in suitcases, tram tickets, picture postcards sent from seaside resorts and inland spas, Rothesay and Llandudno, Matlock and Peebles. *Here for the week. Weather Mixed. Lizzie and Jim.*

The memorabilia of working-class life such as these are more vulnerable but they are surely just as important as gilded antiques. The problem is that the version of the past retailed by the heritage industry is too often selective, and class-specific.

The rise of middle-class culture represented by the countryside and heritage traditions, encapsulated in Hewison's country house and Wright's gentrifying inner city, should not be allowed to hide the reality of a UK that is now probably as culturally diverse as at any time in its history. The

distinctive cultures of Northern Ireland, Scotland and Wales are important, although these are not without their own versions of countryside and
heritage traditions. The following passage from a book by a famous Welsh
historian may strike familiar chords:

> While heartening, all this (remembrance of the Welsh past) is also disturbing:
> one wonders whether it is some kind of symptom. We are living through a
> somewhat desperate hunt after our own past, a time of old militants
> religiously recorded on tape, of quarries and pits turned into tourist
> museums. This recovered tradition is increasingly operating in terms of a
> celebration of a Heroic Past which seems rarely to be brought to bear on
> vulgarly contemporary problems except in terms of a merely rhetorical style
> which absolves its fortunate possessors from the necessity of thought. This is
> not to encapsulate the past, it is to sterilize it. It is not to cultivate an
> historical consciousness; it is to eliminate it. (Williams, 1985, p. 300)

These different national cultures are paralleled by the cultures of the large
number of ethnic communities scattered around the UK, each with their
own distinctive institutions – places of religious worship, cinemas, night
clubs, increasingly distinctive media, and so on. As Clarke and Critcher
(1985) point out, the influence of these communities on British society and
culture should not be belittled. Their cultures and styles have diffused into
the community at large, for example in the realms of fashion, food and
music.

All these differences underline the factor that the UK consists not of one
culture but of many cultures, interlinked certainly but often quite distinctive in their range of meanings and images. Dominant groups such as the
growing middle classes may seek to impose their meanings and images onto
those diverse cultures' interpretations of economic and social change but
they are rarely able to attain complete mastery.

References

BRAGG, M. (1976) *Peak for England: An Essay on England: 1900–1975*, London,
Secker and Warburg.

CLARKE, J. and CRITCHER, C. (1985) *The Devil Makes Work: Leisure in
Capitalist Britain*, London, Macmillan.

HAMNETT, C., McDOWELL, L. and SARRE, P. (eds) (1989) *The Changing
Social Structure*, London, Sage/Open University.

JACK, I. (1987) *Before The Oil Ran Out: Britain 1977–86*, London, Secker and
Warburg.

LAING, S. (1985) *Representations of Working Class Life 1957–1964*, London,
Macmillan.

WILLIAMS, G. A. (1985) *When Was Wales? A History of the Welsh*, Harmondsworth, Penguin.

WRIGHT, P. (1988) 'Brideshead and the tower blocks', *London Review of Books*,
June, pp. 3–7.

15   Cultural change and contemporary holiday-making

John Urry

In much of the current debate on the nature of modern life one particular social activity has been relatively underexamined, namely that of holiday-making. And yet in many of the key texts which adumbrate the character of the modern experience [. . .] it is movement or travel which is the defining characteristic of modernity. And in turn it is travel which is the absolute precondition for the emergence of mass tourism – surely one of the quintessential features of modern life. In this article I shall examine some aspects of recent changes in the nature of contemporary tourism, arguing that if we are moving towards a postmodern culture then that will have its parallel developments in the organization of holiday-making. Is contemporary tourism becoming postmodern?

I shall be particularly interested in the effects that such developments might be having upon the old-fashioned pleasures of going to the seaside. I shall be concerned to describe and begin to explain how and why many people who once thought of 'going to the seaside' as the principal form of extended leisure activity, now consider this to be merely one of a number of potential kinds of such activity. Why have many people now come to see the spending of a week's or fortnight's holiday by the seaside as a much less attractive and meaningful kind of touristic experience than was the case in the decades around the Second World War? Such changes cannot be separated from a set of cultural transformations which are loosely connected with the emergence of so-called postmodernism in many spheres of cultural experience in the past couple of decades. Very broadly 'mass holiday-making' to the British seaside resort was the quintessential form of tourism in *industrial* society. With more recent changes in the direction of a *post-industrial* society, there has been the emergence of what has been journalistically characterized as 'post-tourism' (see Feifer, 1985, Chapter 9).

Before outlining such recent developments it is necessary to consider briefly the nature of mass tourism. It is by definition a leisure activity which presupposes regulated and organized work. It is one form in which leisure, the opposite of work, is socially organized and constructed. Most known human societies have not so organized work and leisure (and tourism) in separate spheres. The development of leisure and hence of tourism is integrally bound up with transformations in the nature of paid work which became constructed as a relatively separate and organized sphere of social activity. It is organized within particular places and occurs for regularized and predictable periods of time. Tourism likewise has come to be developed as something occurring in particular *other* places which in some way or other contrast with those places where paid work occurs. Minimally, there are a number of interrelated features of the social practices known as 'tourism' (see Burkart and Medlik, 1974, Chapter 4; Graburn, 1978; Urry, 1987):

1   Tourist relationships arise from a movement of people to, and their stay in, various destinations which are outside the normal places of residence and work.
2   Periods of residence clsewhere are relatively short-term and temporary – there is a clear intention to return 'home' within a limited period.
3   The places are visited for purposes which are not directly connected with paid work and they generally offer some distinct contrasts with the world of at least *paid* work.
4   The activities engaged in 'on holiday' are chosen because they are pleasurable, non-pecuniary and involve unfamiliar or non-routine sensations.
5   A substantial proportion of the population engages in such tourist practices, and new socialized forms of provision (travel, accommodation and entertainment) are developed to cope with its mass (rather than élite) character. 'Tourism' replaces the individual 'traveller'.
6   'Going on holiday' is part of most people's organization of time over the course of the year. If one is not at work for more than a few days then 'normal adults' will travel. To stay at home is to be pitied; to travel away at least once a year is part of the modern experience.

Mass tourism of this sort, in which people travel away from their place of work and residence, has become an utterly central feature of modern consumer culture. The origins of such processes lay with a number of developments: the growth of sea bathing and then of seaside resorts in the eighteenth century; the emergence of enormous popular resorts in the middle to late nineteenth century; the development of holidays with pay and the exceptionally widespread practice of spending a week or fortnight by the sea; the post-Second World War development of holiday camps, of foreign package holidays, and of a much more varied pattern of holiday-making within Britain (see Urry, 1987, for a summary; and Jakle, 1983, for an account of parallel developments in North America). Tourism is a huge business supporting perhaps 1.4 million jobs in Britain – there are more people employed now in hotels than in coal mines *and* car factories. Tourism has since 1960 or so become highly internationalized. So although in 1983 UK residents made 19 million trips abroad, there has also been a large increase in the number of foreign visitors to the UK. In fact only four other countries in the OECD received more money from foreign visitors than the UK (*Economist*, 1987, pp. 20–1, Lewis and Outram, 1986, pp. 202–3).

There are obviously 'economic' reasons for a number of these shifts, particularly for the fact that there are declining numbers of 'main' holidays taken by UK residents in Britain, that there is a gradual reduction in the number of people staying by the seaside, and that if people want to visit the seaside they are more likely to do so abroad than in the UK. However, in the rest of this article I shall try to show that there are changes occurring in the nature of contemporary tourism which also help to explain why 'going to the seaside' for a week or fortnight in Britain has become a less and less attractive proposition. After all, increasing numbers of holidays are taken in Britain (by British and foreign visitors) – but they are not taken at the typical seaside resort [. . .]

My claim here is that there is one kind of experience of visiting places separate from one's place of work/residence which is roughly describable as that of 'post-(mass) tourism', and that in part parallels wider changes in contemporary culture towards the postmodern or postmodernism [. . .]

This set of cultural changes has only come to be of fairly widespread significance because of the growth of relatively unanchored social groupings which provide much of the 'mass' audience for new postmodern cultural forms. In particular there are groupings which neither own nor individually manage capital, and which cannot because of distinctions of taste be simply regarded as part of the working class (see Bourdicu, 1984). A particularly central place in this complex of social forces is played by the 'service class'. This consists of that set of places within the social division of labour: (1) which do not principally involve the ownership of capital; (2) which are located within a set of interlocking social institutions that 'service' capital; (3) in which superior work and market situations are to be found particularly because of the existence of well-defined careers; and (4) in which entry is generally regulated by the differential possession of credentials which particularly serve to demarcate such a service class from more general white-collar workers (see Lash and Urry, 1987, Chapter 6).

Any class can be said to possess a habitus, a system of classifications which structure the orienting practices and activities of agents. And each class struggles to impose its own classificatory schemes favourable to its particular characteristics upon those of other groups and the whole of society. Moreover, classes and other groups possess differential amounts of economic and cultural capital to impose such a taxonomy favourable to their own characteristics.

My claim here is that the service class comprises a set of powerful yet relatively unanchored social groupings which has begun to impose its framework upon much of the wider society, and hence its distinctions of taste have become highly significant for other classes and social groups. I shall note three aspects of this process by which the tastes of the service class have begun to have such effects especially on the seaside resort.

First, there is the way in which 'culture' is prioritized as opposed to 'nature'. Bourdieu expresses this well:

> The nature against which culture is here constructed is nothing other than what is 'popular', 'low', 'vulgar', 'common'. This means that anyone who wants to 'succeed in life' must pay for his (*sic*) accession to everything which

> defines truly humane humans by a change of nature, a 'social promotion'
> experienced as an ontological promotion, a process of 'civilization'. . . , a
> leap from nature to culture, from the animal to the human; but having
> internalized the class struggle, which is at the very heart of culture, he is
> condemned to shame, horror, even hatred of the old Adam. (1984. p. 251)

With such an elevation of taste and its social distinctions the 'typical
working class holiday resort' would seem the very embodiment of a
particular construction of nature, 'vulgar' and 'basic', and the negation of
culture. As a powerful service class possessing considerable cultural capital
has developed, so it has proclaimed the tastelessness of the 'common',
'low', 'vulgar' holiday resort. Having 'good taste' would be demonstrated
by not visiting such places, although contemporary cultural practices might
involve using or appropriating elements in a postmodern pastiche (e.g.
McGill's postcards). The presumed features of such places have become
constructed as uncivilized, only to be played at and not taken seriously.
And this is because in part of the social class and age-group composition of
the visitors. For example, the North-West Tourist Board has been worried
by the fact that Blackpool mainly appeals to the 'middle-aged working
class' (1972). Such resorts are deemed to attract only those with such 'low'
or 'vulgar' tastes, and this causes major problems for such resorts. In
Morecambe, for example, a clear example of this has revolved around the
Miss Great Britain contest. A particular representation of women as
'cultureless' sex objects (women as 'nature') has increasingly come to be
seen as in 'bad taste' and not appropriate to a contemporary resort – that
is, one in which culture dominates nature.

However, at the same time, the culture/nature division also works *within*
culture. Bourdieu talks of the symbolic subversion by intellectuals (and the
rest of the service class) of the rituals of the bourgeois order through
'ostentatious poverty', through minimal luxury, 'functionalism', and an
'ascetic aestheticism' (1984, p. 287). Such a liking for the natural is reflected in a stunning diversity of cultural symbols and practices: health foods,
real ale, real bread, vegetarianism, 'traditional' non-Western science
and medicine, natural childbirth, wool and cotton rather than 'man-
made' fibres, antiques rather than 'man-made' reproductions, old houses
rather than modern houses, jogging, swimming, cycling, walking, dancing
and mountaineering rather than contrived, organized leisure, and so on.
Bourdieu talks of the liking that these groups have for 'natural, wild
nature' (1984, p. 220) and this is reflected in the wide diversity of
'middle-class' groups concerned with simultaneously using *and* protecting
the countryside. In the UK for example the membership of the National
Trust increased over ten-fold between 1951 and 1971, that of the Camping
Club eight-fold, while that of the Royal Society for the Protection of Birds
rose from about 6000 to nearly 90000 in 1971 and 400000 in 1985
(Robinson, 1976, p. 181; RSPB, 1985). Part of this trend has been an
increased tendency to visit the seaside, but much of this increase went not
to 'organized' resorts where a kind of culture dominates nature, but to

relatively 'unspoilt' (that is, more natural) parts of the coastline. Indeed what has happened has been that the coast has been reappropriated as part of nature, of the relatively unspoilt countryside, rather than the seaside being part of culture. The very features of the typical resort – entertainments, funfairs, bathing beauty contests, arcades, and so on – are a set of cultural practices which have become less highly valued because of the reassertion of the value of the natural, the unspoilt, the uncontrived.

Further, as part of the decentring of identity the service class and other white-collar groups possess less rigid (or grid-like) classificatory structures and can lead lives in the present, less constrained by the controls imposed by collective memories and expectations [. . .] At the same time postmodernism involves attempts to subvert the boundaries of 'group', of age, sex, race, class and place. Many people indeed delight in trying to transgress such boundaries, particularly in a spirit of playfulness, of casting on and taking off identities which have relatively little meaning to the individuals concerned. This is associated with the tendency for many such people to view themselves as 'marginal', as 'unclassifiable', 'anything rather than categorized, assigned to a class, a determinate place in social space' (Bourdieu, 1984, p. 370) [. . .]

This weakening of both grid and group has major significance for traditional centres for holiday-making which were highly focused around very strong classificatory structures and distinctions between groups. On the first, such resorts were based on a specific division of pleasure and pain Pleasure was associated with being away from the pain of work and of the conditions of life in industrial cities, and from exhausting and boring routines of domestic work and home life. Recent changes have in part dissolved such a strong classificatory structure. Pleasure may be experienced in a wide variety of locations, particularly as leisure-based activities have expanded often in or close to the potential holiday-makers' home location. And as I shall consider below, there has been a proliferation of sights which people now deem suitable for the tourist gaze, many of which are less 'cultural' and more 'natural'. In relationship to 'group' there has been a decline in the salience of working-class family-household units and a growth in a wide variety of 'tourist units' which are mostly not based on family-households (see Medlik, 1982, p. 79 on the segments of the tourist–leisure market likely to expand in the 1980s). The seaside holiday was very much based on a family-regulated holiday for people of roughly the same class and from similar areas. But as there has been a decentring of identity, many of those forms of group-identification within space and over time have been dissolved, and hence have reduced the attractiveness of those resorts which were designed to structure the 'formation' of pleasure in particular class-related patterns. The decline of such resorts indicates the relative weakness of the contemporary working class and of the powerful destructuring powers of the service and white-collar classes.

So far I have noted some recent cultural transformations which are at least consistent with certain features of postmodernism. I have also provided some examples of how these transformations are reflected within British seaside resorts. However, the connection between 'culture' and the 'coast' still remains relatively opaque without considering in rather more detail just what is involved in the formation of pleasure in the tourist industry.

Tourist attractions necessarily involve complex processes of production in order that regular, meaningful and profitable 'touristic experiences' can be generated and sustained. These cannot be left merely to chance, because the having of these experiences is essentially constructed and organized. They are not 'natural', although of course they often involve viewing nature. People learn to have such experiences, and they have to be provided with clear markers that this is indeed the kind of site where it is appropriate to have those experiences [. . .]

Potential tourist sights/sites have to offer pleasurable experiences which are out of the ordinary. People must experience, and in particular *anticipate* the experience of particularly intense pleasures, pleasures which are on a different scale, or involve different senses, from those customarily encountered. However, these sensations do not follow 'naturally'; they have to be produced by an array of tourist service providers. Nevertheless, quite often the production contains ambiguities, and these have to be read and experienced in at least a partly appropriate manner by the tourists concerned. Some of the most striking ambiguities involve the attempts to stage events or situations which are supposedly 'authentic' (see Boorstein, 1964, for an extensive critique of such contrived experiences; and see Murphy, 1985, Chapter 8).

Pleasures and their anticipation thus involve highly complex processes of production and consumption in which bodily sensations are worked on and worked at in contexts designed to demarcate the *extra*ordinary. Yet the very production of predictable and easily consumable sensations has become increasingly problematic because of some of the processes noted above. Mercer notes that popular pleasures 'require a wholehearted and unselfconscious involvement in a cultural event, form or text' (1983, p. 84). Yet the postmodern delight in play, distance, mobility, diversity and transgression, challenges 'unself-conscious involvement', and encourages distance, reflection, sophisticated 'coolness'. As a consequence pleasure begins to be constructed and experienced in really different ways than previously: first, people remain less satisfied and they keep demanding *new* out-of-the-ordinary experiences ('Eastender' holiday breaks organized by Islington Council being the latest of these!); second, as a consequence of the universal availability of the mass media in advanced Western societies there has been a massive upward shift in the level of what is 'ordinary' and hence what is 'extraordinary'; third, people expect more, and if unsatisfied will quickly switch to sources of alternative sensations; fourth, the process of production of pleasure can no longer be too contrived, planned or obviously artificial; and finally, and speculatively, it may be that to experience pleasures in a distanced manner is simply less satisfying and makes it almost impossible to *enjoy* 'simple' pleasures. It is fairly clear that all these changes will transform the once 'simple' popular pleasure of going to and staying at the seaside in Britain.

This last point can be illustrated by considering three quintessential sites for the formation of pleasure at the seaside; piers and towers, the pleasure park and the holiday camp. The first both involve an attempt to conquer nature, to construct a 'man-made' object which at all times and for ever is there dominating either the sea or the sky. Their domination is what gives them a reason for being there, that is their function. As Barthes says of the similar Eiffel Tower:

> the Tower must escape reason. The first condition for this victorious flight is that the Tower must be an utterly *useless* monument . . . as a matter of fact, the Tower is *nothing* . . . it participates in no rite, in no cult, not even in Art; you cannot visit the Tower as a museum; there is nothing to see *inside* the Tower. (1979, pp. 5, 7)

Yet twice as many people visit the Tower as the Louvre. And this is because it enables the visitor to participate in a dream. The Tower is no normal spectacle because it gives us a wholly original view of Paris [. . .] Towers and piers more generally permit us to see things in their structure, to link human organization with extraordinary natural phenomena, and to celebrate the participation within, and the victory of, human agency over nature. They are part of that irreducibly extraordinary character of the ideal tourist site [. . .]

Yet consider how things have changed in recent years. Piers have been falling into the sea and do not in any way demonstrate the domination *of* nature; rather the reverse. At the same time, much more spectacular and modern examples of the mastery of the sea can now be found, in bridges, tunnels, hovercraft, marinas and the like. Likewise towers connecting the land and the sky are now dwarfed by skyscrapers, hotels, space capsules and of course by aircraft, all of which are much more obviously 'modern' or even 'postmodern' (see Jencks, 1984, on the postmodern in architecture). The internationalization of the post-war tourist industry has placed all potential tourist sites on a scale of the extraordinary, and as a consequence seaside towers and piers now come very near the bottom of the hierarchy.

This is also the case for the pleasure park, where again a distinct hierarchy is established, although this is on more of a regional or at the most national than international basis. In the north-west of England Blackpool Pleasure Beach is the leading site for such a regime of pleasure. It has always attempted to look resolutely modern. 'Its architecture of pleasure has taken on a streamlined, functional appearance' (Bennett, 1983, p. 145). And it has been periodically updated. The designer of the Festival of Britain, Jack Radcliffe, gave it a new look in the 1950s. In the 1960s new rides were added, and these were mostly based on innovations pioneered in world fairs or were based on futuristic rides from American amusement parks (for example, the Starship Enterprise introduced in 1980). Central to the strategy of the management of the Pleasure Beach has been that of progress, of being first (at least in the UK), biggest and best. It even has its own tower, using latest technology, and which makes *the* Blackpool Tower seem rather quaint (Bennett, 1983, p. 147). The Park is still owned by a local company and it has not gone the way of much of Blackpool's entertainment facilities which have become part of London-based leisure companies, especially THF and EMI (Bennett, 1983, p. 146). It attracts 6.5 million visitors a year. Everywhere else will come off badly in competition with it. People staying in Morecambe often travel to Black-pool to partake of its pleasures, including particuarly the Pleasure Park. The only competition to Blackpool now comes from the new-style amuse-ment and theme parks, the most successful in the north of England being that at Alton Towers. Two points are worth noting here. First, these new parks are generally not located by the seaside, although they often do have a very attractive 'rural' location close to the motorway (rather than the rail) network. Second, the pleasure parks located at the existing resorts will struggle to compete. They *should* exhibit 'modernity', high technology, youth, controlled danger, anticipation and pleasure. But being located in 'old-fashioned' resorts there are considerable counter-messages, of pre-vious technologies, age, danger through neglect, and regret at not being elsewhere. In the case of Morecambe the main pleasure park has been turned into a theme park, although whether it will be able to compete with those better established and nearer major population centres is perhaps doubtful (it has been established by the owners who are the Blackpool Pleasure Beach Co. on the bizarre theme of the 'wildwest').

Third, holiday camps have been found in many resorts (see Ward and Hardy, 1986). They began with the literal camp (of tents) before the First World War. Their development was in part a reaction against the poor quality of accommodation and services in the typical boarding house. Especially with the 'luxury' camps established initially by Billy Butlin in Skegness in 1936, relatively luxurious facilities for the period were provided, with on-site amusement, good-quality food, high-class entertain-ments and modern sanitation, a 'veritable Beveridge of leisure' according to Ray Gosling (quoted in Ward and Hardy, 1986, p. 161). As Butlin himself said, he tried to create 'a holiday centre for the great mass of middle-income families for whom no one seemed to be catering' (quoted in Ward and Hardy, 1986, p. 60).

The heyday of such camps was in the immediate aftermath of the Second World War – this resulted from a number of factors, including the coming into effect of the 1938 Holidays with Pay Act, the high levels of employ-ment, and the reduced age of marriage and the very high rate of family formation. Three points about the 1950s are worth noting: the attempt to restrict the number of 'single' visitors and the centrality to camp life of 'family relationships'; the changing class composition of the camps as they – like their host resorts – became progressively 'working class'; and the shift towards self-catering – especially at Pontin's – and the attempt to construct this as increased 'freedom'. However, this attempted representation of camps as permitting freedom has not succeeded. Holiday camps which were once the very embodiment of 'modernity', of a futuristic 'make-believe', were undeniably rooted in what might be described as 'Fordist holiday-making'. With the shift to 'flexibilization' in tourism such camps seem to have had their day [. . .] Holiday camps look by contrast not to that sort of 'flexible' future but to a somewhat mass organized past, most appreciated now as televised nostalgia (as in *Hi-De-Hi*).

Apart from piers, towers, entertainment complexes and holiday camps, it was believed that resorts were in some sense extraordinary because the sea, the sand and sometimes the sun were to be found there; as well as an absence of the manufacturing industry which characterized much of the rest of the country. However, over the past decade or two the distinctiveness of such resorts has dramatically declined. This is for a number of reasons.

First, there has been the extraordinary valuation that has come to be placed upon the sun-tanned body. In the nineteenth century the development of seaside resorts was based upon the presumed health-giving properties of sea bathing. Sun bathing was relatively uncommon, particularly because of the valuation placed upon the pale skin. However, from the 1920s onwards within the upper class this valuation began to change, so that in the post-war period it has been the sun that is presumed to produce health. *The* ideal body is that which is tanned – and any resort which cannot guarantee tanning will seem distinctively unfashionable. (It is interesting to consider whether the current anxiety about malignant melanoma is about to induce a shift towards the belief that it is smart not to be tanned!)

Second, the resorts have not been able to maintain their distinctiveness as places where entertainment and pleasure is concentrated. This is for a number of reasons: first, television has at a stroke evened out entertainment across all places; second, most resorts are fairly small and so cannot support a high concentration of entertainment services; third, resorts are normally run by Conservative councils who are often unwilling to engage in public expenditure sufficient to provide suitable collective facilities [. . .] and fourth, almost all towns and cities have in the past decade or two begun to develop themselves as sites of consumption, both for their 'own' residents and for potential tourists.

Third, a further paradoxical reason why these resorts now appear as less extraordinary is that the absence of a previous manufacturing industry means that they lack interesting, well-preserved historical sites which can be sacralized, packaged and viewed. And the 'authentic' recreation of the workplaces and houses of the industrial workforce has recently become one of the most expanding areas of tourist development (see Halsall, 1987, on how tourism has become part of the education process). Almost by definition seaside resorts, because of the legacy of the particular built environment, lack such sites in which the 'real lives' of manufacturing/ mining workers can be nostalgically recreated. MacCannell points out the significance of these changes:

> Modern Man (*sic*) is losing his attachment to the work bench, the neighbour-
> hood, the town, the family, which he once called 'his own' but, at the same
> time, he is developing an interest in the 'real life' of others. (1976, p. 91)

In Britain this finds its clearest reflection in the way in which some of the
least prepossessing sites of industrialization have been transformed into
successful tourist sites. It is almost that the worse the 'industrial' experience, the more authentic the resulting attraction thus seems. Examples
include the development of Bradford as a touring centre for the Yorkshire
Dales and West Yorkshire; Wigan Pier; and Black Country World in
Dudley [. . .] A very recent and perhaps even more unexpected example is
the development of the Rhondda Valley as a major tourist attraction, with
a planned museum based in the Lewis Merthyr coalmine, a Rhondda
Heritage Park and a wildwest theme park (see Halsall, 1986). Such
developments have been much encouraged by the English Tourist Board's
Tourism Development Action Programmes (TDAPs) – two of the areas so
specified being Bradford and Tyne and Wear (see Davies, 1987)!

One important feature of such developments has been the enormously
widespread growth of what one might term a postmodern museum culture.
Central to this development has been a two-pronged attack on auratic art.
First, there has been a marked broadening of the objects which are deemed
worthy of being preserved, so much so that one museum opens every
fortnight in Britain (see White, 1987, p. 10). Museums are concerned with
're-presentations' of history, and what has happened has been a marked
increase in the range of historical experiences which are 'represented',
particularly of the mass of ordinary people whose culture did not generate
'great works of art' (see Horne, 1984) [. . .] Second, there has been a
change in the nature of museums themselves, in which considerably greater
emphasis is placed upon participation of the visitor in the exhibits
themselves. This is taken to the furthest extreme in those 'museums' in
which actors play various historical roles and interact with the visitors, and
where the latter may actually participate in simple historical sketches. This
challenges the typical way in which museums prioritize authenticity which,
as Horne maintains, 'provides a radiance of value and scarcity that hallows
the object in itself, so that often a museum provides . . . a collection of
isolated objects, sacred in themselves' (1984, p. 17).

As the publicity for Tyne and Wear's Museum states:

> In our museum, the emphasis is on action, participation and fun. Out are the
> endless old-fashioned glasss cases you pored over in hushed silence. In are
> professionally designed displays, working models to play with, complete
> period room settings to browse through and sound effects to complete the
> picture. (quoted in White, 1987, p. 10)

Aura has also been disrupted by the way that museums often now reveal
the very process by which the objects have been rendered authentic and
made appropriate to the tourist gaze.

Museums, though, cannot be created everywhere, and about anything. They only work because there are certain connections between the past and the present. There has to be something linking the two, and that is normally place; it can also be occupation, industry, famous person or event. The museums that work best are those which are located in places which are 'romantic' (Paris, Vienna) or which involve an individual or culture which is likewise deemed 'romantic' (the Lake District poets). This in some sense means that there is certain 'organic' connection between the place and person, that the former contributes to and endows the latter with peculiarly intense and meaningful emotions over and above the mundane bodily and mental sensations enjoyed by normal mortals. Seaside resorts are not constructed as in any sense 'romantic' (Lyme Regis being an interesting exception). This is partly because of the predominantly working-class nature of many such places. Workers on holiday are not presumed to be able to experience romanticism as opposed to mere romance. Also such places have often not attracted the historical characters, composers, writers, poets, inventors and the like, around whom romantic myths are formed, and which endow places connected with them with an aura of the sacred. It is interesting how there has recently been a 'romanticization' of some kinds of industrial work, and these therefore become fitting objects of sacralization within what has been termed the 'working non-working industry' (see White, 1987).

Two important changes are therefore occurring more generally in the organization of the contemporary town or city First, they have become much more centres of consumption rather than production, or as Harvey argues, they present an immense 'accumulation of spectacles' (1987, p. 35). Cities no longer simply communicate power, authority and corporate domination, but also play, consumption and spectacle. It has recently been suggested that the shopping mall in West Edmonton in Canada represents the ultimate in this postmodern nirvana (see Schields, 1986). The completed mall will be the temple of depthless consumerism, playfulness and hedonism. The mall is over a mile long with over 800 shops, a 2.5-acre indoor lake with four deep-sea mini-submarines, a reproduction Spanish galleon, dolphins, an 18-hole mini-golf course, 40 restaurants, a 10-acre water park, a nineteenth-century imitation Parisian boulevard (Haussmann will no doubt be turning in his grave), a New Orleans street with nightclubs, and a hotel offering a variety of theme rooms, such as Hollywood, Roman and Polynesian! To the extent to which very many towns and cities are developing similar centres of play, spectacle and consumption the 'old-fashioned' resort will have difficulty competing as a site for consumption.

Second, parallel with this has been the exceptional development of 'nostalgia'; so much so that one commentator has suggested that Britain will 'soon be appointing a Curator instead of a Prime Minister' (quoted in Lowenthal, 1985, p. 4). Nostalgia used both to be more specifically confined in time and place, and to be much more limited in its devaluation of the present. Woods argues that until the 1970s nostalgia trips were 'fairly surreptitious and ambivalent because we didn't want to relinquish our hold on the present, on whatever it meant to be modern. . . . Now that the present seems so full of woe . . . a general abdication, an actual desertion from the present' (1974, p. 346). One very clear reflection of this has been the rapid development of vernacular or neo-vernacular architecture (see Jencks, 1984, pp. 96–104). As Relph notes, the overriding characteristic of postmodern townscapes is that of quaintness (1987, pp. 253–4). Such 'quaintness' involves intricate sequences of enclosures, winding passages, little courtyards, canopies over sidewalks, easy transitions, a continuity of appearance between the inside and outside of buildings, few right angles and provision for pedestrians, street theatre and the like. Space is viewed as historically specific, rooted in conventions, particularistic, ambiguous and subordinate to context. All towns and cities have thus become potential objects of the tourist gaze sensitized to 'quaintification'. Seaside resorts thus suffer both from the ubiquitous emergence of potential competitors and from the fact that often they lack the interesting streets and buildings, particularly from the manufacturing past, around which a quaint nostalgic web can be plausibly spun. The growth, therefore, of a series of postmodern cultural developments has left many seaside resorts 'high and dry'!

References

BALLANTYRE, A. (1986) 'Dishing dirt in Dudley', *The Guardian*, 6 August, p. 18.

BARTHES, R. (1979) 'The Eiffel Tower', in *The Eiffel Tower and Other Mythologies*, New York, Hill and Wong.

BAUDRILLARD, J. (1981) *For a Critique of the Political Economy of the Sign*, St Louis, Telos Press.

BAUDRILLARD, J. (1985) 'The ecstacy of communication', in Foster, H. (ed.) *Postmodern Culture*, London, Pluto Press, pp. 126–34.

BELL, D. (1976) *The Cultural Contradictions of Capitalism*, London, Heinemann.

BENNETT, T. (1983) 'A thousand and one troubles, Blackpool Pleasure Beach', in *Formations of Pleasure*, London, Routledge and Kegan Paul, pp. 138–55.

BERMAN, M. (1983) *All That is Solid Melts into Air*, London, Verso.

BOORSTEIN, D. J. (1964) *The Image: A Guide to Pseudo-Events in America*, New York, Harper and Row.

BOURDIEU, P. (1984) *Distinction*, London, Routledge and Kegan Paul.

BURKART, A. J. and MEDLIK, S. (1974) *Tourism, Past, Present and Future*, London, Heinemann.

COHEN, E. (1979) 'A phenomenology of tourist experiences', *Sociology*, Vol. 3, pp. 179–210.

DAVIES, L. (1987) 'If you've got it, flaunt it', *Employment Gazette*, April, pp. 167–71.

DOUGLAS, M. (1973) *Natural Symbols: Explorations in Cosmology*, London, Barrie and Jenkins.

ECONOMIST (1987) 'Making history pay', 1 August, p. 21–2.

EDGAR, D. (1987) 'The new nostalgia', *Marxism Today*, March, p. 30–5.

FEATHERSTONE, M. (1987) 'Lifestyle and consumer culture', *Theory, Culture & Society*, Vol. 4, No. 1, pp. 55–70.

FEIFER, M. (1985) *Going Places*, London, Macmillan.

GRABURN, N. (1978) 'Tourism: the sacred journey', in Smith, V. L. (ed.) *Hosts and Guests*, Oxford, Blackwell, pp. 17–31.

HALSALL, M. (1986) 'Through the valley of the shadow', *The Guardian*, 27 December, p. 21.

HALSALL, M. (1987) 'Lessons loom', *The Guardian*, 6 August, p. 18.

HARVEY, D. (1987) 'Flexible accumulation through urbanization: reflections on "post-modernism" in the American city', Symposium on 'Developing the American City' at the Yale School of Architecture.

HORNE, D. (1984) *The Great Museum*, London, Pluto.

JAKLE, J. (1983) *The Tourist: Travel in Twentieth Century America*, Lincoln and London, University of Nebraska Press.

JAMESON, F. (1984) 'Postmodernism and consumer culture', in Foster, H. (ed.) *Postmodern Culture*, London, Pluto.

JENCKS, C. (1984) *The Language of Post-Modern Architecture*, New York, Academy.

KRIPPENDORF, J. (1986) 'The new tourist – turning point for leisure and travel, *Tourism Management*, Vol. 7, pp. 131–5.

LASCH, C. (1980) *The Culture of Narcissism*, London, Sphere.

LASH, S. and URRY, J. (1987) *The End of Organized Capitalism*, Cambridge, Polity Press.

LEWIS, B. and OUTRAM, M. (1986) 'Customer satisfaction with package holidays', in Moores, B. (ed.) *Are You Being Served?*, Oxford, Philip Allan, pp. 201–13.

LOWENTHAL, D. (1985) *The Past is a Foreign Country*, Cambridge, Cambridge University Press.

MacCANNELL, D. (1976) *The Tourist: A New Theory of the Leisure Class*, New York, Schocken Books.

MEDLIK, S. (1982) *Trends in Tourism: World Experience and England's Prospect*, London, English Tourist Board.

MERCER, C. (1983) 'A poverty of desire: pleasure and popular politics', in Bennett, T. (ed.) *Formations of Pleasure*, London, Routledge and Kegan Paul.

MEYROWITZ, J. (1985) *No Sense of Place: The Impact of Electronic Media on Social Behaviour*, New York, Oxford University Press.

MURPHY, P. E. (1985) *Tourism: A Community Approach*, London, Methuen.

NORTH-WEST TOURIST BOARD (1972) *Annual Report*, Last Drop Village, Bolton, Lancs, North West Tourist Board.

RELPH, E. (1987) *The Modern Urban Landscape*, London, Croom Helm.

ROBINSON, H. (1976) 'The decline of Saint Monday, 1766–1876', *Past and Present*, Vol. 71, pp. 76–101.

ROYAL SOCIETY FOR THE PROTECTION OF BIRDS (RSPB) (1985) *Facts About the RSPB*, Sandy, Beds., RSPB.

SCHIELDS, R. (1986) 'Global spatialization and the built environment: the case of

SMITH, V. L. (ed.) (1978) *Hosts and Guests*, Oxford, Blackwell.

THOMPSON, G. (1983) 'Carnival and the calculable: consumption and the play at Blackpool', in Bennett, T. (ed.) *Formations of Pleasure*, London, Routledge and Kegan Paul, pp. 124–36.

URRY, J. (1987) 'Some social and spatial aspects of services', *Society and Space*, Vol. 5, pp. 5–26.

WARD, M. and HARDY, D. (1986) *Goodnight Campers: The History of the British Holiday Camp*, London and New York, Mansell.

WHITE, D. (1987) 'The born-again museum', *New Society*, 1 May, pp. 10–14.

WICKERS, D. (1987) 'Splashing Out', *The Guardian*, 20 June, p. 8.

WOODS, M. (1974) 'Nostalgia or never: you can't go home again', *New Jersey*, 7 November, pp. 343–6.

16 Brideshead re-revisited

R. Hewison

In 1976 the mournful notes of a plangent, romantic theme tune introduced television audiences to the whispered messages of national loss and decay that echo through Evelyn Waugh's threnody on the decline and fall of the great house of Brideshead [. . .]

It was not entirely accidental that *Brideshead Revisited* should be adopted for television in the mid-1970s, or that its episodes should be in production in 1974 and 1975. The Bridesheads of England were again under threat, just as they had been in 1944 when Evelyn Waugh completed the novel. The menace of 1944 was not foreign invasion and violent destruction, for there was no longer any danger that the war would be lost, but [. . .] there loomed what Waugh called 'the age of Hooper', a bleak featureless future governed by, and in the interests of, the all too common man.[1] Waugh looked gloomily towards a post-war world of mediocrity under a socialist government, whose policies meant that country houses and the values they represented would be swept away. But the country house has proved a more resilient element in British life than was feared in 1944 – and 1974.

Evelyn Waugh's novel demonstrates the peculiarly strong hold such places have on the British – though for once it seems more appropriate to say English – imagination. Because there has been no foreign invasion, civil war or revolution since the seventeenth century these houses both great and small represent a physical continuity which embodies the same adaptability to change within a respect for precedent and tradition that has shaped the common law. With a garden, a park and a greater or lesser estate, they enshrine the rural values that persist in a population that has been predominantly urban for more than a century. Some are works of art in themselves, but continuity, accumulation, even occasional periods of neglect, have meant that the furnishings and pictures of even minor houses have considerable historic and market value. As the great celebration of the country house at the National Gallery of Art in Washington in 1985–86 sought to demonstrate, 'they have become, as it were, vessels of civilization.'[2] [. . .]

The country house is the most familiar symbol of our national heritage, a symbol which, for the most part, has remained in private hands. That it has done so is a remarkable achievement in the face of the egalitarian twentieth century. It may well be that the century is less egalitarian than it might have been, not because the buildings and their contents have survived, but because of the values they enshrine. They are not museums – that is the whole basis on which they are promoted – but living organisms. As such they do not merely preserve certain values of the past: hierarchy, a sturdy individualism on the part of their owners, privilege tempered by social duty, a deference and respect for social order on the part of those who service and support them. They reinforce these values in the present [. . .] By a mystical process of identification the country house becomes the nation, and love of one's country makes obligatory a love of the country house. We have been re-admitted to paradise lost.

Re-admitted, that is, on visiting day. The country house is as much emblem as bricks and mortar, it has no formal architectural definition; consequently it is not possible to say how many country houses there are. The ideal house retains its contents, its parkland, at least the home estate – and its owners. The Historic Houses Association calculates that there are approximately 3500 that retain their contents and supporting land, of which approximately 2000 are in private hands and sustain a long-term family connection.

The uncertainty about the precise number of country houses reflects their privacy, and the fact that such houses, like their families, have come and gone ever since the Saxon settlements. If it is true that the country house is in decline, then it has been in decline for almost a century. It is certain that at least 1116 country houses were demolished between 1875 and 1975 [. . .] 1875 saw the beginnings of a long agricultural depression that lasted almost till the end of the century, and reduced the value of the great houses' supporting estates. In 1894 death duties were introduced, and although these were, to begin with, relatively light, the deaths of many heirs to estates as young officers in the First World War led to sometimes double and treble death duties being paid.

Between 1918 and 1945, 485 houses were demolished. The 1930s were years of economic depression, and with urbanization the sources of agricultural and domestic labour began to dry up. On the outbreak of war in 1939 the government requisitioned virtually every country house for official purposes: for the storage of art works, as secret training establishments, laboratories, hospitals, or simply barracks. The Brideshead that Waugh's narrator revisits at the beginning of the novel, its park a shanty town of Nissen huts, the great fountain empty save for cigarette butts and barbed wire, the furniture in store and the rooms boarded up, faced a future that looked bleak indeed.

That the country house *has* survived is largely due to a private body, the National Trust. It is a private charity, governed by an executive committee appointed by a fifty-person council, of whom half are nominees from other amenity bodies. The Trust depends on donations, admission charges and the subscriptions of its members, and income from its farms and investments. Following a recruitment drive in recent years the membership stands at 1.4 million. In return for a basic subscription of £14.40 they gain free admission to National Trust properties, and have the right to vote for those Council members who are not appointed by related organizations, though most members are content to use their membership simply to visit Trust properties.

The National Trust is the largest private landowner in the United Kingdom, with (in December 1986) 540 000 acres, 470 miles of coastline, and 292 properties open to the public, 87 of them large houses. It owns 1181 farms and some 15 000 agricultural buildings. The National Trust for Scotland owns 100 000 acres with 111 properties open to the public, including 19 castles and historic houses.

In spite of its status as a voluntary organization, however, the Trust has long enjoyed a 'national' position, confirmed by a succession of National Trust Acts. This private body has a highly public funtion. While not directly funded by the government it has a special relationship with the Treasury, both as a repository for properties and objects that are given 'to the nation' in lieu of tax, and because it provides a form of tax haven for private estates which avoid tax by passing to the Trust. It is run by public figures, including members of Parliament and of the House of Lords, and has access to the government through that complex network of interlocking relationships and connections that make up the self-selected aristocracy of the Great and the Good. The formal links through its constitution with other amenity bodies are doubled by personal cross-memberships and common backgrounds in the field of public service [. . .]

The National Trust has been described by one of its former chairmen, Lord Antrim, as 'a self-perpetuating oligarchy';[3] in spite of its large membership it has long been the fiefdom of 'the amenity earls', or those who would like to live like them. In his contribution to *The Treasure Houses of Britain* Mark Girouard has described the attitude of generations of country house owners: 'An independent, property-owning landed class was seen as the right and natural ruling class, but their power and privileges were recognised as bringing corresponding duties.'[4] Such is the attitude inherited by the governors of the National Trust. The Trust has the special status afforded to organizations that have been established for a long time. Yet it is not generally realized, that as it approaches its centenary, the National Trust is a quite different organization to that which its founders intended.

The National Trust has its origins in the Commons, Open Spaces and Footpaths Preservation Society, founded in 1865, and its primary purpose was not the protection of buildings or private property, but public access to the countryside. As is now recognized, landowners regard their property as an asset to be exploited to the owner's best advantage; with rare exceptions, any sense of a responsibility to the general community who enjoy the landscape as a source of aesthetic refreshment is secondary. The conflict is clear in the battles to preserve access to common land against enclosures for farming which the Commons Preservation Society was formed to fight [. . .]

To the founders of the Trust, the landscape, especially that which expressed the spiritually regenerative forces of nature, rather than the civilizing activities of man, was the primary value in danger. But memory, too, had a capacity for moral change, by acting as a reminder of former greatness, and the landscape could not be seen without its human associations. Accordingly, when the Trust was formally registered with the Board of Trade in January 1895 as a body intending to hold land in perpetuity, it was as 'The National Trust for Places of Historic Interest or Natural Beauty'.

The Trust's first acquisition was a stretch of headland above the resort of Barmouth in Wales, the small seed from which the Trust's continuing campaign to preserve the coastline through Enterprise Neptune has grown. It acquired its first house in 1896, the Clergy House at Alfriston, but this late fourteenth-century structure of timber, plaster and thatch expresses the medievalizing tastes of the first members. The purchase price was ten pounds. Other small buildings followed. The only acquisition that would qualify as a country house was the early sixteenth-century Barrington Court in 1907. In that year the Trust's inevitable responsibility for buildings as well as land was officially recognized [. . .] by the first National Trust Act, which empowered it to promote 'the permanent preservation for the benefit of the nation lands and tenements (including buildings) of beauty or historic interest'. The Act introduced the concept that the Trust's property was 'inalienable', that is to say it could never be disposed of or taken away from the Trust, even by compulsory purchase, except by express will of Parliament. Many of the early properties acquired were small, but there were important protective acquisitions in the Lake District, and by 1914 the Trust controlled 5500 acres.

While the early members of the National Trust, 725 in 1914, cannot be said to have been promoters of the cult of the country house, they were sympathetic to the cult of the countryside which expressed itself in the Arts and Crafts movement, and the idealization of rural values felt by an increasingly urbanized population. This vicarious enjoyment of the countryside was cunningly exploited by the magazine publisher Edward Hudson, who bought a not very successful paper *Racing Illustrated*, and relaunched it in 1897 as *Country Life*. The magazine was a skilful mixture of traditional aristocratic values with the open air principles of the reformed public schools. It combined farming, field sports and golf with articles on society figures, fashion and interior decoration. Alongside articles on the new recreation of motoring came discussions of dying rural crafts.

Since the country house is central to this gentry's eye view of rural existence, *Country Life* naturally featured country houses in its pages, and the magazine became the obvious place for estate agents to advertise such properties, which were coming more frequently onto the market as a result of the agricultural depression and the effect of death duties [. . .] The magazine continues to play a central role in the promotion and protection of the country house [. . .]

In the 1920s, as the original founders of the National Trust began to die off, the focus of policy started to shift. Short of funds, it was no longer eager to accept any parcel of land however small, while the impact of death duties on the great estates became a cause of alarm [. . .] In 1931, however, the Treasury conceded an important change in the tax laws as an incentive to landowners to give property to the Trust. The 1931 Finance Act allowed land or buildings given to the Trust to escape death duties; owners or their heirs could reduce their tax liabilities by judicious gifts to the Trust, and thus keep the rest of the estate intact, while the Trust stood to gain considerable land and buildings. In 1937 the exemption was extended to cases where the donor retained a life interest in the property.

The National Trust began to adapt to the new circumstances. In 1932 it acquired a new chairman, the Marquess of Zetland [. . .] who had had no previous experience of the Trust, but who had the aristocratic connections that would give the Trust access to the owners of great estates who might see the advantages of passing land to the Trust. The emphasis was still on land, but [. . .] in 1934 the Marquess of Lothian proposed that the Trust should adopt a positive policy for the acquisition of country houses, and press for the creation of a fiscal scheme that would ensure their survival [and] in 1937 a fresh National Trust Act confirmed the Trust's new role as the protector of the country house [. . .] As a result of the 1937 Act the Trust was able formally to launch its Country House Scheme.

The essence of the scheme was that wherever possible the Trust arranged for the owners to continue living in the house, either as tenants on a long lease, or under the terms of what is known as a 'memorandum of wishes', which is not legally enforceable, but gives the owner long-term security for himself and his heirs. Thus, in exchange for often quite limited rights of access to the public, the owner was able to continue his life very much as before, without the financial burden of maintaining the house in which he lived.

This extension of the power and influence of the National Trust coincided with a shift in the tastes of those influential within it. Before the early 1930s most of the buildings it had shown interest in were medieval or Tudor and Jacobean. The only country house it acquired in the 1930s, Montacute in Somerset in 1931, dates from the late sixteenth century. But, partially because of the threat to later country houses resulting from the depression, and redevelopment in London [. . .] the architecture of the eighteenth century began to acquire a new value in the experts' eyes. The Society for the Protection of Ancient Buildings could hold no brief for neo-classical architecture: accordingly, the Georgian Group came into being in 1937 [. . .]

By 1939, the Trust's holdings had increased to 410 properties and 58 900 acres. In 1940, on the death of Lord Lothian, the original proponent of the scheme, the Trust acquired Blickling in Norfolk, its first property under the Country House Scheme. The need to preserve and record what was now perceived as an expression of the civilized values for which the country was fighting had become urgent.

Throughout the war the National Trust steadily acquired important properties [. . .] The scheme's secretary, James Lees-Milne toured the country, inspecting potential properties and talking to their owners [. . .] By the end of the war the Trust had acquired Wallington, Cliveden, Great Chatfield, Polesden Lacy, Speke Hall, West Wycombe and Lacock Abbey among other properties, so that in 1945 it controlled 112 000 acres and was responsible for nearly a hundred historic buildings [. . .]

In 1945, Britain seemed on the verge of a social revolution. The new Labour government was busy nationalizing the mines and the railways, increasing taxes, rationing luxuries and substituting a bureaucratic order and equality for the old system of social privilege and respect. Country house owners and their allies viewed this new world with suspicion, none more so than James Lees-Milne, as he surveyed the contents of Brock-hampton House, which had passed to the Trust on the death of its last owner in 1946:

> This evening the whole tragedy of England impressed itself upon me. This small, not very important seat in the heart of our secluded country, is now deprived of its last squire. A whole social system has broken down. What will replace it beyond government by the masses, uncultivated, rancorous, savage, philistine, the enemies of all things beautiful? How I detest democracy. More and more I believe in benevolent autocracy.[5]

The new régime however did not prove to be entirely philistine. The 1947 Town and Country Planning Act, for all its faults (which favoured landowners), remains the foundation for our present system of land use. It introduced the concept of green belts, and sought to improve on the principle, first introduced in the Town and Country Planning Act of 1944, that specific buildings, graded according to architectural merit, should be listed, and therefore protected from demolition or alteration without local authority – or, on appeal, government – consent. Local authorities were empowered to issue building preservation orders for the first time.

The Labour government was also sympathetic to the plight of the country house: in 1946 the Chancellor of the Exchequer, Hugh Dalton, decided to use powers that had lain virtually dormant since they were first created in 1910, to accept property in lieu of tax in such a way as to be able to hand the houses or land on to the National Trust or other suitable bodies [. . .]

While ready to accept houses [. . .] the National Trust was anxious that its independence would not be compromised by too close cooperation with the government [. . .]

The rapid expansion of the Trust's holdings during and immediately after the war presented the Trust with a severe problem: it held a rich store of land and buildings, but it was short of the revenue to restore or maintain them. During the 1930s its lands had enjoyed a benevolent neglect – thus creating an almost accidental group of nature reserves – but from 1945 there was an urgent need to generate income from its agricultural land and modernize the farms let to tenants [. . .]

At the best of times the Trust could only cope with a limited number of rescue operations, and it became increasingly wary of accepting houses without an endowment of land or investments that could ensure their upkeep. In the late 1940s, as demolitions continued, the country house seemed more endangered than ever. Many needed major repairs following their wartime occupation; owners who had moved out in 1939 had neither the means nor the inclination to move back in again [. . .] Country houses were being taken over by schools, nursing homes, and even prisons. The Labour government recognized that there was a growing problem, and in 1948 appointed a committee under Sir Ernest Gowers to investigate.

The Gowers Report on *Houses of Outstanding Historic or Architectural Interest* (1950) concluded that 'owing to the economic and social changes we are faced with a disaster comparable only to that which the country suffered by the Dissolution of the Monasteries in the sixteenth century'.[6] The report strongly favoured private ownership, and recommended a number of tax changes that would improve their chances of survival. In the event, only one of the Gowers recommendations passed into law, although it was to be of substantial benefit to the Trust. In 1953 the Historic Buildings and Monuments Act established quasi-independent Historic Buildings Councils for England, Scotland and Wales with government funds to assist in the repair of historic buildings. Private owners qualified if they could prove financial need, and they were expected to reciprocate by granting a measure of public access to their properties. The National Trust quickly became a major recipient of Historic Buildings Council funds [. . .]

The position of the country house began to improve. Demolitions reached their peak in 1955, when seventy-six were lost, but after that declined rapidly. The steady rise in the value of agricultural land and of investments in the stock market over the next decade meant that fewer owners felt their homes to be an insupportable burden. In 1955 the present Duke and Duchess of Devonshire decided that they would move back into the great house at Chatsworth.

Some owners enterprisingly recognized that it was possible to secure their future by satisfying the public's increasing curiosity about the great houses, and (continuing a tradition that goes back to the eighteenth century) open them to the public and charge admission. The pioneer was the Marquess of Bath, who opened Longleat in 1949, followed by Lord Montagu of Beaulieu in 1952 and the Duke of Bedford at Woburn Abbey in 1955. It was quickly recognized that it was not enough simply to open the doors: there had to be an attraction, so the lions were installed at Longleat, the motor cars at Beaulieu, and nudist camps and jazz festivals held at Woburn. The age of marketing the heritage had begun: the secret of such houses was that they were marketed as stately *homes*.

The country house was not only financially, but culturally more secure. During the period of post-war austerity the nostalgic note struck by *Brideshead Revisited* in 1945 had become a popular refrain. Plays and novels set in country houses were a staple source of entertainment, and with the increase in car ownership, visiting National Trust and other properties became a popular recreation [. . .]

Society had re-oriented itself in relation to the values that the country house represented: nostalgia for the past ensured the continuation of the country house into the present. The National Trust played an important role, not only in taking a significant number of houses into its care, but by changing the perception of country house ownership from one of privileged possession (though that of course had its own snobbish appeal) to one of responsible guardianship [. . .] The rescue of so many Bridesheads placed a considerable strain on the finances of the Trust, and there were those who questioned not only the wisdom, but the morality of the Country House Scheme [. . .] In response to criticisms that it was neglecting its original purposes, in 1963 the Trust decided to launch Enterprise Neptune, a special appeal to enable it to take into care as much of the unspoiled coastline as possible [. . .]

The consequences of the Country House Scheme have now come into conflict with the more recent growth of an environmental lobby, which argues that the financial needs of the Trust's houses have caused it to neglect its primary responsibility to the landscape [. . .] In 1985 the British Association of Nature Conservationists attempted an assessment of the Trust's performance.

The authors of the report acknowledged that some Trust properties do receive good nature conservation management, but other areas of con-servation interest had 'while in the possession of the National Trust, been destroyed or seriously degraded'. They challenge the National Trust's priorities:

> Although conservation is now accepted as desirable, the land is still seen primarily as a source of income. Wherever possible the estate makes money for the maintenance of the organisation and the built properties. Within the Trust there is an appreciation of fine houses and their content: there is even an acceptance of the need to conserve the urban commonplace. In contrast, there is no apparent level of appreciation and zest for conservation in the rural estate. This attitude reflects the composition of the leadership of the Trust.

Their conclusion is that 'in many respects the Trust has failed in its function to resist the destruction of the rural beauties its founders were so passionately concerned about'.[7]

The chairman of the National Trust, Dame Jennifer Jenkins, has dismissed the conservationists' report as 'a wholly unacceptable and unproven attack on the Trust'.[8] The Trust continues to hold a secure position as the repository and expression of cultural values that are distinctly British: a respect for privacy and private ownership, and a disinclination to question the privileges of class. In the shadow of the Trust, private owners have been able to claim to be doing no more than carrying on the Trust's work at their own expense.

The cult of the country house has ensured their survival – even when in 1974 the call to arms sounded again [. . .]

From 1972 onwards alarming rumours began to circulate that the Labour

Party – out of office since 1970 – intended to introduce a tax on capital and assets that would forcibly carry out the redistribution of wealth that, in spite of a top rate of income tax of ninety-eight per cent had failed to occur since 1945. In March 1974 Labour was returned to power, and in August published a green paper outlining proposals both for a wealth tax on current capital, and a capital transfer tax to replace death duty.

The wealth tax would be an annual tax on assets, including houses worth £100000 or more, and would take in securities, life assurance, copyrights, patents and all but minor works of art. (House prices have risen so much since then that it is important to remember that the government originally calculated that the tax would be paid by only one per cent of the population.) The government was well aware that for those people whose wealth largely consisted of works of art, collections of books or other objects of cultural significance the only way to pay the tax would be by selling off part of the collection, and accordingly it was prepared to consider exemption in the same way that exemptions already existed from death duty. The green paper also acknowledged that historic houses faced a similar difficulty [. . .]

This assurance was hardly sufficient for those who might have to pay such a tax. The threat to the heritage from a wealth tax was used to justify resistance to the tax altogether. Even before the green paper was published opposition to the idea had found a focus in the formation of a campaign committee, Heritage in Danger [. . .] Opposition to the tax proved almost universal, and a Parliamentary Select Committee appointed to consider the scheme heard a stream of witnesses [. . .] The National Trust spoke up for the private owner. It told the committee 'The National Trust's anxieties arise from the fear that private owners, in whose ownership the bulk of the national heritage at present lies, may be forced by the new taxes and inflation to dispose of their property and that as a result the national heritage will be greatly reduced or dispersed'.[9]

Shortly before the Select Committee reported in December 1975 a petition against the tax, bearing a million signatures gathered in at country houses during the summer, was presented to Parliament. The only voices in favour of the tax came from a small group of left-wing art critics, and the Labour government's Minister for the Arts, Hugh Jenkins.

It is impossible not to conclude that the campaign against the wealth tax was a powerful stimulus to the spread of the word 'heritage'. 1975 was indeed to be European Architectural Heritage Year, but Heritage in Danger proved a powerful rallying cry for the wealth tax lobby, and a number of projects associated with Architectural Heritage Year were recruited to the campaign.

One such was a report by the architectural writer John Cornforth commissioned in 1972 by the Historic Houses Committee of the British Tourist Authority, a committee of country house owners which became the foundation of the Historic Houses Association in 1973. When Cornforth's report was published with the help of *Country Life* in the Autumn of 1974 the wealth tax debate was at its height, and it was appropriately titled *Country Houses in Britain – Can They Survive?* Cornforth's answer was that they could, provided that they were allowed to live in a favourable tax climate.

Publication of Cornforth's report coincided with an exhibition at the Victoria and Albert Museum which his research had helped to inspire. Although the Minister for the Arts, Hugh Jenkins, was able to force Sir Roy Strong – technically a civil servant – to resign from Heritage in Danger, there was nothing he could do to stop the V&A's director from mounting an exhibition that spoke powerfully for the country house lobby. *The Destruction of the Country House: 1875–1975* gave the impression that the private country house was about to disappear altogether. The exhibition began with an evocative roll call of the one thousand and more that had gone in the past century, including 250 since the war, and Sir Roy Strong's catalogue essay painted a bitter picture of the rising costs of insurance, Value Added Tax, security and staffing [. . .] He wrote 'the historic houses of this country belong to everybody, or at least everybody who cares about this country and its traditions'.[10]

The same message was hammered home in Patrick Cormack's *Heritage in Danger*, first published in 1976, and reissued [. . .] in 1978, after it had formed the basis for a television series. 'It is a sobering thought that more houses are now under siege than at any time since the Civil War, though the weapons menacing them are fiscal rather than military, and those directing them are Government forces,'[11] [. . .]

But, by 1976, the wealth tax was a dead letter [. . .] it was clear that the heritage campaign had succeeded. Hugh Jenkins lost his post as Minister for the Arts a few months later. If anything the position of country house owners was improved by the Capital Transfer Tax Act of 1975 which gave exemptions to houses where owners permitted them to open to the public for a minimum of sixty days, and exempted agricultural land which the owner farmed himself. It also permitted the setting up of private charitable trusts as a complete haven for houses and supporting land. The wealth tax drew its last gasp in the run up to the 1979 general election: Heritage in Danger warned that £200 million worth of art and books would go on the market if the tax were introduced. When the Chancellor Denis Healey replied that it was no longer considered practical to apply the tax to works of art, but that no decision had been taken on historic houses, the chairman of the Historic Houses Association, George Howard, owner of the television Brideshead, Castle Howard, warned that Labour's election manifesto meant that there would be no more privately owned historic houses. The wealth tax disappeared with the defeat of the Labour government.

Although Brideshead, once more at the centre of the national conscious-ness thanks to television, was safe from the menace of the wealth tax, nowhere in the United Kingdom was it possible to escape the effects of the economic crisis of the mid-1970s. The Department of the Environment, which had first encouraged local authorities to participate in Architectural Heritage Year in 1975, found itself imposing cuts in a desperate attempt to save money. The following year a hard pressed government found itself with a heritage issue of embarrassing proportions.

Though a short-term defeat, the battle of Mentmore Towers led to a significant victory for the heritage lobby. In 1974 the Seventh Earl of Rosebery was faced with a considerable tax bill on the death of his father. In order to retain the family estate at Dalmeny intact he offered another property, Mentmore, built and furnished in high Victorian style by Baron Mayer de Rothschild, in lieu of death duties. The valuation first put on the house and its contents for tax purposes was two million pounds [. . .] [But] the government could only offer Lord Rosebery a million pounds. The haggling went on into 1976, by which time the tax bill had risen to three million. Finally Lord Rosebery lost patience, and in May 1977 Sothebys' held a sale at Mentmore. Before the sale the government agreed to accept four pieces of furniture in lieu of £1 million in tax, but the sale of the contents of Mentmore alone raised £6 million. The house itself changed hands for an undisclosed sum, and is now a centre for transcendental meditation. [. . .]

As a result of the Mentmore *débâcle* a Select Committee of the House of Commons was established to enquire into the whole functioning of the Land Fund. It reported in March 1978 [. . .] but the general election in May meant that it was a Conservative government which finally introduced a National Heritage Bill in the Autumn [. . .] The heritage achieved a new legislative status, protected by a quango, the National Heritage Memorial Fund, empowered to make grants or loans to preserve not just buildings, but any land or object which, in the opinion of the trustees, is of outstanding scenic, historic, aesthetic or scientific interest [. . .]

In the 1980s country houses have become more than ever symbols of continuity and security, as *The National Trust Book of the English House* (1985) reminds us: 'They look back to periods of apparent stability and order that, to some people, seem preferable to the chaos of the present.[12] The National Trust's role as the guardian of this order has been acknowledged by its present director-general, Angus Stirling, who wrote in his 1985 report 'The concept of benefit deriving from the Trust's care of much of the country's finest landscape and buildings has special significance at this time, when the nation is so troubled by the effect of unemployment, the deprivation of inner cities and the rapidity of change in society.'[13] [. . .]

Throughout the post-war period the country house has retained a central position as one of the definitive emblems of the British cultural tradition – principally through appeals to its 'national' significance in the face of economic threat. The National Trust's commitment to the continued occupation of houses for whom it accepts responsibility by the families that formerly owned them has preserved a set of social values as well as dining chairs and family portraits. Some sixty National Trust properties retain accommodation of some kind for the family of their original donors. That these houses are therefore not perceived as museums is presented as a great virtue. The Trust's policy is to show objects 'in their natural setting and in the ambience of the past'.[14] But the 'ambience of the past' raises questions of definition and interpretation: a museum has as its objective not just the preservation of evidences of the past but the interpretation of that evidence to the present, yet this is precisely what the National Trust approach refuses to do.

Even when the facts of history mean that a house cannot be lived in because the line has died out, it is still presented, in the view of the Trust's chief expert on interior decoration in the 1950s and '60s, so that it 'should look like one where the family had just gone out for the afternoon'.[15] This suggests that history is treated, not as a process of development and change, but something achieved on arrival at the present day. However scholarly the presentation of each item, there is an implicit decision to present the house and its history in the best possible light [. . .]

It is the Trust's present policy to concentrate more on the acquisition of open countryside and coastline – Enterprise Neptune was relaunched in 1985 – and in the case of country houses act 'only as a safety net when other solutions have been explored'.[16] The focus is now on the smaller, vernacular buildings on its estates, but this has not meant that it has ceased to acquire major new responsibilities: Calke Abbey in 1984, Nostell Priory and Kedleston Hall in 1986. Now that the public's taste has shifted towards a nostalgia for the everyday, the Trust is opening the kitchens as well as the state rooms. Calke Abbey is a case in point. The house, acquired with the help of £5 million from the National Heritage Memorial Fund, is not architecturally especially distinguished, but it had not been touched for years, and its rooms were stuffed with the relics of pre-war life. Calke Abbey is to be treated 'as a document of social history, complete with its kitchens and laundries, stables and riding school, joiner's and blacksmith's shops, church and park – a quintessence of all that is magical about English country house life'.[17] A life not just preserved, but revived.

Part of the magic of the country house is that the privilege of private ownership has become a question of national prestige. Those who have held on to their houses, and the majority of all country houses remain in private hands, have had to concede a greater degree of public access in exchange for tax exemptions and repair grants, others have turned their historic houses into commercial enterprises, but the hierarchy of cultural values that created the country houses remains the same. Private owner-ship has been elided into a vague conception of public trusteeship. The Earl of March, prominent during the wealth tax campaign, has said of his successful enterprise at Goodwood House in Sussex: 'I never feel that I am the owner – only a steward for my lifetime, and not principally for the benefit of the family but for the whole community.'[18] [. . .] Financially, politically and culturally country houses and their owners appear to be more secure than we have been led to suppose.

Notes

1   Evelyn Waugh, *Brideshead Revisited* (first published, 1945, revised 1960), Penguin, 1962, p. 7; p. 331.
2   *The Treasure Houses of Britain: 500 Years of Private Patronage and Art Collecting*, ed. G. Jackson-Stops, Yale University Press, 1985, p. 11.
3   Quoted in Montagu of Beaulieu, *The Gilt and the Gingerbread: or How to Live in a Stately Home and Make Money*, Michael Joseph, 1967, p. 89.
4   *Treasure Houses*, op. cit., p. 27.
5   James Lees-Milne, *Caves of Ice* (first published 1983), Faber, 1984, p. 172.
6   Quoted in *Britain's Historic Buildings*, op. cit., p. 10.
7   Clive Chatters and Rick Minter, 'Nature Conservation and the National Trust', *Ecos: A Review of Conservatism*, Vol. 7, No. 4 (Autumn, 1986), pp. 25–32.
8   Anne Spackman, 'National Trust accused of nature neglect', *Independent*, 6 December, 1986.
9   Memorandum of the National Trust to the Select Committee on a Wealth Tax, House of Commons 696, Vol. II, 384, HMSO, November, 1975.
10   Roy Strong, *The Destruction of the Country House 1875–1975*, Thames and Hudson, 1974, p. 7–10.
11   *Heritage in Danger*, New English Library, 1976, p. 35.
12   Arthur Jones, *Britain's Heritage: The Creation of the National Heritage Memorial Fund*, Weidenfeld, 1985, p. 120.
13   National Trust, *Annual Report*, 1985, p. 4.
14   Robin Fedden, *The Continuing Purpose: A History of the National Trust, Its Aims and Work*, Longman, 1968, p. 129.
15   John Cornforth 'John Fowler', *National Trust Studies 1979*, ed. G. Jackson-Stops, Sotheby Parke Bernet, 1978, p. 40.
16   National Trust, *Annual Report*, 1986, p. 4.
17   *Treasure Houses*, op. cit., p. 76.
18   Quoted in *Heritage in Danger*, 1976, op. cit., p. 39.

17 The ghosting of the inner city

P. Wright

'Anyone seeking refuge in a genuine, but purchased, period-style house, embalms himself alive.'

Theodore Adorno (*Minima Moralia*)

George Orwell located the imaginary prole quarter [of his novel *Nineteen Eighty-Four*] somewhere vaguely to the 'north and east' of a no longer existing Saint Pancras Station. While there is certainly no point in searching out any literal reality which may be conceived to lie 'behind' the prole quarter, there are certainly things to be said about the sense of history and tradition as it actually exists in the inner-city areas of the 1980s. There is a place some miles to the 'north and east' of a still existing Saint Pancras Station called Stoke Newington. In this area (which has the convenience of being where I live) the terraced houses have a yard or two of space between their doors and the street. A few years ago one could probably have distanced Stoke Newington still further from the prole quarter by saying quite unequivocally that the streets are of tarmac rather than cobblestones. In Thatcher's years, however, these incurably Labour voting inner-city areas have been deliberately deprived of what to start with were less than adequate public funds. The pavements seem more cracked and broken than in the recent past and the area's elderly people are falling down more often than they should be. Similarly, an increasing number of houses – even in the face of an intense housing shortage – are boarded up empty awaiting repairs which are currently beyond the means of the financially strapped local authority. As for the roads, they also lack repair; tarmac is being worn away and in many places the underlying cobbles have recently risen up into view again. Doubtless we'll be seeing a lot of them in the rate-capped years to come.

The past reappears in other ways too. Stoke Newington is fairly typical of many inner-city areas in which a white working class coexists with a diversity of minority groups and an incoming middle class, and it is seeing changes which are familiar to other such areas as well. Thus an increasingly *preservational* emphasis has established itself in this area over recent years – an emphasis which is more contemporary and ambitious than the one rather tired blue plaque which was put up in 1932 to 'indicate' the spot where Daniel Defoe once lived and wrote *Robinson Crusoe*. This newer emphasis is closely connected with what is often called 'gentrification' – a process which has certainly taken place here between the 1940s (when the area's Victorian terraced houses were scarcely marketable at all) and a present day rich in mortgages (for those who can afford them), tax relief (for those who have mortgages) and (until very recently) improvement grants. Even the most caved-in old 'rathole' (to use Orwell's term) is now likely to fetch well over £40000 as long as it has been emptied of sitting tenants [£100000 in 1988].

The houses which the planners of the 1960s so loudly decried as slums are being refitted in more senses than one. As any observer who walked the streets of this area would be likely to notice, the whirring of industrial sewing machines (on which Asian and Cypriot homeworkers labour for the small sums which must be won in direct competition with Third World manufacturers) has recently been augmented to produce a modified soundscape. There may indeed be reggae and funk in the air, but these days there is also more of the quiet purring associated with consumer durables – along with the resounding bangs and crashes of middle-class self-sufficiency and house renovation. Robinson Crusoe may now be drawing a salary from a job in lecturing, teaching, local government or the probation service, but he's still doing it himself in his own time. His island in the late twentieth century may be no larger than a terraced house, but the same sky stretches out overhead and his garden – with a little extra planting, some additional fencing and the odd trellis – is still idyllic enough. What Raymond Williams has called 'mobile privatization' – that movable if not entirely atomized life which brings with it the interior styles of the new *biedermeier* – has certainly found its way into this area of late.[1]

If possessed of a remotely wry inclination, our observer might be impressed by the extent to which such paradoxical forms of coexistence have become the mode in places like this. The clapped out but still powerful old Daimler-Jaguar, even if it is just broken down and rusting at the side of the road (testimony, perhaps, to the long term financial impossibility of a dream-laden purchase), finds itself alongside increasing numbers of expensively renovated Morris Minors [. . .] The traditional pushbike rider is liable to be overtaken – especially taking off wheezily from the traffic lights – by more and more correctly clad (sensible shoes included) and non-smoking owners of shining, light-weight Claud Butler or Peugeot racing bicycles. As for the area's many working-class dogs, they are more aggressively regarded by people for whom brown heaps on the pavement or in the park constitute a pressing social problem. The sweated immigrant textile industry has also seen some changes recently, now finding itself in co-existence with a white assertion of ethnicity as style – not just skin-heads but also a somewhat wealthier and more 'cultured' appropriation which finds expression in Palestinian scarves, central American or Indian rugs and fabrics, the hand-knitted sweaters and even the leg-warmers of late 1970s post-eroticism. So comes the time to diversify – into restaurants perhaps.

The middle classes, in short, have been moving in since the late 1960s, and the signs are everywhere to be seen. This new population brings with it a market for wine bars and a new range of culturally defined shops (some of which appeal to tradition directly while others display their more discontinuous modernism against a surrounding background of tradition). It enters the area with an attention of its own – with particular ways of appropriating the place in which it finds and must sustain and understand itself. Alongside the ethnic restaurants (the latest of which is 'Californian' and eking out a living one flight up from Seval and Son's sweatshop), therefore, this is also where a sense of the past comes in. Suddenly this hard-pressed inner-city area is a settlement again – a new town in the wood as the name Stoke Newington would suggest to those interested in the historical meanings of place names. Because this upwardly mobile slum is in an old country, we could easily enough push the reference back to the Domesday Book (which registers this place as 'Newtowne'), but a more informative starting point is provided by Sir Walter Besant who took an interested stroll through the area and reported back to his public in a book called *London North of the Thames* which was published in 1911.[2] Besant concluded that 'almost all there is of history in the Parish' was concentrated around Church Street. Seventy years later (and if one excludes a cluster of Queen Anne houses on the north end of the High Street) many of the newcomers – owner-occupying residents of what Besant dismissed as the 'little villa houses which the modern builder strings up by the row' along the streets off Church Street – would agree. The new focus is certainly centred on Church Street, even though the commercial and retailing centres are firmly established elsewhere (on the more recession-struck High Street for example), and even though the old Borough of Stoke Newington has been integrated into the bigger administrative quagmire known as Hackney. Of course, Church Street, being westerly, is just that little bit closer to respectable Highbury and further from the rather less gentrified wastes of Clapton and other places east. For this reason among others, perhaps it is not so surprising that a sense of local history should be making its way down to meet the newcomers along this particular road. This, after all, is the road in which the area's great names tend to congregate. Daniel Defoe lived on Church Street and Harriet Beecher Stowe stayed in a house at what used to be its junction with Carysfort Road; Isaac Watts wrote his hymns in a no longer existing mansion off to the north and as a young boy Edgar Allan Poe went to school at the connection with Edwards Lane. There is also the old Victorian Free Library in which this sort of information can be looked up, and eighteenth century 'Tall Houses', as they were known locally, survive on the south side of the road. For those who want to round the whole atmosphere off, a tradition of dissent can with some limited (in this case that is to say seventeenth century) historical accuracy be imagined to hang over the whole village scene.

I'm not suggesting that these new settlers have exactly researched the history of the area, only that a certain appreciation of the remaining past has facilitated their settlement in the area. This appreciation has much more to do with attitudes towards surviving physical presences than with any formulated historiography. So it happens that old rotting bricks take on an aesthetic aura [. . .] testifying now to valued age rather than to bad manufacture, cheap building, dampness or recent urban dereliction and decay. So it happens that there is a market for those very nineteenth century fittings (cast iron fireplaces, sash windows, cheap pine – which can always be stripped) which the renovators were ripping out only a couple of years ago when *modernization* was still the essence of conversion. So it happens that small voluntary associations with an interest in the area's architectural heritage spring up, organizing tours of the area and producing booklets like The Hackney Society's *The Victorian Villas of Hackney*. So it happens that the few enamelled signs – 'Win her affection with A1 Confections' – remaining above shop fronts or the barely visible traces of wartime camouflage paint on the townhall are brought to a new kind of focus by some passers-by. So it happens that the classical junkshops of Orwell's prole quarter – shops in which a few ordinary but irreplaceable 'treasures' might be found among the general accumulation of undeniably local detritus – are being augmented by a new kind of 'not-quite-antique' shop in which the selection (which includes nineteenth century engravings of noteworthy Stoke Newington buildings) has already been made by well-travelled proprietors who value old things rather as Orwell himself did, and who fit well with Orwell's identification of antique dealers as more like collectors than tradesmen. So it happens that one of the several building societies opening branches in the area (often on the back of booming estate agents) fills its windows with eighteenth and nineteenth century images of the place. So it also happens that this contemporary preservational emphasis comes to be linked with official policy. Stoke Newington Church Street has recently been declared a preservation area, and the newly rediscovered grave of the nineteenth century Chartist Bronterre O'Brien is said to be undergoing some sort of restoration (with the GLC's financial assistance) in the local cemetery.

In this new perspective Stoke Newington is not so much a literal place as a cultural oscillation between the prosaic reality of the contemporary inner city and an imaginative reconstruction of the area's past as a dissenting settlement (which it was in Defoe's time) [. . .] For those who want it, this imagined past will keep looming into view. In the midst of the greyness, the filth and the many evidences of grinding poverty, the incoming imagination can dwell on those redeeming traces which still indicate a momentary 'absence of modernity' [. . .] The same old brick that testifies to the eighteenth century at one moment can speak of the early 1940s at the next.

The stroll down Church Street can be full of such moments for those who are inclined to tune into them. What looks like nothing more than a Spar supermarket redeclares itself on the second glance as an eighteenth century hostelry. And underneath the greengrocer's next door there are apparently cellars where the horses used to be stabled. Meanwhile those run-down and densely tenanted houses further to the east are actually four storey eighteenth century townhouses – the 'Tall Houses' of Besant's account. Small wonder that one has been bought, emptied of its tenants and done up by an art-historian – true 'restoration' indeed (and doubtless the new owner's pride in the place is only enhanced by the derelict state of an identical council owned house next door but one). Traces remain, as one might say, except that this preservationist attention is not automatically granted to residues which have survived neglect, decay and the barbarism of post-war planning. It has a more subjective side as well, involving as it does a contemporary *orientation* towards the past rather than just the survival of old things. As so few guide books ever recognize, this is not merely a matter of noticing old objects situated in a self-evident reality: the present meaning of historical traces such as these is only to be grasped if one takes account of the doubletake or second glance in which they are recognized [. . .] This past doesn't just endure: it displays itself against the tawdry present which it also actively indicts.

So while there are indeed some fine eighteenth century town houses, the odd bow window, and other such remains along Church Street, there is also on the subjective side an increased inclination to value the past, to notice and cherish it, to move into it and maintain it as a presence in our lives. To a considerable extent, I suggest, middle-class incomers have brought with them Orwell's fond perspective on the prole quarter – a perspective which is not based on cherishing things and places which have been near and lived with for years, but which finds its basis in a more abstract and artificial aestheticization of the ordinary and the old. These flashes of redemptive disclosure in which the past is glimpsed as both other and miraculously still present may seem, and in some cases may also be, innocent enough. But before anyone gets too excited about the modernist possibilities of an alienated past which keeps breaking into view in the present it should also be recognized that such moments of sudden disclosure can be deeply problematic in their significance [. . .]

For if the 1970s brought the Habitat and Laura Ashley styles of interior decor into this area, they also saw the rise of the National Front. Likewise, if the early 1980s have seen the intensified restoration of Victorian Villas in old inner-city areas like Stoke Newington, they have also – and still almost unbelievably to many – heard a prime minister advocating what she was pleased to define as a return to Victorian values.

What exactly is it that keeps breaking through? The reappearance is not simply of the past as it 'really' was: indeed, sometimes the authentic trace of history is precisely what just has to go. In Thatcher's years old ideas of 'charity' and 'philanthropy' may indeed have been in the air again, but if the 'deserving poor' are still sometimes to be found living in 'model dwellings' [. . .] the terms of residence are different and a certain remodelling of the original nineteenth century edifice may also have become necessary. Towards the end of 1984, for example, a small improvement was made to Gibson Gardens, a large model dwelling tenement (dating from 1880) in which flats – among the very cheapest in the area – seem now to be permanently for sale. A chimney had to come down, although not exactly for structural reasons. In these times when the deserving poor are somewhat more likely to become modest owner occupiers (happily relinquishing their status as tenants in council owned post-war tower-blocks?)

the problem had far more to do with the old words which were still cut in bold letters on the public face of that chimney: 'The Metropolitan Association for the Improvement of the Dwellings of the Industrious Classes . . .'

Past against past

Although it can be imagined as an English settlement with roots in the Domesday Book, ('There is land for two ploughs and a half . . . There are four villanes and thirty seven cottagers with ten acres'), we should remember that Stoke Newington has recently been administratively integrated into Hackney, a borough which in 1983 was declared to be the poorest in Britain. This suggests other perceptions of the place, and these certainly exist. For a start there are clear indications of the ongoing and customary practices of a white working class – indications which may well be resignified and mythologized in the incoming middle-class perspective, but which are not in themselves mere hallucinations.

Within this white working class there is also a sense of the area and its past – one that is significantly different, going to the considerably less aesthetic High Street for its focus far more automatically than to Church Street. There are many older people who remember a more prosperous High Street as it was in the 1950s – there was at least one large department store, and the pavements could be so crowded on Saturdays that people had to walk in the road. This remembered past exists in stark contrast with the present, for if the High Street is still the place to shop it has clearly also seen better days. A recently introduced one-way system drove some trade out of what is also an arterial road leading in the direction of Cambridge and other august locations [. . .] The big department store was demolished – after years of dereliction – by the beginning of 1984, and many of the more recent shops (like Marks and Spencer) have relocated in the current economic decline. As for the large supermarkets of recent years (Sains bury's, Safeway and so on), these have started as they mean to go on – elsewhere. Little has improved from this point of view [. . .]

While some of the cultural relations of the white working class have survived the upheavals of the post-war period they have done so most strongly off either of the main streets, in amongst those rows of 'little village houses' which Besant found so meaningless. Here the pub may still be the 'local', but it is also clear that cultural survival has often occurred alongside a growing sense of anxiety [. . .]

As for the embitterment and reaction which grows in such a context, it will take me a few years to forget the somewhat dishevelled elderly man who happened to make his way down the pavement as we were moving in. 'People moving in,' he said with affected surprise and a certain amount of contempt in his voice: 'people (by which he meant white people) still moving in.' He went on to comment that had he been able to he would have moved *out* years ago, along with the many he had known leave for the suburbs and new towns in the 1960s and '70s. Too many 'rusty spoons' around here as it's sometimes put in rhyming slang. Encounters such as these indicate the extent to which this traditional white working class has been affected by a dislocation of culture and memory like that which Orwell describes in *Nineteen Eighty-Four*. In this situation the recourse to racism can provide easy compensation [. . .]

When we come to the minority communities that form a significant part of the Hackney population we ought to leave Orwell behind completely, and not just out of recognition for settlements which have occurred since Orwell was writing in the 1940s. There is a long established Jewish population in the area with its Hasidic community concentrated slightly to the north of Stoke Newington in Stamford Hill. There are Irish, African, Italian, Asian, Cypriot (both Greek and Turkish) and West Indian people in the area – people who have their own routes through the place, although not necessarily ones that move in any easy accordance with the imaginative reconstructions and memories which hold the measure of the place for many white inhabitants. Given the prevailing white criteria, which measure belonging and cultural authenticity in terms of continuity of place and an imaginary valuation of the remaining trace, it is entirely consistent that the belonging for these people should seem (and I speak here from a dominant point of view) more makeshift and improvised. For people excluded from conventional identification with the area's historical geography, the traditional structure of the place is still there to be dealt with. Sometimes, courtesy not least of imperial history, old centres can be adopted – like the sixteenth century church on the edge of Clissold Park which, while it looks exactly like the fragment of old Elizabethan village that in one limited respect it is, seems now to be used most actively by a West Indian congregation – but at other times the connections seem more strained. Thus on the High Street there is a Turkish mosque and community centre. This is housed in a building which until recently was being used as a cinema and which was originally built as an entertainment palace with exotic domes thrown in for orientalist effect [. . .]

The different populations in the Stoke Newington area have different senses of the place and these are certainly not always congruent with one another. Thus, for example, I recall walking through Stoke Newington with Annette, a twenty-one year old white woman who has lived her entire life in Hoxton (a more thoroughly working-class area which lies a few miles south of Stoke Newington). Annette comes from what years of ethnographic sociology have treated as the classic East End background and she finds it hard to believe that anyone would ever *choose* to live in this borough: she herself has eyes set on Kent or, failing that, Essex. As we walk through streets of Besant's 'little villa houses', she comments approvingly on a house which from any culturally sanctioned perspective is a complete eyesore. Its bricks have recently been covered with a fake stone cladding, the sash windows have been replaced with cheap louvres, and the whole place is painted up in gloss so that it shines like a birthday cake. These 'improvements' certainly stand out, and it seems very likely that the quieter neighbours (subtler greys and whites, carefully restored wooden shutters . . .) might be among those who see them as acts of vandalism [. . .]

Annette, meanwhile, sees it differently. Somebody *owns* this place and their renovation of it speaks of pride, self-determination and freedom to this woman who has lived her whole life in council flats. For her it is exactly the point that this house stands out from the rest. The uniformity of the street is merely the grey background against which this improved house glows – a well packaged interior and 'home'. As for all that stripped pine to be seen in other houses around here, what about painting it? And what are all these enormous plants doing in some front windows – the ones without net curtains [. . .]

These tensions between different appropriations of the place are articulated around many different phenomena or issues. Thus, for example, middle-class incomers value Abney Park cemetery precisely because it is overgrown and four-fifths wild – a good place for a Gothic stroll. A very different view is taken by some working-class people (far more likely to have relatives buried in the place), who find the unknown and neglected appearance of this nineteenth century cemetery a mark of decay, and argue that it should definitely be tidied up.[3] The same contest of views occurs over the bay windows in the area's terraced houses. Many house owners – working class, black, Cypriot (although very rarely if ever incoming middle class) rip these out, throw the whole front of the house forward with an extension which opens up considerably increased space inside. None of this looks good from the point of view of the Hackney Society. In his preservationist pamphlet on *The Victorian Villas of Hackney* Michael Hunter (himself a relatively early settler in the area) celebrates every feature of these little villa houses – from plaster cornices, ceiling roses, moulded skirting boards and door frames through to the floral capitals above the bay windows and those touches of Italianate influence which come to these slum houses 'from the Renaissance palaces of Venice, Florence and Rome' no less. The plea is straightforward and direct:[4]

> Above all, if you live in a Victorian house and are considering altering it in any way, please respect the aesthetic merits of this type of building which have been outlined here. Each Victorian house is, in its way, a period piece and worth respecting as such; many form part of terraces which have an aesthetic unity that is easily destroyed by piecemeal, unsympathetic alterations to individual houses.

The row is no longer the line along which speculative jerry-builders strung their cheap 'little villa houses'. Since 1911, when Besant found nothing of historical or aesthetic interest in streets of this sort, the row has become a precious aesthetic unity which present-day inhabitants are all too likely to misunderstand and abuse – especially those whose history goes back into a very different experience of the nineteenth century. All is well with the buildings, and with an impoverished local state planning less demolition these days the problem now seems increasingly to lie with the heedless people who live in them. Perhaps this is why so many of the photographs in books like this evict the contemporary inhabitants and their various furnishings altogether, concentrating instead on bare rooms and empty streets. They are like stills of a clear and surviving old world – the aesthetic attention can evidently work like a neutron bomb. What would the Hackney Society say to the Irish carpet layer who looked up at the cornices in our front room and said that he would love to own one of these houses – he would start by putting strip lighting *inside* the cornices? Is it all just a matter of bad taste? Certainly not. Here was another person who as a financially hard-pressed council tenant imagined a freedom of action that he currently lacked.

The point should be clear enough. People live in different worlds even though they share the same locality: *there is no single community or quarter*. What is pleasantly 'old' for one person is decayed and broken for another. Just as a person with money has a different experience of shopping in the area than someone with almost none, a white home owner is likely to have a different experience of the police (the considerate homebeat officer who comes round to commiserate after yet another stereo or colour television has been stolen) than a black person – home owner or not. Likewise, if I read *The Guardian* or *The Times* and can substantially determine my own relation to the borough, then maybe I don't actually need to read the *Hackney Gazette*. Those stories of daily misery and violent horror can stay local to someone else's paper, together with the job advertisements (although, of course, I'll keep a close eye on the rising house prices) [. . .]

The sense of history plays its part in all this [. . .] For in the midst of all this romantic attachment to old brick and earth, the large and mixed ethnic minority and black populations in the Hackney area are still struggling against formidable odds for the basic constitutional and cultural rights of a citizenship which is itself far from secure. History from this point of view remains to be made, as do the cultural means of developing and expressing a different past or, in wider terms, a different experience of the same imperialist history. From this perspective (a perspective which, far from being a 'minority' matter, is central to the democratic development of the borough) the other appropriations of the area's past may well constitute part of the problem, valuing as they do a time before much recent immigration took place. In the case of preservationism this danger is almost self-evident. What should also be said is that the problem may also be expressed in the historio-ophical dreams of the area's new Robinson Crusoes – figures who, left-leaning or not, can certainly be caught in an imaginary and less than emancipatory relation to Friday. After all, progressive credentials can be drawn from living in mixed areas without anything actually being done to contribute to the social welfare or development of the minority groups which lend such exuberant colour to incoming life. I recently heard a woman say that she wanted her child to go to a school with children of all races. Why not indeed, but isn't the wish itself curiously specific to an incoming white imagination, and isn't it insultingly abstract? While this sort of cultural consumerism may not be deliberately practised, it doesn't exist any the less for the fact that it is passive. Similar questions are brought to mind by Fox's Winebar – a relatively new establishment on Church Street which is already fabled as a convenient day-time rendezvous for those young women from the north who are now finding employment as resident (if not precisely Victorian) nannies with the area's new middle class.[5] Fox's has the somewhat curious distinction of being remarkably white in its clientele whilst at the same time being packed to the ceiling with members of the anti-racist and professional left.

Such difficulties were raised into the sharpest relief in the reception which greeted publication of Paul Harrison's book *Inside the Inner City* in 1983.[6] Here were over four hundred pages of closely described social disaster. Harrison describes the miseries and deprivations of Hackney with an eye to shattering national myths about the adequacy of the welfare state, the absence of real poverty in Britain. This is not a book that seeks to be local in its solidarity with the poor. In the view of this modern-day Charles Booth, Hackney is (as a policeman put it to Harrison) a 'bloody awful place, a stinking cesspit' – a strong contender for the title of most awful place in Britain. Brittle romanticizations of the area don't last a minute here, and certain local myths also come under attack. As Harrison writes, 'there are many people who live in Hackney who will deny this: middle-class owner occupiers who will tell you aggressively that it is not at all such a bad place to live'. Harrison hints that it is not just houses that can be gentrified: the number of councillors who are graduates has risen dramatically in recent years, and the local Labour Party has a new kind of membership as well. As for that 'rich diversity of colourful cultures' which the 'chic radical' may see in this area, this is just so much voyeurism. Harrison reports on (yet more) grinding poverty and concludes in an Orwellian mode that the oppressed are hopelessly divided against themselves. Turkish against Greek Cypriots, people from large West Indian islands against those from small islands, Indians against Pakistanis, Muslims against Hindus. The spiral plunges downward, in his view, with nothing to check it.

If there were some cavills from the local left when Harrison's book came out (some complained, truthfully enough, that Harrison overlooked the things that Hackney people were doing to overcome their plight, while others dismissed it all as more middle-class parasitism and issued another of those timeless calls for imminent revolution), the right also felt the need to reply and for a while the national press was full of discussion. Paul Johnson dutifully hacked out a repudiation of 'the poverty myth that can make us all paupers'.[7] Disregarding all the evidences of the book, Johnson blithely reasserted his own pet dogmas: people are poor because they are paid too much, or because they are robbed and crime is unchecked (in turn because the police are distrusted); housing is inadequate and insecure because private tenants still have some security of tenure. . . . As for the profusion of one parent families, all this goes to show that the priests are behaving like 'social workers' rather than doing their jobs. Hackney needs the Ten Commandments rather than public money or the social services department, says this deeply caring and Christian man – a soothing message, no doubt, for an autocratic government which has cheated this borough of funding even according to the already corrupt norms of a system of allocation devised to redistribute wealth from the inner city areas to the rich Tory shires.

If this was the *Daily Mail*'s predictable response, *The Times* came up with more interesting goods. David Walker replied to the book, arguing that the poor are 'inadequate' and that, contrary to the suggestions of the 'poverty lobby' and the ethos of the 1960s (that evil decade), the poor need 'to be taught the virtues of thrift'. As Walker continued, 'affecting vignettes of life among the Hackney poor do not of themselves make a case for increased social security payments. They might, instead, suggest that the women of poor families need help and guidance on household management'.[8]

This, of course, is not to exclude 'affecting vignettes' of life among the Hackney gentrifiers, which is precisely what Philippa Toomey hastened to contribute in an article entitled 'Hooray for Hackney' and published in next day's *The Times*. For Toomey the fuss was frankly unbelievable – she actually *lives* in Hackney and, like a good pioneer (a middle-class plotlander in this urban jungle), she intends to stay there for the rest of her days. Her article (which reeks of De Beauvoir, that part of East Islington which somehow slipped over the borough line into Hackney one night) denies it all: 'As I walked home along the canal in blazing sunshine. . . .' Her folksong continues in the Percy Grainger mode: there are ducks and ducklings on the canal rather than condoms and cadavers; little boys fish and lovers 'dawdle' on the towpath. Can this be a 'no-go area for almost all except those compelled to remain here?' Toomey thinks of her 'gracious home' (perhaps even older than a Victorian Villa), of the public libraries, of her Church with its mixed congregation, of the improvements which she and her friends have brought to the area. She thinks of walking home safely, of her good neighbours (who once helped the police apprehend her burglars), and of the ethnic radiance of Ridley Road with its 'lively' street market. Here is yet another way of camping out in the modern world. What can the problem be?[9] [. . .]

Notes

1   Raymond Williams, *Towards 2000*, London 1983.
2   Sir Walter Besant, *London North of the Thames*, London 1911, pp. 573–87.
3   Paul Joyce's *A Guide to Abney Park Cemetery* was published in 1984 by the

London Borough of Hackney and a voluntary association of fairly recent origin called Save Abney Park Cemetery. Joyce's booklet treats the cemetery as part historical testimony and part wilderness – preservation and conservation together. The Hackney Society has also found occasion to comment on Abney Park Cemetery in its survey of the *Parks and Open Spaces in Hackney* (London 1980). There is little satisfaction here for those who make the error of mistaking this 'open space' for a cemetery rather than a park. As it is put, 'any attempt to "tidy up" this park should be treated with suspicion. Yet soon after Hackney took the cemetery over, flowerbeds were inserted into its main avenues as if no public park could be complete without them, thus displaying a simplistic and uniform attitude to park design which it is hoped will in future be avoided' (p. 7). The real point, however, is not to do with 'park design' so much as with the use of this 'park' as a cemetery at all. The Hackney Society laments the fact that burials have taken place 'on the grass verges and other unsuitable positions' and hopes with winning sympathy that 'these could perhaps be deprived of their headstones in due course' (p. 18). Fortunately, however, no burials are now taking place 'except for insertions into existing family graves', so the era of disgraceful and predominantly working-class indiscretions is coming to an end. In future, strolling incomers will be less and less disturbed in their musings by the vulgar glare of new stone, crudely exposed soil, plastic flowers or any well-trimmed and excessively decorous verge. As somebody who enjoys the occasional Gothic stroll himself, I find the Hackney Society's aesthetic remarkably sympathetic. What remains problematic is the way this aesthetic is forced over other forms of life with such stunning disregard for what it would disconnect. With blithe confidence the Hackney Society elevates its own particular choice to the level of aesthetic and universal law. 'In the name of memory history has been abolished.'

4   Michael Hunter, *The Victorian Villas of Hackney*, The Hackney Society, 1981.
5   See Amanda Root, 'The Return of the Nanny', *New Socialist*, No. 22, December 1984, pp. 16–19. A good riposte to this article came from Susan Black, *New Socialist*, No. 24, February 1985, p. 47.
6   Paul Harrison, *Inside the Inner City*, Harmondsworth 1983.
7   Paul Johnson, 'The poverty myth that can make us all paupers', *Daily Mail*, 30 August 1983.
8   David Walker in *The Times*, 25 August 1983.
9   Philippa Toomey, 'Hooray for Hackney', *The Times*, 26 August 1983.

Parts of this essay appeared in C. Aubrey and P. Chilton (eds), *Nineteen Eighty-Four in 1984*, London 1983.

Index